Indian-White Relations

in the United States

Indian-White Relations

in the United States

A Bibliography of Works Published
1975–1980

Francis Paul Prucha

University of Nebraska Press
Lincoln and London

Publication of this book has been aided by a grant from The
Andrew W. Mellon Foundation.

Library of Congress Cataloging in Publication Data
Prucha, Francis Paul.
    Indian-white relations in the United States.
    Supplement to: A bibliographical guide to the history of
Indian-white relations in the United States / Francis Paul
Prucha. Chicago: University of Chicago Press, 1977.
    Includes index.
    1. Indians of North America—Government relations—Bib-
liography. I. Prucha, Francis Paul. Bibliographical guide to
the history of Indian-white relations in the United States. II.
Title.
Z1209.2.U5P67 Suppl. [E93]   016.3231'197073
AACR2   81–14722
ISBN 0–8032–3665–4
ISBN 0–8032–8705–4 (pbk.)

E
93
.P78
1982

Contents

Preface

This bibliography of works dealing with Indian-white relations in the United States is designed as a supplement to A Bibliographical Guide to the History of Indian-White Relations in the United States, published by the University of Chicago Press in 1977. That volume provided an extensive listing of reference books and guides and a classified bibliography of studies published through 1974. The present work extends the bibliography to cover studies published 1975-1980. The few items in the original Bibliographical Guide dated later than 1974 are repeated here.

The classification is fundamentally the same as in the original volume, so users of that work will find a familiar arrangement. The number of subheadings, however, has been reduced because of the smaller number of items, and a few new subheadings have been added to correspond to new areas of interest in writing about Indian affairs. The following categories of material are excluded except for special cases: unpublished master's theses, reports and studies originating in agencies of the federal government, strictly anthropological works, mimeographed materials, and reprints of books or other studies.

Emphasis is on United States history, but British colonial Indian affairs have been included. By and large, Canadian items have been excluded, and no attempt has been made to provide material dealing with Spanish-Indian relations in what is now the United States. The classification is primarily by topics, not by tribal groups. Studies dealing with specific tribes, however, can be located by consulting the index. Each item has been entered only once, so it will be necessary to make frequent use of the detailed index. As in the original Guide, problems of selection and classification arose at many points. It is too much to hope that they were all solved in a way that will satisfy everyone, but I do hope that this supplementary bibliography will prove useful to many.

I have been helped in gathering, verifying, and classifying titles for this supplement by Phillip M. Runkel, Michael Meagher, and Susan Cooney. Work on the bibliography was done principally in the following libraries: Marquette University Library, Milwaukee Public Library, University of Wisconsin-Milwaukee Library, Library of the State Historical Society of Wisconsin, Newberry Library, Huntington Library, University of Wisconsin-Madison Library, and the Library of the Medical College of Wisconsin.

The preparation of the bibliography has been materially aided by a research grant from the DeRance Foundation.

Francis Paul Prucha, S.J.
Marquette University

1
Materials of the Federal Government

Because the federal government conducts official relations with American Indian groups, the largest and most important sources of records for Indian-white relations in the United States are the published and unpublished documents of the federal government.

RECORDS IN THE NATIONAL ARCHIVES

Guides to records in the National Archives are given in A Bibliographical Guide to the History of Indian-White Relations in the United States, pp. 3-5.

Microfilm Publications

Numerous Indian records available in the microfilm publications of the National Archives are listed in The American Indian: Subject Catalog of National Archives Microfilm Publications (1972) and Catalog of National Archives Microfilm Publications (1974). For microfilm published since those listings, see the following supplement.

1. "Supplementary List of National Archives Microfilm Publications, 1974-80." Prologue 13 (Spring 1981): 60-72.

Specific collections pertinent to Indian affairs microfilmed since 1974 are listed below. The symbol DP indicates that a descriptive pamphlet for the microfilm is available.

2. Interior Department Territorial Papers: Oklahoma, 1889-1912. RG 48. M-828. 5 Rolls. DP.

3. Miscellaneous Letters Sent by the Pueblo Indian Agency, 1874-1891. RG 75. M-941. 10 Rolls. DP.

4. Records of the Bureau of Indian Affairs, Procedural Issuances: Orders and Circulars, 1854-1955. RG 75. M-1121. 17 Rolls.

5. Records of the Central Superintendency of Indian Affairs, 1813-1878. RG 75. M-856. 108 Rolls. DP.

6. Records of the Dakota Superintendency of Indian Affairs, 1861-1870, and 1877-1878, and the Wyoming Superintendency, 1870. RG 75. M-1016. 13 Rolls. DP.

7. Records of the Idaho Superintendency of Indian Affairs, 1863-1870. RG 75. M-832. 3 Rolls. DP.

8. Records of the Minnesota Superintendency of Indian Affairs, 1849-1856. RG 75. M-842. 9 Rolls. DP.

9. Records of the Montana Superintendency of Indian Affairs, 1867-1873. RG 75. M-833. 3 Rolls. DP.

10. Records of the Nevada Superintendency of Indian Affairs, 1869-1870. RG 75. M-837. 1 Roll. DP.

11. Records of the Utah Superintendency of Indian Affairs, 1853-1870. RG 75. M-834. 2 Rolls. DP.

12. Records of the Wisconsin Superintendency of Indian Affairs, 1836-1848, and the Green Bay Subagency, 1850. RG 75. M-951. 4 Rolls. DP.

13. Reports of Inspections of the Field Jurisdictions of the Office of Indian Affairs, 1873-1900. RG 48/RG 75. M-1070. 60 Rolls. DP.

14. Selected Classes of Letters Received by the Indian Division of the Office of the Secretary of the Interior, 1849-1880. RG 48. M-825. 32 Rolls. DP.

15. Selected Letters Received by the Office of Indian Affairs Relating to the Cherokees of North Carolina, 1851-1905. RG 75. M-1059. 7 Rolls. DP.

16. Superintendents' Annual Narrative and Statistical Reports from Field Jurisdictions of the Bureau of Indian Affairs, 1907-1938. RG 75. M-1011. 174 Rolls. DP.

17. The Territorial Papers of the United States: The Territory of Iowa, 1838-1846. M-325. 102 Rolls. DP.

18. The Territorial Papers of the United States: The Territory of Minnesota, 1849-1858. M-1050. 11 Rolls.

19. The Territorial Papers of the United States: The Territory of Oregon, 1848-1859. M-1049. 12 Rolls.

Other Publications Relating to National Archives Material

20. Butler, John P. Index to the Papers of the Continental Congress, 1774-89. 5 volumes. Washington: Government Printing Office, 1978.

21. Holmes, Oliver W. "Indian-Related Records in the National Archives and Their Use: Observations over a Third of a Century." In Indian-White Relations; A Persistent Paradox, edited by Jane F. Smith and Robert M. Kvasnicka, pp. 13-32. Washington: Howard University Press, 1976.

22. Ryan, Carmelita S. "Special Study of the Appraisal of Indian Records." In Indian-White Relations: A Persistent Paradox, edited by Jane F. Smith and Robert M. Kvasnicka, pp. 33-42. Washington: Howard University Press, 1976.

23. _____. "The Written Record and the American Indian: The Archives of the United States." Western Historical Quarterly 6 (April 1975): 163-173.

DOCUMENTS OF THE FEDERAL GOVERNMENT

The most important guides, indexes, catalogs, and printed compilations are listed in A Bibliographical Guide to the History of Indian-White Relations in the United States, pp. 6-12.

New Guides and Indexes

24. Johnson, Steven L. Guide to American Indian Documents in the Congressional Serial Set: 1817-1899. New York: Clearwater Publishing Company, 1977.

25. CIS Index to Publications of the United States. Washington: Congressional Information Service. Index, published bi-monthly; Articles, published monthly. See annual cumulations.

26. CIS Annual. Washington: Congressionaal Information Service, 1970--. Part 1, Abstracts of Congressional Publications and Legislative Histories; part 2, Index to Congressional Publications and Public Laws.

27. CIS Five-Year Cumulative Index, 1970-1974. 2 volumes. Washington: Congressional Information Service, 1975. Subjest and name index.

28. CIS Four-Year Cumulative Index, 1975-1978. 3 volumes. Washington: Congressional Information Service, 1979. Subject and name index.

29. CIS US Congressional Committee Prints Index from the Earliest Publications through 1969. 5 volumes. Washington: Congressional Information Service, 1980.

30. CIS US Serial Set Index. 36 volumes. Washington: Congressional Information Service, 1975-1978. Covers period 1789-1969.

31. Witness Index. Microfiche. Westport, Connecticut: Greenwood Press. Alphabetical list of witnesses before U.S. Congressional committees, 25th-89th Congresses.

Collection of Documents

32. Prucha, Francis Paul, ed. Documents of United States Indian Policy. Lincoln: University of Nebraska Press, 1975.

2
Guides to Sources

General guides to manuscripts and printed sources of value to a researcher studying Indian-white relations are listed in A Bibliographical Guide to the History of Indian-White Relations in the United States, pp. 13-25. Useful guides published 1975-1980 are listed here.

GUIDES TO MANUSCRIPTS AND OTHER COLLECTIONS

33. Arguimbau, Ellen, and John A. Brennan. A Guide to Manuscript Collections. Boulder: University of Colorado, Western Historical Collections, 1977.

34. Carriker, Robert, Jennifer Ann Boharski, Eleanor R. Carriker, and Clifford A. Carroll. Guide to the Microfilm Edition of the Oregon Province Archives of the Society of Jesus Alaska Mission Collection. Spokane: Gonzaga University, 1980.

35. Catalog to Manuscripts at the National Anthropological Archives. 4 volumes. Boston: G. K. Hall and Company, 1975.

36. Davenport, John B. "The Manuscript Collections of the University of North Dakota." Great Plains Journal 15 (Spring 1976): 134-143.

37. Davis, Richard C., and Linda Angle Miller. Guide to the Catalogued Collections in the Manuscript Department of the William R. Perkins Library, Duke University. Santa Barbara, California; Clio Books, 1980.

38. Debo, Angie. "Major Indian Record Collections in Oklahoma." In Indian-White Relations: A Persistent Paradox, edited by Jane F. Smith and Robert B. Kvasnicka, pp. 112-118. Washington: Howard University Press, 1976.

39. Directory of Archives and Manuscript Repositories in the United States. Washington: National Historical Publications and Records Commission, 1978.

40. Ewers, John C. "Artifacts and Pictures as Documents in the History of

of Indian-White Relations." In Indian-White Relations: A Persistent Paradox, edited by Jane F. Smith and Robert M. Kvasnicka, pp. 101-111. Washington: Howard University Press, 1976.

41. Gehring, Charles. A Guide to Dutch Manuscripts Relating to New Netherland in United States Repositories. Albany: University of the State of New York, 1978.

42. Guide to American Historical Manuscripts in the Huntington Library. San Marino: Huntington Library, 1979.

43. Hohler, Joanne Stanberg, ed. The Papers of Carlos Montezuma, 1892-1937: Guide to a Microfilm Edition. Madison: State Historical Society of Wisconsin, 1975.

44. Jordan, H. Glenn. "The Western History Collections and the Great Plains; Opportunities for Research in Regional History." Great Plains Journal 15 (Fall 1975): 55-64.

45. _____. "Western History Collections at the University of Oklahoma." Chronicles of Oklahoma 54 (Fall 1976): 370-392.

46. _____. "The Western History Collection of the University of Oklahoma Library." Great Plains Journal 14 (Fall 1975): 55-64.

47. Kelly, Lawrence C. "Indian Records in the Oklahoma Historical Society Archives." Chronicles of Oklahoma 54 (Summer 1976): 227-244.

48. Logsdon, Guy. "Indian Studies Resources at the University of Tulsa." Chronicles of Oklahoma 55 (Spring 1977): 64-77.

49. Lucas, Lydia A. Manuscripts Collections of the Minnesota Historical Society. Guide No. 3. St. Paul: Minnesota Historical Society, 1977.

50. Mills, Todd. "Western Manuscripts in the University of Arizona Library."

Arizona and the West 22 (Spring 1980):
5-66.

51. Moltke-Hansen, David, and Sallie
Doscher. South Carolina Historical
Society Manuscript Guide. Supplement to
South Carolina Historical Magazine 80
(July 1979). Charleston: South Carolina
Historical Society, 1979.

52. Robertson, James I., Jr., ed. An In-
dex-Guide to the Southern Historical
Society Papers, 1876-1959. 2 volumes.
Millwood, New York: Kraus International
Publications, 1980.

53. Shy, Arlene Phillips, and Barbara A.
Mitchell. Guide to the Manuscript Col-
lections of the William L. Clements
Library. Third edition. Boston: G.K.
Hall and Company, 1978.

54. Skemer, Don C., and Robert C. Morris.
Guide to the Manuscript Collections of
the New Jersey Historical Society.
Newark: New Jersey Historical Society,
1979.

55. Spindel, Donna. Introductory Guide
to Indian-Related Records (to 1876) in
the North Carolina State Archives.
Raleigh, North Carolina: Division of
Archives and History, Department of
Cultural Resources, 1977.

56. Wehrkamp, Tim. "Manuscript Sources
in Sioux Indian History at the Historical Resource Center." South Dakota
History 8 (Spring 1978): 143-156.

57. Wheat, Helen, and Brad Agnew. "Special
Collections Department at Northeastern
Oklahoma State University." Chronicles
of Oklahoma 56 (Spring 1978): 73-84.

58. Whipkey, Harry E. Guide to the Manu-
script Groups in the Pennsylvania State
Archives. Harrisburg: Pennsylvania
Historical and Museum Commission, 1976.

BIBLIOGRAPHIES OF INDIAN MATERIALS

Listed here are general bibliographies
specifically on Indians or with substantial
Indian material. Bibliographies that deal
with particular tribes, areas, or topics
will be found in appropriate sections
below.

59. A Bibliography of Books on Indians of
North America: Holdings in the Forrest
R. Polk Library. Oshkosh: Reference
Department, Forrest R. Polk Library,
University of Wisconsin-Oshkosh, 1975.

60. Buchanan, Jim, and Fran Burkert. A
Bibliography of Current American Indian
Policy. Monticello, Illinois: Vance
Bibliographies, 1979.

61. Cashman, Marc. Bibliography of American Ethnology. Rye, New York: Todd
Publications, 1976.

62. Ellis, Richard N. "Published Source
Materials on Native Americans." Western
Historical Quarterly 7 (April 19-6):
187-192.

63. Gagala, Kenneth L., ed. The Economics
of Minorities: A Guide to Information
Sources. Detroit: Gale Research Company, 1975.

64. Hodge, William H. A Bibliography of
Contemporary North American Indians:
Selected and Partially Annotated with
Study Guides. New York: Interland
Publishing, 1976.

65. "The Indians of the Midwest: A Partially Annotated Bibliography." Great
Lakes Review 11 (Winter 1976): 54-74.

66. Miller, Wayne Charles, with Faye
Nell Vowell and others. A Comprehensive
Bibliography for the Study of American
Minorities. 2 volumes. New York: New
York University Press, 1976.

67. Murdock, George Peter, and Timothy
J. O'Leary. Ethnographic Bibliography
of North America. 4th edition. 5
volumes. New Haven: Human Relations
Area Files Press, 1975.

68. The North American Indian: A Bibliography of Community Development. Washington: U.S. Department of Housing and
Urban Development, 1975.

69. Oaks, Priscilla. Minority Studies:
A Selective Annotated Bibliography.
Boston: G.K. Hall and Company, 1975.

70. Perkins, David, and Norman Tanis.
Native Americans of North America:
A Bibliography Based on Collections in
the Libraries of California State
University, Northridge. Northridge:
California State University, 1975.

71. Prucha, Francis Paul. A Bibliographical Guide to the History of Indian-
White Relations in the United States.
Chicago: University of Chicago Press,
1977.

72. _____. United States Indian Policy:
A Critical Bibliography. Bloomington:
Indiana University Press, 1977.

73. Thornton, Russell, and Mary K. Gras-
mick. Bibliography of Social Science
Research and Writings on American
Indians. Minneapolis: Center for Urban
and Regional Affairs, University of
Minnesota, 1979.

74. _____. Sociology of American In-

dians: A Critical Bibliography. Bloomington: Indiana University Press, 1980.

OTHER GUIDES AND REFERENCE BOOKS

75. The Arizona Index: A Subject Index to Periodical Articles about the State. Compiled by Donald M. Powell and Virginia E. Rice. 2 volumes. Boston: G.K. Hall and Company, 1978.

76. Bibliographic Guide to North American History. Boston: G.K. Hall and Company, 1978--.

77. Buchanan, Jim. "American Indian Periodical Literature: A Selective Bibliography." RQ 16 (Spring 1977): 225-230.

78. The Combined Retrospective Index Set to Journals in History, 1838-1974. Introduction and User's Guide by Evan I. Farber. 11 Volumes. Washington: Carrollton Press, 1977. See listing under "Indians" in volume 8, pp. 230-329.

79. Klein, Barry T., ed. Reference Encyclopedia of the American Indian. 3rd edition. 2 volumes. Rye, New York: Todd Publications, 1978.

80. Leitch, Barbara A. A Concise Dictionary of Indian Tribes of North America. Algonac, Michigan: Reference Publications, 1979.

81. Nickerson, Gifford S. Native North Americans in Doctoral Dissertations, 1971-1975: A Classified and Indexed Research Bibliography. Monticello, Illinois: Council of Planning Librarians, 1977.

82. North American Indians: A Dissertation Index. Ann Arbor, Michigan: University Microfilms International, 1977. Supplement I covers dissertations published in 1977 and 1978.

ORAL HISTORY

83. Crampton, C. Gregory. "The Archives of the Duke Projects in American Indian Oral History." In Indian-White Rela-

tions: A Persistent Paradox, edited by Jane F. Smith and Robert M. Kvasnicka, pp. 119-128. Washington: Howard University Press, 1976.

84. Listening to Indians: An Oral History Collection from St. Louis Community College at Florissant Valley. Microfiche. Sanford, North Carolina: Microfilming Corporation of America, 1979. Checklisted in The New York Times Oral History Program: Oral History Guide No. 2.

85. Meckler, Alan M., and Ruth McMullin, eds. Oral History Collections. New York: R. R. Bowker Company, 1975.

86. Proctor, Samuel. "The Southeastern Indian Oral History Program at the University of Florida." In Indians of the Lower South: Past and Present, edited by John K. Mahon, pp. 1-5. Pensacola: Gulf Coast History and Humanities Conference, 1975.

87. University of South Dakota American Indian Oral History Research Project. Microfiche. Sanford, North Carolina: Microfilming Corporation of America, 1979. Checklisted in The New York Times Oral History Program: Oral History Guide No. 2.

INDIAN PERIODICALS

88. Danky, James P., and Michael Fox. "Alternative Periodicals: Native Americans." Wilson Library Bulletin 51 (February 1977): 481-485; (April 1977): 662-664.

Among new Indian periodicals are the following.

89. American Indian Journal, 1975--. Published by the Institute for the Development of Indian Law; a continuation of Legislative Review and Education Journal.

90. Journal of Cherokee Studies, 1976--.

91. Wassaja/The Indian Historian, 1980--. A combination of previous publications.

3
Indian Affairs/Indian Policy

Much of the writing about Indian-white relations in the United States has dealt with what might be called the political status of the Indians. In this general category fall such topics as the policy of the federal government, humanitarian reform movements directed toward the Indians, and public concern over Indian affairs.

GENERAL WORKS ON INDIAN-WHITE RELATIONS

Comprehensive Works

92. Chamberlin, J. E. The Harrowing of Eden: White Attitudes toward North American Natives. New York: Seabury Press, 1975.

93. Coffer, William E. Phoenix: The Decline and Rebirth of the Indian People. New York: Van Nostrand Reinhold Company, 1979.

94. Dennis, Henry C., ed. The American Indian, 1492-1976: A Chronology and Fact Book. Second edition. Dobbs Ferry, New York: Oceana Publications, 1977.

95. Gates, Paul Wallace, ed. The Rape of Indian Lands. New York: Arno Press, 1979.

96. Gibson, Arrell Morgan. The American Indian: Prehistory to the Present. Lexington, Massachusetts: D.C. Heath and Company, 1980.

97. Hagan, William T. American Indians. Revised edition. Chicago: University of Chicago Press, 1979.

98. Hassrick, Royal B. Cowboys and Indians; An Illustrated History. New York: Promontory Press, 1976.

99. Hecht, Robert A. Continents in Collision: The Impact of Europe on the North American Indian Societies. Lanham, Maryland: University Press of America, 1980.

100. Kickingbird, Lynn, and Kirke Kickingbird. Indians and the U.S. Government. Washington: Institute for the Develop-

ment of Indian Law, 1977.

101. Leitch, Barbara A. Chronology of the American Indian. St. Clair Shores, Michigan: Scholarly Press, 1975.

102. McNickle, D'Arcy. They Came Here First: The Epic of the American Indian. Revised edition. New York: Octagon Books, 1975.

103. Price, John A. Native Studies: American and Canadian Indians. Toronto: McGraw-Hill Ryerson, 1978.

104. Washburn, Wilcomb E. The Indian in America. New York: Harper and Row, 1975.

Brief or Specialized Accounts

105. Bee, Robert, and Ronald Gingerich. "Colonialism, Classes and Ethnic Identity: Native Americans and the National Political Economy." Studies in Comparative International Development 12 (Summer 1977): 70-93.

106. Downs, Ernest C. "How the East Was Lost." American Indian Journal 1 (November 1975): 6-10.

107. Eggan, Fred. "Beyond the Bicentennial: The Future of the American Indian in the Perspectives of the Past. Journal of Anthropological Research 34 (Summer 1978): 161-180.

108. _____. "The Politics of Power: Indian-White Relations in a Changing World." In Political Organization of Native North Americans, edited by Ernest L. Schusky, pp. 283-297. Washington: University Press of America, 1980.

109. Ellis, Richard N. "Hispanic Americans and Indians in New Mexico State Politics." New Mexico Historical Review 53 (October 1978): 361-364.

110. Guillemin, Jeanne. "American Indian Resistance and Protest." In Violence in America, edited by Hugh Davis Graham and Ted Robert Gurr, pp. 287-305. Beverly Hills, California: Sage Publications, 1979.

111. Gurian, Jay. "The Importance of Dependency in Native American-White Contact." <u>American Indian Quarterly</u> 3 (Spring 1977): 16-36.

112. Highwater, Jamake. <u>Many Smokes, Many Moons: A Chronology of American Indian History through Indian Art</u>. Philadelphia: J.B. Lippincott Company, 1978.

113. Hoxie, Frederick Eugene. "Beyond Savagery: The Campaign to Assimilate the American Indians, 1880-1920." Ph.D. dissertation, Brandeis University, 1977.

114. Jorgensen, Joseph G. " Century of Political Economic Effects on American Indian Society, 1880-1980." <u>Journal of Ethnic Studies</u> 6 (Fall 1978): 1-82.

115. Jorgensen, Joseph, and Richard Clemmer. "America in the Indian's Past: A Review." <u>Indian Historian</u> 11 (December 1978): 38-44. Review of Wilcomb E. Washburn, <u>The Indian in America</u>.

116. Josephy, Alvin M., Jr. "The Historical and Cultural Context of White-Native American Conflicts." <u>Indian Historian</u> 12 (Summer 1979): 6-14.

117. Larrabee, Edward McM. <u>Recurrent Themes and Sequences in North American Indian-European Culture Contact</u>. Transactions of the American Philosophical Society, volume 66, part 7. Philadelphia: American Philosophical Society, 1976.

118. Levitan, Sar A., and William B. Johnston. <u>Indian Giving: Federal Programs for Native Americans</u>. Baltimore: Johns Hopkins University Press, 1975.

119. McNickle, D'Arcy. "An Historical Review of Federal-Indian Relationships." <u>American Indian Journal</u> 1 (December 1975): 16-18.

120. Miner, H. Craig, and William E. Unrau. <u>The End of Indian Kansas: A Study of Cultural Revolution, 1854-1871</u>. Lawrence: Regents Press of Kansas, 1978.

121. Munkres, Robert L. "The Arrival of Emigrants and Soldiers: Curiosity, Contempt, Confusion and Conflict." In <u>Red Men and Hat Wearers: Viewpoints in Indian History</u>, edited by Daniel Tyler, pp. 63-91. Boulder, Colorado: Pruett Publishing Company, 1976.

122. Ortiz, Roxanne Dunbar. "Wounded Knee 1890 to Wounded Knee 1973: A Study in United States Colonialism." <u>Journal of Ethnic Studies</u> 8 (Summer 1980): 1-15.

123. Schusky, Ernest L., ed. <u>Political Organization of Native North Americans</u>. Washington: University Press of America, 1980.

124. Sheehan, Bernard W. "The American Indian as Victim." <u>Alternative: An American Spectator</u> 8 (January 1975): 5-8.

125. Spicer, Edward H. "American Indians, Federal Policy toward." In <u>Harvard Encyclopedia of American Ethnic Groups</u>, edited by Stephan Thernstrom, Ann Orlov, and Oscar Handlin, pp. 114-122. Cambridge: Harvard University Press, 1980.

126. Stineback, David C. "White Nationalism and Native Cultures." <u>American Indian Culture and Research Journal</u> 2 (No. 2, 1978): 9-13.

127. Strickland, Rennard. "Friends and Enemies of the American Indian: An Essay Review on Native American Law and Public Policy." <u>American Indian Law Review</u> 3 (No. 2, 1975): 313-331.

128. Stuart, Paul. "United States Indian Policy: From the Dawes Act to the American Indian Policy Review Commission." <u>Social Service Review</u> 51 (September 1977): 451-463.

129. Svensson, Frances. "Liberal Democracy and Group Rights: The Legacy of Individualism and Its Impact on American Indian Tribes." <u>Political Studies</u> 27 (September 1979): 421-439.

130. Unrau, William E. "An International Perspective on American Indian Policy: The South Australian Protector and Aborigines Protection Society." <u>Pacific Historical Review</u> 45 (November 1976): 519-538.

131. Wessel, Thomas R. "Agriculture, Indians and American History." <u>Agricultural History</u> 50 (January 1976): 9-20.

132. Whitney, Ellen M. "Indian History and the Indians of Illinois." <u>Journal of the Illinois State Historical Society</u> 69 (May 1976): 139-146.

133. Williams, Walter L. "United States Indian Policy and the Debate over Philippine Annexation: Implications for the Origins of American Imperialism." <u>Journal of American History</u> 66 (March 1980): 810-831.

Collected Essays

134. Cortes, Carlos E., Arlin I. Ginsburg, Alan W. F. Green, and James A. Joseph, <u>Three Perspectives on Ethnicity--Blacks, Chicanos, and Native Americans</u>. New York: G.P. Putnam's Sons, 1976.

135. Smith, Jane F., and Robert M. Kvasnicka, eds. <u>Indian-White Relations: A</u>

Persistent Paradox. Washington: Howard University Press, 1976. Proceedings of the National Archives Conference on Research in the History of Indian-White Relations, 1972.

136. Tyler, Daniel, ed. <u>Red Men and Hat Wearers: Viewpoints in Indian History</u>. Boulder, Colorado: Pruett Publishing Company, 1976. Papers from the Colorado State University Conference on Indian History, August 1976.

137. Worcester, Donald E., ed. <u>Forked Tongues and Broken Treaties</u>. Caldwell, Idaho: Caxton Printers, 1975.

COLONIAL INDIAN AFFAIRS

General and Miscellaneous Studies

138. Bailey, Kenneth P. <u>Christopher Gist: Frontiersman, Explorer, and Indian Agent</u>. Hamden, Connecticut: Archon Books, 1976.

139. Del Papa, Eugene M. "The Royal Proclamation of 1763: Its Effect upon Virginia Land Companies." <u>Virginia Magazine of History and Biography</u> 83 (October 1975): 406-411.

140. Edmunds, R. David. "Pickawillany: French Military Power versus British Economics." <u>Western Pennsylvania Historical Magazine</u> 58 (April 1975): 169-184.

141. Hamilton, Milton. <u>Sir William Johnson, Colonial American, 1715-1763</u>. Port Washington, New York: Kennikat Press, 1976.

142. Jaenen, Cornelius J. <u>Friend and Foe: Aspects of French-Amerindian Cultural Contact in the Sixteenth and Seventeenth Centuries</u>. Toronto: McClelland and Stewart, 1976.

143. Kupperman, Karen O. "English Perceptions of Treachery, 1583-1640: The Case of the American Savages." <u>Historical Journal</u> 20 (June 1977): 263-287.

144. _____. <u>Settling with the Indians: The Meeting of English and Indian Cultures in America, 1580-1640</u>. Totowa, New Jersey: Rowman and Littlefield, 1980.

145. Willy, Todd G. "Defaming the American Indian in the Parliament of 1777." <u>Indian Historian</u> 10 (Summer 1977): 3-8, 62.

146. York, Everett L. "Ethnocentricity or Racism: Some Thoughts on the Nature of Early Indian-White Relations." <u>American Indian Quarterly</u> 1 (Winter 1974-1975): 281-291.

Colonial New England

147. Burton, William John. "Hellish Fiends and Brutish Men: Amerindian-Euroamerican Interaction in Southern New England: An Interdisciplinary Analysis, 1600-1750." Ph.D. dissertation, Kent State University, 1976.

148. Eisen, George. "Voyageurs, Black-Robes, Saints, and Indians." <u>Ethnohistory</u> 24 (Summer 1977): 191-205.

149. Gragg, Larry. "'This Troublesome Planter,' Thomas Morton of Merry Mount." <u>History Today</u> 27 (October 1977): 667-672.

150. Harper, Susanne Banta. "John Brainerd and the First Indian Reservation." <u>Indian Historian</u> 12 (No. 4, 1979): 20-21.

151. Jennings, Francis. <u>The Invasion of America: Indians, Colonialism and the Cant of Conquest</u>. Chapel Hill: University of North Carolina Press, 1975.

152. Kawashima, Yasuhide. "Forced Conformity: Puritan Criminal Justice and Indians." <u>Kansas Law Review</u> 25 (Spring 1977): 361-373.

153. Koehler, Lyle. "Red-White Power Relations and Justice in the Courts of Seventeenth-Century New England." <u>American Indian Culture and Research Journal</u> 3 (No. 4, 1979): 1-31.

154. Kupperman, Karen Ordahl. "Thomas Morton, Historian." <u>New England Quarterly</u> 50 (December 1977): 660-664.

155. Lloyd, Peter. "The Emergence of a Racial Prejudice towards the Indians in Seventeenth-Century New England: Some Notes on an Explanation." Ph.D. dissertation, Ohio State University, 1975.

156. Moynihan, Ruth Barnes. "The Patent and the Indians: The Problem of Jurisdiction in Seventeenth-Century New England." <u>American Indian Culture and Research Journal</u> 2 (No. 1, 1977): 8-18.

157. Sainsbury, John A. "Indian Labor in Early Rhode Island." <u>New England Quarterly</u> 48 (September 1975): 378-393.

158. Segal, Charles M., and David C. Stineback. <u>Puritans, Indians, and Manifest Destiny</u>. New York: G.P. Putnam's Sons, 1977.

159. Sehr, Timothy J. "Ninigret's Tactics of Accommodation--Indian Diplomacy in New England, 1637-1675." <u>Rhode Island History</u> 36 (May 1977): 43-53.

160. Shuffelton, Frank. "Indian Devils

and Pilgrim Fathers: Squanto, Hobomok, and the English Conception of Indian Religion." New England Quarterly 49 (March 1976): 108-116.

161. Stineback, David C. "The Status of Puritan-Indian Scholarship." New England Quarterly 51 (March 1978): 80-90.

162. Thomas, G. E. "Puritans, Indians, and the Concept of Race." New England Quarterly 48 (March 1975): 3-27.

163. Thomas, Peter A. "Contrastive Subsistence Strategies and Land Use as Factors for Understanding Indian-White Relations in New England." Ethnohistory 23 (Winter 1976): 1-18.

164. Vaughan, Alden T. New England Frontier: Puritans and Indians, 1620-1675. Revised edition. New York: W. W. Norton and Company, 1979.

165. Vaughan, Alden T., and Daniel K. Richter. "Crossing the Cultural Divide: Indians and New Englanders, 1605-1763." Proceedings of the American Antiquarian Society 90 (Part 1, 1980): 23-99.

166. Walker, Willard. "A Chronological Account of the Wabanaki Confederacy." In Political Organization of Native North Americans, edited by Ernest L. Schusky, pp. 41-84. Washington: University Press of America, 1980.

The Middle Colonies

167. Bridenbaugh, Carl. "The Old and New Societies of the Delaware Valley in the Seventeenth Century." Pennsylvania Magazine of History and Biography 100 (April 1976): 143-172.

168. Esposito, Frank John. "Indian-White Relations in New Jersey, 1609-1802." Ph.D. dissertation, Rutgers University, 1976.

169. Haan, Richard L. "The Covenant Chain: Iroquois Diplomacy on the Niagara Frontier, 1697-1730." Ph.D. dissertation, University of California, Santa Barbara, 1976.

170. Rouse, Parke, Jr. "Conquistadors on the Chesapeake." Americas 32 (August 1980): 28-33.

171. Russell, Marvin G. "Thomas Barton and Pennsylvania's Colonial Frontier." Pennsylvania History 46 (October 1979): 313-334.

The Southern Colonies

172. Cashion, Jerry Clyde. "North Carolina and the Cherokee: The Quest for Land on the Eve of the American Revolution, 1754-1776." Ph.D. dissertation,

University of North Carolina, 1979.

173. Davis, Richard Beale. "The Indian as Image and Factor in Southern Colonial Life." In Intellectual Life in the Colonial South, 1585-1763, 1: 103-256. 3 volumes. Knoxville: University of Tennessee Press, 1978. Bibliographical essay on Indians, 1: 415-429.

174. Fausz, J. Frederick, and Jon Kukla. "A Letter of Advice to the Governor of Virginia, 1624." William and Mary Quarterly, 3d series 34 (January 1977): 104-129.

175. Morgan, Edmund S. American Slavery--American Freedom: The Ordeal of Colonial Virginia. New York: W.W. Norton and Company, 1975. Deals with Indian relations passim.

176. Morgan, Timothy Everett. "Turmoil in an Orderly Society: Colonial Virginia, 1607-1754: A History and Analysis." Ph.D. dissertation, College of William and Mary, 1976.

177. Robinson, W. Stitt. The Southern Colonial Frontier, 1607-1763. Albuquerque: University of New Mexico Press, 1979.

178. Vaughan, Alden T. "'Expulsion of the Salvages': English Policy and the Virginia Massacre of 1622." William and Mary Quarterly, 3d series 35 (January 1978): 57-84.

179. Woods, Patricia Dillon. "The Relations between the French of Colonial Louisiana and the Choctaw, Chickasaw and Natchez Indians, 1699-1762." Ph.D. dissertation, Louisiana State University, 1978.

See also Sheehan, Savagism and Civility (3123a) and Porter, The Inconstant Savage (3119).

INDIAN AFFAIRS DURING THE REVOLUTION

180. Barsh, Russel Lawrence. "Native American Loyalists and Patriots: Reflections on the American Revolution in Native American History." Indian Historian 10 (Summer 1977): 9-19.

181. Chalou, George C. "George Rogers Clark and Indian America, 1778-1780." In The French, the Indians, and George Rogers Clark in the Illinois Country, pp. 34-46. Proceedings of an Indiana American Revolution Bicentennial Symposium. Indianapolis: Indiana Historical Society, 1977.

182. Hagan, William T. Longhouse Diplomacy and Frontier Warfare: The Iroquois Confederacy in the American Revolution.

Albany: New York State American Revolution Bicentennial Commission, n.d.

183. Jennings, Francis. "The Indians' Revolution." In The American Revolution: Explorations in the History of American Radicalism, edited by Alfred F. Young, pp. 319-348. DeKalb, Illinois: Northern Illinois University Press, 1976.

184. Levinson, David. "An Explanation for the Oneida-Colonist Alliance in the American Revolution." Ethnohistory 23 (Summer 1976): 265-289.

185. Nash, Gary. "The Forgotten Experience: Indians, Blacks, and the American Revolution." In The American Revolution: Changing Perspectives, edited by William M. Fowler, Jr., and Wallace Coyle, pp. 27-46. Boston: Northeastern University Press, 1979.

186. O'Donnell, James H. III. "The Florida Revolutionary Indian Frontier: Abode of the Blessed or Field of Battle?" In Eighteenth-Century Florida: Life on the Frontier, edited by Samuel Proctor, pp. 60-74. Gainesville: University Presses of Florida, 1976.

187. _____. "The Plight of the Ohio Indians during the American Revolution." In The Historic Indian in Ohio, edited by Randall Buchman, pp. 14-20. Columbus: Ohio Historical Society, 1976.

188. _____. "The Southern Indians in the War for American Independence, 1775-1783." In Four Centuries of Southern Indians, edited by Charles M. Hudson, pp. 46-64. Athens: University of Georgia Press, 1975.

189. _____. "The South on the Eve of the Revolution: The Native Americans." In The Revolutionary War in the South: Power, Conflict, and Leadership: Essays in Honor of John Richard Alden, edited by W. Robert Higgins, pp. 64-78. Durham: Duke University Press, 1979.

190. _____. "Who Is There To Mourn for Logan? No One! The Native American Crisis in the Ohio Country, 1774-1783." In Ohio in the American Revolution, edited by Thomas H. Smith, pp. 17-21. Columbus: Ohio Historical Society, 1976.

191. Rice, Otis K. "The Ohio Valley in the American Revolution: A General View." In Ohio in the American Revolution, edited by Thomas H. Smith, pp. 5-13. Columbus: Ohio Historical Society, 1976.

192. Smith, Thomas H., ed. Ohio in the American Revolution. Ohio American Revolution Bicentennial Conference Series, No. 1. Columbus: Ohio Historical Society, 1976.

193. Tanner, Helen Hornbeck. "Pipesmoke and Muskets: Florida Indian Intrigues of the Revolutionary Era." In Eighteenth-Century Florida and Its Borderlands, edited by Samuel Proctor, pp. 13-39. Gainesville: University Presses of Florida, 1975. Commentary by William C. Sturtevant, pp. 40-47.

See also studies of military relations between Indians and whites during the Revolutionary War (880 to 886).

INDIAN AFFAIRS, 1780-1815

194. Anderson, Gary. "American Agents vs. British Traders: Prelude to the War of 1812 in the Far West." In The American West: Essays in Honor of W. Eugene Hollon, edited by Ronald Lora, pp. 3-24. Toledo: University of Toledo, 1980.

195. Carter, Harvey Lewis. "A Frontier Tragedy: Little Turtle and William Wells." Old Northwest 6 (Spring 1980): 3-18.

196. Clarfield, Gerard. "Protecting the Frontiers: Defense Policy and the Tariff Question in the First Washington Administration." William and Mary Quarterly, 3d series 32 (July 1975): 443-464.

197. Drinnon, Richard. "The Metaphysics of Empire-Building: American Imperialism in the Age of Jefferson and Monroe." Massachusetts Review 16 (Autumn 1975): 666-688.

198. Ferguson, Clyde R. "Confrontation at Coleraine: Creeks, Georgians, and Federalist Indian Policy." South Atlantic Quarterly 78 (Spring 1979): 224-243.

199. Foley, William E., and Charles David Rice. "Visiting the President: An Exercise in Jeffersonian Indian Diplomacy." American West 16 (November-December 1979): 4-14, 56. Illustrated by drawings by Saint-Memin.

200. Graymont, Barbara. "New York State Indian Policy after the Revolution." New York History 57 (October 1976): 438-474.

201. Holmes, Jack D. L. "The Southern Boundary Commission, the Chattahoochee River, and the Florida Seminoles, 1799." In Four Centuries of Southern Indians, edited by Charles M. Hudson, pp. 65-82. Athens: University of Georgia Press, 1975.

202. Horsman, Reginald. "United States Indian Policy and Expansion into Ohio." In The Historic Indian in Ohio, edited by Randall Buchman, pp. 6-13. Columbus:

Ohio Historical Society, 1976.

203. Isern, Thomas D., ed. "Exploration and Diplomacy: George Champlin Sibley's Report to William Clark, 1811." Missouri Historical Review 73 (October 1978): 85-102.

204. McDaniel, Mary Jane. "Tecumseh's Visits to the Creeks." Alabama Review 33 (January 1980): 3-14.

205. Penick, James, Jr. "I Will Stamp on the Ground with My Foot and Shake Down Every House." American Heritage 27 (December 1975): 82-87. Tecumseh's prediction of an earthquake.

206. Roberts, Gary L. "The Chief of State and the Chief." American Heritage 26 (October 1975): 28-33, 86-89. George Washington and Alexander McGillivray.

207. Ross, Daniel J. J., and Bruce S. Chappell, eds. "Visit to the Indian Nations: The Diary of John Hambley." Florida Historical Quarterly 55 (July 1976): 60-73.

208. Schusky, Ernest L. "Thoughts and Deeds of the Founding Fathers: The Beginning of United States and Indian Relations." In Political Organization of Native North Americans, edited by Ernest L. Schusky, pp. 7-39. Washington: University Press of America, 1980.

209. Sturtevant, William C. "The Cherokee Frontiers, the French Revolution, and William Augustus Bowles." In The Cheorkee Indian Nation: A Troubled History, edited by Duane H. King, pp. 61-91. Knoxville: University of Tennessee Press, 1979.

210. Symonds, Craig. "The Failure of America's Indian Policy on the Southwestern Frontier, 1785-1793." Tennessee Historical Quarterly 35 (Spring 1976): 29-45.

211. Watson, Thomas D. "Strivings for Sovereignty: Alexander McGillivray, Creek Warfare, and Diplomacy, 1783-1790." Florida Historical Quarterly 58 (April 1980): 400-414.

212. Weeks, Philip. "Genocide in Ohio: Gnadenhutten 1782." Wassaja/The Indian Historian 13 (November 1980): 32-33.

213. White, David H. "The Spaniards and William Augustus Bowles in Florida, 1799-1803." Florida Historical Quarterly 54 (October 1975): 145-155.

214. Whittenburg, James P. "'The Common Farmer (Number 2)': Herman Husband's Plan for Peace between the United States and the Indians, 1792." William and Mary Quarterly, 3d series 34 (October 1977): 647-650.

215. Williams, Joyce G., and Jill E. Farrelly. Diplomacy on the Indiana-Ohio Frontier, 1783-1791. Bloomington: Indiana University Bicentennial Committee, 1976.

216. Wright, J. Leitch, Jr. Britain and the American Frontier, 1783-1815. Athens: University of Georgia Press, 1975.

Works on Indian wars, 1780-1812 (902 to 907) and on the War of 1812 (908 to 912) should also be consulted.

FROM THE WAR OF 1812 TO THE CIVIL WAR

General and Miscellaneous Studies

217. Beeton, Beverly. "Teach Them to Till the Soil: An Experiment with Indian Farms, 1850-1862." American Indian Quarterly 3 (Winter 1977-1978): 299-320.

218. Bolt, Christine. "The Anti-Slavery Origins of Concern for the American Indians." In Anti-Slavery, Religion and Reform: Essays in Memory of Roger Anstey, edited by Christine Bolt and Seymour Drescher, pp. 233-253. Folkestone, England: Dawson, 1980.

219. Christy, Howard A. "Open Hand and Mailed Fist: Mormon-Indian Relations in Utah, 1847-52." Utah Historical Quarterly 46 (Summer 1978): 216-235.

220. Doran, Michael F. "Antebellum Cattle Herding in the Indian Territory." Geographical Review 66 (January 1976): 48-58.

221. Ewers, John C. "Indian Views of the White Man Prior to 1850: An Interpretation." In Red Men and Hat Wearers: Viewpoints in Indian History, edited by Daniel Tyler, pp. 7-23. Boulder: Colorado: Pruett Publishing Company, 1976.

222. Hurtado, Albert L. "Controlling California's Indian Labor Force: Federal Administration of California Indian Affairs during the Mexican War." Southern California Quarterly 61 (Fall 1979): 217-238.

223. Magnaghi, Russell M. "The Red River Valley North of the Natchitoches, 1817-1818: The Letters of John Fowler." Louisiana Studies 15 (Fall 1976): 287-293.

224. _____. "Sulphur Fork Factory, 1817-1822." Arkansas Historical Quarterly 27 (Summer 1978): 168-183.

225. Rogin, Michael Paul. Fathers and

Children: Andrew Jackson and the Sub-
jugation of the American Indian. New
York: Alfred A. Knopf, 1975.

226. Satz, Ronald N. American Indian Policy
in the Jacksonian Era. Lincoln: University of Nebraska Press, 1975.

227. _____. "Indian Policy in the Jacksonian Era: The Old Northwest as a Test
Case." Michigan History 60 (Spring
1976): 71-93.

228. _____. "Remini's Andrew Jackson
(1767-1821): Jackson and the Indians."
Tennessee Historical Quarterly 38
(Summer 1979): 158-166.

229. Schulte, Steven C. "American Indian
Historiography and the Myth of the
Origins of the Plains Wars." Nebraska
History 61 (Winter 1980): 437-446.

230. Smith, Robert E. "The Wyandot Exploring Expedition of 1839." Chronicles of
Oklahoma 55 (Fall 1977): 282-292.

231. Stein, Gary Carl. "Federal Indian
Policy As Seen by British Travelers in
America: 1783-1860." Ph.D. dissertation,
University of New Mexico, 1975.

232. Trennert, Robert A., Jr. Alternative
to Extinction: Federal Indian Policy
and the Beginnings of the Reservation
System, 1846-51. Philadelphia: Temple
University Press, 1975.

233. _____. "Indian Policy on the Santa
Fe Road: The Fitzpatrick Controversy
of 1847-1848." Kansas History 1 (Winter
1978): 243-253.

234. Unruh, John D., Jr. The Plains Across:
The Overland Emigrants and the Trans-
Mississippi West, 1840-1860. Urbana:
University of Illinois Press, 1979.
Chapter 5, "Emigrant-Indian Interaction,"
pp. 156-200.

235. Viola, Herman J. "From Civilization
to Removal: Early American Indian Policy."
In Indian-White Relations: A Persistent
Paradox, edited by Jane F. Smith and
Robert M. Kvasnicka, pp. 45-56. Wash-
ington: Howard University Press, 1976.

236. Wise, William. Massacre at Mountain
Meadows: An American Legend and a Mon-
umental Crime. New York: Thomas Y.
Crowell Company, 1976.

See also studies on Indian removal (237
to 272) and on the Indian wars of the
period.

Indian Removal

237. Anderson, Gary Clayton. "The Removal
of the Mdewakanton Dakota in 1837: A

Case for Jacksonian Paternalism."
South Dakota History 10 (Fall 1980): 310-
333.

238. Blais, M. Jeanne. "The Imposing Alliance: Jackson, Georgia, and Indian Removal, 1825-1832." Indian Historian 8
(Winter 1975): 47-53.

239. Carter, Samuel III. Cherokee Sunset,
a Nation Betrayed: A Narrative of Tra-
vail and Triumph, Persecution and Exile.
Garden City, New York: Doubleday and
Company, 1976.

240. Clark, Carter Blue. "Chickasaw
Colonization in Oklahoma." Chronicles
of Oklahoma 54 (Spring 1976): 44-59.

241. _____. "'Drove off Like Dogs'--
Creek Removal." In Indians of the Lower
South: Past and Present, edited by John
K. Mahon, pp. 118-124. Pensacola
Gulf Coast History and Humanities Con-
ference, 1975.

242. Clifton, James A. "The Post-Removal
Aftermath." In The Historic Indian in
Ohio, edited by Randall Buchman, pp.
38-46. Columbus: Ohio Historical
Society, 1976.

243. Corn, James F. "Conscience or Duty:
General John E. Wool's Dilemma with
Cherokee Removal." Journal of Cherokee
Studies 3 (Winter 1978): 35-39.

244. DeRosier, Arthur H., Jr. "Myths and
Realities in Indian Westward Removal:
The Choctaw Example." In Four Centuries
of Southern Indians, edited by Charles
M. Hudson, pp. 83-100. Athens: Univer-
sity of Georgia Press, 1975.

245. Edwards, John Carver. "'Oh God the
Horror of That Night Will Never Be
Forgot': Ann Margaret McCall and the
Creek War of 1836." Manuscripts 28
(Spring 1976): 140-145.

246. Evans, E. Raymond. "Fort Marr Block-
house: The Last Evidence of America's
First Concentration Camps." Journal of
Cherokee Studies 2 (Spring 1977): 256-
263.

247. Feder, Bernard. "The Ridge Family
and the Death of a Nation." American
West 15 (September-October 1978): 28-31,
61-63.

248. French, Laurence. "The Death of a
Nation." American Indian Journal 4
(June 1978): 2-9.

249. Gibson, Arrell Morgan. "America's
Exiles." Chronicles of Oklahoma 54
(Spring 1976): 3-15.

250. _____. "The Great Plains as a

Colonization Zone for Eastern Indians."
In Ethnicity on the Great Plains,
edited by Frederick C. Luebke, pp. 19-
37. Lincoln: University of Nebraska
Press, 1980.

251. Gibson, Arrell Morgan, ed. America's
Exiles: Indian Colonization in Oklahoma.
Oklahoma City: Oklahoma Historical Soci-
ety, 1976. Reprint of Chronicles of
Oklahoma 54 (Spring 1976).

252. Grinde, Donald. "Cherokee Removal
and American Politics." Indian Historian
8 (Summer 1975): 33-42, 56.

253. Holm, Tom. "Cherokee Colonization
in Oklahoma." Chronicles of Oklahoma
54 (Spring 1976): 60-76.

254. Jahoda, Gloria. The Trail of Tears.
New York: Holt, Rinehart and Winston,
1975.

255. Jordan, H. Glenn. "Choctaw Colonization in Oklahoma." Chronicles of Oklahoma 54 (Spring 1976): 16-33.

256. Kersey, Harry A., Jr. "The Cherokee,
Creek, and Seminole Responses to Removal:
A Comparison." In Indians of the Lower
South: Past and Present, edited by John
K. Mahon, pp. 112-117. Pensacola:
Gulf Coast History and Humanities Con-
ference, 1975.

257. King, Duane H., and E. Raymond Evans,
eds. "The Trail of Tears: Primary
Documents of the Cherokee Removal."
Journal of Cherokee Studies 3 (Summer
1978): 131-185.

258. Klopfenstein, Carl G. "The Removal
of the Indians from Ohio." In The
Historic Indian in Ohio, edited by Randall Buchman, pp. 28-38. Columbus:
Ohio Historical Society, 1976.

259. Manzo, Joseph Theodore. "Native
American Perceptions of the Prairie-
Plains Environment." Ph.D. dissertation,
University of Kansas, 1978.

260. Norgren, Jill L., and Petra T.
Shattuck. "Limits of Legal Action: The
Cherokee Cases." American Indian Culture and Research Journal 2 (No. 2,
1978): 14-25.

261. Norwood, Frederick A. "Strangers
in a Strange Land: Removal of the Wyandot Indians." Methodist History 13
(April 1975): 45-60.

262. Parker, Linda. "Indian Colonization
in Northeastern and Central Indian
Territory." Chronicles of Oklahoma
54 (Spring 1976): 104-129.

263. Payne, John Howard. "The Cherokee

Cause." Journal of Cherokee Studies
1 (Summer 1976): 17-22. A 1835 letter.

264. Savage, William W., Jr. "Creek Colonization in Oklahoma." Chronicles of Oklahoma 54 (Spring 1976): 34-43.

265. Strickland, William Murrell. "The
Rhetoric of Cherokee Indian Removal from
Georgia, 1828-1832." Ph.D. dissertation,
Louisiana State University, 1975.

266. Swindler, William F. "Politics as
Law: The Cherokee Cases." American
Indian Law Review 3 (No. 1, 1975): 7-20.

267. Trennert, Robert A. "The Business
of Indian Removal: Deporting the Potawatomi from Wisconsin, 1851." Wisconsin Magazine of History 63 (Autumn
1979): 36-50.

268. _____. "A Trader's Role in the
Potawatomi Removal from Indiana: The
Case of George W. Ewing." Old Northwest
4 (March 1978): 3-24.

269. Venables, Robert W. "Victim versus
Victim: The Irony of the New York Indians' Removal to Wisconsin." In American Indian Environments: Ecological
Issues in Native American History, edited by Christopher Vecsey and Robert W.
Venables, pp. 140-151. Syracuse: Syracuse University Press, 1980.

270. Vipperman, Carl J. "'Forcibly If
We Must': The Georgia Case for Cherokee
Removal, 1802-1832." Journal of Chero-
kee Studies 3 (Spring 1978): 103-110.

271. Welsh, Louise. "Seminole Colonization in Oklahoma." Chronicles of Oklahoma 54 (Spring 1976): 77-103.

272. Young, Mary. "Indian Removal and the
Attack on Tribal Autonomy: The Cherokee
Case." In Indians of the Lower South:
Past and Present, edited by John K.
Mahon, pp. 125-142. Pensacola: Gulf
Coast History and Humanities Conference,
1975.

THE CIVIL WAR YEARS

273. Chandler, Robert. "The Failure of
Reform: White Attitudes and Indian
Response in California during the Civil
War Era." Pacific Historian 24 (Fall
1980): 284-294.

274. Fischer, LeRoy H., and William L.
McMurry. "Confederate Refugees from
Indian Territory." Chronicles of Ok-
lahoma 57 (Winter 1979): 451-462.

275. Kelsey, Harry. "Abraham Lincoln and
American Indian Policy." Lincoln Herald
77 (Fall 1975): 139-148.

276. Morgan, James F. "The Choctaw Warrants of 1863." Chronicles of Oklahoma 57 (Spring 1979): 55-66.

277. Nichols, David A. Lincoln and the Indians: Civil War Policy and Politics. Columbia: University of Missouri Press, 1978.

278. Rampp, Lary C., and Donald L. Rampp. The Civil War in the Indian Territory. Austin, Texas: Presidial Press, 1975.

279. Tyler, S. Lyman. "Ute Indians along Civil War Communication Lines." Utah Historical Quarterly 46 (Summer 1978): 251-261.

280. Viola, Herman J. Lincoln and the Indians. Historical Bulletin No. 31. Madison: Lincoln Fellowship of Wisconsin, 1976.

281. Ware, James W. "Indian Territory." Journal of the West 16 (April 1977): 101-113.

282. Wilson, T. Paul. "Delegates of the Five Civilized Tribes to the Confederate Congress." Chronicles of Oklahoma 53 (Fall 1975): 353-366.

INDIAN AFFAIRS, 1865-1900

General and Miscellaneous Studies

283. Anderson, Grant K. "Samuel D. Hinman and the Opening of the Black Hills." Nebraska History 60 (Winter 1979): 520-542.

284. Bigart, Robert, and Clarence Woodcock. "The Trans-Mississippi Exposition and the Flathead Delegation." Montana, the Magazine of Western History 29 (October 1979): 14-23.

285. Blinderman, Abraham. "Congressional Social Darwinism and the American Indian." Indian Historian 11 (Spring 1978): 15-17.

286. Cash, Joseph H. "The Reservation Indian Meets the White Man (1860-1914)." In Red Men and Hat Wearers: Viewpoints in Indian History, edited by Daniel Tyler, pp. 93-111. Boulder, Colorado: Pruett Publishing Company, 1976.

287. Crowder, David L. "Nineteenth-Century Indian-White Conflict in Southern Idaho." Idaho Yesterdays 23 (Summer 1979): 13-18.

288. Hauptman, Laurence M. "Governor Theodore Roosevelt and the Indians of New York State." Proceedings of the American Philosophical Society 119 (February 21, 1975): 1-7.

289. Heizer, Robert F., ed. Federal Concern about Conditions of California Indians, 1853 to 1913: Eight Documents. Socorro, New Mexico: Ballena Press, 1979.

290. Hoopes, Alban W. The Road to the Little Big Horn--and Beyond. New York: Vantage Press, 1975.

291. Hoxie, Frederick E. "The End of the Savage: Indian Policy in the United States Senate, 1880-1900." Chronicles of Oklahoma 55 (Summer 1977): 157-179.

292. Kelsey, Harry. "The Doolittle Report of 1867: Its Preparation and Shortcomings." Arizona and the West 17 (Summer 1975): 107-120.

293. Malone, Michael P., and Richard B. Roeder. "1876 on the Reservations: The Indian 'Question.'" Montana, the Magazine of Western History 25 (October 1975): 52-61.

294. Mattingly, Arthur P. "The Great Plains Peace Commission of 1867." Journal of the West 15 (July 1976): 23-37.

295. Milner, Clyde A. II. "With Good Intentions: Quaker Work and Indian Survival, the Nebraska Case, 1869-1882." Ph.D. dissertation, Yale University, 1979.

296. Nicklason, Fred. "The American Indians' 'White Problem': The Case of the Jicarilla Apache." Prologue 12 (Spring 1980): 41-55.

297. Pennington, William D. "Government Agricultural Policy on the Kiowa Reservation, 1869-1901." Indian Historian 11 (Winter 1978): 11-16.

298. _____. "Government Policy and Indian Farming on the Cheyenne and Arapaho Reservation, 1869-1880." Chronicles of Oklahoma 57 (Summer 1979): 171-189.

299. Proceedings of the Great Peace Commission of 1867-1868. Introduction by Vine Deloria, Jr., and Raymond DeMallie. Washington: Institute for the Development of Indian Law, 1975.

300. Prucha, Francis Paul. American Indian Policy in Crisis: Christian Reformers and the Indian, 1865-1900. Norman: University of Oklahoma Press, 1976.

301. _____. "The Board of Indian Commissioners and the Delegates of the Five Tribes." Chronicles of Oklahoma 56 (Fall 1978): 247-264.

302. Remsberg, Stanley Ray. "United States Administration of Alaska: The Army Phase, 1867-1877: A Study in Federal Governance of an Overseas Possession."

Ph.D. dissertation, University of Wisconsin-Madison, 1975.

303. Tate, Michael L. "John P. Clum and the Origins of an Apache Constabulary, 1874-1877." *American Indian Quarterly* 3 (Summer 1977): 99-120.

304. Trennert, Robert A. "The Indian Role in the 1876 Centennial Celebration." *American Indian Culture and Research Journal* 1 (No. 4, 1976): 7-13.

305. _____. "Popular Imagery and the American Indian: A Centennial View." *New Mexico Historical Review* 51 (July 1976): 215-232.

306. Vantine, J. Liessman. "The Metal Breasts." *North Dakota History* 45 (Summer 1978): back cover. Indian police.

307. White, Lonnie J., ed. *Chronicle of a Congressional Journey: The Doolittle Committee in the Southwest, 1865.* Boulder, Colorado: Pruett Publishing Company, 1975.

308. Worcester, Donald E. "The Friends of the Indian and the Peace Policy." In *Forked Tongues and Broken Treaties,* edited by Donald E. Worcester, pp. 254-291. Caldwell, Idaho: Caxton Printers, 1975.

309. Zegas, Judy Braun. "North American Indian Exhibit at the Centennial Exposition." *Curator* 19 (June 1976): 162-173.

Reformers and Reform Organizations

310. Ahern, Wilbert H. "Assimilationist Racism: The Case of the 'Friends of the Indian.'" *Journal of Ethnic Studies* 4 (Summer 1976): 23-32.

311. Bannan, Helen M. "The Idea of Civilization and American Indian Policy Reformers in the 1880s." *Journal of American Culture* 1 (Winter 1978): 787-799.

312. _____. "Reformers and the 'Indian Problem,' 1878-1887 and 1922-1934." Ph.D. dissertation, Syracuse University, 1976.

313. _____. "'True Womanhood' and Indian Assimilation." In *Selected Proceedings of the 3rd Annual Conference on Minority Studies,* edited by George E. Carter and James R. Parker, 2: 187-194. 2 volumes. LaCrosse, Wisconsin: Institute for Minority Studies, 1976.

314. Banning, Evelyn I. "Helen Hunt Jackson in San Diego." *Journal of San Diego History* 24 (Fall 1978): 457-467.

315. Burgess, Larry E. *The Lake Mohonk Conference of Friends of the Indian: Guide to the Annual Reports.* New York: Clearwater Publishing Company, 1975.

316. Byers, John R., Jr. "The Indian Matter of Helen Hunt Jackson's *Ramona*: From Fact to Fiction." *American Indian Quarterly* 2 (Winter 1975-1976): 331-346.

317. Fritz, Henry E. "The Board of Indian Commissioners and Ethnocentric Reform, 1878-1893." In *Indian-White Relations: A Persistent Paradox,* edited by Jane F. Smith and Robert M. Kvasnicka, pp. 57-78. Washington: Howard University Press, 1976.

318. Hagan, William T. "Civil Service Commissioner Theodore Roosevelt and the Indian Rights Association." *Pacific Historical Review* 44 (May 1975): 187-200.

319. Mardock, Robert W. "Standing Bear and the Reformers." In *Indian Leaders: Oklahoma's First Statesmen,* edited by H. Glenn Jordan and Thomas M. Holm, pp. 101-113. Oklahoma City: Oklahoma Historical Society, 1979.

320. Marsden, Michael T. "A Dedication to the Memory of Helen Hunt Jackson, 1830-1885." *Arizona and the West* 21 (Summer 1979): 109-112.

321. *Papers of the Indian Rights Association, 1864 (1882-1968) 1973.* Glen Rock, New Jersey: Microfilming Corporation of America, 1973. The publisher has issued a *Guide to the Microfilm Edition* (1975).

Indian Affairs in the Indian Territory

322. Ford, Jeanette W. "Federal Law Comes to Indian Territory." *Chronicles of Oklahoma* 58 (Winter 1980-1981): 432-439.

323. Goble, Danney Glenn. "A New Kind of State: Settlement and State-Making in Oklahoma to 1907." Ph.D. dissertation, University of Missouri-Columbia, 1976.

324. Hampton, Carol. "Indian Colonization in the Cherokee Outlet and Western Indian Territory." *Chronicles of Oklahoma* 54 (Spring 1976): 130-148.

325. Miner, H. Craig. *The Corporation and the Indian: Tribal Sovereignty and Industrial Civilization in Indian Territory, 1865-1907.* Columbia: University of Missouri Press, 1976.

326. _____. "'A Corps of Clerks': The Bureaucracy of Industrialization in Indian Territory, 1866-1907." *Chronicles of Oklahoma* 53 (Fall 1975): 322-331.

327. Morgan, James F. "William Cary Renfrow: Governor of Oklahoma Territory, 1893-1897." Chronicles of Oklahoma 53 (Spring 1975): 46-65.

328. Nolen, Curtis L. "The Okmulgee Constitution: A Step towards Indian Self-Determination." Chronicles of Oklahoma 58 (Fall 1980): 264-281.

329. Osborne, Alan. "The Exile of the Nez Perce in Indian Territory, 1878-1885." Chronicles of Oklahoma 56 (Winter 1978-1979): 450-471.

330. Williams, Ronnie. "Pictorial Essay on the Dawes Commission." Chronicles of Oklahoma 53 (Summer 1975): 225-238.

See also studies of the post-Civil War Indian wars.

INDIAN AFFAIRS, 1901-1932

331. Berens, John F. "'Old Campaigners, New Realities': Indian Policy Reform in the Progressive Era, 1900-1912." Mid-America 59 (January 1977): 51-64.

332. Briley, Ronald. "Lynn J. Frazier and Progressive Reform: A Plodder in the Ranks of a Ragged Regiment." South Dakota History 7 (Fall 1977): 438-454.

333. Dippie, Brian W. "'Now or Never Is the Time': Anthropology, Government Policy, and the Concept of the Vanishing Indian." In Hemispheric Perspectives on the United States: Papers from the New York Conference, edited by Joseph S. Tulchin, pp. 404-415. Westport: Connecticut: Greenwood Press, 1978.

334. Dorcy, Michael Morgan. "Friends of the American Indian, 1922-1934: Patterns of Patronage and Philanthropy." Ph.D. dissertation, University of Pennsylvania, 1978.

335. Ellis, Richard N. "'Indians at Ibapah in Revolt': Goshutes, the Draft and the Indian Bureau, 1917-1919." Nevada Historical Society Quarterly 19 (Fall 1976): 163-170.

336. Holm, Thomas M. "Indians and Progressives: From Vanishing Policy to the Indian New Deal." Ph.D. dissertation, University of Oklahoma, 1978.

337. Knapp, Ronald, and Laurence Hauptman. "'Civilization over Savagery': The Japanese, the Formosan Frontier, and United States Indian Policy, 1895-1915." Pacific Historical Review 49 (November 1980): 647-652.

338. Littlefield, Daniel F., Jr., and Lonnie E. Underhill. "The 'Crazy Snake Uprising' of 1909: A Red, Black or White Affair?" Arizona and the West 20 (Winter 1978): 307-324.

339. Nugent, Ann. Regulation of the Lummi Indians by Government Officials between 1900-1920. Bellingham, Washington: Lummi Communications, 1977.

340. Parman, Donald L. "The 'Big Stick' in Indian Affairs: The Bai-a-lil-le Incident in 1909." Arizona and the West 20 (Winter 1978): 343-360.

341. _____. "A White Man's Fight: The Crow Scandal, 1906-1913." In The American West: Essays in Honor of W. Eugene Hollon, edited by Ronald Lora, pp. 73-96. Toledo: University of Toledo, 1980.

342. Stefon, Frederick J. "Significance of the Meriam Report of 1928. Indian Historian 8 (Summer 1975): 2-7, 46.

THE INDIAN NEW DEAL

343. Berkey, Curtis. "Implementation of the Indian Reorganization Act." American Indian Journal 2 (August 1976): 2-7.

344. _____. "John Collier and the Indian Reorganization Act." American Indian Journal 2 (July 1976): 2-7.

345. _____. "The Legislative History of the Indian Reorganization Act." American Indian Journal 2 (July 1976): 15-22.

346. Bromert, Roger. "The Sioux and the Indian-CCC." South Dakota History 8 (Fall 1978): 340-356.

347. _____. "The Sioux and the Indian New Deal, 1933-1944." Ph.D. dissertation, University of Toledo, 1980.

348. Ducheneaux, Frank. "The Indian Reorganization Act and the Cheyenne River Sioux." American Indian Journal 2 (August 1976): 8-14.

349. Kelly, Lawrence C. "The Indian Reorganization Act: The Dream and the Reality." Pacific Historical Review 44 (August 1975): 291-312.

350. _____. "John Collier and the Indian New Deal: An Assessment." In Indian-White Relations: A Persistent Paradox, edited by Jane F. Smith and Robert M. Kvasnicka, pp. 227-241. Washington: Howard University Press, 1976.

351. Kickingbird, Lynn. "Attitudes toward the Indian Reorganization Bill." American Indian Journal 2 (July 1976): 8-14.

352. Koppes, Clayton R. "From New Deal to Termination: Liberalism and Indian

Policy, 1933-1953." Pacific Historical Review 46 (November 1977): 543-566.

353. McNickle, D'Arcy. "The Indian New Deal as Mirror of the Future." In Political Organization of Native North Americans, edited by Ernest L. Schusky, pp. 107-119. Washington: University Press of America, 1980.

354. Philp, Kenneth R. "John Collier and the Controversy over the Wheeler-Howard Bill." In Indian-White Relations: A Persistent Paradox, edited by Jane F. Smith and Robert M. Kvasnicka, pp. 171-200. Washington: Howard University Press, 1976.

355. _____. "John Collier and the Indians of the Americas: The Dream and the Reality." Prologue 11 (Spring 1979): 5-21.

356. _____. John Collier's Crusade for Indian Reform, 1920-1954. Tucson: University of Arizona Press, 1977.

357. _____. "Turmoil at Big Cypress: Seminole Deer and the Florida Cattle Tick Controversy." Florida Historical Quarterly 56 (July 1977): 28-44.

358. Taylor, Graham D. "Anthropologists, Reformers, and the Indian New Deal." Prologue 7 (Fall 1975): 151-162.

359. _____. The New Deal and American Indian Tribalism: The Administration of the Indian Reorganization Act, 1934-45. Lincoln: University of Nebraska Press, 1980.

360. Weeks, Charles J. "The Eastern Cherokee and the New Deal." North Carolina Historical Review 53 (July 1976): 303-319.

INDIAN AFFAIRS AFTER 1945

General and Miscellaneous Studies

361. Bodine, John J. "Taos Blue Lake Controversy." Journal of Ethnic Studies 6 (Spring 1978): 42-48.

362. Bonney, Rachel A. "The Role of AIM Leaders in Indian Nationalism." American Indian Quarterly 3 (Autumn 1977): 209-224.

363. Flannery, Thomas Patrick, Jr. "The Indian Self-Determination Act: An Analysis of Federal Policy." Ph.D. dissertation, Northwestern University, 1980.

364. Porto, Brian L. "The Pattern Process in American Indian Affairs: Patterns of Interaction between American Indian Interest Groups, the Bureau of Indian Affairs, and the Indian Affairs Committees of the Congress." Ph.D. dissertation, Miami University, 1979.

365. White, David R. M. "The American Indian Religious Freedom Act: Native American Religious Issues . . . also Land Issues." Wassaja/The Indian Historian 13 (September 1980): 39-44.

Termination

366. Boender, Debra R. "Termination and the Administration of Glenn L. Emmons as Commissioner of Indian Affairs, 1953-1961." New Mexico Historical Review 54 (October 1979): 287-304.

367. Burt, Larry Wayne. "United States Expansion and Federal Policy toward Native Americans, 1953-60." Ph.D. dissertation, University of Toledo, 1979.

368. Fixico, Donald Lee. "Termination and Relocation: Federal Indian Policy in the 1950's." Ph.D. dissertation, University of Oklahoma 1980.

369. Herzberg, Stephen J. "The Menominee Indians: Termination to Restoration." American Indian Law Review 6 (No. 1, 1978): 143-204.

370. Peroff, Nicholas Carl. "Menominee Termination and Restoration." Ph.D. dissertation, University of Wisconsin-Madison, 1977.

371. Stefon, Frederick J. "The Irony of Termination: 1943-1958." Indian Historian 11 (September 1978): 3-14.

372. Underdal, Stanley James. "On the Road toward Termination: The Pyramid Lake Paiutes and the Indian Attorney Controversy of the 1950s." Ph.D. dissertation, Columbia University, 1977.

373. Wilkinson, Charles F., and Eric R. Biggs. "Evolution of the Termination Policy." American Indian Law Review 5 (No. 1, 1977): 139-184.

Indian Claims Commission

374. Carriker, Robert C. "The Kalispel Tribe and the Indian Claims Commission Experience." Western Historical Quarterly 9 (January 1978): 19-31.

375. Cutter, Donald C. "Clio and the California Indian Claims." Journal of the West 14 (October 1975): 35-48.

376. Downes, Randolph C., ed. "How a Historical Society Helped Bring About the Award to the Ottawa Tribe." Northwest Ohio Quarterly 47 (Winter 1974-1975): 4-14.

377. Gamino, John. "Indian Claims Commission: Discretion and Limitation in the Allowance of Attorneys' Fees." American Indian Law Review 3 (No. 1, 1975): 115-135.

378. Heizer, Robert F., ed. The California Indians vs. The United States of America (HR 4497). Socorro, New Mexico: Ballena Press, 1978.

379. Hoover, Herbert T. "Yankton Sioux Tribal Claims against the United States, 1917-1975." Western Historical Quarterly 7 (April 1976): 125-142.

380. "Indian Claims Commission 1975 Annual Report." American Indian Law Review 4 (No. 1, 1976): 175-188.

381. Lurie, Nancy Oestreich. "Indian Claims Commission." Annals of the American Academy of Political and Social Science 436 (March 1978): 97-110.

382. Pierce, Margaret Hunter. "The Work of the Indian Claims Commission." American Bar Association Journal 63 (February 1977): 227-232.

383. Rosenthal, Harvey Daniel. "Their Day in Court: A History of the Indian Claims Commission." Ph.D. dissertation, Kent State University, 1976.

384. "Seminole Land Rights in Florida and the Award of the Indian Claims Commission." American Indian Journal 4 (August 1978): 2-27.

385. "Special Recent Development: Indian Claims Commission 1975 Annual Report." American Indian Law Review 4 (No. 1, 1976): 175-188.

386. Stewart, Omer C. "The Western Shoshone of Nevada and the U.S. Government, 1863-1950." In Selected Papers from the 14th Great Basin Anthropological Conference, edited by Donald R. Tuohy, pp. 78-114. Socorro, New Mexico, 1978.

387. United States Indian Claims Commission, August 13, 1946--September 30, 1978: Final Report. Washington: Government Printing Office, 1979. Contains a history of the Commission, an alphabetical index of Indian Claims Commission cases, and a map showing "Indian Land Areas Judicially Established."

388. White, John R. "Barmecide Revisited: The Gratuitous Offset in Indian Claims Cases." Ethnohistory 25 (Spring 1978): 179-192.

Alaska Native Claims Settlement Act

389. "Alaska Native Claims Settlement Act: Long-Term Prospects." American Indian Journal 3 (May 1977): 10-17.

390. Branson, Douglas M. "Square Pegs in Round Holes: Alaska Native Claims Settlement Corporations under Corporate Law." UCLA-Alaska Law Review 8 (Spring 1979): 103-138

391. Fuller, Lauren L. "Alaska Native Claims Settlement Act: Analysis of the Protective Clauses of the Act through a Comparison with the Dawes Act of 1887." American Indian Law Review 4 (No. 2, 1976): 269-278.

392. Gruenstein, Peter. "Alaska's Natives, Inc." Progressive 41 (March 1977): 33-38.

393. Haynes, James B. "The Alaska Native Claims Settlement Act and Changing Patterns of Land Ownership in Alaska." Professional Geographer 28 (February 1976): 66-71.

394. Hopkins, Regina Marie. "The Alaskan National Monuments of 1978: Another Chapter in the Great Alaskan Land War." Boston College Environmental Affairs Law Review 8 (No. 1, 1979): 59-87.

395. Lazarus, Arthur, Jr., and W. Richard West, Jr. "The Alaska Native Claims Settlement Act: A Flawed Victory." Law and Contemporary Problems 40 (Winter 1976): 132-165.

396. Perret, Karen. "The Alaska Native Claims Settlement Act and the Alaskans." Indian Historian 11 (Winter 1978): 1-10.

397. Price, Monroe E. "A Moment in History: The Alaska Native Claims Settlement Act." UCLA-Alaska Law Review 8 (Spring 1979): 89-101.

398. _____. "Region-Village Relations under the Alaska Native Claims Settlement Act." UCLA-Alaska Law Review 5 (Fall 1975): 58-99; (Spring 1976): 237-265.

399. Reitze, Arnold W., Jr., and Glenn L. Reitze. "The Northwestern Frontier." Environment 17 (March 1975): 4, 34.

400. Schuyten, Peter J. "A Novel Corporation Takes Charge in Alaska's Wilderness." Fortune 92 (October 1975): 158-162, 164-168.

401. Treisman, Eric. "The Last Treaty." Harper's Magazine 250 (January 1975): 37-39.

American Indian Policy Review Commission

402. "AIPRC--BIA Management Study." American Indian Journal 2 (October 1976): 10-15.

403. "AIPRC--BIA Management Study: Budget Process." American Indian Journal 2 (November 1976): 2-9.

404. "AIPRC--BIA Management Study: Management Information." American Indian Journal 2 (December 1976): 7-11.

405. AIPRC--BIA Management Study: Personnel Management." American Indian Journal 2 (December 1976): 2-6.

406. "AIPRC--Interim Task Forces Report." American Indian Journal 2 (October 1976): 2-9.

407. "The AIPRC Report." Journal of American Indian Education 16 (May 1977): 1-14.

408. "AIPRC's Report on Indian Health." American Indian Journal 3 (February 1977): 17-23.

409. Ayres, Mary Ellen. "Federal Indian Policy and Labor Statistics--A Review Essay." Monthly Labor Review 101 (April 1978): 22-27.

410. Doss, Michael Peter. "The American Indian Policy Review Commission: A Case Study and Analysis of an Attempted Large System Change by a Temporary Organization." Ed.D. dissertation, Harvard University, 1977.

411. Grinde, Donald A., Jr. "Politics and the American Indian Policy Review Commission." In New Directions in Federal Indian Policy: A Review of the American Indian Policy Review Commission, pp. 19-28. Los Angeles: American Indian Studies Center, University of California, Los Angeles, 1979.

412. Kickingbird, Kirke. "The American Indian Policy Review Commission: A Prospect for Future Change in Federal Indian Policy." American Indian Law Review 3 (No. 2, 1975): 243-253.

413. Meeds, Lloyd. "The Indian Policy Review Commission." Law and Contemporary Problems 40 (Winter 1976): 9-11.

414. Muskrat, Jerry. "Recommendations of the American Indian Policy Review Commission and the Supreme Court." In New Directions in Federal Indian Policy: A Review of the American Indian Policy Review Commission, pp. 99-114. Los Angeles: American Indian Studies Center, University of California, Los Angeles, 1979.

415. New Directions in Federal Indian Policy: A Review of the American Indian Policy Review Commission. Introduction by Anthony D. Brown. Los Angeles: American Indian Studies Center, University of California, Los Angeles, 1979.

416. Slagle, Al Logan. "The American Indian Policy Review Commission: Repercussions and Aftermath." In New Directions in Federal Indian Policy: A Review of the American Indian Policy Review Commission, pp. 115-132. Los Angeles: American Indian Studies Center, University of California, Los Angeles, 1979.

417. Thompson, Mark. "Nurturing the Forked Tree: Conception and Formation of the American Indian Policy Review Commission." In New Directions in Federal Indian Policy: A Review of the American Indian Policy Review Commission, pp. 5-18. Los Angeles: American Indian Studies Center, University of California, Los Angeles, 1979.

The reports of the task forces and the final report of the Commission (which includes a minority report) are listed here.

418. Bureau of Indian Affairs Management Study: Report on BIA Management Practices to the American Indian Policy Review Commission. Washington: Government Printing Office, 1976.

419. Final Report: Report on Trust Responsibilities and the Federal-Indian Relationship, Including Treaty Review (Task Force 1). Washington: Government Printing Office, 1976.

420. Final Report: Report on Tribal Government (Task Force 2). Washington: Government Printing Office, 1976.

421. Final Report: Report on Federal Administration and Structure of Indian Affairs (Task Force 3). Washington: Government Printing Office, 1976.

422. Final Report: Report on Federal, State, and Tribal Jurisdiction (Task Force 4). Washington: Government Printing Office, 1976.

423. Final Report: Report on Indian Education (Task Force 5). Washington: Government Printing Office, 1976.

424. Final Report: Report on Indian Health (Task Force 6). Washington: Government Printing Office, 1976.

425. Final Report: Report on Reservation and Resource Development and Protection (Task Force 7). Washington: Government Printing Office, 1976.

426. Final Report: Report on Urban and Rural Non-Reservation Indians (Task Force 8). Washington: Government Printing Office, 1976.

427. Final Report: Law Consolidation, Revision, and Codification (Task Force 9). 2 volumes. Washington: Government Printing Office, 1977.

428. Final Report: Report on Terminated
and Nonfederally Recognized Indians
(Task Force 10). Washington: Government
Printing Office, 1976.

429. Final Report: Report on Alcohol and
Drug Abuse (Task Force 11). Washington;
Government Printing Office, 1976.

430. Special Joint Task Force Report on
Alaskan Native Issues. Washington:
Government Printing Office, 1976.

431. Final Report. 2 volumes. Washington:
Government Printing Office, 1977. The
final report of the Commission, submitted
to Congress, May 17, 1977.

Current Comment 1975

432. Adams, John P. "AIM and the FBI."
Christian Century 92 (April 2, 1975):
325-326.

433. _____. "AIM, the Church and the
FBI: The Douglas Durham Case." Christian
Century 92 (May 14, 1975): 489-495.

434. _____. "Why the Alexians Gave the
Abbey to the Indians." Christian Century
92 (March 5, 1975): 223-228.

435. "Alexians Cancel Indian Gift." Christian Century 92 (August 6-13, 1975): 704.

436. Banks, Dennis. "Consciousness Raising."
Engage/Social Action 3 (January 1975):
37-39. AIM leader on group's purpose.

437. Bee, Robert L. "The Washington Connection: American Indian Leaders and
American Indian Policy." Indian Historian
12 (Winter 1979): 2-11, 36.

438. Deloria, Vine, Jr. "God Is Also Red:
An Interview with Vine Deloria, Jr.,
by James R. McGraw." Christianity and
Crisis 35 (September 15, 1975): 198-206.

439. _____. "The Indian Movement: Out
of a Wounded Past." Ramparts 13 (March
1975): 28-32.

440. _____. "The North Americans."
Crisis 82 (December 1975): 385-387.

441. deMontigny, Lionel H. "The Bureau-
cratic Game and a Proposed Indian Ploy."
Indian Historian 8 (Fall 1975): 25-30.

442. Feaver, George. "An Indian Melodrama."
Encounter 44 (May 1975): 23-24. Wounded
Knee 1973.

443. _____. "The True Adventure."
Encounter 45 (October 1975): 25-32.

444. _____. "Wounded Knee and the New
Tribalism." Encounter 44 (February
1975): 28-35; (March 1975): 16-14.

445. Hastings, Doris. "From the People Who
Gave You America." Arts and Activities
78 (December 1975): 36-37.

446. Henry, Jeannette. "The Native American and Revolutions." Indian Historian
8 (Winter 1975): 10-12.

447. "Hollywood, Academia and Red Pride."
Human Behavior 4 (January 1975): 46.

448. "The Lengthening Shadow of Wounded
Knee." Moody Monthly 75 (March 1975):
24-27.

449. Lewis, Ronald G., and Man Keung Ho.
"Social Work with Native Americans."
Social Work 20 (September 1975): 379-382.

450. Lyles, Jean Caffey. "Gresham: Occupation and Aftermath." Christian
Century 92 (February 19, 1975): 155-157.

451. McCall, Cheryl. "Burying Still at
Wounded Knee." New Times 4 (May 30
1975): 42-43, 45-47.

452. McGuire, Diarmuid. "Ghost Dance
at Pine Ridge: FBI Loses Two in New
Indian War on U.S." Rolling Stone, No.
194 (August 28, 1975): 26, 28.

453. Mencarelli, James, and Steve Severin.
Protest: Red, Black, Brown Experience
in America. Grand Rapids, Michigan:
Eerdmans, 1975.

454. "Menominee Troubles." Christian
Century 92 (February 5-12, 1975): 103-
104.

455. "The New Indian-Treaty Wars." Newsweek 85 (January 13, 1975): 58-59.

456. "Pine Ridge Shoot-Out." Newsweek
86 (July 7, 1975): 15-16.

457. "A Report from Pine Ridge: Conditions
on the Oglala Sioux Reservation."
Civil Rights Digest 7 (Summer 1975):
28-38.

458. Seabury, Paul. "Burying the Hatchet."
Commentary 59 (April 1975): 72-73.

459. "The Siletz Restoration Bill." American Indian Journal 1 (November 1975):
11-13.

460. Stang, Alan. "Red Indians." American Opinion 18 (September 1975): 1-10,
73+.

461. Stephens, Suzanne. "Of Nature and
Modernity." Progressive Architecture
56 (October 1975): 66-69. Native
American Center, Minneapolis, Minnesota.

462. "Still Hunted." Economist 256 (July
12, 1975): 63.

463. Stuewer, John. "Incident at Gresham." *Progressive* 39 (December 1975): 47-51.

464. Turner, Frederick W. III. "The Century after *A Century of Dishonor*: American Conscience and Consciousness." *Massachusetts Review* 16 (Autumn 1975): 715-731.

466. "U.S. Indians: On Legal Trail--and Winning." *U.S. News and World Report* 78 (May 26, 1975): 52-53.

467. Wantland, William C. "An Essay: The Ignorance of Ignorance: Cultural Barriers between Indians and Non-Indians." *American Indian Law Review* 3 (No. 1, 1975): 1-5.

468. Weisman, Joel. "About That 'Ambush' at Wounded Knee." *Columbia Journalism Review* 14 (September-October 1975): 28-31.

469. "Whatever Happened to . . . That Billion-Dollar Windfall for Alaska's Natives." *U.S. News and World Report* 79 (December 8, 1975): 45.

470. Zimmerman, Bill. *Airlift to Wounded Knee*. Chicago: Swallow Press, 1976.

Current Comment 1976

471. "Arizona Project Helps Elderly Native Americans Sustain Tribal Heritage." *Aging*, Nos. 263-264 (September-October 1976): 7-8.

472. Baird, Bruce. "Is It Worth the Climb? Programming Efforts for Native Americans." *Public Telecommunications Review* 4 (July-August 1976): 50-52.

473. Banks, Dennis. "The Black Scholar Interviews: Dennis Banks." *Black Scholar* 7 (June 1976): 28-36.

474. Berry, Thomas. "The Indian Future." *Cross Currents* 26 (Summer 1976): 133-142.

475. Berry, Wendell. "The Unsettling of America." *Nation* 222 (February 7, 1976): 149-151; (February 14, 1976): 181-182.

476. Binyon, Michael. "Reservations about the White Man's Culture." *Times Educational Supplement* 3207 (November 19, 1976): 17.

477. Braudy, Susan. "'We Will Remember' Survival School: A Visit with Women and Children of the American Indian Movement." *Ms.* 5 (July 1976): 77-80, 94, 120.

478. Clavir, Judy Gumbo, and Stew Albert. "Open Fire or, The FBI's History Lesson." *Crawdaddy*, November 1976, pp. 52-57.

479. Deloria, Vine, Jr. "Completing the Theological Circle; Civil Religion in America. *Religious Education* 71 (May-June 1976): 278-287.

480. _____. "A Last Word from the First Americans." *New York Times Magazine*, July 4, 1976, p. 80.

481. _____. "The Twentieth Century." In *Red Men and Hat Wearers: Viewpoints in Indian History*, edited by Daniel Tyler, pp. 155-166. Boulder, Colorado: Pruett Publishing Company, 1976.

482. _____. "Why the U.S. Never Fought the Indians." *Christian Century* 93 (January 7-14, 1976): 9-12.

483. Edward, J. "Trail of Tears to 1976: A Look at the Bicentennial." *Ms.* 5 (July 1976): 100-101.

484. Folsom, R. D. "The Climate in Congress: Indians Face Period of Uncertainty." *American Indian Law Review* 4 (No. 2, 1976): 349-354.

485. Gordon, Henry. "The Cut Bank Case." *Progressive* 40 (March 1976): 26.

486. Griessman, B. Eugene. "The Tukabatchi Pow Wow and the Spirit of Tecumseh; or, How to Hold a Pow Wow without Indians." *Phylon* 37 (June 1976): 172-173.

487. "Indian Is . . . Seminars." *American Indian Journal* 2 (February 1976): 13

488. Keller, Charles. "Prison Reform and Indians." *Indian Historian* 9 (Winter 1976): 34-38.

489. Koster, John. "American Indians and the Media." *Cross Currents* 26 (Summer 1976): 164-171. Treatment of Wounded Knee 1973.

490. Lurie, Nancy Oestreich. "The Will-o'-the-Wisp of Indian Unity." *Indian Historian* 9 (Summer 1976): 19-24.

491. McIntyre, Michael. "International Indian Treaty Council." *Engage/Social Action* 4 (April 1976): 57-59.

492. McKale, Michael. "From Reservation to Global Society: American Culture, Liberation and the Native American-- An Interview with Vine Deloria, Jr. *Radical Religion* 2 (No. 4, 1976): 49-58.

493. Olguin, John Phillip, and Mary T. Olguin. "Isleta--The Pueblo That Roared." *Indian Historian* 9 (Fall 1976): 2-13.

494. Paredes, J. Anthony. "The Need for

Cohesion and American Isolates."
American Anthropologist 78 (June 1976):
335-337.

495. Parman, Donald L. "American Indians
and the Bicentennial." New Mexico Historical Review 51 (July 1976): 233-249.

496. "Projects in Nevada Succeed in Helping
Indians Help Themselves." Aging, Nos.
263-264 (September-October 1976): 18-20.

497. Ranck, Lee. "A Voice Speaking inside
the Drum." Engage/Social Action 4
(August 1976): 7-16, 57-60. International
Indian Treaty Conference.

498. Rogal, Kim C. "Indians and Ranchers:
Bad Days on the Reservation." Nation
223 (November 20, 1976): 525-530.

499. "Statement Concerning Improved Services to Elderly American Indians. American Indian Journal 2 (September 1976):
18-21.

500. Steiner, Stan. The Vanishing White
Man. New York: Harper and Row, 1976.

501. Sullivan, John A. "Native Americans'
Right To Be Different." Christian
Century 93 (November 3, 1976): 960, 962.

502. Trillin, Calvin. "U.S. Journal: The
Southwest: Cultural Differences." New
Yorker 51 (January 5, 1976): 63-67.

503. Tyler, Daniel. "The Indian Welt-
anshauung: A Summary of Views Expressed
by Indians at the 'Viewpoints in Indian
History' Conference, August 1974,
Colorado State University." In Red Men
and Hat Wearers: Viewpoints in Indian
History, edited by Daniel Tyler, pp.
135-139. Boulder, Colorado: Pruett
Publishing Company, 1976.

504. Vizenor, Gerald. Tribal Scenes and
Ceremonies. Minneapolis: Nodin Press,
1976.

505. Wasser, Martin. "The Six Nations and
the State." Conservationist 30 (January 1976): 36-37.

506. White, Dale. "We Can Never Go Back
into the Woods Again." Conservationist
30 (January 1976): 29-32.

507. Witt, Shirley Hill. "The Brave-
Hearted Women: The Struggle at Wounded
Knee." Civil Rights Digest 8 (Summer
1976): 38-45.

Current Comment 1977

508. Blackburn, Dan. "Skyhorse and Mohawk:
More Than a Murder Trial." Nation 225
(December 24, 1977): 682-686.

509. Brasch, Beatty. "The Y-Indian Guide

and Y-Indian Princess Program." Indian
Historian 10 (Summer 1977): 49-60.

510. Chapman, William. "Native Americans'
New Clout." Progressive 41 (August 1977):
30-32.

511. Dillingham, Brint. "Recent Development in the Skyhorse Mohawk Case." American Indian Journal 3 (August 1977):
18-19.

512. Friedenberg, Edgar Z. "The News
about Leonard Peltier." Canadian Forum
56 (March 1977): 26-28.

513. "The Geneva Conference." American
Indian Journal 3 (November 1977): 4-23.
A series of articles and statements.

514. Goldman, Martin S. "Teaching the
Holocaust: Some Suggestions for Comparative Analysis." Journal of Intergroup Relations 6 (December 1977):
23-30.

515. Hart, Donna. "Enlarging the American Dream." American Education 13
(May 1977): 10-16.

516. Huck, Susan L. M. "Giving It Back
to the Indians." American Opinion 20
(June 1977): 39-54.

517. Johansen, Bruce. "Leonard Peltier
and the Posse: Still Fighting the Indian Wars." Nation 225 (October 1,
1977): 304-307.

518. Kanter, Elliot. "The FBI Takes
Aim at AIM." American Indian Journal
3 (August 1977): 14-18.

519. Kovler, Peter. "Still Scalping
the Indians: Congress Is the Problem."
Nation 225 (September 17, 1977): 233-
236.

520. Lounberg, Dan. "The New Face of the
American Indian Movement." Crisis 84
(December 1977): 463-466.

521. "Native Americana." Rights 23
(January-February 1977): 8-9.

522. "Native Americans before the U.N."
American Indian Journal 3 (September
1977): 3-4.

523. "NCAI Resolutions." American Indian
Journal 3 (January 1977): 21-26.

524. Otway, H. Edward. "On Behalf of
the Indian Community." Engage/Social
Action 5 (August 1977): 49-52.

525. Ryan, Joe. "Compared to Other Nations." American Indian Journal 3
(August 1977): 2-13.

526. Schroeter, Gerd. "The Buckskin

Curtain as Shibboleth and Security-Blanket." Journal of Ethnic Studies 4 (Winter 1977): 85-94.

527. Taylor, Stuart. "Indians on the Lawpath." New Republic 176 (April 30, 1977): 16-21.

528. Trippett, Frank. "Should We Give the U.S. Back to the Indians?" Time 109 (April 11, 1977): 51-52.

529. "The Washington Report." American Indian Journal 3 (November 1977): 24-25.

Current Comment 1978

530. "American Indians: Backlash." Current 204 (July 1978): 20-22.

531. "A Backlash Stalks the Indians." Business Week, No. 2551 (September 11, 1978): 153, 156.

532. Castile, George Pierre. "The Headless Horsemen: Recapitating the Beheaded Community." Indian Historian 11 (Summer 1978): 38-45.

533. Dorris, Michael. "Case History of a Conscience-Based Protest." Interracial Books for Children Bulletin 9 (No. 2, 1978): 4-5, 22.

534. Duval, Vincent. "Human Rights Begin at Home, Washington!" World Marxist Review 21 (October 1978): 136-144.

535. "GAO Report on Indian Self-Determination." American Indian Journal 4 (June 1978): 35-36.

536. Garriott, Charlie. "Captives in Their Homeland: An Introduction to the Survival Struggles of Native Americans." Sojourners 7 (July 1978): 12-13.

537. Guillemin, Jeanne. "The Politics of National Integration: A Comparison of United States and Canadian Indian Administrations." Social Problems 25 (February 1978): 319-332.

538. Highwater, Jamake. "In Search of Indian America." Retirement Living 18 (April 1978): 21-27; (May 1978): 38-41; (June 1978): 23-25.

539. Hraba, Joseph. "The American Indian and Ethnicity in Iowa's Future." In The Worlds between Two Rivers: Perspectives on American Indians in Iowa, edited by Gretchen M. Bataille and others, pp. 112-121. Ames: Iowa State University Press, 1978.

540. "Indians on March toward Self-Rule." U.S. News and World Report 84 (March 27, 1978): 72-74.

541. Johansen, Bruce. "Indians for Sover-

eignty; The Reservation Offensive." Nation 226 (February 25, 1978): 204-207.

542. Kellogg, Mark. "Indian Rights: Fighting Back with White Man's Weapons." Saturday Review, November 25, 1978, pp. 24-27.

543. Langston, Maxine M. "Religious Community Support." Engage/Social Action 6 (September 1978): 42-44. The "Longest Walk."

544. _____. "A Walk of Love for All Humanity." Engage/Social Action 6 (July 1978): 4-7. The "Longest Walk."

545. Margolis, Richard J. "Red-White Relations." New Leader 61 (April 10, 1978): 17-18.

546. Monkres, Peter. "The Longest Walk: An Indian Pilgrimage." Christian Century 95 (April 5, 1978): 350-352.

547. Page, James K., Jr. "Phenomena, Comment and Notes." Smithsonian 9 (September 1978): 34-38. Thoughts on the "Longest Walk."

548. "A Paleface Uprising." Newsweek 91 (April 10, 1978): 39-40. Interstate Congress for Equal Rights and Responsibilities.

549. "Papago Indians Go Solar." Chemistry 51 (September 1978): 3.

550. "Profits in the Tundra." Newsweek 92 (August 21, 1978): 62, 65. Alaska's regional corporations.

551. Ranck, Lee. "To Save Their Indian Way of Life." Engage/Social Action 6 (September 1978): 4-7, 41. The "Longest Walk."

552. "The Rich Indians." Newsweek 91 (March 20, 1978): 61-64.

553. Shattuck, Petra, and Jill Norgren. "Indian Rights: The Cost of Justice." Nation 227 (July 22, 1978): 70-72.

554. Shenk, Phil. "The Longest Walk: Marching for Indian Self-Preservation." Sojourners 7 (July 1978): 10-12.

555. Solomon, Bill. "Indians and Nuclear 'Progress.'" Progressive 42 (August 1978): 38.

556. Talbot, Steve. "Free Alcatraz: The Culture of Native American Liberation." Journal of Ethnic Studies 6 (Fall 1978): 83-96.

557. "Tepees on the Mall." Newsweek 92 (July 31, 1978): 27.

558. Tullberg, Steve. "Carter, Indian

Sovereignty, and the Supreme Court: New Twists and Doubletalk?" American Indian Journal 4 (March 1978): 40-42.

559. "War Pipe." Economist 267 (April 29, 1978): 54. Extradition of Dennis Banks.

Current Comment 1979

560. Bee, Robert L. "To Get Something for the People: The Predicament of the American Indian Leader." Human Organization 38 (Fall 1979): 239-247.

561. "Brando's Gift Stirs a Quarrel." Newsweek 93 (May 14, 1979): 20, 22.

562. Durham, Jimmie. "American Indians and Carter's Human Rights Sermons." Black Scholar 10 (March-April 1979): 48-53.

563. Hecht, Robert A. "The American Indian Mystique." America 140 (February 3, 1979): 71-73.

564. _____. "The Right To Remain Indian." Commonweal 106 (March 30, 1979): 176-179.

565. Matthiessen, Peter. "Last Stand at the Western Gate." Nation 229 (August 25, 1979): 135-138. Construction at a sacred Indian site.

566. Miller, Mark, and Judith Miller. "The Politics of Energy vs. the American Indian." USA Today 107 (March 1979): 8-11.

567. Panzarella, Robert, and Ansley LaMar. "Attitudes of Blacks and Whites toward Native American Revolutionary Tactics for Social Change." Human Relations 32 (January 1979): 69-75.

568. Raines, Howell. "American Indians: Struggling for Power and Identity." New York Times Magazine, February 11, 1979, pp. 21-24+.

569. Stephens, Richard C., and Michael H. Agar. "Red Tape--White Tape: Federal-Indian Funding Relationships." Human Organization 38 (Fall 1979): 283-293.

570. Strickland, Rennard. "The Absurd Ballet of American Indian Policy or American Indian Struggling with Ape on Tropical Landscape: An Afterword." Maine Law Review 31 (No. 1, 1979): 212-221.

571. Trosper, Ronald L. "Public Welfare and the American Indian." Urban and Social Change Review 12 (Summer 1979): 28-31.

572. Wilkinson, Charles F. "Shall the Islands Be Preserved?" American West 16 (May-June 1979): 33-37, 66-69.

Current Comment 1980

573. Batzle, Peter, and Melanie Oliviero. "The Congress." American Indian Journal 6 (January 1980): 16-20.

574. "Bingo Is the Best Revenge." Time 116 (July 7, 1980): 18. Seminole Indian bingo games.

575. Carpenter, Edward M. "Social Services, Policies, and Issues." Social Casework 61 (October 1980): 455-461.

576. Castile, George Pierre. "Who Speaks for the People?" Wassaja/The Indian Historian 13 (June 1980): 33-37.

577. Gedicks, Al. "Exxon, Copper, and the Sokaogon." Progressive 44 (February 1980): 43-46.

578. Giago, Tim A., Jr. "The Broadcast Media: Can the American Indian Get In?" Wassaja/The Indian Historian 13 (March 1980): 11-14.

579. Guillemin, Jeanne. "Federal Policies and Indian Politics." Society 17 (May-June 1980): 29-34.

580. Henry, Jeannette, and Rupert Costo. "Who Is an Indian?" Wassaja/The Indian Historian 13 (June 1980): 15-18.

581. Hutchins, Francis G. "Righting Old Wrongs." New Republic 183 (August 30, 1980): 14-17.

582. Lubick, George. "Sacred Mountains, Kachinas, and Skiers: The Controversy over the San Francisco Peaks." In The American West: Essays in Honor of W. Eugene Hollon, edited by Ronald Lora, pp. 133-154. Toledo: University of Toledo, 1980.

583. Lujan, Lance. "Education." American Indian Journal 6 (January 1980): 24-25.

584. MacDonald, Peter. "Both Political Parties Are in a Dead Heat to Wipe Out Tribal Sovereignty." Wassaja/The Indian Historian 13 (September 1980): 9-12.

585. "The New Commissioner Gets Down to Business." American Indian Journal 6 (March 1980): 16-21. Interview with William Hallett.

586. "Preparing To Meet New Raiders." Economist 275 (May 3, 1980): 29-30.

587. "Reagan on Indian Affairs." American Indian Journal 6 (October 1980): 10-13.

588. Roos, Philip D., Dowell H. Smith,

Stephen Langley, and James McDonald. "The Impact of the American Indian Movement on the Pine Ridge Indian Reservation." Phylon 41 (March 1980): 89-99.

589. Sherman, Bob. "The News." American Indian Journal 6 (January 1980): 3-9. History of AIM.

590. "What the People Say." American Indian Journal 6 (October 1980): 7-9. The 1980 Presidential election.

591. Webb-Vignery, June. "Won't Anybody Hire an Indian?" Wassaja/The Indian Historian 13 (June 1980): 30-32.

592. Wilkinson, Gerald Thomas. "On Assisting Indian People." Social Casework 61 (October 1980): 451-454.

593. Winchell, Dick. "The Treachery of Orme Dam." Wassaja/The Indian Historian 13 (November 1980): 45-47.

See the Readers' Guide, other periodical indexes, and newspaper indexes for further current materials.

4
The Indian Department

The Bureau of Indian Affairs and the Indian superintendencies and agencies, with their numerous personnel, made up what was often called the "Indian Department."

BUREAU OF INDIAN AFFAIRS

594. Alexander, Thomas G. A Clash of Interests: Interior Department and Mountain West, 1863-96. Provo, Utah: Brigham Young University Press, 1977.

595. Bruce, Louis R. "The Bureau of Indian Affairs, 1972." In Indian-White Relations: A Persistent Paradox, edited by Jane F. Smith and Robert M. Kvasnicka, pp. 242-250. Washington: Howard University Press, 1976.

596. Butler, Raymond V. "The Bureau of Indian Affairs: Activities since 1945." Annals of the American Academy of Political and Social Science 436 (March 1978): 50-60.

597. Jackson, Curtis E., and Marcia J. Galli. A History of the Bureau of Indian Affairs and Its Activities among Indians. San Francisco: R and E Research Associates, 1977.

598. Lawson, Michael L. "How the Bureau of Indian Affairs Discourages Historical Research." Indian Historian 10 (Fall 1977): 25-27.

599. Nickeson, Steve. "The Structure of the Bureau of Indian Affairs." Law and Contemporary Problems 40 (Winter 1976): 61-76.

600. Officer, James E. "The Bureau of Indian Affairs since 1945: An Assessment." Annals of the American Academy of Political and Social Science 436 (March 1978): 61-72.

601. Peone, Chuck. "Critical Problem Areas Involving Fund Management in the Bureau of Indian Affairs." American Indian Journal 2 (November 1976): 10-11.

602. Sigelman, Lee, and Robert Carter.

"American Indians in the Political Kingdom: A Note on the Bureau of Indian Affairs." Administration and Society 8 (November 1976): 343-354.

603. Stuart, Paul. The Indian Office: Growth and Development of an American Institution, 1865-1900. Ann Arbor, Michigan: UMI Research Press, 1979.

COMMISSIONERS OF INDIAN AFFAIRS

Biographical sketches of all the Commissioners of Indian Affairs from 1824 to 1977 are included in the following book. The individual chapters are listed separately in chronological order.

604. Kvasnicka, Robert M., and Herman J. Viola, eds. The Commissioners of Indian Affairs, 1824-1977. Lincoln: University of Nebraska Press, 1979.

605. "Thomas L. McKenney, 1824-30," By Herman J. Viola. Pp. 1-7.

606. "Samuel S. Hamilton, 1830-31." By R. David Edmunds. Pp. 9-11.

607. "Elbert Herring, 1831-36." By Ronald N. Satz. Pp. 13-16.

608. "Carey Allen Harris, 1836-38." By Ronald N. Satz. Pp. 17-22.

609. "Thomas Hartley Crawford, 1838-45." By Ronald N. Satz. Pp. 23-27.

610. "William Medill, 1845-49." By Robert A. Trennert. Pp. 29-39.

611. "Orlando Brown, 1849-50." By Robert A. Trennert. Pp. 41-47.

612. "Luke Lea, 1850-53." By Robert A. Trennert. Pp. 49-56.

613. "George W. Manypenny, 1853-57." By Robert M. Kvasnicka. Pp. 57-67.

614. "James W. Denver, 1857, 1858-59." By Donald Chaput. Pp. 69-75.

615. "Charles E. Mix, 1858." By Harry Kelsey. Pp. 77-79.

616. "Alfred Burton Greenwood, 1859-61." By Gary L. Roberts. Pp. 81-87.

617. "William P. Dole, 1861-65." By Harry Kelsey. Pp. 89-98.

618. "Dennis Nelson Cooley, 1865-66." By Gary L. Roberts. Pp. 99-108.

619. "Lewis Vital Bogy, 1866-67." By William E. Unrau. Pp. 109-114.

620. "Nathaniel Green Taylor, 1867-69." By William E. Unrau. Pp. 115-122.

621. "Ely Samuel Parker, 1869-71." By Henry G. Waltmann. Pp. 123-133.

622. "Francis A. Walker, 1871-73." By H. Craig Miner. Pp. 135-140.

623. "Edward Parmelee Smith, 1873-75." By Richard C. Crawford. Pp. 141-147.

624. "John Q. Smith, 1875-77." By Edward E. Hill. Pp. 149-153.

625. "Ezra A. Hayt, 1877-80." By Roy W. Meyer. Pp. 155-166.

626. "Roland E. Trowbridge, 1880-81." By Michael A. Goldman. Pp. 167-172.

627. "Hiram Price, 1881-85." By Floyd A. O'Neil. Pp. 173-179.

628. "John D. C. Atkins, 1885-88." By Gregory C. Thompson. Pp. 181-188.

629. "John H. Oberly, 1888-89." By Floyd A. O'Neil. Pp. 189-191.

630. "Thomas Jefferson Morgan, 1889-93." By Francis Paul Prucha. Pp. 193-203.

631. "Daniel M. Browning, 1893-97." By William T. Hagan. Pp. 205-209.

632. "William A. Jones, 1897-1904." By W. David Baird. Pp. 211-220.

633. "Francis Ellington Leupp, 1905-1909." By Donald L. Parman. Pp. 221-232.

634. "Robert Grosvenor Valentine, 1909-12." By Diane T. Putney. Pp. 233-242.

635. "Cato Sells, 1913-21." By Lawrence C. Kelly. Pp. 243-250.

636. "Charles Henry Burke, 1921-29." By Lawrence C. Kelly. Pp. 251-261.

637. "Charles James Rhoads, 1929-33." By Lawrence C. Kelly. Pp. 263-271.

638. "John Collier, 1933-45." By Kenneth R. Philp. Pp. 273-282.

639. "William A. Brophy, 1945-48. By S. Lyman Tyler. Pp. 283-287.

640. "John Ralph Nichols, 1949-50." By William J. Dennehy. Pp. 289-292.

641. "Dillon Seymour Myer, 1950-53." By Patricia K. Ourada. Pp. 293-299.

642. "Glenn L. Emmons, 1953-61." By Patricia K. Ourada. Pp. 301-310.

643. "Philleo Nash, 1961-66." By Margaret Connell Szasz. Pp. 311-323.

644. "Robert L. Bennett, 1966-69." By Richard N. Ellis. Pp. 325-331.

645. "Louis Rook Bruce, 1969-73." By Joseph H. Cash. Pp. 333-340.

646. "Morris Thompson, 1973-76." By Michael T. Smith. Pp. 341-346.

647. "Benjamin Reifel, 1976-77." By Michael T. Smith. Pp. 347-348.

Other studies of individual commissioners are listed below.

648. Faust, Richard H. "William Medill: Commissioner of Indian Affairs, 1845-1849." Old Northwest 1 (June 1975): 129-140.

649. Furman, Necah. "Seedtime for Indian Reform: An Evaluation of the Administration of Commissioner Francis Ellington Leupp." Red River Valley Historical Review 2 (Winter 1975): 495-517.

650. Unrau, William E. "Politics, Bureaucracy and the Bogus Administration of Indian Commissioner Lewis Vital Bogy, 1866-1867." American Indian Law Review 5 (No. 1, 1977): 185-194.

AGENTS AND SUPERINTENDENTS

651. Altshuler, Constance Wynn. "Poston and the Pimas: The 'Father of Arizona' as Indian Superintendent." Journal of Arizona History 18 (Spring 1977): 23-42. Charles D. Poston.

652. Apostol, Jane. "Horatio Nelson Rust: Abolitionist, Archaeologist, Indian Agent." California History 58 (Winter 1979-1980): 304-315.

653. Balman, Gail Eugene. "Douglas Hancock Cooper: Southerner." Ph.D. dissertation, Oklahoma State University, 1976.

654. Bret Harte, John. "The Strange Case of Joseph C. Tiffany: Indian Agent in Disgrace." Journal of Arizona History 16 (Winter 1975): 383-404. San Carlos Agency, Arizona, 1880-1882.

655. Cramer, Harry G. III. "Tom Jeffords--Indian Agent." *Journal of Arizona History* 17 (Autumn 1976): 265-300.

656. Foley, William E., and Charles David Rice. "Pierre Chouteau, Entrepreneur as Indian Agent." *Missouri Historical Review* 72 (July 1978): 365-387.

657. Grant, C. L., and Gerald H. Davis, eds. "The Wedding of Col. Benjamin Hawkins." *North Carolina Historical Review* 54 (Summer 1977): 308-316.

658. Grissom, Donald B. "William Wells, Indian Agent." *Old Fort News* 42 (No. 2, 1979): 51-59.

659. Humins, John Harold. "George Boyd: Indian Agent of the Upper Great Lakes, 1819-1842." Ph.D. dissertation, Michigan State University, 1975.

660. Hutton, Paul A. "William Wells: Frontier Scout and Indian Agent." *Indiana Magazine of History* 74 (September 1978): 183-222.

661. Isern, Thomas D. "The Controversial Career of Edward W. Wynkoop." *Colorado Magazine* 56 (Winter-Spring 1979): 1-18.

662. Jensen, Richard E. "The Oto, Missouria, and Agent Dennison." *Nebraska History* 59 (Spring 1978): 47-55. William Wallace Dennison.

663. Johnson, Ben H. "Hum-pa-zee." *Montana, the Magazine of Western History* 28 (January 1978): 56-64. Charles B. Lohmiller of Fort Peck Agency.

664. Littlefield, Daniel F., Jr. "Abraham G. Mayers." *Arkansas Historical Quarterly* 34 (Summer 1975): 122-148.

665. Munkres, Robert L. "Broken Hand and the Indians: A Case Study of Mid-19th Century White Attitudes." *Annals of Wyoming* 50 (Spring 1978): 157-171. Thomas Fitzpatrick.

666. _____. "Thomas Fitzpatrick and the Santa Fe Road." *Westerners Brand Book* (Chicago) 34 (July-August 1977): 25-27, 30-32.

667. Neighbours, Kenneth Franklin. *Robert Simpson Neighbors and the Texas Frontier, 1836-1859.* Waco, Texas: Texian Press, 1975.

668. O'Neil, Floyd A., and Stanford J. Layton. "Of Pride and Politics: Brigham Young as Indian Superintendent." *Utah Historical Quarterly* 46 (Summer 1978): 236-250.

669. Pfaller, Louis L. "Indian Diplomat at Large: Two Incidents in the Career of Major McLaughlin." *North Dakota History* 42 (Spring 1975): 4-17.

670. _____. "James McLaughlin and the Rodman Wanamaker Expedition of 1913." *North Dakota History* 44 (Spring 1977): 4-11.

671. _____. James McLaughlin: The Man with an Indian Heart. New York: Vantage Press, 1978.

672. Rayman, Ronald. "Confrontation at the Fever River Lead Mining District: Joseph Montfort Street vs. Henry Dodge, 1827-1828." *Annals of Iowa* 44 (Spring 1978): 278-295.

673. _____. "Joseph Montfort Street: Establishing the Sac and Fox Indian Agency in Iowa Territory, 1838-1840." *Annals of Iowa* 43 (Spring 1976): 261-274.

674. Smith, Robert E. "Thomas Mosely, Jr. and the Last Years of the Wyandot Subagency." *Pacific Historian* 21 (Spring 1977): 1-20.

675. Steffen, Jerome O. *William Clark: Jeffersonian Man on the Frontier.* Norman: University of Oklahoma Press, 1977.

676. Stern, Norton B. "Herman Bendell: Superintendent of Indian Affairs, Arizona Territory, 1871-1873." *Western States Jewish Historical Quarterly* 8 (April 1976): 265-282.

677. Zwink, T. Ashley. "On the White Man's Road: Lawrie Tatum and the Formative Years of the Kiowa Agency, 1869-1873." *Chronicles of Oklahoma* 56 (Winter 1978-1979): 431-441.

AGENCIES AND SUPERINTENDENCIES

678. Best, J. J. "Letters from Dakota, or Life and Scenes among the Indians: Fort Berthold Agency, 1889-1890." Edited by Stuart E. Brown, Jr. *North Dakota History* 43 (Winter 1976): 4-31.

679. Clow, Richmond L. "The Whetstone Indian Agency, 1868-1872." *South Dakota History* 7 (Summer 1977): 291-308.

680. Sievers, Michael A. "Funding the California Indian Superintendency: A Case Study of Congressional Appropriations." *Southern California Quarterly* 59 (Spring 1977): 49-73.

681. Smith, Robert E. "The Clash of Leadership at the Grand Reserve: The Wyandot Subagency and the Methodist Mission, 1820-1824." *Ohio History* 89 (Spring 1980): 181-205.

682. Theisen, Lee Scott. "The Oregon

Superintendency of Indian Affairs, 1853-1856." Pacific Historian 22 (Summer 1978): 184-195.

683. Youngkin, S. Douglas. "'Hostile and Friendly': The 'Pygmalion Effect' at Cheyenne River Agency, 1873-1877." South Dakota History 7 (Fall 1977): 402-421.

RESERVATIONS

684. Barker, Raleigh E. Tales from a Reservation Storekeeper. Edited by John Hicks. Tampa, Florida: American Studies Press, 1979. Pine Ridge Reservation.

685. Bekken, James M. "Indians--Reservations--Jurisdictional Effect of Surplus Land Statute upon Traditional Boundaries of an Indian Reservation." North Dakota Law Review 52 (Winter 1975): 411-419.

686. Blossom, Katherine Eleanor. "Culture Change and Leadership in a Modern Indian Community--The Colorado River Indian Reservation." Ph.D. dissertation, University of North Carolina at Chapel Hill, 1976.

687. Browne, William P., and Michael Davis. "Community Control and the Reservation; Self-Interest as a Factor Limiting Reform." Ethnicity 3 (December 1976): 368-377. Isabella Reservation (Chippewa), Michigan.

688. Carlson, Robert. "Grace Lambert--Fort Totten Indian Reservation." North Dakota History 44 (Fall 1977): 8-10.

689. Cole, D. C. "Reorganization, Consolidation, and the Expropriation of the Chiricahua Apache Reservation." Indian Historian 10 (Spring 1977): 3-7.

690. Covington, James W. "Brighton Reservation, Florida, 1935-1938." Tequesta, No. 36 (1976): 54-65.

691. Gidley, M. With One Sky above Us: Life on an Indian Reservation at the Turn of the Century. New York: G.P. Putnam's Sons, 1979. Photographs by Edward H. Latham at Colville Reservation.

692. Hagan, William T. "The Reservation Policy: Too Little and Too Late." In Indian-White Relations: A Persistent Paradox, edited by Jane F. Smith and Robert M. Kvasnicka, pp. 157-169. Washington: Howard University Press, 1976

693. Hislop, Donald Lindsay. The Nome Lackee Indian Reservation, 1854-1870. Chico, California: Association for Northern California Records and Research, 1978.

694. Hoxie, Frederick E. "From Prison to Homeland: The Cheyenne River Indian Reservation before WW I." South Dakota History 10 (Winter 1979): 1-24.

695. Johnson, Ronald N., and Gary D. Libecap. "Agency Costs and the Assignment of Property Rights: The Case of Southwestern Indian Reservations." Southern Economic Journal 47 (October 1980): 332-347.

696. Kennedy, James Bradford. "The Umatilla Indian Reservation, 1855-1975: Factors Contributing to a Diminished Land Resource Base." Ph.D. dissertation, Oregon State University, 1977.

697. Knack, Martha C. "A Short Resource History of Pyramid Lake, Nevada." Ethnohistory 24 (Winter 1977): 47-63.

698. Schusky, Ernest L. "The Lower Brule Sioux Reservation: A Century of Misunderstanding." South Dakota History 7 (Fall 1977): 422-437.

699. Slagle, Richard M. "The Puyallup Indians and the Reservation Disestablishment Test." Washington Law Review 54 (June 1979): 653-668.

700. Thompson, Gerald. The Army and the Navajo. Tucson: University of Arizona Press, 1976. An administrative study of the Bosque Redondo.

701. Trosper, Ronald L. "Native American Boundary Maintenance: The Flathead Indian Reservation, Montana--1860-1970." Ethnicity 3 (September 1976): 256-274.

702. Twiss, Gayla. "A Short History of Pine Ridge." Indian Historian 11 (Winter 1978): 36-39.

703. Vogeler, Ingolf, and Terry Simmons. "Settlement Morphology of South Dakota Indian Reservations." Yearbook of the Association of Pacific Coast Geographers 38 (1975): 91-108.

704. Wachtel, David. "An Historical Look at BIA Police on the Reservations." American Indian Journal 6 (May 1980): 13-18.

5
Treaties and Councils

COLONIAL INDIAN TREATIES

705. Early American Indian Documents: Treaties and Laws, 1607-1789, general editor, Alden T. Vaughan. Volume 1, Pennsylvania and Delaware Treaties, 1629-1737, edited by Donald H. Kent. Washington: University Publications of America, 1979.

706. Kinnaird, Lawrence. "Spanish Treaties with Indian Tribes." Western Historical Quarterly 10 (January 1979): 39-48.

707. Pham, Augustine Lan Van. "English Colonial Treaties with American Indians: Observations on a Neglected Genre." Ph.D. dissertation, Fordham University, 1977.

UNITED STATES TREATIES AND COUNCILS

708. Anderson, George E., W. H. Ellison, and Robert F. Heizer. Treaty Making and Treaty Rejection by the Federal Government in California, 1850-1852. Socorro, New Mexico: Ballena Press, 1978.

709. Campisi, Jack. "New York-Oneida Treaty of 1795: A Finding of Fact." American Indian Law Review 4 (No. 1, 1976): 71-82.

710. Carpenter, William Geoffrey. "Treaties--Termination by War--Provisions of Article III of the Jay Treaty of 1794 Exempting Indians from Payment of Customs Duties on Goods Purchased in Canada and Brought into the United States for Personal Use Were Abrogated by the War of 1812." Virginia Journal of International Law 16 (Summer 1976): 951-963.

711. Clark, Thomas D. "The Jackson Purchase: A Dramatic Chapter in Southern Indian Policy and Relations." Filson Club History Quarterly 50 (July 1976): 302-320.

712. Clifton, James A. "Chicago, September 14, 1833: The Last Great Indian Treaty in the Old Northwest." Chicago History 9 (Summer 1980): 86-97.

713. Costo, Rupert, and Jeannette Henry. Indian Treaties: Two Centuries of Dishonor. San Francisco: Indian Historian Press, 1977. A discussion of current Indian affairs.

714. Decker, Craig A. "The Construction of Indian Treaties, Agreements, and Statutes." American Indian Law Review 5 (No. 2, 1977): 299-311.

715. Deloria, Vine, Jr. "Researching American Indian Treaties: Northwest and Southwest." American Indian Journal 1 (November 1975): 14-17.

716. DeMallie, Raymond J. "American Indian Treaty Making: Motives and Meanings." American Indian Journal 3 (January 1977): 2-10.

717. _____. "Touching the Pen: Plains Indian Treaty Councils in Ethnohistorical Perspective." In Ethnicity on the Great Plains, edited by Frederick C. Luebke, pp. 38-53. Lincoln: University of Nebraska Press, 1980.

718. DeRosier, Arthur H., Jr. "The Cherokee Indians: Disaster through Negotiation." In Forked Tongues and Broken Treaties, edited by Donald E. Worcester, pp. 33-70. Caldwell, Idaho: Caxton Printers, 1975.

719. _____. "The Choctaw Indians: Negotiations for Survival." In Forked Tongues and Broken Treaties, edited by Donald E. Worcester, pp. 1-31. Caldwell, Idaho: Caxton Printers, 1975.

720. _____. "The Destruction of the Creek Confederacy." In Forked Tongues and Broken Treaties, edited by Donald E. Worcester, pp. 72-108. Caldwell, Idaho: Caxton Printers, 1975.

721. Doty, James. Journal of Operations of Governor Isaac Ingalls Stevens of Washington Territory in 1855. Edited by Edward J. Kowrach. Fairfield, Washington: Ye Galleon Press, 1978.

722. Edmunds, R. David. "'Nothing Has Been Effected': The Vincennes Treaty of 1792." Indiana Magazine of History 74 (March 1978): 23-35.

723. Essin, Emmett M. III. "The Southern Cheyennes." In Forked Tongues and Broken Treaties, edited by Donald E. Worcester, pp. 110-162. Caldwell, Idaho: Caxton Printers, 1975.

724. Gill, E. Ann. "An Analysis of the 1868 Oglala Sioux Treaty and the Wounded Knee Trial." Columbia Journal of Transnational Law 14 (No. 1, 1975): 119-146.

725. Hoopes, Chad L. Domesticate or Exterminate: California Indian Treaties, Unratified and Made Secret in 1852. N.p. Redwood Coast Publications, 1975.

726. Keller, Robert H. "An Economic History of Indian Treaties in the Great Lakes Region." American Indian Journal 4 (February 1978): 2-20.

727. Kickingbird, Kirke, Lynn Kickingbird, Alexander Tallchief Skibine, and Charles Chibitty. Indian Treaties. Washington: Institute for the Development of Indian Law, 1980.

728. Kickingbird, Lynn, and Curtis Berkey. "American Indian Treaties--Their Importance Today." American Indian Journal 1 (October 1975): 3-7.

729. Lane, Barbara. "Background of Treaty Making in Western Washington." American Indian Journal 3 (April 1977): 2-11.

730. Magnaghi, Russell M. "The Isle Royale Compact of 1844." Inland Seas 33 (Winter 1977): 287-292.

731. Mathes, Valerie Sherer. "Treaties with the Comanches." In Forked Tongues and Broken Treaties, edited by Donald E. Worcester, pp. 169-211. Caldwell, Idaho: Caxton Printers, 1975.

732. Meinhardt, Nick, and Diane Payne. "Reviewing U.S. Treaty Commitments to the Lakota Nation." American Indian Journal 4 (January 1978): 2-12.

733. Murray, Robert A. "Treaty Presents at Fort Laramie, 1867-68: Prices and Quantities from the Seth E. Ward Ledger." Museum of the Fur Trade Quarterly 13 (Fall 1977): 1-5.

734. Newcombe, Barbara T. "'A Portion of the American People': The Sioux Sign a Treaty in Washington in 1858." Minnesota History 45 (Fall 1976): 82-96.

735. Sievers, Michael A. "Westward by Indian Treaty: The Upper Missouri Example." Nebraska History 56 (Spring 1975): 77-107.

736. Wilkinson, Charles F., and John M. Volkman. "Judicial Review of Indian Treaty Abrogation: 'As Long As Water Flows, or Grass Grows upon the Earth'-- How Long a Time Is That?" California Law Review 63 (May 1975): 601-661.

737. Worcester, Donald E. "Treaties with the Teton Sioux." In Forked Tongues and Broken Treaties, edited by Donald E. Worcester, pp. 214-252. Caldwell, Idaho: Caxton Printers, 1975.

738. Zwink, Timothy A. "E. W. Wynkoop and the Bluff Creek Council, 1866." Kansas Historical Quarterly 43 (Summer 1977): 217-239.

6
Land and the Indians

GENERAL AND MISCELLANEOUS STUDIES

739. Carter, Nancy Carol. "Race and
Power Politics as Aspects of Federal
Guardianship over American Indians:
Land-Related Cases, 1887-1924." Ameri-
can Indian Law Review 4 (No. 2, 1976):
197-248.

740. Chapman, Berlin B. Federal Management and Disposition of the Lands of
Oklahoma Territory, 1866-1907. New
York: Arno Press, 1979. Ph.D. dissertation, University of Wisconsin,
1931.

741. Corbett, William P. "Pipestone: The
Origin and Development of a National
Monument." Minnesota History 47 (Fall
1980): 83-92.

742. _____. "The Red Pipestone Quarry:
The Yanktons Defend a Sacred Tradition,
1858-1929." South Dakota History 8
(Spring 1978): 99-116.

743. Dobyns, Henry F. "Brief Perspective
on a Scholarly Transformation: Widowing
the 'Virgin' Land." Ethnohistory 23
(Spring 1976): 95-104.

744. Hagan, William T. "Justifying Dispossession of the Indians: The Land
Utilization Argument." In American Indian Environments: Ecological Issues
in Native American History, edited by
Christopher Vecsey and Robert W.
Venables, pp. 65-80. Syracuse: Syracuse University Press, 1980.

745. Hampton, David Keith. Cherokee
Reserves. Oklahoma City: Baker Publishing Company, 1979.

746. Janke, Ronald Arthur. "The Development and Persistence of U.S. Indian
Land Problems As Shown by a Detailed
Study of the Chippewa Indian." Ph.D.
dissertation, University of Minnesota,
1976.

747. Kelley, Klara B. "Federal Indian
Land Policy and Economic Development in
the United States." In Economic Develop-

ment in American Indian Reservations,
edited by Roxanne Dunbar Ortiz, pp.
30-42. Albuquerque: Native American
Studies, University of New Mexico, 1979.

748. McDonnell, Janet Ann. "The Disintegration of the Indian Estate: Indian
Land Policy, 1913-1929." Ph.D. dissertation, Marquette University, 1980.

749. Sutton, Imre. Indian Land Tenure:
Bibliographical Essays and a Guide to
the Literature. New York: Clearwater
Publishing Company, 1975.

750. Townley, John M. "Reclamation and
the Red Man: Relationships on the
Truckee-Carson Project, Nevada." Indian Historian 11 (Winter 1978): 21-28.

751. Webber, Joe D. "Indian Cessions
within the Northwest Territory." Illinois Libraries 61 (June 1979): 507-
564.

752. Will, J. Kemper. "Indian Lands
Environment--Who Should Protect It?"
Natural Resources Journal 18 (July
1978): 465-504.

753. Worcester, Donald E. "The Sioux
Land Grab." In Forked Tongues and Broken
Treaties, edited by Donald E. Worcester,
pp. 293-326. Caldwell, Idaho: Caxton
Printers, 1975.

TITLES AND LAND CLAIMS

754. Anderson, James D. "Samuel Wharton
and the Indians' Rights To Sell Their
Land: An Eighteenth-Century View."
Western Pennsylvania Historical Magazine 63 (April 1980): 121-140.

755. Antos, Susan C. "Indian Land Claims
under the Nonintercourse Act." Albany
Law Review 44 (October 1979): 110-138.

756. Arnold, Robert D. Alaska Native Land
Claims. Anchorage: Alaska Native Foundation, 1978.

757. Berry, Mary Clay. The Alaska Pipe-

line: The Politics of Oil and Native Land Claims. Bloomington: Indiana University Press, 1975.

758. Bissonnette, Andrew P. "An Overview of the Question of Access across Indian Lands." Land and Water Law Review 10 (No. 1, 1975): 93-117.

759. Camp, Laurie Smith. "Land Accretion and Avulsion: The Battle of Blackbird Bend." Nebraska Law Review 56 (No. 4, 1977): 814-835.

760. Clinton, Robert N., and Margaret Tobey Hotopp. "Judicial Enforcement of the Federal Restraints on Alienation of Indian Land: The Origins of the Eastern Land Claims." Maine Law Review 31 (No. 1, 1979): 17-90.

761. Davis, John Joseph. "Land Claims under the Indian Trade and Intercourse Acts: The White Settlement Exception Defense." Boston University Law Review 60 (November 1980): 911-932.

762. Dillsaver, Joe D. "Land Use: Exclusion of Non-Indians from Tribal Lands--An Established Right." American Indian Law Review 4 (No. 1, 1976): 135-140.

763. Dwyer, William E., Jr. "Land Claims under the Indian Nonintercourse Act: 25 U.S.C. §177." Boston College Environmental Affairs Law Review 7 (No. 2, 1978): 259-292.

764. Dyer, Ruth Caroline. The Indians' Land Title in California: A Case in Federal Equity, 1851-1942. San Francisco: R and E Research Associates, 1975. Reprint of thesis, University of California, 1944.

765. Formanek, Rjean K. "Blackbird Hills Indian Land Dispute Settled by Placing the Burden of Proving Title on the Non-Indian Party and Incorporating Nebraska Water Law into the Federal Standard." Creighton Law Review 13 (Summer 1980): 1098-1102.

766. Francisco, William P. "Land Is Still the Issue." Tulsa Law Journal 10 (No. 3, 1975): 340-361.

767. Gibson, Michael M. "Indian Claims in the Beds of Oklahoma Watercourses." American Indian Law Review 4 (No. 1, 1976): 83-90.

768. Goodman, James M., and Gary L. Thompson. "The Hopi-Navaho Land Dispute." American Indian Law Review 3 (No. 2, 1975): 397-417.

769. Henderson, J. Youngblood. "Unraveling the Riddle of Aboriginal Title." American Indian Law Review 5 (No. 1, 1977): 75-137.

770. Hotopp, Margaret. "Preferential Burden of Proof Allocation in Indian Land Claims Cases." Iowa Law Review 64 (January 1979): 386-407.

771. Kammer, Jerry. The Second Long Walk: The Navajo-Hopi Land Dispute. Albuquerque: University of New Mexico Press, 1980.

772. Kelly, Daniel G., Jr. "Indian Title: The Rights of American Natives in Lands They Have Occupied since Time Immemorial." Columbia Law Review 75 (April 1975): 654-686.

773. Ludtke, Jean E. "Mashpee, Town or Tribe?: Current Wampanoag Land Claims Suit." American Anthropologist 80 (June 1979): 377-379.

774. Lyons, David. "The New Indian Claims and Original Rights to Land." Social Theory and Practice 4 (Fall 1977): 249-272.

775. McClure, Kade. "Termination: Interpreting Legislative Intent--De Coteau v. District County Court." American Indian Law Review 3 (No. 2, 1975): 489-496.

776. McLaughlin, Robert. "Who Owns the Land?--A Native American Challenge." Juris Doctor 6 (September 1976): 17-25.

777. "The Meaning and Implications of 'Indian Country': State v. Dana." Maine Law Review 31 (No. 1, 1979): 171-211.

778. Nebel, Reynold, Jr. "Resolution of Eastern Indian Land Claims: A Proposal for Negotiated Settlements." American University Law Review 27 (Spring 1978): 695-731.

779. Newton, Nell Jessup. "At the Whim of the Sovereign: Aboriginal Title Reconsidered." Hastings Law Journal 31 (July 1980): 1215-1285.

780. Ortiz, Roxanne Dunbar. Roots of Resistance: Land Tenure in New Mexico, 1680-1980. Los Angeles: Chicano Studies Research Center Publications and American Indian Studies Center, University of California, Los Angeles, 1980.

781. _____. "The Roots of Resistance: Pueblo Land Tenure and Spanish Colonization." Journal of Ethnic Studies 5 (Winter 1978): 33-53.

782. Paterson, John M. R., and David Roseman. "A Reexamination of Passamaquoddy v. Morton." Maine Law Review 31 (No. 1, 1979): 115-152.

783. Powell, Burt Edward. "Land Tenure on Northern Plains Indian Reservations."

Ph.D. dissertation, Duke University, 1975.

784. Ringold, A. F. "Indian Land Law--Some Fundamental Concepts for the Title Examiner." Tulsa Law Journal 10 (No. 3, 1975): 321-339.

785. Rubenstein, Bruce A. "Justice Denied: Indian Land Frauds in Michigan, 1855-1900." Old Northwest 2 (June 1976): 131-140.

786. St. Clair, James D., and William F. Lee. "Defense of Nonintercourse Act Claims: The Requirement of Tribal Existence." Maine Law Review 31 (No. 1, 1979): 91-113.

787. Shanahan, Donald G., Jr. "Compensation for the Loss of the Aboriginal Lands of the California Indians." Southern California Quarterly 57 (Fall 1975): 297-320.

788. Smith, Dwight L. "The Land Cession Treaty: A Valid Instrument of Transfer of Indian Title." In This Land of Ours: The Acquisition and Disposition of the Public Domain, pp. 87-102. Indianapolis: Indiana Historical Society, 1978.

789. Smith, E. B., ed. Indian Tribal Claims Decided in the Court of Claims of the United States, Briefed and Compiled to June 30, 1947. 2 volumes. Arlington, Virginia: University Publications of America, 1976.

790. Tehan, Kevin. "Of Indians, Land, and the Federal Government: The Navajo-Hopi Land Dispute." Arizona State Law Journal, 1976, pp. 173-212.

791. Thiem, Rebecca S. "Indian Rights to Lands Underlying Navigable Waters: State Jurisdiction under the Equal Footing Doctrine vs. Tribal Sovereignty." North Dakota Law Review 55 (1979): 453-474.

792. Thompson, Robert. "Indian Land Claims--A Question of Congress' Right to Unilaterally Abrogate Indian Treaty Provisions: Rosebud Sioux Tribe v. Richard Kneip." Howard Law Journal 21 (1978): 625-644.

793. Tilleman, Paul J. "Indian Law--Boundary Disestablishment through the Operation of Surplus Land Acts." Wisconsin Law Review, 1976, pp. 1305-1331.

794. Vollmann, Tim. "A Survey of Eastern Indian Land Claims: 1970-1979." Maine Law Review 31 (No. 1, 1979): 5-16.

See also current comment on Indian land claims (806 to 836). Land claims are also discussed in some studies dealing with Indian treaties.

ALLOTMENT OF LAND IN SEVERALTY

795. Berthrong, Donald J. "Legacies of the Dawes Act: Bureaucrats and Land Thieves at the Cheyenne-Arapaho Agencies of Oklahoma." Arizona and the West 21 (Winter 1979): 335-354.

796. Carlson, Leonard Albert. "The Dawes Act and the Decline of Indian Farming." Ph.D. dissertation, Stanford University, 1977.

797. Carson, Ruth. "Indians Called Her 'The Measuring Woman': Alice Fletcher and the Apportionment of Reservation Lands." American West 12 (July 1975): 12-15.

798. Fontana, Bernard L. "Meanwhile, Back at the Rancheria . . ." Indian Historian 8 (Winter 1975): 13-18. Papago allotments.

799. Hauptman, Laurence M. "Senecas and Subdividers: Resistance to Allotment of Indian Lands in New York, 1875-1906." Prologue 9 (Summer 1977): 105-116.

800. Holford, David M. "The Subversion of the Indian Land Allotment System, 1887-1934." Indian Historian 8 (Spring 1975): 11-21.

801. Moore, John H. "Aboriginal Indian Residence Patterns Preserved in Censuses and Allotments." Science 207 (January 11, 1980): 201-202.

802. Odell, Marcia Larson. Divide and Conquer: Allotment among the Cherokee. New York: Arno Press, 1979. Ph.D. dissertation, Cornell University, 1975.

803. Smith, Burton M. "The Politics of Allotment: The Flathead Indian Reservation as a Test Case." Pacific Northwest Quarterly 70 (July 1979): 131-140.

804. Washburn, Wilcomb E. The Assault on Indian Tribalism: The General Allotment Law (Dawes Act) of 1887. Philadelphia: J.B. Lippincott Company, 1975.

805. Young, Rowland L. "American Indians . . . Land Allotments." American Bar Association Journal 66 (June 1980): 772-773.

CURRENT COMMENT ON INDIAN CLAIMS

806. "About Nonintercourse." Time 108 (November 15, 1976): 92-93. Maine Indian land claims.

807. "As Maine Goes . . .?" Time 109 (March 14, 1977): 21. Claims of the Passamaquoddy and Penobscot Indians.

808. Blagden, Nellie. "Lawyer Tom Tureen Has Bad News for Maine: The Indians Want, and May Get, Most of the State." People Weekly 7 (January 31, 1977): 30-32.

809. "Carter's First Indian Test." Christian Century 94 (August 3, 1977): 680-681. Maine Indian cases.

810. Cleaves, Robert. "A Betrayal of Trust: The Maine Settlement Act and the Houlton Band of Maliseets." American Indian Journal 6 (November 1980): 2-8.

811. Dillingham, Brint. "Maine: Gunter's Proposed Solution." American Indian Journal 3 (September 1977): 25-26.

812. Dumanoski, Dianne. "Battling to Regain a Lost Past: Martha's Vineyard Indians Want Their Land Back." Civil Rights Digest 8 (Fall 1975): 2-9.

813. Hanlon, William. "Is There a Frog in the House?" America 138 (March 4, 1978): 168. Indian claims, Mashpee, Massachusetts.

814. "If Indian Tribes Win Legal War To Regain Half of Maine." U.S. News and World Report 82 (April 4, 1977): 53-54.

815. "Indians Take to the Courts." Senior Scholastic 110 (February 9, 1978): 16-17.

816. Jensen, Ros. "Blackbird Bend: Landmark Victory in Land Dispute." Christian Century 95 (June 7, 1978): 606-608.

817. Kickingbird, Kirke. "New Concepts for Indian Land." Engage/Social Action 3 (August 1975): 36-38.

818. Kovler, Peter. "Native American Land Rights: Indians Are Suing--Locals Get Restless." Current 204 (July-August 1978): 11-20.

819. Larson, Janet Karsten. "Redeeming the Time and the Land: Epilogue to '1776.'" Christian Century 95 (April 13, 1977): 356-361. Maine Indian land claims.

820. McLaughlin, Robert. "Giving It Back to the Indians." Atlantic 239 (February 1977): 70-85.

821. Morner, Aimee L. "How the Indians Frightened Great Northern Nekoosa: Land Claims by the Passamaquoddy and the Penobscot Tribes." Fortune 98 (July 31, 1978): 98-100.

822. "Navajo against Hopi!" Senior Scholastic 110 (February 9, 1978): 6-8.

823. Norgren, Jill, and Petra T. Shattuck. "Black Hills Whitewash." Nation 230 (May 10, 1980): 557-560. Sioux land claims.

824. "Peace Treaty." Forbes 122 (October 16, 1978): 187-188. Narragansett land claims.

825. Richer, Paul. "Red Man's Revenge." Saturday Review 5 (September 30, 1978): 10. Maine Indian claims.

826. Rudnitsky, Howard. "Those Friendly Indians." Forbes 123 (January 22, 1979): 40-42. Maine Indian land claims.

827. Skibine, A. T. "The Latest Word from the Supreme Court." American Indian Journal 6 (August 1980): 23-29. Sioux land claims.

828. Starnes, Richard. "New Indian Rip-off." Outdoor Life 164 (October 1979): 15-18.

829. Tallchief, A. "Money vs. Sovereignty: An Analysis of the Maine Settlement." American Indian Journal 6 (May 1980): 19-22.

830. "This Land Is My Land." Newsweek 89 (March 14, 1977): 18, 23. Maine Indian land claims.

831. "U.S. Peace-Pipe Offering: Money." U.S. News and World Report 89 (July 14, 1980): 10. Sioux land claims.

832. Weir, David, and Howard Kohn. "Chief Chiloquin's Last Stand." New Times 4 (May 16, 1975): 40-41.

833. "What Is a Tribe." Economist 266 (January 14, 1978): 34-36.

834. Willwerth, James. "In Arizona: A New 'Long Walk'?" Time 115 (June 30, 1980): 4-5. Navajo-Hopi land dispute.

835. Winter, Bill. "Indian Claims Mount: 'Broken Treaties' Cited." American Bar Association Journal 66 (January 1980): 22.

836. "Your Land Is Our Land." Economist 261 (December 25, 1976): 25. New England Indian land claims.

See also studies on titles and land claims (754 to 794).

7
Military Relations

GENERAL AND MISCELLANEOUS STUDIES

837. Berthrong, Donald J. "Changing Concepts: The Indians Learn about the 'Long Knives' and Settlers (1849-1890s)." In Red Men and Hat Wearers: Viewpoints in Indian History, edited by Daniel Tyler, pp. 47-61. Boulder, Colorado: Pruett Publishing Company, 1976.

838. Carroll, John M. The Indian Wars Campaign Medal: Its History and Its Recipients. Bryan, Texas: Privately printed, 1979.

839. _____. The Medal of Honor: Its History and Recipients for the Indian Wars. Bryan, Texas: Privately printed, 1979.

840. Carroll, John M., ed. The Papers of the Order of Indian Wars. Preface by George S. Pappas. Fort Collins, Colorado: Old Army Press, 1975.

841. Ewers, John C. "Intertribal Warfare as the Precursor of Indian-White Warfare on the Northern Great Plains." Western Historical Quarterly 6 (October 1975): 397-410.

842. _____. "The Making and Uses of Maps by Plains Indian Warriors." By Valor and Arms 3 (No. 1, 1977): 36-43.

843. Knight, Oliver. Life and Manners in the Frontier Army. Norman: University of Oklahoma Press, 1978.

844. McChristian, Douglas C. "The Bug Juice War." Annals of Wyoming 49 (Fall 1977): 253-261. Alcohol abuse by soldiers.

845. Morton, Desmond. "Comparison of U.S./Canadian Military Experience on the Frontier." In The American Military on the Frontier, edited by James P. Tate, pp. 17-35. Washington: Office of Air Force History and United States Air Force Academy, 1978.

846. Murray, Robert A. "Water Walking War Wagons: Steamboats in the Western Indian Campaigns." By Valor and Arms 3 (No. 1, 1977): 48-56.

847. Selby, John. The Conquest of the American West. London: George Allen and Unwin, 1975.

848. Stallard, Patricia Y. Glittering Misery: Dependents of the Indian Fighting Army. San Rafael, California: Presidio Press, and Fort Collins, Colorado: Old Army Press, 1978.

849. Tate, James P., ed. The American Military on the Frontier: Proceedings of the 7th Military History Symposium, United States Air Force Academy, 30 September--1 October 1976. Washington: Office of Air Force History, Headquarters USAF, and United States Air Force Academy, 1978.

850. Tate, Michael L. "The Multi-Purpose Army on the Frontier: A Call for Further Research." In The American West: Essays in Honor of W. Eugene Hollon, edited by Ronald Lora, pp. 171-208. Toledo: University of Toledo, 1980.

851. Thian, Raphael P. Notes Illustrating the Military Geography of the United States, 1813-1880. Austin: University of Texas Press, 1979. Original edition published in 1881.

852. Utley, Robert M. "The Bluecoats." American History Illustrated 14 (October 1979): 20-24, 32-34; (November 1979): 32-40.

853. _____. "The Contribution of the Frontier to the American Military Tradition." In The American Military on the Frontier, edited by James P. Tate, pp. 3-13. Washington: Office of Air Force History and United States Air Force Academy, 1978.

854. _____. "The Frontier Army: John Ford or Arthur Penn?" In Indian-White Relations: A Persistent Paradox, edited by Jane F. Smith and Robert M. Kvasnicka, pp. 133-145. Washington: Howard University Press, 1976.

855. _____. Indian, Soldier, and Settler: Experiences in the Struggle for the American West. St. Louis: Jefferson National Expansion Historical Association, 1979.

856. Utley, Robert M., and Wilcomb E. Washburn. The American Heritage History of the Indian Wars. New York: American Heritage Publishing Company, 1977.

COLONIAL INDIAN WARS

857. Brand, Irene B. "Dunmore's War." West Virginia History 40 (Fall 1978): 28-46.

858. Calmes, Alan. "The Lyttelton Expedition of 1759: Military Failures and Financial Successes." South Carolina Historical Magazine 77 (January 1976): 10-33.

859. Champion, Walter T., Jr. "The Road to Destruction: The Effect of the French and Indian War on the Six Nations." Indian Historian 10 (Summer 1977): 20-33.

860. Church, Benjamin. Diary of King Philip's War, 1675-76. Introduction by Alan and Mary Simpson. Chester, Connecticut: Pequot Press, 1975.

861. Edward, Brother C. "The Wyoming Valley Massacre." American History Illustrated 13 (October 1978): 32-40.

862. Farrell, David R. "Pontiac, Gladwin and the Myths of 1763." Indiana Military History Journal 4 (May 1979): 5-14. Major Henry Gladwin.

863. Fausz, J. Frederick. "Fighting 'Fire' with Firearms: The Anglo-Powhatan Arms Race in Early Virginia." American Indian Culture and Research Journal 3 (No. 4, 1979): 33-50.

864. _____. "The Powhatan Uprising of 1622: A Historical Study of Ethnocentrism and Cultural Conflict." Ph.D. dissertation, College of William and Mary, 1977.

865. Horowitz, David. The First Frontier: The Indian Wars and America's Origins, 1606-1776. New York: Simon and Schuster, 1978.

866. Johnson, Richard R. "The Search for a Usable Indian: An Aspect of the Defense of Colonial New England." Journal of American History 64 (December 1977): 623-651.

867. Keller, Allan. "Pontiac's Conspiracy." American History Illustrated 12 (May 1977): 4-8, 42-49.

868. Monguia, Anna R. "The Pequot War Reexamined." American Indian Culture and Research Journal 1 (No. 3, 1975): 13-21.

869. Morrison, Kenneth M. "The Bias of Colonial Law: English Paranoia and the Abenaki Arena of King Philip's War, 1675-1678." New England Quarterly 53 (September 1980): 363-387.

870. Pinkos, Richard J. "'A Lamentable and Woeful Sight': The Indian Attack on Springfield." Historical Journal of Western Massachusetts 4 (Fall 1975): 1-11.

871. Purdy, Barbara A. "Weapons, Strategies, and Tactics of the Europeans and the Indians in Sixteenth- and Seventeenth-Century Florida." Florida Historical Quarterly 55 (January 1977): 259-276.

872. Shea, William Lee. "To Defend Virginia: The Evolution of the First Colonial Militia, 1607-1677." Ph.D. dissertation, Rice University, 1975.

873. _____. "Virginia at War, 1644-1646." Military Affairs 41 (October 1977): 142-147.

874. Shy, John W. "Dunmore, the Upper Ohio Valley, and the American Revolution." In Ohio in the American Revolution, edited by Thomas H. Smith, pp. 13-16. Columbus: Ohio Historical Society, 1976.

875. Sloan, David. "'A Time of Sifting and Winnowing': The Paxton Riots and Quaker Non-Violence in Pennsylvania." Quaker History 66 (Spring 1977): 3-22.

876. Slotkin, Richard, and James K. Folsom, eds. So Dreadfull a Judgment: Puritan Responses to King Philip's War, 1676-1677. Middletown, Connecticut: Wesleyan University Press, 1978.

877. Thomas, William H. B., and Howard McKnight Wilson. "The Battle of Point Pleasant, 1774." Virginia Cavalcade 24 (Winter 1975): 100-107.

878. Williams, Edward G., ed. Bouquet's March to the Ohio: The Forbes Road. Pittsburgh: Historical Society of Western Pennsylvania, 1975.

879. Worrall, Arthur J. "Persecution, Politics, and War: Roger Williams, Quakers, and King Philip's War." Quaker History 66 (Autumn 1977): 73-86.

REVOLUTIONARY WAR

880. Allen, Richard S. "1779--The Revolution Moves West." Conservationist 34 (September-October 1979): 28-32.

881. Almeida, Deirdre. "The Stockbridge Indian in the American Revolution." Historical Journal of Western Massachusetts 4 (Fall 1975): 34-39.

882. Brophy, Marion, and Wendell Tripp, eds. "Supplies for General Sullivan: The Correspondence of Colonel Charles Stewart, May-September, 1979." New York History 60 (July 1979): 244-281; (October 1979): 439-467; 61 (January 1980): 43-80.

883. Burns, Brian. "Massacre or Muster: Burgoyne's Indians and the Militia at Bennington." Vermont History 45 (Summer 1977): 133-144.

884. Livingood, James W. "The American Revolution in the Tennessee Valley." Tennessee Valley Perspective 6 (Summer 1976): 4-10.

885. Sutton, Robert M. "George Rogers Clark and the Campaign in the West: The Five Major Documents." Indiana Magazine of History 76 (December 1980): 334-345.

886. Waller, George M. The American Revolution in the West. Chicago: Nelson-Hall, 1976.

FROM THE REVOLUTION TO THE CIVIL WAR

General and Miscellaneous Studies

887. Agnew, Brad. "The Dodge-Leavenworth Expedition of 1834." Chronicles of Oklahoma 53 (Fall 1975): 376-396.

888. Amos, Alcione M. "Captain Hugh Young's Map of Jackson's 1818 Seminole Campaign in Florida." Florida Historical Quarterly 55 (January 1977): 336-346.

889. Christy, Howard A. "The Walker War: Defense and Conciliation as Strategy." Utah Historical Quarterly 47 (Fall 1979): 395-420.

890. Clow, Richmond L. "Mad Bear: William S. Harney and the Sioux Expedition of 1855-1856." Nebraska History 61 (Summer 1980): 133-151.

891. Dibble, Ernest F. "Captain Hugh Young and His 1818 Topographical Memoir to Andrew Jackson." Florida Historical Quarterly 55 (January 1977): 321-335.

892. Graham, Stanley S. "Routine at Western Cavalry Posts, 1833-1861." Journal of the West 15 (July 1976): 49-59.

893. Hunter, Leslie Gene. "The Mojave Expedition of 1858-59." Arizona and the West 21 (Summer 1979): 137-156.

894. Layton, Thomas N. "Massacre! What Massacre? An Inquiry into the Massacre of 1850." Nevada Historical Society Quarterly 20 (Winter 1977): 240-251.

895. Nackman, Mark E. "The Making of the Texan Citizen Soldier, 1835-1860." Southwestern Historical Quarterly 73 (January 1975): 231-253.

896. Peters, Virginia Bergman. The Florida Wars. Hamden, Connecticut: Archon Books, Shoe String Press, 1979.

897. Strickland, Rex W. "The Birth and Death of a Legend: The Johnson 'Massacre' of 1837." Arizona and the West 18 (Autumn 1976): 257-286.

898. Valliere, Kenneth L. "The Creek War of 1836: A Military History." Chronicles of Oklahoma 57 (Winter 1979): 463-485.

899. Wert, Jeffry. "Old Hickory and the Seminoles." American History Illustrated 15 (October 1980): 28-35.

900. Whitney, Ellen M., ed. The Black Hawk War, 1831-1832. Volume 2, part 3, Appendices and Index. Collections of the Illinois State Historical Library, volume 38. Springfield: Illinois State Historical Library, 1978.

901. Wooster, Robert. "Military Strategy in the Southwest, 1848-1860." Military History of Texas and the Southwest 15 (No. 2): 5-15.

Indian Wars, 1780-1812

902. Carlson, Richard G., ed. "George P. Peters' Version of the Battle of Tippecanoe (November 7, 1811)." Vermont History 45 (Winter 1977): 38-43.

903. Guthman, William H. March to Massacre: A History of the First Seven Years of the United States Army, 1784-1791. New York: McGraw-Hill Book Company, 1975.

904. Haffner, Gerald O. "The Pigeon Roost Massacre: An Eyewitness Acount." Indiana History Bulletin 53 (November-December 1976): 158-161.

905. Johnson, Leland R. "The Doyle Mission to Massac, 1794." Journal of the Illinois State Historical Society 73 (Spring 1980): 2-16.

906. Knopf, Richard C. "'Cool Cat George' and the Indian Wars in Ohio." In The Historic Indian in Ohio, edited by Randall Buchman, pp. 20-28. Columbus: Ohio Historical Society, 1976. George Washington.

907. Walsh, William Patrick. "The Defeat of Major General Arthur St. Clair,

November 4, 1791: A Study of the Nation's Response, 1791-1793." Ph.D. dissertation, Loyola University of Chicago, 1977.

Indians in the War of 1812

908. Akers, Frank Herman, Jr. "The Unexpected Challenge: The Creek War of 1813-1814." Ph.D. dissertation, Duke University, 1975.

909. Dunnigan, Brian Leigh. "The Battle of Mackinac Island." Michigan History 59 (Winter 1975): 239-254.

910. Faust, Richard H. "Another Look at General Jackson and the Indians of the Mississippi Territory." Alabama Review 28 (July 1975): 202-217.

911. Lengel, Leland L. "The Road to Fort Mims: Judge Harry Toulmin's Observations on the Creek War, 1811-1813." Alabama Review 29 (January 1976): 16-36.

912. Melton, Maurice. "War Trail of the Red Sticks." American History Illustrated 10 (February 1976): 32-42.

Second Seminole War

913. Buker, George E. "The Mosquito Fleet's Guides and the Second Seminole War." Florida Historical Quarterly 57 (January 1979): 308-326.

914. _____. Swamp Sailors: Riverine Warfare in the Everglades, 1835-1842. Gainesville: University Presses of Florida, 1975.

915. Fiorato, Jacqueline. "The Cherokee Mediation in Florida." Journal of Cherokee Studies 3 (Spring 1978): 111-119.

916. Moulton, Gary E. "Cherokees and the Second Seminole War." Florida Historical Quarterly 53 (January 1975): 296-305.

917. "Proposal for Ending the Second Seminole War." American Indian Journal 2 (September 1976): 12-14. Letters of John H. Sherburne.

918. Schene, Michael G. "Ballooning in the Second Seminole War." Florida Historical Quarterly 55 (April 1977): 480-482.

919. Walton, George. Fearless and Free: The Seminole Indian War, 1835-1842. Indianapolis: Bobbs-Merrill Company, 1977.

920. Welsh, Michael E. "Legislating a Homestead Bill: Thomas Hart Benton and the Second Seminole War." Florida Historical Quarterly 57 (October 1978): 157-172. Armed Occupation Bill of 1842.

Wars in the Pacific Northwest

921. Guie, H. Dean. Bugles in the Valley: Garnett's Fort Simcoe. Revised edition. Portland: Oregon Historical Society, 1977.

922. Holbrook, Francis X., and John Nikol. "The Navy in the Puget Sound War, 1855-1857: A Documentary Study." Pacific Northwest Quarterly 67 (January 1976): 10-20.

923. Kelly, Plympton J. We Were Not Summer Soldiers: The Indian War Diary of Plympton J. Kelly, 1855-1856. Introductory essay and annotations by William N. Bischoff. Tacoma: Washington State Historical Society, 1976.

924. Moomaw, Juliana P. "Oregon: Patrolling the New Northwest." Journal of the West 14 (January 1975): 5-24.

THE CIVIL WAR AND AFTER

General and Miscellaneous Studies

925. Ambrose, Stephen E. Crazy Horse and Custer: The Parallel Lives of Two American Warriors. Garden City, New York: Doubleday and Company, 1975.

926. Carroll, John M., and Lawrence A. Frost, eds. Private Theodore Ewert's Diary of the Black Hills Expedition of 1874. Piscataway, New Jersey, CRI Books, 1976.

927. Coleman, Ronald G. "The Buffalo Soldiers: Guardians of the Uintah Frontier, 1886-1901." Utah Historical Quarterly 47 (Fall 1979): 421-439.

928. Dobyns, Henry F., and Robert C. Euler. "The Dunn-Howland Killings: Additional Insights." Journal of Arizona History 21 (Spring 1980): 87-95.

929. Feaver, Eric. "Indian Soldiers, 1891-95: An Experiment on the Closing Frontier." Prologue 7 (Summer 1975): 109-118.

930. Guentzel, Richard. "The Department of the Platte and Western Settlement, 1866-1877." Nebraska History 56 (Fall 1975): 389-417.

931. Hoig, Stan. "Silas S. Soule: Partizan of the Frontier." Montana, the Magazine of Western History 26 (January 1976): 70-77. Soule participated in the Sand Creek Massacre.

932. Hurtt, Clarence M. "The Role of Black Infantry in the Expansion of the West." West Virginia History 40 (Winter 1979): 123-157.

933. Hutcheson, Grove. "The Ninth Cavalry." By Valor and Arms 1 (Spring 1975): 48-55.

934. Kelver, Gerald O., ed. 15 Years on the Western Frontier, 1866-1881: A True Story As Told by E.H.L., 2nd Lt., USA, and Jack, Army Scout. Fort Collins, Colorado: Robinson Press, 1975.

935. McClellan, Val J. This Is Our Land. Volume 1, New York: Vantage Press, 1977. Volume 2, Jamestown, Ohio, Western Publishers, 1979. White River Massacre.

936. Millbrook, Minnie Dubbs. "An Old Trail Plowed Under: Hays to Dodge." Kansas Historical Quarterly 43 (Autumn 1977): 264-281.

937. Morton, Desmond. "Cavalry or Police: Keeping the Peace on Two Adjacent Frontiers, 1870-1900.: Journal of Canadian Studies 12 (Spring 1977): 27-37.

938. Murray, Keith A. "The Modoc Indian War: 1872-1873." Studies in History and Society 1 (Spring 1976): 1-27.

939. Palmquist, Peter. "Imagemakers of the Modoc War: Louis Heller and Eadweard Muybridge." Journal of California Anthropology 4 (Winter 1977): 206-241.

940. Parker, Watson, ed. "The Report of Captain John Mix of a Scout to the Black Hills, March-April 1875." South Dakota History 7 (Fall 1977): 385-401.

941. Porter, Kenneth Wiggins. "'The Boys' War': A Study in Frontier Racial Conflict, Journalism and Folk History." Pacific Northwest Quarterly 68 (October 1977): 175-190.

942. Price, Byron. "The Utopian Experiment: The Army and the Indians, 1890-1897." By Valor and Arms 3 (No. 1, 1977): 15-35.

943. Quinn, Joan Corbett. "A Mountain Charade: The Sheepeater Campaign--1879." Montana, the Magazine of Western History 28 (January 1978): 16-27.

944. Reber, Bruce. The United States Army and the Indian Wars in the Trans-Mississippi West, 1860-1898. Special Bibliography No. 17. Carlisle Barracks, Pennsylvania: U.S. Army Military History Institute, 1978.

945. Reedstrom, Ernest Lisle. Bugles, Banners and War Bonnets. Caldwell, Idaho: Caxton Printers, 1977. History of Seventh Cavalry.

946. Rickey, Don. "An Indian Wars Combat Record." By Valor and Arms 2 (Fall 1975): 4-11. Black soldiers.

947. Thompson, Neil Baird. Crazy Horse Called Them Walk-a-Heaps: The Story of the Foot Soldier in the Prairie Indian Wars. St. Cloud, Minnesota: North Star Press, 1979.

948. Underhill, Lonnie E., and Daniel F. Littlefield, Jr. "Disturbances in Jackson's Hole, Wyoming, 1895." Indian Historian 12 (No. 4, 1979): 10-19.

949. Voigt, Barton R. "The Lightning Creek Fight." Annals of Wyoming 49 (Spring 1977): 5-21.

950. Wade, Arthur P. "The Military Command Structure: The Great Plains, 1853-1891." Journal of the West 15 (July 1976): 5-22.

951. Weems, John Edward. Death Song: The Last of the Indian Wars. Garden City, New York: Doubleday and Company, 1976.

952. White, Lonnie. "Indian Soldiers of the 36th Division." Military History of Texas and the Southwest 15 (No. 1): 7-20. World War I.

953. White, W. Bruce. "The American Indian as Soldier, 1890-1919." Canadian Review of American Studies 7 (Spring 1976): 15-25.

954. Wilkinson, Dave. "The Modoc Indian War." American History Illustrated 13 (August 1978): 18-30.

Sioux Uprising of 1862

955. Carley, Kenneth. The Sioux Uprising of 1862. 2nd edition. St. Paul: Minnesota Historical Society, 1976.

956. Daniels, Arthur M. A Journal of Sibley's Indian Expedition during the Summer of 1863 and Record of the Troops Employed. Minneapolis: James D. Thueson, 1980.

957. Dietz, Charlton. "Henry Behnkte: New Ulm's Paul Revere." Minnesota History 45 (Fall 1976): 111-115.

958. Gray, John S. "The Santee Sioux and the Settlers at Lake Shetek." Montana, the Magazine of Western History 25 (January 1975): 42-54.

959. Henig, Gerald S. "A Neglected Cause of the Sioux Uprising." Minnesota History 45 (Fall 1976): 107-110.

960. Jacobson, Clair. "The Battle of Whitestone Hill." North Dakota History 44 (Spring 1977): 4-14.

961. Noyes, Edward. "Neighbors 'To the Rescue': Wisconsin and Iowa Troops Fight Boredom, Not Indians in Minnesota in 1862." Minnesota History 46 (Winter

1979): 312-327.

962. Russo, Priscilla Ann. "The Time To Speak Is Over: The Onset of the Sioux Uprising." Minnesota History 45 (Fall 1976): 97-106.

War on the Southern Plains

963. Bentley, Charles A. "Captain Frederick W. Benteen and the Kiowas." Chronicles of Oklahoma 56 (Summer 1978): 344-347.

964. Carlson, Paul H. "William R. Shafter, Black Troops, and the Finale to the Red River War." Red River Valley Historical Review 3 (Spring 1978): 247-258.

965. _____. "William R. Shafter, Black Troops, and the Opening of the Llano Estacado, 1870-1875." Panhandle-Plains Historical Review 47 (1974): 1-18.

966. Carroll, John M., ed. General Custer and the Battle of the Washita: The Federal View. Bryan, Texas: Guidon Press, 1978. Reprint of documents of the U.S. Government.

967. Gibson, Arrell Morgan. "The St. Augustine Prisoners." Red River Valley Historical Review 3 (Spring 1978): 259-270.

968. Guy, Duane F., ed. "The Canadian River Expedition of 1868." Panhandle-Plains Historical Review 48 (1975): 1-26.

969. Haley, James L. The Buffalo War: The History of the Red River Indian Uprising of 1874. Garden City, New York: Doubleday and Company, 1976.

970. _____. "Prelude to War: The Slaughter of the Buffalo." American Heritage 27 (February 1976): 36-41, 82-87.

971. Harris, Charles W. "The Red River War of 1874-75: The End of an Era on the Great Plains." Red River Valley Historical Review 3 (Spring 1978): 271-277.

972. Hoig, Stan. The Battle of the Washita: The Sheridan-Custer Indian Campaign of 1867-69. Garden City, New York: Doubleday and Company, 1976.

973. Howard, William. "The Beecher Island Battleground." Kansas Quarterly 10 (Summer 1978): 45-51.

974. Leckie, William H. "Buell's Campaign." Red River Valley Historical Review 3 (Spring 1978): 186-193.

975. Millbrook, Minnie Dubbs. "The Jordan Massacre." Kansas History 2 (Winter 1979): 219-230.

976. Murray, Robert A. "Wagons on the Plains." By Valor and Arms 2 (No. 4, 1976): 37-40.

977. Pate, J'Nell. "The Battles of Adobe Walls." Great Plains Journal 16 (Fall 1976): 3-44.

978. _____. "The Red River War of 1874--An Enlisted Man's Contribution." Chronicles of Oklahoma 54 (Summer 1976): 263-275. Sgt. John Bontwell Charlton.

979. Stout, Joseph A., Jr. "Davidson's Campaign." Red River Valley Historical Review 3 (Spring 1978): 194-201.

980. Tate, Michael L. "Indian Scouting Detachments in the Red River War, 1874-1875." Red River Valley Historical Review 3 (Spring 1978): 202-225.

981. Utley, Robert M., ed. "Campaigning with Custer: Letters and Diaries Sketch Life in Camp and Field during the Indian Wars." American West 14 (July-August 1977): 4-9, 58-60. Letters and diaries of Albert and Jennie Barnitz, 1867-1868.

982. _____. Life in Custer's Cavalry: Diaries and Letters of Albert and Jennie Barnitz, 1867-1868. New Haven: Yale University Press, 1977.

983. Wallace, Ernest, ed. "The Journal of Ranald S. Mackenzie's Messenger to the Kwahadi Comanches." Red River Valley Historical Review 3 (Spring 1978): 227-246.

984. Weingardt, Richard. Sound the Charge: The Western Frontier, Spillman Creek to Summit Springs. Englewood, Colorado: Jacqueline Enterprises, 1978.

985. White, Lonnie J., ed. "The Nineteenth Kansas Cavalry in the Indian Territory, 1868-1869: Eyewitness Accounts of Sheridan's Winter Campaign." Red River Valley Historical Review 3 (Spring 1978): 164-185.

War on the Northern Plains

986. Anderson, Grant K. "The Black Hills Exclusion Policy: Judicial Challenges." Nebraska History 58 (Spring 1977): 1-24.

987. _____. "The Prairie Paul Revere." South Dakota History 8 (Winter 1977): 24-33.

988. Clow, Richmond L. "General Philip Sheridan's Legacy: The Sioux Pony Campaign of 1876." Nebraska History 57 (Winter 1976): 461-477.

989. Freeman, Henry B. The Freeman Jour-

nal: The Infantry in the Sioux Campaign of 1876. Edited by George A. Schneider. San Rafael, California: Presidio Press, 1977.

990. Frost, Lawrence A. "The Black Hills Expedition of 1874." Red River Valley Historical Review 4 (Fall 1979): 5-19.

991. Frost, Lawrence A., ed. With Custer in '74: James Calhoun's Diary of the Black Hills Expedition. Provo, Utah: Brigham Young University Press, 1979.

992. Gray, John S. "Blazing the Bridger and Bozeman Trails." Annals of Wyoming 49 (Spring 1977): 23-51.

993. Greene, Jerome A., ed. "'We Do Not Know What the Government Intends To Do . . .': Lt. Palmer Writes from the Bozeman Trail, 1867-68." Montana, the Magazine of Western History 28 (July 1978): 16-35. George Henry Palmer.

994. Hedren, Paul L. First Scalp for Custer: The Skirmish at Warbonnet Creek, Nebraska, July 17, 1876, with a Short History of the Warbonnet Battlefield. Glendale, California: Arthur H. Clark Company, 1980.

995. Lemly, H. R. "The Fight on the Rosebud." By Valor and Arms 1 (Summer 1975): 7-12.

996. Liddic, Bruce R., ed. I Buried Custer: The Diary of Pvt. Thomas W. Coleman, 7th U.S. Cavalry. College Station, Texas: Creative Publishing Company, 1979.

997. McGinnis, Anthony. "Strike and Retreat: Intertribal Warfare and the Powder River War, 1865-1868." Montana, the Magazine of Western History 30 (October 1980): 30-41.

998. Marquis, Thomas B. "Indian Warrior Ways." By Valor and Arms 2 (No. 2, 1976): 36-54.

999. Powell, Peter J. "High Bull's Victory Roster." Montana, the Magazine of Western History 25 (January 1975): 14-21.

1000. Starr, Michael L. "The Battle of Warbonnet Creek." American History Illustrated 12 (February 1978): 4-11, 48-49.

1001. Sumner, E. V. "Besieged by the Utes: The Massacre of 1879." By Valor and Arms 2 (Fall 1975): 12-22. Reprint of 1891 article.

1002. Turchen, Lesta V., and James D. McLaird. The Black Hills Expedition of 1875. Mitchell, South Dakota: Dakota Wesleyan University Press, 1975.

1003. Turner, C. Frank. "Custer and the Canadian Connections." Beaver, Outfit 307 (Summer 1976): 4-11.

1004. Unrau, William E., ed. Tending the Talking Wire: A Buck Soldier's View of Indian Country, 1863-1866. Salt Lake City: University of Utah Press, 1979. Letters of Hervey Johnson.

1005. White, Lonnie J., ed. "Hugh Kirkendall's Wagon Train on the Bozeman Trail, 1866: Letters of C.M.S. Millard." Annals of Wyoming 47 (Spring 1975): 45-58.

1006. White, William. Custer, Cavalry, and Crows: The Story of William White As Told to Thomas Marquis. Annotated by John A. Popovich. Fort Collins, Colorado: Old Army Press, 1975.

Little Big Horn

1007. Allison, E. H. "Harrington's Death." By Valor and Arms 1 (January 1975): 26-28.

1008. Bookwalter, Thomas E. "The Custer Battle: An Aerial Analysis." Westerners Brand Book (Chicago) 34 (April 1977): 9-11, 15-16.

1009. Brereton, J. M. "Consummation at Little Big Horn." Blackwood's Magazine 318 (December 1975): 516-530.

1010. Carroll, John M., ed. General Custer and the Battle of the Little Big Horn: The Federal View. New Brunswick: Garry Owen Press, 1976.

1011. Dippie, Brian W. Custer's Last Stand: The Anatomy of an American Myth. Missoula: University of Montana Publications in History, 1976.

1012. Downey, Fairfax. "Bugler at the Little Big Horn." By Valor and Arms 2 (No. 2, 1976): 58-66. Giovanni Martini.

1013. Gray, John S. Centennial Campaign: The Sioux War of 1876. Fort Collins: Colorado: Old Army Press, 1976.

1014. _____. "The Pack Train on George A. Custer's Last Campaign." Nebraska History 57 (Spring 1976): 53-68.

1015. _____. "Sutler on Custer's Last Campaign." North Dakota History 43 (Summer 1976): 14-21.

1016. Hammer, Kenneth. "Notes from the Custer Battlefield: Walter Mason Camp's Interviews with Survivors of the Little Bighorn." American West 13 (March-April 1976): 36-45.

1017. Hammer, Kenneth, ed. Custer in

'76: Walter Camp's Notes on the Custer Fight. Provo, Utah: Brigham Young University Press, 1976.

1019. Hammer, Kenneth, and Dennis Rowley. "Custer's Man Camp: Oral Historian without Peer." Manuscripts 27 (Spring 1975): 112-120. Walter Mason Camp.

1020. Hutton, Paul A. "From Little Big-horn to Little Big Man: The Changing Image of a Western Hero in Popular Culture." Western Historical Quarterly 7 (January 1976): 19-45.

1021. Jones, Archer. "The United States in the Little Big Horn Campaign." North Dakota History 42 (Spring 1975): 22-27.

1022. King, Charles. "Custer's Last Battle." Introduction by Paul L. Hedren. Annals of Wyoming 48 (Spring 1976): 109-125. Originally published in Harper's New Monthly Magazine 81 (August 1890): 378-387.

1023. Liberty, Margot. "The Symbolic Value of the Little Big Horn in the Northern Plains." In Political Organization of Native North Americans, edited by Ernest L. Schusky, pp. 121-136. Washington: University Press of America, 1980.

1024. McGreevy, Patrick S. "Surgeons at the Little Big Horn." Surgery, Gynecology and Obstetrics 140 (May 1975): 774-780.

1025. Magruder, T. L. "General Custer and the Spencer Carbine, or Custer Would Not Have Died for Our Sins with the Connecticut Rifle." Connecticut Historical Society Bulletin 45 (January 1980): 16-21.

1026. Marquis, Thomas B. Keep the Last Bullet for Yourself: The True Story of Custer's Last Stand. New York: Two Continents Publishing Group, 1976.

1027. Myers, Rex C. "Montana Editors and the Custer Battle." Montana, the Magazine of Western History 26 (April 1976): 18-31.

1028. Pearson, Carl L. "Sadie and the Missing Custer Battle Papers." Montana, the Magazine of Western History 26 (Autumn 1976): 12-17. Sadie Whiteman. See article by Kathryn Wright (1036).

1029. Penrod, Mike. "The Big Horn Expedition of 1876." Kansas Quarterly 10 (Summer 1978): 79-90.

1030. Pomplun, Ray. "Belated Justice." Kansas Quarterly 10 (Summer 1978): 91-93.

1031. Russell, Don. "What Really Happened at Custer's Last Stand?" Art News 77 (December 1978): 63-70.

1032. Sievers, Michael A. "The Literature of the Little Bighorn: A Centennial Historiography." Arizona and the West 18 (Summer 1976): 149-176.

1033. Tillett, Leslie, ed. Wind on the Buffalo Grass: The Indians' Own Account of the Battle at the Little Big Horn River, and the Death of Their Life on the Plains. New York: Thomas Y. Crowell Company, 1976.

1034. Upton, Richard, ed. The Custer Adventure. Fort Collins, Colorado: Old Army Press, 1975. Stories told by participants.

1035. Willert, James. Little Big Horn Diary: Chronicle of the 1876 Indian War. La Mirada, California: James Willert, Publisher, 1977.

1036. Wright, Kathryn. "An Epilogue and a Final Answer Deferred." Montana, the Magazine of Western History 26 (October 1976): 18-21. See article by Carl L. Pearson (1028).

Nez Perce War

1037. Davison, Stanley R. "A Century Ago: The Tortuous Pursuit." Montana, the Magazine of Western History 27 (October 1977): 2-19.

1038. d'Easum, C. G. (Dick). "White Bird without a Bugle." Pacific Northwesterner 21 (Spring 1977): 41-48.

1039. McDermott, John D. Forlorn Hope: The Battle of White Bird Canyon and the Beginning of the Nez Perce War. Boise: Idaho State Historical Society, 1978.

1040. MacDonald, Duncan. "The Nez Perces: The History of Their Troubles and the Campaign of 1877." Introduction by Merle W. Wells. Idaho Yesterdays 21 (Winter 1978): 2-15, 26-30.

1041. Myers, Rex C. "The Settlers and the Nez Perce." Montana, the Magazine of Western History 27 (October 1977): 20-29.

1042. Park, Edwards. "Big Hole: Still a Gaping Wound to Nez Perce." Smithsonian 9 (May 1978): 92-99.

1043. Tchakmakian, Pascal. The Great Retreat: The Nez Perces War in Words and Pictures. San Francisco: Chronicle Books, 1976.

1044. Thompson, Erwin N. "The Summer of '77 at Fort Lapwai." Idaho Yesterdays 21 (Summer 1977): 11-15.

1045. "We Have Joseph and All His People . . . A Soldier Writes Home about the Final Battle." Montana, the Magazine of Western History 27 (October 1977): 30-33.

War in the Southwest

1046. Davisson, Lori. "New Light on the Cibecue Fight: Untangling Apache Identities." Journal of Arizona History 20 (Winter 1979): 423-444.

1047. Gale, Jack C. "Hatfield under Fire, May 15, 1886: An Episode of the Geronimo Campaigns." Journal of Arizona History 18 (Winter 1977): 447-468.

1048. _____. "Lebo in Pursuit." Journal of Arizona History 21 (Spring 1980): 11-24. Captain Thomas C. Lebo's pursuit of Geronimo.

1049. Gilbert, Robert M. "The Battle of the Hay Camp." Far-Westerner 16 (July 1975): 7-11.

1050. Hedren, Paul L. "Captain Charles King at Sunset Pass." Journal of Arizona History 17 (Autumn 1976): 253-264.

1051. Kessel, William B. "The Battle of Cibecue and Its Aftermath: A White Mountain Apache's Account." Ethnohistory 21 (Spring 1974): 123-134.

1052. Kutz, Jack. "Battles of Dog Canyon." Desert Magazine 38 (April 1975): 20-23.

1053. Langellier, J. Phillip. "Camp Grant Affair, 1871: Milestone in Federal Indian Policy?" Military History of Texas and the Southwest 15 (No. 2): 17-29.

1054. Lummis, Charles Fletcher. Dateline Fort Bowie: Charles Fletcher Lummis Reports on an Apache War. Edited by Dan L. Thrapp. Norman: University of Oklahoma Press, 1979.

1055. Rolak, Bruno J. "General Miles' Mirrors: The Heliograph in the Geronimo Campaign of 1886." Journal of Arizona History 16 (Summer 1975): 145-160.

1056. Trafzer, Cliff. "Mr. Lincoln's Army Fights the Navajos, 1863-1864." Lincoln Herald 77 (Fall 1975): 148-158.

1057. Turcheneske, John Anthony, Jr. "The Apache Prisoners of War at Fort Sill, 1894-1914." Ph.D. dissertation, University of New Mexico, 1978.

1058. _____. "The United States Congress and the Release of the Apache Prisoners of War at Fort Sill." Chronicles of Oklahoma 54 (Summer 1976): 199-226.

1059. Wilson, John P. "Retreat to the Rio Grande: The Report of Captain Isaiah N. Moore." Rio Grande History 2 (Winter 1974-1975): 4-8.

Wounded Knee, 1890

1060. Bosma, Boyd. "An Interview with Jim Mesteth." Indian Historian 11 (Spring 1978): 18-21. Survivor of Wounded Knee.

1061. Byers, Cece, and Mary Alexander. "A Resolution on 'The Indian Question.'" Social Education 42 (April 1978): 301-303.

1062. McCormick, L. S. "Wounded Knee and the Drexel Mission Fights." By Valor and Arms 1 (January 1975): 3-15.

1063. Marshall, Julian, and Jerome Peltier. "Wounded Knee--Battle or Tragedy?" Pacific Northwesterner 23 (Summer 1979): 41-48.

1064. Sievers, Michael A. "The Historiography of 'The Bloody Field . . . That Kept the Secret of the Everlasting Word': Wounded Knee." South Dakota History 6 (Winter 1975): 33-54.

1065. Smith, Rex Alan. Moon of Popping Trees. New York: Reader's Digest Press, 1975.

1066. Stewart, Omer C. "Contemporary Document on Wovoka (Jack Wilson), Prophet of the Ghost Dance in 1890." Ethnohistory 24 (Summer 1977): 219-222.

1067. Utley, Robert M. "Wounded Knee and Other Dark Images: The West of Dewey Horn Cloud." American West 16 (May-June 1979): 4-11.

UNITED STATES MILITARY POSTS

1068. Agnew, Brad. Fort Gibson: Terminal on the Trail of Tears. Norman: University of Oklahoma Press, 1980.

1069. Anderson, H. Allen. "Fort Phantom Hill: Outpost on the Clear Fork on the Brazos." Museum Journal 16 (1976): 1-110.

1070. Boydstun, Q. B. "The Restoration of Old Fort Gibson." Chronicles of Oklahoma 58 (Summer 1980): 176-191.

1071. Cook, Fred S. "A Nostalgic Look at Texas' Fort Stockton." Desert Magazine 39 (August 1976): 10-13.

1072. Corbett, William P. "Confederate Strongholds in Indian Territory: Forts Davis and McCulloch." In Early Military Forts and Posts of Oklahoma, edited by

Odie Faulk and others, pp. 65-77. Oklahoma City: Oklahoma Historical Society, 1978.

1073. Davisson, Lori. "Fifty Years at Fort Apache." Journal of Arizona History 17 (Autumn 1976): 301-320.

1074. Derrick, W. Edwin. "Fort Reno: Defender of the Southern Plains." In Early Military Forts and Posts of Oklahoma, edited by Odie Faulk and others, pp. 113-121. Oklahoma City: Oklahoma Historical Society, 1978.

1075. Everman, Michael. "Outposts in Post-Civil War Indian Territory." In Early Military Forts and Posts of Oklahoma, edited by Odie Faulk and others, pp. 90-102. Oklahoma City: Oklahoma Historical Society, 1978.

1076. Faulk, Odie, Kenny A. Franks, and Paul F. Lambert, eds. Early Military Forts and Posts of Oklahoma. Oklahoma City: Oklahoma Historical Society, 1978.

1077. Frazier, Arthur H. "The Military Frontier: Fort Dearborn." Chicago History 9 (Summer 1980): 81-85.

1078. Freedom, Gary Stuart. "U.S. Military Forts on the Northern Great Plains, 1866-1891: An Historical Geography." Ph.D. dissertation, University of Tennessee, 1976.

1079. Friggens, Thomas. "Fort Wilkins: Army Life on the Frontier." Michigan History 61 (Fall 1977): 220-250.

1080. Hammer, Kenneth M. "Railroads and the Frontier Garrisons of Dakota Territory." North Dakota History 46 (Summer 1979): 24-34.

1081. Hardeman, Nicholas P. "Brick Stronghold of the Border: Fort Assinniboine, 1879-1911." Montana, the Magazine of Western History 29 (April 1979): 54-67.

1082. Harris, Mac R. "Early Military Forts, Posts and Camps in Oklahoma." In Early Military Forts and Posts of Oklahoma, edited by Odie Faulk and others, pp. 122-127. Oklahoma City: Oklahoma Historical Society, 1978.

1083. Hedren, Paul L. "Captain King's Centennial Year Look at Fort Laramie, Wyoming." Annals of Wyoming 48 (Spring 1976): 103-108.

1084. _____. "On Duty at Fort Ridgely, Minnesota: 1853-1867." South Dakota History 7 (Spring 1977): 168-192.

1085. Howard, Helen Addison. "Unique History of Fort Tejon." Journal of the West 18 (January 1979): 41-51.

1086. Howard, James A. II. "Fort Washita." In Early Military Forts and Posts of Oklahoma, edited by Odie Faulk and others, pp. 54-64. Oklahoma City: Oklahoma Historical Society, 1978.

1087. Hughes, J. Patrick. "Forts and Camps in Oklahoma before the Civil War." In Early Military Forts and Posts of Oklahoma, edited by Odie Faulk and others, pp. 39-53. Oklahoma City: Oklahoma Historical Society, 1978.

1088. Hurt, R. Douglas. "The Construction and Development of Fort Wallace, Kansas, 1865-1882." Kansas Historical Quarterly 43 (Spring 1977): 44-55.

1089. Kraus, Joe. "Old Forts of Northern Arizona." Desert Magazine 38 (October 1975): 6-9.

1090. Littlefield, Daniel F., Jr., and Lonnie E. Underhill. "Fort Coffee and Frontier Affairs, 1834-1838." Chronicles of Oklahoma 54 (Fall 1976): 314-338.

1091. _____. "Fort Wayne and Border Violence, 1840-1847." Arkansas Historical Quarterly 36 (Spring 1977): 3-30.

1092. _____. "Fort Wayne and the Arkansas Frontier, 1838-1840." Arkansas Historical Quarterly 35 (Winter 1976): 334-359.

1093. Lupton, David W. "Fort Platte, Wyoming, 1841-1845: Rival of Fort Laramie." Annals of Wyoming 49 (Spring 1977): 83-96.

1094. McGuigan, Patrick B. "Bulwark of the American Frontier: A History of Fort Towson." In Early Military Forts and Posts of Oklahoma, edited by Odie Faulk and others, pp. 9-25. Oklahoma City: Oklahoma Historical Society, 1978.

1095. Mayes, William B., Jr. "Did Morphy Blunder?: The Closing of Fort Hays, Kansas." Journal of the West 15 (July 1976): 38-48.

1096. Mentzer, Raymond A., Jr. "Camp Baker/Fort Logan: Microcosm of the Frontier Military Experience." Montana, the Magazine of Western History 27 (April 1977): 34-43.

1097. Murray, Robert A. "Cantonment Reno/Fort McKinney No. 1--New Views of an Old Wyoming Army Post." Annals of Wyoming 48 (Fall 1976): 275-279.

1098. _____. "Trading Posts, Forts and Bridges of the Casper Area--Unravel-

ing the Tangle on the Upper Platte."
Annals of Wyoming 47 (Spring 1975):
4-30.

1099. Ney, Virgil. "Daily Life at Fort
Atkinson--on the Missouri--1820-27."
Military Review 57 (January 1977):
36-48; (February 1977): 50-66.

1100. _____. Fort on the Prairie:
Fort Atkinson, on the Council Bluff,
1819-1827. Washington: Command Publications, 1978.

1101. _____. "Prairie Generals and
Colonels at Cantonment Missouri and Fort
Atkinson." Nebraska History 56 (Spring
1975): 51-76.

1102. Notson, William M. "Fort Concho,
1868-1872: The Medical Officers Observations." Military History of Texas
and the Southwest 12 (No. 2): 125-149.

1103. Peterson, Susan. "Fort Supply,
Isolated Outpost." In Early Military
Forts and Posts of Oklahoma, edited by
Odie Faulk and others, pp. 78-89.
Oklahoma City: Oklahoma Historical Soci-
ety, 1978.

1104. Reed, Bill. "Fort McDowell--The
'Most Unhappy Post.'" Journal of Arizona History 17 (Autumn 1976): 321-340.

1105. _____. The Last Bugle Call: A
History of Fort McDowell, Arizona
Territory, 1865-1890. Parsons, West
Virginia: McClain Printing Company,
1977.

1106. Robinson, Willard B. American Forts:
Architectural Form and Function. Urbana: University of Illinois Press, 1977.

1107. Robrock, David P. "A History of
Fort Fetterman, Wyoming, 1867-1882."
Annals of Wyoming 48 (Spring 1976):
5-76.

1108. Rohrs, Richard C. "Fort Gibson:
Forgotten Glory." In Early Military
Forts and Posts of Oklahoma, edited by
Odie Faulk and others, pp. 26-38. Ok-
lahoma City: Oklahoma Historical Society,
1978.

1109. Schene, Michael G. "Fort Foster:
A Second Seminole War Fort." Florida
Historical Quarterly 54 (January 1976):
319-339.

1110. Schubert, Frank Nicholas. "Fort
Robinson, Nebraska: The History of a
Military Community, 1874-1916." Ph.D.
dissertation, University of Toledo,
1977.

1111. Smith, G. Hubert. "A Frontier Fort
in Peacetime." Minnesota History 45

(Fall 1976); 116-128. Fort Ridgely.

1112. Stanley, Arthur J., Jr. "Fort
Leavenworth: Dowager Queen of Frontier
Posts." Kansas Historical Quarterly
42 (Spring 1976): 1-23.

1113. Utley, Robert M. "The Presence of
the Past: Fort Bowie." American West
16 (March-April 1979): 14-15, 55.

1114. Williams, Edward G. "Fort Pitt and
the Revolution on the Western Frontier."
Western Pennsylvania Historical Magazine 59 (January 1976): 1-37; (April
1976): 129-152; (July 1976): 251-287;
(October 1976): 379-444.

1115. _____. Fort Pitt and the Revolution on the Western Frontier. Pittsburgh: Historical Society of Western
Pennsylvania, 1978.

1116. _____. "A Note on Fort Pitt
and the Revolution on the Western Frontier." Western Pennsylvania Historical
Magazine 60 (July 1977): 265-276.

1117. Woods, H. Merle. Fort Reno, the
Protector. El Reno, Oklahoma: El Reno
American, 1975.

1118. Zwink, Timothy A. "Fort Sill: The
Formative Years." In Early Military
Forts and Posts of Oklahoma, edited by
Odie Faulk and others, pp. 103-112.
Oklahoma City: Oklahoma Historical
Society, 1978.

MILITARY PERSONNEL

Army Officers

1119. Alberts, Don Edward. "General
Wesley Merritt: Nineteenth Century
Cavalryman." Ph.D. dissertation, Uni-
versity of New Mexico, 1975.

1120. Altshuler, Constance Wynn. "Men
and Brothers." Journal of Arizona
History 19 (Autumn 1978): 315-322.
Major General Irvin McDowell and Juan
Chivaria, Maricopa chief.

1121. Anderson, Harry H. "Charles King's
Campaigning with Crook: A New and Personal Version Revealed in Family
Letters." Westerners Brand Book (Chicago) 32 (January 1976): 65-67, 70-72.

1122. Averell, William Woods. Ten Years
in the Saddle: The Memoir of William
Woods Averell. Edited by Edward K.
Eckert and Nicholas J. Amato. San
Rafael, California: Presidio Press, 1978.

1123. Bailey, John W. Pacifying the Plains:
General Alfred Terry and the Decline of
the Sioux, 1866-1890. Westport, Connecticut: Greenwood Press, 1979.

1124. Bell, William Gardner. *John Gregory Bourke: A Soldier-Scientist on the Frontier.* Washington: Potomac Corral of Westerners, 1978.

1125. Benner, Judith Ann. "Lone Star Soldier: A Study of the Military Career of Lawrence Sullivan Ross." Ph.D. dissertation, Texas Christian University, 1975. Served on the Indian frontier in Texas.

1126. Bookwalter, Thomas E. *Honor Tarnished: The Reno Court of Inquiry.* N.p., Little Horn Press, 1979.

1127. Burg, Maclyn P. "Service on the Vanishing Frontier, 1887-1898." *Military History of Texas and the Southwest* 13 (No. 3): 5-21. Alonzo Gray's career.

1128. _____. "Service on the Vanishing Frontier, 1898-1922." *Military History of Texas and the Southwest* 13 (No. 4): 19-28.

1129. Davidson, William. "Ranald Mackenzie: Forgotten Hero?" *American West* 13 (March-April 1976): 52, 62.

1130. Dawson, Joseph G. III. "The Alpha-Omega Man: General Phil Sheridan." *Red River Valley Historical Review* 3 (Spring 1978): 147-163.

1131. Denney, William Homer. "Soldier of the Republic: The Life of Major Ebenezer Denny." Ph.D. dissertation, Miami University, 1978.

1132. Dunlay, Thomas W. "General Crook and the White Man Problem." *Journal of the West* 18 (April 1979): 3-10.

1133. Hedren, Paul L., ed. "Eben Swift's Army Service on the Plains, 1876-1879." *Annals of Wyoming* 50 (Spring 1978): 141-153.

1134. Hofling, Charles K. "Custer's Marriage and Domestic Life." *Psychohistory Review* 9 (Fall 1980): 59-70.

1135. Hutton, Paul A. "The Celluloid Custer." *Red River Valley Historical Review* 4 (Fall 1979): 20-43.

1136. Kieffer, Chester L. *Maligned General: The Biography of Thomas Sidney Jesup.* San Rafael, California: Presidio Press, 1979.

1137. Kroeker, Marvin E. *Great Plains Command: William B. Hazen in the Frontier West.* Norman: University of Oklahoma Press, 1976.

1138. Leonard, Thomas C. "The Reluctant Conquerors: How the Generals Viewed the Indians." *American Heritage* 27 (August 1976): 34-40.

1139. Morris, Robert E. "Custer Made a Good Decision: A Leavenworth Appreciation." *Journal of the West* 16 (October 1977): 5-11.

1140. Rosenberg, Bruce A. "Custer and the Epic of Defeat." *Journal of American Folklore* 88 (April-June 1975): 165-177.

1141. Simmons, David A. "The Military and Administrative Abilities of James Wilkinson in the Old Northwest, 1792-1793." *Old Northwest* 3 (September 1977): 237-250.

1142. Skelton, William B. "Army Officers' Attitudes toward Indians, 1830-1860." *Pacific Northwest Quarterly* 67 (July 1976): 113-124.

1143. Trafzer, Cliff. "Comanche Killer or Commentator: Captain Marcy the Ethnographer." *Chronicles of Oklahoma* 58 (Spring 1980): 53-64.

1144. Utley, Robert M. "The Enduring Custer Legend." *American History Illustrated* 11 (June 1976): 4-9, 42-49.

1145. Wallace, Andrew. "Duty in the District of New Mexico: A Military Memoir." *New Mexico Historical Review* 50 (July 1975): 231-262. The diary of Col. August V. Kautz, 1869.

Indian Scouts

1146. Clark, Keith, and Donna Clark. "William McKay's Journal, 1866-67: Indian Scouts." *Oregon Historical Quarterly* 79 (Summer 1978): 120-171; (Fall 1978): 268-333.

1147. Dunlay, Thomas William. "Indian Scouts and Auxiliaries with the U.S. Army in the Trans-Mississippi West, 1860-1890." Ph.D. dissertation, University of Nebraska, 1980.

1148. Keenan, Jerry. "Little-Man-with-the-Strong-Heart: Yellowstone Kelly." *By Valor and Arms* 2 (No. 4, 1976): 45-48. Indian scout.

1149. Radbourne, Allan. "The Naming of Mickey Free." *Journal of Arizona History* 17 (Autumn 1976): 341-346.

1150. Weist, Katherine M. "Ned Casey and His Cheyenne Scouts: A Noble Experiment in an Atmosphere of Tension." *Montana, the Magazine of Western History* 27 (January 1977): 26-39.

GOVERNMENT EXPLORATIONS

1151. Abrams, Rochonne. "Meriwether Lewis: The Logistical Imagination." *Bulletin of the Missouri Historical*

Society 36 (July 1980): 228-240.

1152. Appelman, Roy E. Lewis and Clark: Historic Places Assoicated with Their Transcontinental Exploration (1804-06). Washington: United States Department of the Interior, National Park Service, 1975.

1153. Baker, T. Lindsay. "The Survey of the Santa Fe Trail, 1825-1827." Great Plains Journal 14 (Spring 1975): 210-234.

1154. Chuinard, Eldon G. Only One Man Died: The Medical Aspects of the Lewis and Clark Expedition. Glendale, California: Arthur H. Clark Company, 1979.

1155. Hawke, David Freeman. Those Tremendous Mountains: The Story of the Lewis and Clark Expedition. New York: W.W. Norton Company, 1980.

1156. Kane, Lucile, June D. Holmquist, and Carolyn Gilman, eds. The Northern Expeditions of Stephen H. Long: The Journals of 1817 and 1823 and Related Documents. St. Paul: Minnesota Historical Society Press, 1978.

1158. Moulton, Gary E. "The Journals of the Lewis and Clark Expedition: Beginning Again." We Proceeded On 6 (November 1980): 14-16.

1159. Murphy, Dan, and David Muench. Lewis and Clark: Voyage of Discovery. Las Vegas: KC Publications, 1977.

1160. Nicollet, Joseph N. Joseph N. Nicollet on the Plains and Prairies: The Expeditions of 1838-39, with Journal, Letters, and Notes on the Dakota Indians. Translated and edited by Edmund C. Bray and Martha Coleman Bray. St. Paul: Minnesota Historical Society Press, 1976.

1161. Parker, John, ed. The Journals of Jonathan Carver and Related Documents, 1766-1770. St. Paul: Minnesota Historical Society Press, 1976.

1162. Satterfield, Archie. The Lewis and Clark Trail. Harrisburg, Pennsylvania: Stackpole Books, 1978.

1163. Tate, Michael. "Randolph B. Marcy: First Explorer of the Wichitas." Great Plains Journal 15 (Spring 1976): 80-113.

8
Trade and Traders

GENERAL AND MISCELLANEOUS STUDIES

1164. Gonzalez, Mario. "Regulation of Indian Traders: A Historical Perspective." American Indian Law Review 5 (No. 2, 1977): 313-342.

1165. Hanson, Charles, Jr. "Henry Deringer and the Indian Trade." Museum of the Fur Trade Quarterly 15 (Fall 1979): 5-11.

1166. Martin, Calvin. Keepers of the Game: Indian-Animal Relationships and the Fur Trade. Berkeley: University of California Press, 1978.

1167. _____. "The War between the Indians and Animals." Natural History 87 (June-July 1978): 92-96.

1168. Miller, David. "The Fur Men and Explorers Meet the Indians." In Red Men and Hat Wearers: Viewpoints in Indian History, edited by Daniel Tyler, pp. 25-45. Boulder, Colorado: Pruett Publishing Company, 1976.

COLONIAL INDIAN TRADE

1169. Brown, Philip M. "Early Indian Trade in the Development of South Carolina: Politics, Economics, and Social Mobility during the Proprietary Period, 1670-1719." South Carolina Historical Magazine 76 (July 1975): 118-128.

1170. Cutcliffe, Stephen Hosmer. "Indians, Furs, and Empires: The Changing Policies of New York and Pennsylvania, 1674-1768." Ph.D. dissertation, Lehigh University, 1976.

1171. Hanson, Charles, Jr. "Trade Goods in Colonial New England." Museum of the Fur Trade Quarterly 13 (Fall 1977): 6-11.

1172. Ray, Arthur J., and Donald B. Freeman. "Give Us Good Measure": An Economic Analysis of Relations between the Indians and the Hudson's Bay Company before 1763. Toronto: University of Toronto Press, 1978.

1173. Wilcoxen, Charlotte. "Indian-Trade Silver on the New York Colonial Frontier." Antiques 116 (December 1979): 1356-1361.

THE EAST AND THE MISSISSIPPI VALLEY

1174. Auge, Thomas. "Destruction of a Culture." Gateway Heritage 1 (Fall 1980): 32-45.

1175. _____. "The Life and Times of Julien Dubuque." Palimpsest 57 (January-February 1976): 2-13.

1176. Birk, Douglas A., and Bruce M. White. "Who Wrote the 'Diary of Thomas Connor'? A Fur Trade Mystery." Minnesota History 46 (Spring 1979): 170-188.

1177. Gramly, Richard Michael. "Deerskins and Hunting Territories: Competition for a Scarce Resource of the Northeastern Woodlands." American Antiquity 42 (October 1977): 601-605.

1178. Hanson, Charles E., Jr. "Lead in the Fur Trade." Museum of the Fur Trade Quarterly 14 (Fall 1978): 7-12.

1179. Kay, Jeanne. "John Lawe, Green Bay Trader." Wisconsin Magazine of History 64 (Autumn 1980): 3-27.

1180. _____. "The Land of La Baye: The Ecological Impact of the Green Bay Fur Trade, 1634-1836." Ph.D. dissertation, University of Wisconsin-Madison, 1977.

1181. Kersey, Harry A., Jr. Pelts, Plumes, and Hides: White Traders among the Seminole Indians, 1870-1930. Gainesville: University Presses of Florida, 1975.

1182. White, Bruce M. The Fur Trade in Minnesota: An Introductory Guide to Manuscript Sources. St. Paul: Minnesota Historical Society Press, 1977.

TRANS-MISSISSIPPI WEST

1183. Aldrich, Duncan M. "General Stores, Retail Merchants, and Assimilation: Retail Trade in the Cherokee Nation, 1838-1890." Chronicles of Oklahoma 57 (Summer 1979): 119-136.

1184. Alwin, John A. "Pelts, Provisions and Perceptions: The Hudson's Bay Company Mandan Indian Trade, 1795-1812." Montana, the Magazine of Western History 29 (July 1979): 16-27.

1185. Anderson, Irving W. "Fort Manuel: Its Historical Significance." South Dakota History 6 (Spring 1976): 131-151.

1186. "Bent's Old Fort." Colorado Magazine 54 (Fall 1977): special issue. Articles by Enid Thompson, Louisa Ward Arps, Merrill Mattes, George A. Thorson, and Sarah M. Olson.

1187. Berry, James Jesse. "Arikara Middlemen: The Effects of Trade on an Upper Missouri Society." Ph.D. dissertation, Indiana University, 1978.

1188. Briggs, Walter, and Glenn Cuerden. "Castle in the Desert: A Historical Tour of Reconstructed Bent's Fort." American West 13 (September-October 1976): 10-17.

1189. Clokey, Richard M. William H. Ashley: Enterprise and Politics in the Trans-Mississippi West. Norman: University of Oklahoma Press, 1980.

1190. Danoff, Hyman O. "Indian Traders of the Southwest: The Danoffs of New Mexico." Western States Jewish Historical Quarterly 12 (July 1980): 291-303.

1191. De Lauer, Marjel. "A Century of Indian Traders and Trading Posts." Arizona Highways 51 (March 1975): 6-15.

1192. Dickson, Frank H. "Hard on the Heels of Lewis and Clark." Montana, the Magazine of Western History 26 (January 1976): 14-25.

1193. Foley, William E., and Charles David Rice. "Compounding the Risks: International Politics, Wartime Dislocations and Auguste Chouteau's Fur Trading Operations, 1792-1815." Missouri Historical Society Bulletin 34 (April 1978): 131-139.

1194. Garber, D. W. "Jedediah Strong Smith--Fur Trader from Ohio: A Postscript." Pacific Historian 22 (Spring 1978): 9-25.

1195. Goetzmann, William H. "The Mountain Men." American West 15 (July-August 1978): 4-17.

1196. Gowans, Fred R. Rocky Mountain Rendezvous; A History of the Fur Trade Rendezvous, 1825-1840. Provo, Utah: Brigham Young University Publications, 1976.

1197. Gowans, Fred R., and Eugene E. Campbell. Fort Bridger: Island in the Wilderness. Provo, Utah: Brigham Young University Press, 1975.

1198. Gray, John S. "Honore Picotte, Fur Trader." South Dakota History 6 (Spring 1976): 186-202.

1199. Hanson, Charles, Jr. "Joseph Bissonette's Last Trading Post." Museum of the Fur Trade Quarterly 16 (Fall 1980): 2-4.

1200. Hanson, Charles E., Jr., and Veronica Sue Walters. "The Early Fur Trade in Northwestern Nebraska." Nebraska History 57 (Fall 1976): 291-314.

1201. Henn, Roger. "Trials of an Indian Trader." Westerners Brand Book (Chicago) 33 (March 1976): 1-3, 7-8; (April 1976): 11, 15-16; (May-June 1976): 23; (July-August 1976): 26-27.

1202. Hussey, John A. "Fort Vancouver: Fur Trade Capital of the Pacific Northwest." American West 14 (September-October 1977): 12-19, 68-71.

1203. Jensen, Richard E. "Bellevue: The First Twenty Years, 1822-1842." Nebraska History 56 (Fall 1975): 339-374.

1204. Jensen, Richard E., ed. "A Description of the Fur Trade in 1831 by John Dougherty." Nebraska History 56 (Spring 1975): 109-120.

1205. Lamar, Howard R. The Trader on the American Frontier: Myth's Victim. College Station: Texas A and M University Press, 1977.

1206. Leader, Jeanne P. "The Pottawatomies and Alcohol: An Illustration of the Illegal Trade." Kansas History 2 (Autumn 1979): 157-165.

1207. Lupton, David Walker. "Fort Bernard on the Oregon Trail." Nebraska History 60 (Spring 1979): 21-35.

1208. Murray, Robert A. "First Tracks in the Big Horns." Montana, the Magazine of Western History 26 (January 1976): 2-13.

1209. Ottoson, Dennis R. "Toussaint Charbonneau, a Most Durable Man." South Dakota History 6 (Spring 1976): 152-185.

1210. Strayer, Brian F. "Fur Trappers' Attitudes toward the Upper Missouri Sioux, 1820-1860." Indian Historian

12 (No. 4, 1979): 34-40.

1211. Swagerty, William R. "Marriage and Settlement Patterns of Rocky Mountain Trappers and Traders." Western Historical Quarterly 11 (April 1980): 159-180.

1212. Thompson, Enid. "Life in an Adobe Castle, 1833-1849." Colorado Magazine 54 (Fall 1977): 7-27. Bent's Old Fort.

1213. Utley, Robert M. "Portrait for a Western Album." American West 15 (September-October 1978): 10-11. Indian trader John Lorenzo Hubbell.

1214. Wishart, David J. "Cultures in Co-operation and Conflict: Indians in the Fur Trade in the Northern Great Plains, 1807-1840." Journal of Historical Geography 2 (October 1976): 311-328.

1215. _____. The Fur Trade of the Ameri-can West, 1807-1840: A Geographical Synthesis. Lincoln: University of Nebraska Press, 1979.

1216. _____. "The Fur Trade of the West, 1807-1840: A Geographic Synthesis." In The Frontier: Comparative Studies, edited by David Harry Miller and Jerome O. Steffen, pp. 161-200. Norman: University of Oklahoma Press, 1977.

1217. _____. "Images of the Northern Great Plains from the Fur Trade, 1806-1843." In Images of the Plains: The Role of Human Nature in Settlement, edited by Brian W. Blouet and Merlin P. Lawson, pp. 45-55. Lincoln: University of Nebraska Press, 1975.

1218. Woolworth, Nancy L., "Gingras, St. Joseph and the Metis in the Northern Red River Valley: 1848-1873." North Dakota History 42 (Fall 1975): 17-27.

9
Missions and Missionaries

GENERAL AND MISCELLANEOUS STUDIES

1219. Axtell, James. "The European Failure
to Convert the Indians: An Autopsy."
In Papers of the Sixth Algonquian Conference, 1974, edited by William Cowan,
pp. 272-290. Ottawa: National Museum
of Canada, 1975.

1220. Beaver, R. Pierce. The Native Ameri-
can Christian Community: A Directory of
Indian, Aleut, and Eskimo Churches.
Monrovia, California: Missions Advanced
Research and Communications Center, 1979.

1221. Blanchard, Kendall. "Changing Sex
Roles and Protestantism among the Navajo Women in Ramah.' Journal for the
Scientific Study of Religion 14 (March
1975): 43-50.

1222. Cumming, John, ed. "A Missionary
among the Senecas: The Journal of Abel
Bingham, 1822-1828." New York History
60 (April 1979): 157-193.

1223. DeGroot, A. T. Churches and the
North American Indians: A Chronology
and Sample Denominational Bibliographies.
Peoria, Arizona: Privately printed,
1979. Contains bibliographies on the
Christian Church (Disciples of Christ)
and the Southern Baptists and the Indians.

1224. Derrick, W. Edwin. "Coweta Mission:
Struggle for the Mind and Soul of the
Creek Indians." Red River Valley His-
torical Review 4 (Winter 1979): 4-13.

1225. Forbes, Bruce David. "Evangeliza-
tion and Acculturation among the Santee
Dakota Indians, 1834-1864." Ph.D. dissertation, Princeton Theological Semi-
nary, 1977.

1226. Fraser, Gordon H. Rain on the
Desert. Chicago: Moody Press, 1975.

1227. Gowans, Fred R., and Eugene E. Campbell. Fort Supply: Brigham Young's
Green River Experiment. Provo, Utah:
Brigham Young University Publications,
1976. Mormon mission

1228. Hobday, Jose. "Forced Assimilation

and the Native American Dance."
Cross Currents 26 (Summer 1976): 189-
194.

1229. Jennings, George J. "The American
Indian Ethos: A Key for Christian Missions?" Missiology 5 (October 1977):
487-898.

1230. Juhnke, James C. "General Conference Mennonite Missions to the American Indians in the Late Nineteenth
Century." Mennonite Quarterly Review
54 (April 1980): 117-134.

1231. Kleber, Louis C. "Religion among
the American Indians." History Today
28 (February 1978): 81-87.

1232. Kucharsky, David. "Toward a Red
Theology?" Christianity Today 19
(May 9, 1975): 46-47.

1233. McGraw, James R. "God Is Also
Red: An Interview with Vine Deloria,
Jr." Christianity and Crisis 35
(September 15, 1975): 198-206.

1234. Peterson, Charles S. "Jacob Hamblin,
Apostle to the Lamanites, and the Indian Mission." Journal of Mormon History 2 (1975): 21-34.

1235. Ramsey, Jarold. "The Bible in
Western Indian Mythology." Journal of
American Folklore 90 (October-Decem-
ber 1977): 442-454.

1236. Ronda, James P., and James Axtell.
Indian Missions: A Critical Bibliogra-
phy. Bloomington: Indiana University
Press, 1978.

1237. Schusky, Ernest L. "American Indians
on Their Own." Christian Century 94
(March 30, 1977): 303-306. Response
to article by Carl F. Starkloff (1238).

1238. Starkloff, Carl F. "Church between
Cultures: Missions on Indian Reservations." Christian Century 93 (November 3, 1976): 955-959. See response
by Ernest L. Schusky (1237).

1239. _____. "Cultural Problems in

Mission Catechesis among Native Americans." Occasional Bulletin of Missionary Research 3 (October 1979): 138-140.

1240. _____. "Mission Method and the American Indian." Theological Studies 38 (December 1977): 621-653.

1241. Terrell, John Upton. The Arrow and the Cross: A History of the American Indian and the Missionaries. Santa Barbara, California: Capra Press, 1979.

1242. Warner, Michael J. "Protestant Missionary Work with the Navajo Indians from 1846 to 1912." Ph.D. dissertation, University of New Mexico, 1977.

1243. Wax, Murray L., and Rosalie H. Wax. "Religion among American Indians." Annals of the American Academy of Political and Social Science 436 (March 1978): 27-39.

1244. Wiebe, Menno. "Indian Talk-Back--Church Back-Track." Occasional Bulletin of Missionary Research 2 (April 1978): 43-48.

1245. Williams, William H. "A Means to and End: Oregon's Protestant Missionaries View the Indian." Pacific Historian 20 (Summer 1976): 147-156.

1246. Witheridge, David E. "No Freedom of Religion for American Indians." Journal of Church and State 18 (Winter 1976): 5-19.

COLONIAL MISSIONS

1247. Bowden, Henry W., and James P. Ronda, eds. John Eliot's Indian Dialogues: A Study in Cultural Interaction. Westport, Connecticut: Greenwood Press, 1980.

1248. Gaston, Leroy Clifton III. "Crucifix and Calumet: French Missionary Efforts in the Great Lakes Region, 1615-1650." Ph.D. dissertation, Tulane University, 1978.

1249. Guzzardo, John C. "The Superintendent and the Ministers: The Battle for Oneida Allegiances, 1761-75." New York History 57 (July 1976): 255-283.

1250. Jacob, J. R. "The New England Company, the Royal Society, and the Indians." Social Studies of Science 5 (November 1975): 450-455.

1251. Nash, Gary B. "Notes on the History of Seventeenth-Century Missionization in Colonial America." American Indian Culture and Research Journal 2 (No. 2, 1978): 3-8.

1252. Otis, Virginia Ladd. "John Eliot, Missionary to the Indians." New-England Galaxy 17 (Fall 1975): 25-31.

1253. Rogers, George Truett. "American Baptist Missionaries to Indians in the Northeast in Colonial Times." Foundations 18 (April-June 1975): 153-164.

1254. Ronda, James P. "'We Are Well As We Are': An Indian Critique of Seventeenth-Century Christian Missions." William and Mary Quarterly, 3d series 34 (January 1977): 166-183.

1255. Salisbury, Neal. "Prospero in New England: The Puritan Missionary as Colonist." In Papers of the Sixth Algonquian Conference, 1974, edited by William Cowan, pp. 253-273. Ottawa: National Museum of Canada, 1975.

1256. Simmons, William S. "Conversion from Indian to Puritan." New England Quarterly 52 (June 1979): 197-218.

1257. Stevens, Michael Edward. "The Ideas and Attitudes of Protestant Missionaries to the North American Indians, 1643-1776." Ph.D. dissertation, University of Wisconsin-Madison, 1978.

1258. Wakely, Francis E. "Mission Activity among the Iroquois, 1642-1719." Rochester History 38 (October 1976): 1-24.

BAPTIST MISSIONS

1259. Mondello, Salvatore. "Isabel Crawford and the Kiowa Indians." Foundations 22 (January-March 1979): 28-42.

1260. _____. "Isabel Crawford, Champion of the American Indians." Foundations 22 (April-June 1979): 99-115.

1261. _____. "Isabel Crawford: The Making of a Missionary." Foundations 21 (October-December 1978): 322-339.

1262. Wiggins, Lexie Oliver, Jr. "A Critical History of the Southern Baptist Indian Mission Movement, 1855-1861." Ph.D. dissertation, University of Oklahoma, 1980.

CATHOLIC MISSIONS

1263. Curtis, Ralph E., Jr. "Relations between the Quapaw National Council and the Roman Catholic Church, 1876-1927." Chronicles of Oklahoma 55 (Summer 1977): 211-221.

1264. Duchschere, Kevin A. "John Shanley: North Dakota's First Catholic Bishop." North Dakota History 46 (Spring 1979): 4-13.

1265. Fittipaldi, Silvio E. "The Catholic Church and the American Indians." Horizons 5 (Spring 1978): 73-75. Response by Carl F. Starkloff (1286).

1266. Flecky, Michael, and Harold Moore. Photo Album: St. Francis Mission, School, and Community, 1886-1976. St. Francis, South Dakota: Rosebud Educational Society, 1976.

1267. Garrand, Victor. Augustine Laure, S.J., Missionary to Yakimas. Edited by Edward J. Kowrach. Fairfield, Washinton: Ye Galleon Press, 1977.

1268. Griffith, James S. "The Folk-Catholic Chapels of the Papagueria." Pioneer America 7 (July 1975): 21-36.

1269. Kaminsky, Larry. "Reservation Renewal." Extension 73 (December 1978): 12-18. Lower Brule Indian Reservation.

1270. Lundy, George. "Chapel of Logs." Extension 73 (November 1978): 5-11. Fort Hall Indian Reservation.

1271. _____. "High Achievers." Extension 73 (January-February 1979): 5-11.

1272. _____. "No Nonsense Missioner." Extension 72 (July-August 1977): 5-11.

1273. _____. "River of Life." Extension 70 (April-May 1976): 5-11. St. Peters Mission School, Pima Reservation.

1274. _____. "The St. John's Story." Extension 70 (December 1975): 5-11. St. John's Indian School, Komatke Village, Arizona.

1275. Mathes, Valerie Sherer. "American Indian Women and the Catholic Church." North Dakota History 47 (Fall 1980): 20-25.

1276. Mengarini, Gregory. Recollections of the Flathead Mission, Containing Brief Observations Both Ancient and Contemporary Concerning This Particular Nation. Translated and edited by Gloria Ricci Lothrop. Glendale, California: Arthur H. Clark Company, 1977.

1277. "A New Beginning: Catholic Bishops of Minnesota." Catholic Mind 74 (September 1975): 7-10. Pastoral letter on Indians.

1278. Rahill, Peter. "Catholics Penetrated Missouri's Indian Border." Social Justice Review 68 (June 1975): 87-92; (July-August 1975): 120-123.

1279. Reilly, Robert T. "Indian Catholics: Bringing Prayer Back Down to Earth." U.S. Catholic 44 (February 1979): 25-30.

1280. Renner, Louis L. "Farming at Holy Cross Mission on the Yukon." Alaska Journal 9 (Winter 1979): 32-37.

1281. _____. "Julius Jette: Distinguished Scholar in Alaska." Alaska Journal 5 (Autumn 1975): 239-247.

1282. Robertson, Dario F. "The Catholic Mission and Indian Reservations." Social Thought 3 (Fall 1977): 15-29.

1283. Rosholt, Malcolm, and John Britten Gehl. Florimond J. Bonduel: Missionary to Wisconsin Territory. Rosholt, Wisconsin: Rosholt House, 1976.

1284. Ryan, Patrick J. "Indians and Martyrs Reconsidered." America 133 (October 18, 1975): 226-228.

1285. Scott, John M. "Red Cloud's Dream." Social Justice Review 71 (July-August 1980): 138-148.

1286. Starkloff, Carl F. "A Reflection on 'The Catholic Church and the American Indian.'" Horizons 5 (Fall 1978): 255-258. See Fittipaldi article (1265).

1287. Weber, Francis J. "Bishop Salpointe and the Indians." Records of the American Catholic Historical Society of Philadelphia 90 (March-December 1979): 53-59.

1288. Wintz, Jack. "Respect Our Indian Values." St. Anthony Messenger 83 (July 1975): 34-40.

1289. Wolff, Gerald W. "Father Sylvester Eisenman and Marty Mission." South Dakota History 5 (Fall 1975): 360-389.

News items on Indians in the National Catholic Reporter and articles in other Catholic periodicals are indexed in the Catholic Periodical and Literature Index.

EPISCOPAL CHURCH MISSIONS

1290. Deloria, Vine. "The Confusion of History: A Review Essay." Historical Magazine of the Protestant Episcopal Church 46 (September 1977): 349-353.

1291. Franks, Kenny A. "Missionaries in the West: An Expedition of the Protestant Episcopal Church in 1844." Historical Magazine of the Protestant Episcopal Church 44 (September 1975): 318-333.

1292. Jessett, Thomas E. "Anglican Indians in the Pacific Northwest before the Coming of White Missionaries." Historical Magazine of the Protestant Episcopal Church 45 (December 1976): 401-412.

LUTHERAN MISSIONS

1293. Doederlein, Ferdinand. "The Doederlein Diary: 17 May 1859--February 1860." Concordia Historical Institute Quarterly 51 (Fall 1978): 99-135. Introduction by Roger Moldenhaver.

1294. Miessler, E. G. H. "Pioneer Lutheran Missionary to the Chippewas: Autobiography of E.G.H. Miessler, 1826-1916." Translated by H.C. Miessler. Concordia Historical Institute Quarterly 52 (Winter 1979): 146-174.

1295. Morstad, Alexander E. "Erik Morstad's Missionary Work among Wisconsin Indians." Norwegian American Studies 27 (1977): 111-150.

1296. Vittands, Alexander T. "The Trials of Pastor Cloeter: Indian Mission to Minnesota Territory, 1856-1868." Old Northwest 2 (September 1976): 253-280.

METHODIST MISSIONS

1297. Brockway, Allan R., ed. The American Indian Today." Engage/Social Action 5 (July 1977): 17-47. Methodist Church Task Force on Indians.

1298. Fassett, Thom. The Untimely Survivors." Engage/Social Action 5 (July 1979): 19-47.

1299. Forbes, Bruce David. "Thomas Fullerton's Sketch of Chippewa Missions, 1841-1844." Methodist History 17 (January 1979): 106-114.

1300. Loewenberg, Robert J. Equality on the Oregon Frontier: Jason Lee and the Methodist Mission, 1834-43. Seattle: University of Washington Press, 1976.

1301. Miller, Virginia P. "The 1870 Ghost Dance and the Methodists: An Unexpected Turn of Events in Round Valley." Journal of California Anthropology 3 (Winter 1976): 66-74.

1302. Norwood, Frederick A. "Conflict of Cultures: Methodist Efforts with the Ojibway, 1830-1880." Religion in Life 48 (Autumn 1979): 360-376.

1303. _____. "Native Americans and Frontier Justice." Christian Century 97 (May 28, 1980): 614-615.

1304. _____. "Serpents and Savages." Religion in Life 46 (Autumn 1977): 301-315.

1305. _____. "Two Contrasting Views of the Indians: Methodist Involvement in the Indian Troubles in Oregon and Washington." Church History 49 (June 1980): 178-187.

1306. Vernon, Walter N. "Beginnings of Indian Methodism in Oklahoma." Methodist History 17 (April 1979): 127-154.

1307. _____. "Methodist Beginnings among Southwest Oklahoma Indians." Chronicles of Oklahoma 58 (Winter 1980-1981): 392-411.

QUAKER MISSIONS

1308. Rothenberg, Diane Brodatz. "Friends Like These: An Ethnohistorical Analysis of the Interaction between Allegany Senecas and Quakers, 1798-1823." Ph.D. dissertation, City University of New York, 1976.

1309. Walker, Joseph E., ed. "Plowshares and Pruning Hooks for the Miami and Potawatomi: The Journal of Gerard T. Hopkins, 1804." Ohio History 88 (Autumn 1979): 361-407.

1310. Williams, Dorothy M. "Feathers of Peace." Quaker History 65 (Spring 1976): 32-34.

PRESBYTERIAN, CONGREGATIONAL, AND ABCFM MISSIONS

1311. Bigglestone, William E. "Oberlin College and the Beginning of the Red Lake Mission." Minnesota History 45 (Spring 1976): 21-31.

1312. Brown, Nettie Terry. "The Missionary World of Ann Eliza Worcester Robertson." Ph.D. dissertation, North Texas State University, 1978.

1313. Cocks, James F. III. "The Selfish Savage: Protestant Missionaries and Nez Perce and Cayuse Indians, 1835-1847." Ph.D. dissertation, University of Michigan, 1975.

1314. Coleman, Michael C. "Christianizing and Americanizing the Nez Perce: Sue L. McBeth and Her Attitudes to the Indians." Journal of Presbyterian History 53 (Winter 1975): 339-361.

1315. _____. "Not Race, but Grace: Presbyterian Missionaries and American Indians, 1837-1893." Journal of American History 67 (June 1980): 41-60.

1316. _____. "Presbyterian Missionaries and Their Attitudes to the American Indians, 1837-1893." Ph.D. dissertation, University of Pennsylvania, 1977.

1317. Conard, A. Mark. "The Cherokee Mission of Virginia Presbyterians."

Journal of Presbyterian History 58 (Spring 1980): 35-48.

1318. Davies, Phillips G. "David Jones and Gwen Davies, Missionaries in Nebraska Territory, 1853-1860." *Nebraska History* 60 (Spring 1979): 77-91.

1319. Drury, Clifford M. "The Spokane Indian Mission at Tshimakain, 1838-1848." *Pacific Northwest Quarterly* 67 (January 1976): 1-9.

1320. _____. "Wilderness Diaries: A Missionary Couple in the Pacific Northwest, 1839-48." *American West* 13 (November-December 1976): 4-9, 62-63. Diaries of Elkanah and Mary Walker.

1321. Forbes, Bruce David. "Presbyterian Beginnings in South Dakota, 1840-1900." *South Dakota History* 7 (Spring 1977): 115-153.

1322. Higginbotham, Mary Alves. "The Creek Path Mission." *Journal of Cherokee Studies* 1 (Fall 1976): 72-86.

1323. Hutchins, John. "The Trial of Reverend Samuel A. Worcester." *Journal of Cherokee Studies* 2 (Fall 1977): 356-374.

1324. Lynch, Claire. "William Thurston Boutwell and the Chippewas." *Journal of Presbyterian History* 58 (Fall 1980): 239-253.

1325. Morrill, Allen Conrad, and Eleanor Dunlop Morrill. *Out of the Blanket.* Moscow: University Press of Idaho, 1978. Story of Sue and Kate McBeth.

1326. Perdue, Theda. "Letters from Brainerd." *Journal of Cherokee Studies* 4 (Winter 1979): 4-9.

1327. Pilkington, Walter, ed. *The Journals of Samuel Kirkland: 18th-Century Missionary to the Iroquois, Government Agent, Father of Hamilton College.* Clinton, New York: Hamilton College, 1980.

1328. Saunders, Mary. *The Whitman Massacre.* Fairfield, Washington: Ye Galleon Press, 1977. A survivor's account.

1329. Snell, William R. "Candy's Creek Mission Station, 1824-1837." *Journal of Cherokee Studies* 4 (Summer 1979): 163-185.

1330. Spalding, Arminta Scott. "Cyrus Kingsbury: Missionary to the Choctaws." Ph.D. dissertation, University of Oklahoma, 1975.

1331. *User's Guide to the American Indian Correspondence: The Presbyterian Historical Society Collection of Missionaries' Letters, 1833-1893.* Westport, Connecticut: Greenwood Press, n.d. Guide to microfilm edition of documents.

1332. Vaughn, Courtney Ann. "Job's Legacy: Cyrus Byington, Missionary to the Choctaws in Indian Territory." *Red River Valley Historical Review* 3 (Fall 1978): 5-18.

1333. Walker, Elkanah. *Nine Years with the Spokane Indians: The Diary, 1838-1848, of Elkanah Walker.* Edited by Clifford M. Drury. Glendale, California: Arthur H. Clark Company, 1976.

1334. Waltmann, Henry G. "John C. Lowrie and Presbyterian Indian Administration, 1870-1882." *Journal of Presbyterian History* 54 (Summer 1976): 259-276.

10
Legal Relations

REFERENCE WORKS

1335. <u>Current Law Index</u>. Menlo Park, California: Information Access Corporation. Volume 1, 1980--.

1336. Dees, Harry. "Basic Bibliography for Native American Law." <u>Law Library Journal</u> 69 (February 1976): 78-89.

1337. Gasaway, Laura N., James L. Hoover, and Dorothy M. Warden. <u>American Indian Legal Materials: A Union List</u>. Stanfordville, New York: Earl L. Coleman, 1980.

1338. <u>National Indian Law Library Catalogue: An Index to Indian Legal Materials and Resources</u>. Boulder, Colorado: Native American Rights Fund, 1976.

1339. Webb, Vincent J. <u>Indian Justice: A Research Bibliography</u>. Monticello, Illinois: Council of Planning Librarians, 1976.

GENERAL AND MISCELLANEOUS STUDIES

1340. Bloom, Joseph D., Spero M. Manson, and Gordon Neligh. "Civil Commitment of American Indians." <u>Bulletin of the American Academy of Psychiatry and the Law</u> 8 (March 1980): 94-103.

1341. Coulter, Robert T. "Indian Conflicts and Nonjudicial Dispute Settlement." <u>Arbitration Journal</u> 33 (December 1978): 28-31.

1342. Deloria, Vine, Jr. "Indian Law and the Reach of History." <u>Journal of Contemporary Law</u> 4 (Winter 1977): 1-13.

1343. _____. "Legislation and Litigation Concerning American Indians." <u>Annals of the American Academy of Political and Social Science</u> 436 (March 1978): 86-96.

1344. Funke, Karl A., and Kirke Kickingbird. "The Role of Native Americans in American Legal History." <u>Law Library Journal</u> 69 (November 1976): 474-493.

1345. "A History of Indian Jurisdiction." <u>American Indian Journal</u> 2 (April 1976): 2-15.

1346. Iverson, Peter. "Legal Assistance and Navajo Economic Revitalization." <u>Journal of Ethnic Studies</u> 4 (Fall 1976): 21-34.

1347. _____. "Legal Counsel and the Navajo Nation since 1945." <u>American Indian Quarterly</u> 3 (Spring 1977): 1-15.

1348. Kawashima, Yasuhide. "The Native Americans and White Man's Law before 1800." <u>Indian Historian</u> 11 (Spring 1978): 22-27.

1349. Kearl, Russell C. "On Teaching Federal Indian Law: A Commentary on Getches, Rosenfelt and Wilkinson's <u>Cases and Materials on Federal Indian Law</u>." <u>Journal of Contemporary Law</u> 6 (Winter 1979): 1-54.

1350. Keller, Robert H., Jr. "William O. Douglas, the Supreme Court, and American Indians." <u>American Indian Law Review</u> 3 (No. 2, 1975): 333-360.

1351. <u>Laws of the Colonial and State Governments Relating to Indians and Indian Affairs, from 1633 to 1831 Inclusive</u>. Stanfordville, New York: Earl M. Coleman, 1979. Reprint of 1832 edition.

1352. Medcalf, Linda Joy. "The American Legal Ideology in Theory and Practice: Lawyers Who Represent Native Americans." Ph.D. dissertation, University of Washington, 1976.

1353. Muskrat, Jerry. "The Constitution and the American Indian: Past and Prologue." <u>Hastings Constitutional Law Quarterly</u> 3 (Summer 1976): 657-677.

1354. Newton, Nell Jessup. "Indian Tribal Trust Funds." <u>Hastings Law Journal</u> 27 (November 1975): 519-543.

1355. Schomp, Bonnie. "Administrative Law: Current Progress of Native American

Broadcasting--Status of Indian Ownership." American Indian Law Review 4
(No. 1, 1976): 91-98.

1356. Shattuck, Petra T., and Jill Norgren.
"Indian Lawsuits and White Power."
Nation 225 (July 2, 1977): 12-16.

1357. Singer, Scott N. "Federal Indian
Law: The Bureau of Indian Affairs."
Annual Survey of American Law, 1976,
pp. 41-58.

1358. Stauss, Joseph H., Bruce Chadwick,
Howard M. Bahr, and Lowell K. Halverson.
"An Experimental Outreach Legal Aid
Program for an Urban Native American
Population Utilizing Legal Parapro-
fessionals." Human Organization 38 (Win-
ter 1979): 386-394.

1359. Stockdale, Linda. "A Legal Advo-
cate's Experience." Amicus 2 (December
1976): 27-32.

1360. Strickland, Rennard. "Indian Law and
Policy: The Historian's Viewpoint." Washington Law Review 54 (June 1979); 475-
478.

1361. _____. "The Price of a Free Man:
Resources for the Study of Indian Law,
History, and Policy at the University
of Tulsa." Tulsa Law Journal 15 (Summer 1980): 720-732.

1362. "Update on Indian Probate Problems."
Real Property, Probate and Trust Journal 10 (Spring 1975): 220-222.

1363. Veeder, William H. "Greed and
Bigotry: Hallmark of American Indian
Law." American Indian Journal 3 (Decem-
ber 1977): 2-15.

1364. Washburn, Wilcomb E. "The Historical Context of American Indian Legal
Problems." Law and Contemporary Problems 40 (Winter 1976): 12-24.

LEGAL STATUS/INDIAN SOVEREIGNTY

1365. Ainsworth, Diane. "Indians on the
Warpath: Can They Still Call Themselves
Tribes?" Human Behavior 7 (May 1978):
36-37.

1366. Andrade, Ron. "Are Tribes Too
Exclusive?" American Indian Journal 6
(July 1980): 12-13.

1367. Barsh, Russel Lawrence. "The Omen:
Three Affiliated Tribes v. Moe and the
Future of Tribal Self-Government."
American Indian Law Review 5 (No. 1,
1977): 1-73.

1368. _____. "U.S. v. Mitchell Decision
Narrows Trust Responsibility." Ameri-

can Indian Journal 6 (August 1980):
2-14.

1369. Barsh, Russel Lawrence, and James
Youngblood Henderson. The Road: Indian
Tribes and Political Liberty. Berkeley:
University of California Press, 1980.

1370. Barsh, Russel Lawrence, and Ronald
L. Trosper. "Title I of the Indian
Self-Determination and Education As-
sistance Act of 1975." American Indian
Law Review 3 (No. 2, 1975): 361-395.

1371. Berkey, Curtis. "Federal Administrative Power and Indian Sovereignty."
American Indian Journal 2 (June 1976):
12-15.

1372. _____. "The Inherent Powers of
Indian Governments." American Indian
Journal 2 (May 1976): 15-18.

1373. Blake, James F. "Federal Legal
Status of the American Indian." Rendezvous 11 (Spring 1977): 17-27.

1374. Brecher, Joseph J. "Federal Regu-
latory Statutes and Indian Self-Determination: Some Problems and Proposed Legislative Solutions." Arizona Law Review
19 (No. 2, 1977): 285-312.

1375. Bysiewicz, Shirley R., and Ruth E.
Van de Mark. "The Legal Status of the
Dakota Indian Woman." American Indian
Law Review 3 (No. 2, 1975): 255-312.

1376. Chambers, Reid Peyton. "Judicial
Enforcement of the Federal Trust Re-
sponsibility to Indians." Stanford
Law Review 27 (May 1975): 1213-1248.

1377. Clinebell, John Howard, and Jim
Thomson. "Sovereignty and Self-
Determination: The Rights of Native
Americans under International Law."
Buffalo Law Review 27 (Fall 1978):
669-714.

1378. Deloria, Vine, Jr. "Self-Determina-
tion and the Concept of Sovereignty."
In Economic Development in American
Indian Reservations, edited by Roxanne
Dunbar Ortiz, pp. 22-28. Albuquerque:
Native American Studies, University of
New Mexico, 1979.

1379. Fairbanks, Robert Alvin. "A Discussion of the Nation-State Status of
American Indian Tribes: A Case Study
of the Cheyenne Nation." American
Indian Journal 3 (October 1977): 2-24.

1380. Funke, Karl A. "Education Assist-
ance and Employment Preference: Who
Is an Indian?" American Indian Law
Review 4 (No. 1, 1976): 1-45.

1381. Green, Jessie D., and Susan Work.

"Comment: Inherent Indian Sovereignty." American Indian Law Review 4 (No. 2, 1976): 311-342.

1382. Green, L. C. "North America's Indians and the Trusteeship Concept." Anglo-American Law Review 4 (April-June 1975): 137-162.

1383. Gross, Michael P. "Indian Self-Determination and Tribal Sovereignty: An Analysis of Recent Federal Indian Policy." Texas Law Review 56 (August 1978): 1195-1244.

1384. Hall, Gilbert L. The Federal-Indian Trust Relationship. Washington: Institute for the Development of Indian Law, 1979.

1385. Holyoak, William D. "Tribal Sovereignty and the Supreme Court's 1977-1978 Term." Brigham Young University Law Review, 1978, pp. 911-936.

1386. Hughes, Sharman E. "Immigration/Importation: Exemption of Indian Tribes--Akins v. Saxbe." American Indian Law Review 3 (No. 2, 1975): 469-477.

1387. Israel, Daniel H. "The Reemergence of Tribal Nationalism and Its Impact on Reservation Resource Development." University of Colorado Law Review 47 (Summer 1976): 617-652.

1388. Joyner, Christopher C. "The Historical Status of American Indians under International Law." Indian Historian 11 (December 1978): 30-36.

1389. Kickingbird, Kirke, Charles J. Chibitty, Lynn Kickingbird, and Curtis Berkey. Indian Sovereignty. Washington: Institute for the Development of Indian Law, 1977.

1390. Kissel, Benedetta A. "The Ninth Circuit's Federal Instrumentality Doctrine--A Threat to Tribal Sovereignty." Notre Dame Lawyer 53 (December 1977): 358-384.

1391. Knecht, Steven A. "Tribal Status and the Indian Nonintercourse Act: An Alternative to the Montoya Definition of Tribe." Catholic University Law Review 29 (Spring 1980): 625-639.

1392. McCoy, Robert G. "The Doctrine of Tribal Sovereignty: Accommodating Tribal, State, and Federal Interests." Harvard Civil Rights Law Review 13 (Spring 1978): 357-423.

1393. McLaughlin, Robert. "The Native American Challenge: In Pursuit of Tribal Sovereignty." Juris Doctor 6 (October 1976): 51-58.

1394. Martone, Frederick J. "American In-dian Tribal Self-Government in the Federal System: Inherent Right or Congressional License?" Notre Dame Lawyer 51 (April 1976): 600-635.

1395. Mettler, Earl. "A Unified Theory of Indian Tribal Sovereignty." Hastings Law Journal 30 (September 1978): 89-136.

1396. Murdock, Donald B. "The Case for Native American Tribal Citizenship." Indian Historian 8 (Fall 1975): 2-5.

1397. Pipestem, F. Browning, and G. William Rice. "The Mythology of the Oklahoma Indians: A Survey of the Legal Status of Indian Tribes in Oklahoma." American Indian Law Review 6 (No. 2, 1979): 259-328.

1398. Rice, George William. "Indian Rights: 25 U.S.C. §71: The End of Indian Sovereignty or a Self-Limitation of Contractual Ability?" American Indian Law Review 5 (No. 1, 1977): 239-253.

1399. Rivers, Theodore John. "The Nez Perce Laws (1842): The Introduction of Laws Foreign to an Independent People." Indian Historian 11 (Summer 1978): 15-24.

1400. Robertson, Dario F. "A New Constitutional Approach to the Doctrine of Tribal Sovereignty." American Indian Law Review 6 (No. 2, 1978): 371-394.

1401. Scott, Charles. "Administrative Law: Self-Determination and the Consent Power: The Role of the Government in Indian Decisions." American Indian Law Review 5 (No. 1, 1977): 195-215.

1402. Simpson, Garrett William. "Constitutional Law: Reapportionment--The Navahos and the Trials of Apache County." American Indian Law Review 3 (No. 2, 1975): 445-458.

1403. Swagerty, William R., ed. Indian Sovereignty. Proceedings of the Second Annual Conference on Problems and Issues Concerning American Indians Today. Chicago: Newberry Library, 1979. Papers by Francis Jennings, Arthur Lazarus, Jr., Wendell Chino, and John Redhouse and discussion.

1404. Thomas, Mark W. "Constitutional Law--Equal Protection--Supreme Court Upholds the Validity of Preferential Treatment of Indians in Land Disputes--Wilson v. Omaha Indian Tribe, 99 S. Ct. 2529, 1979." Creighton Law Review 13 (Winter 1979): 619-632.

1405. Thomson, J. S. "Federal Indian Policy: A Violation of International Treaty Law." Western State University

Law Review 4 (Spring 1977): 229-271.

1406. "Tribal Sovereignty: Another Look." Washington University Law Quarterly, Summer 1975, pp. 815-823.

1407. "The Unilateral Termination of Tribal Status: Mashpee Tribe v. New Seabury Corp." Maine Law Review 31 (No. 1, 1979): 153-170.

1408. Werhan, Keith M. "The Sovereignty of Indian Tribes: A Reaffirmation and Strengthening in the 1970's." Notre Dame Lawyer 54 (October 1978): 5-25.

1409. Young, Owen. "Aborigines and the Constitutions of Australia, Canada, and the United States." University of Toronto Faculty Law Review 35 (Spring 1977): 87-106.

1410. Young, Rowland L. "American Indians . . . Treaty Abrogation." American Bar Association Journal 66 (October 1980): 1274-1280.

1411. Zobel, Ron. "Tribal Courts, Double Jeopardy and the Dual Sovereignty Doctrine." Gonzaga Law Review 13 (No. 2, 1978): 467-492.

INDIAN RIGHTS

1412. Alstad, Milva M. "Martinez v. Santa Clara Pueblo: The Scope of Indian Equal Protection." Utah Law Review, 1976, pp. 547-557.

1412. Anderson, Kevin N. "Indian Employment Preference: Legal Foundations and Limitations." Tulsa Law Journal 15 (Summer 1980): 733-771.

1414. Baird, Brian Douglas. "Morton v. Mancari: New Vitality for the Indian Preference Statutes." Tulsa Law Journal 10 (No. 3, 1975): 454-462.

1415. Begay, Harold G. "An Abridgement of Constitutional Rights?" Journal of American Indian Education 18 (May 1979): 1-4.

1416. Berman, Howard R. "The Concept of Aboriginal Rights in the Early Legal History of the United States." Buffalo Law Review 27 (Fall 1978): 637-667.

1417. Blair, Bowen. "Indian Rights: Native Americans versus American Museums-- A Battle for Artifacts." American Indian Law Review 7 (No. 1, 1979): 125-154.

1418. Brothers, Lynda L. "Preserving Indian Archaeological Sites through the California Environmental Quality Act." Golden Gate University Law Review 6

(Fall 1975); 1-21.

1419. Cooper, Robert L. "Constitutional Law: Preserving Native American Cultural and Archeological Artifacts." American Indian Law Review 4 (No. 1, 1976): 99-103.

1420. Coulter, Robert T. "Lack of Redress." Civil Rights Digest 10 (Spring 1978): 30-37.

1421. Coulter, Robert T., assisted by Curtis Berkey and Kerry Stoebner. "The Denial of Legal Remedies to Indian Nations under U.S. Law." American Indian Journal 3 (September 1977): 5-11.

1422. Cross, Raymond, and Barbara Rath. "Indian Monies and Welfare Eligibility." Clearing House Review 14 (June 1980): 120-123.

1423. Davis, Kenneth Culp. "Administrative Law Surprises in the Ruiz Case." Columbia Law Review 75 (May 1975): 823-844.

1424. "The Denial of Indian Civil and Religious Rights." Indian Historian 8 (Summer 1975): 43-46.

1425. Dillsaver, Joe D. "Indian Rights: Eligibility of Indians for State Assistance." American Indian Law Review 4 (No. 2, 1976): 289-294.

1426. Doty, Peggy. "Constitutional Law: The Right To Wear a Traditional Indian Hair Style--Recognition of a Heritage." American Indian Law Review 4 (No. 1, 1976): 105-120.

1427. Folsom, Roy D. "Equal Opportunity for Indian Children--The Legal Basis for Compelling Bilingual and Bicultural Education." American Indian Law Review 3 (No. 1, 1975): 51-82.

1428. Garbani, Ledonna. "The California Native American Heritage Commission." America 142 (June 7, 1980): 483-484.

1429. Gave, Howard B. "Juries--Voir Dire--Due Process Requires Inquiry into a Prospective Juror's Possible Prejudice toward Indians." Journal of Urban Law 53 (August 1975): 119-133.

1430. Gurich, Noma D. "Due Process: Tom v. Sutton--Right to Appointed Counsel for an Indigent Indian in a Tribal Court Criminal Proceeding." American Indian Law Review 5 (No. 2, 1977): 381-392.

1431. Haught, Steven. "Due Process: Delaware Tribal Business Committee v. Weeks: The Participation of Kansas

Delawares in Tribal Awards." American Indian Law Review 5 (No. 2, 1977): 369-380.

1432. Henderson, J. Youngblood. "The Question of Nonresident Tuition for Tribal Citizens." American Indian Law Review 4 (No. 1, 1976): 47-70.

1433. "'Hypocrisy and an Outrage': Human Rights from a Native Perspective." American Indian Journal 4 (August 1978): 46-48.

1434. Ingber, Jeffrey. "Equal Protection As Applied to Tribal Membership and Enrollment Provisions." New York University Review of Law and Social Change 7 (Winter 1978): 15-60.

1435. Johnson, Ralph W., and E. Susan Crystal. "Indians and Equal Protection." Washington Law Review 54 (June 1979): 587-631.

1436. Johnston, Robert. "Constitutional Law: Whitehorn v. State: Peyote and Religious Freedom in Oklahoma." American Indian Law Review 5 (No. 1, 1977): 229-238.

1437. Kasen, Larry M. "Federal Indian Burden of Proof Statute: 5th Amendment Due Process Considerations." Natural Resources Journal 19 (July 1979): 725-734.

1438. Loy, Debra K. "Criminal Law: Equal Protection and Unequal Punishment under the Major Crimes Act—United States v. Cleveland." American Indian Law Review 3 (No. 1, 1975): 103-108.

1439. Lyles, Jean Caffey. "Gods, Graves and Scholars in Elm Grove, Wisconsin." Christian Century 95 (October 11, 1978): 942-943.

1440. Martin, S. Lee. "Indian Rights and Constitutional Implications of the Major Crimes Act." Notre Dame Lawyer 52 (October 1976): 109-135.

1441. Meyer, Carol. "The Louisiana Purchase and Indian Rights." American Indian Journal 2 (October 1976): 16-17.

1442. Pilling, Arnold R. "Native American Religious Rights: Constitutional Considerations." Indian Historian 12 (Winter 1979): 13-19.

1443. Rice, Randolf J. "Native Americans and the Free Exercise Clause." Hastings Law Journal 28 (July 1977): 1509-1536.

1444. Rosen, Cathryn-Jo. "Constitutional Law: Unequal Protection for the American Indian under the Major Crimes Act—United States v. Antelope." Temple Law Quarterly 50 (No. 1, 1976): 109-123.

1445. Rosen, Lawrence. "The Excavation of American Indian Burial Sites: A Problem in Law and Professional Responsibility." American Anthropologist 82 (March 1980): 5-27.

1446. Senkel, David P. "Constitutional Law—Equal Protection—Major Crimes Act, 18 U.S.C. § 1153, Which Subjects Indian Convicted of Certain Offenses to Greater Sentence Than Non-Indian Convicted for Same Offense, Violates Equal Protection Principles Inherent in Fifth Amendment Due Process Clause—United States v. Big Crow, 523 F 2d 955 (8th Cir. 1975)." Creighton Law Review 9 (June 1976): 717-738.

1447. Shattuck, Petra T., and Jill Norgren. "Political Use of the Legal Process by Black and American Indian Minorities." Howard Law Journal 22 (1979): 1-26.

1448. Silvestro, Jo-Nell. "Indian Crimes Act of 1976: Another Amendment to the Major Crimes Act—But How Many More To Come?" South Dakota Law Review 22 (Spring 1977): 407-430.

1449. "United Nations Representatives Study Discrimination against Indigenous People." American Indian Journal 2 (September 1976): 2-11.

1450. Vernon, Howard A. "The Cayuga Claims: A Background Study." American Indian Culture and Research Journal 4 (No. 3, 1980): 21-35.

1451. Wasser, Martin B., and Louis Grumet. "Indian Rights—The Reality of Symbolism." New York State Bar Journal 50 (October 1978): 482-485, 514-518.

1452. Werntz, Joseph Lee III. "Constitutional Law—Title VII—Indian Hiring Preference Does Not Contravene Fourteenth Amendment Equal Protection Clause." New Mexico Law Review 10 (Summer 1980): 461-469.

1453. Woodward, David. "The Rights of Reservation Parents and Children: Cultural Survival or the Final Termination?" American Indian Law Review 3 (No. 1, 1975): 21-50.

1454. Ziontz, Alvin J. "After Martinez: Civil Rights under Tribal Government." University of California-Davis Law Review 12 (March 1979): 1-35.

CIVIL RIGHTS ACT 1968

1455. Beaver, Jennifer B. "Political Advocacy and Freedom of Expression under the Indian Civil Rights Act of 1968."

Arizona State Law Journal, 1976, pp. 479-498.

1456. de Raismes, Joseph. "Indian Civil Rights Act of 1968 and the Pursuit of Reponsible Tribal Self-Government." South Dakota Law Review 20 (Winter 1975): 59-106.

1457. "Equal Protection under the Indian Civil Rights Act: Martinez v. Santa Clara Pueblo." Harvard Law Review 90 (January 1977): 627-636.

1458. Hardin, John T. "Santa Clara Pueblo v. Martinez: Tribal Sovereignty and the Indian Civil Rights Act of 1968." Arkansas Law Review 53 (Summer 1979): 399-421.

1459. Holmes, Dennis R. "Political Rights under the Indian Civil Rights Act." South Dakota Law Review 24 (Spring 1979): 419-446.

1460. "Implication of Civil Remedies under the Indian Civil Rights Act." Michigan Law Review 75 (November 1976): 210-235.

1461. Jones, Cliff A. "Remedies: Tribal Deprivation of Civil Rights: Should Indians Have a Cause of Action under 42 U.S.C. § 1983?" American Indian Law Review 3 (No. 1, 1975): 183-195.

1462. Kennedy, Gary D. "Tribal Elections: An Appraisal after the Indian Civil Rights Act." American Indian Law Review 3 (No. 2, 1975): 497-508.

1463. Lindstrom, Vieno. "Constitutional Law: Santa Clara Pueblo v. Martinez: Tribal Membership and the Indian Civil Rights Act." American Indian Law Review 6 (Summer 1978): 205-216.

1464. Lynch, Judy D. "Indian Sovereignty and Judicial Interpretations of the Indian Civil Rights Act." Washington University Law Quarterly, Summer 1979, pp. 897-918.

1465. Molander, Susan Sanders. "Indian Civil Rights Act and Sex Discrimination--Martinez v. Santa Clara Pueblo." Arizona State Law Journal, 1977, pp. 227-239.

1466. Pearldaughter, Andra. "Constitutional Law: Equal Protection: Martinez v. Santa Clara Pueblo--Sexual Equality under the Indian Civil Rights Act." American Indian Law Review 6 (No. 1, 1978): 187-204.

1467. Stevens, Carl. "Remedies: Indian Civil Rights Act--Exhaustion of Tribal Remedies Prior to Removal to Federal Court." American Indian Law Review 3

(No. 1, 1975): 169-182.

1468. Ziontz, Alvin J. "In Defense of Tribal Sovereignty: An Analysis of Judicial Error in Construction of the Indian Civil Rights Act." South Dakota Law Review 20 (Winter 1975): 1-58.

CHILD WELFARE

1469. Barsh, Russel Lawrence. "The Indian Child Welfare Act of 1978: A Critical Analysis." Hastings Law Journal 31 (July 1980): 1287-1336.

1470. Berlin, Irving N. "Anglo Adoptions of Native Americans: Repercussions in Adolescence." Journal of the American Academy of Child Psychiatry 17 (Spring 1978): 387-388.

1471. Blanchard, Evelyn Lance, and Steven Unger. "Destruction of American Indian Families." Social Casework 58 (May 1977): 312-314.

1472. Byler, William. "Removing Children." Civil Rights Digest 9 (Summer 1977): 19-27.

1473. Guerrero, Manuel P. "Indian Child Welfare Act of 1978: A Response to the Threat to Indian Culture Caused by Foster and Adoptive Placements of Indian Children." American Indian Law Review 7 (No. 1, 1979): 51-77.

1474. Hall, Sarah Moore. "A Sioux Mother Battles White In-Laws for Her Child in the Bitter Case of Brokenleg v. Butts." People Weekly 11 (June 25, 1979): 71-72.

1475. Ishisaka, Hideki. "American Indians and Foster Care: Cultural Factors and Separation." Child Welfare 57 (May 1978): 299-308.

1476. Jones, Mack T. "Indian Child Welfare: A Jurisdictional Approach." Arizona Law Review 21 (1979): 1123-1145.

1477. Limprecht, Jane. "The Indian Child Welfare Act--Tribal Self-Determination through Participation in Child Custody Proceedings." Wisconsin Law Review 1979, pp. 1202-1227.

1478. McCartney, Gaylene J. "The American Indian Child-Welfare Crisis: Cultural Genocide or First Amendment Preservation." Columbia Human Rights Law Review 7 (Fall-Winter 1975-1976): 529-551.

1479. Marousek, Linda A. "The Indian Child Welfare Act of 1978: Provisions and Policy." South Dakota Law Review 25 (Winter 1980): 98-115.

1480. Miles, Marilyn Meissner. "Custody Provisions of the Indian Child Welfare Act of 1978: The Effect on California Dependency Law." University of California-Davis Law Review 12 (Summer 1979): 647-672.

1481. Miller, Dorothy L., Fred Hoffman, and Denis Turner. "A Perspective on the Indian Child Welfare Act." Social Casework 61 (October 1980): 468-471.

1482. Printz, Jane G. "Navajo Grandparents--'Parent' or 'Stranger'--a Child Custody Determination." New Mexico Law Review 9 (Winter 1978-1979): 187-194.

1483. Unger, Steven, ed. The Destruction of American Indian Families. New York: Association on American Indian Affairs, 1977.

1484. Wamser, Garry. "Child Welfare under the Indian Child Welfare Act of 1978: A New Mexico Focus." New Mexico Law Review 10 (Summer 1980): 413-429.

JURISDICTION

1485. Bamberger, James A. "Public Law 280: The Status of State Legal Jurisdiction over Indians after Washington v. Confederated Bands and Tribes of the Yakima Indian Nation." Gonzaga Law Review 15 (No. 1, 1979): 133-169.

1486. Baris, Allan. "Washington's Public Law 280 Jurisdiction on Indian Reservations." Washington Law Review 53 (October 1978): 701-727.

1487. Barsh, Russel Lawrence. "Kennedy's Criminal Code Reform Bill and What It Doesn't Do for the Tribes." American Indian Journal 6 (March 1980): 2-15.

1488. Barsh, Russel Lawrence, and James Youngblood Henderson. "The Betrayal: Oliphant v. Suquamish Indian Tribe and the Hunting of the Snark." Minnesota Law Review 63 (April 1978): 609-640.

1489. Berkey, Curtis G. "Indian Law--Indian Tribes Have No Inherent Authority To Exercise Criminal Jurisdiction over Non-Indians Violating Criminal Laws within Reservation Boundaries--Oliphant v. Suquamish Indian Tribe, 435 U.S. 191 (1978)." Catholic University Law Review 28 (Spring 1979): 663-687.

1490. Biggs, Eric R. "Tribal Preemption." Washington Law Review 54 (June 1979): 633-652.

1491. Bishop, Bruce A. "The States and Indian Jurisdiction: Another Approach." State Government 51 (Autumn 1978): 230-234.

1492. Bubrow, Jonathan. "PL-280 Jurisdiction: Although Partial Assumption of Jurisdiction by Washington over Indian Land Is Authorized by Public Law 280, the State's Exercise of That Jurisdiction Violates Equal Protection." Gonzaga Law Review 13 (Fall 1977): 225-239.

1493. Burns, Larry Alan. "Criminal Jurisdiction: Double Jeopardy in Indian Country." American Indian Law Review 6 (No. 2, 1978): 395-402.

1494. Clinton, Robert N. "Criminal Jurisdiction over Indian Lands: A Journey through a Jurisdictional Maze." Arizona Law Review 18 (No. 3, 1976): 503-583.

1495. _____. "Development of Criminal Jurisdiction over Indian Lands: The Historical Perspective." Arizona Law Review 17 (No. 4, 1975): 951-991.

1496. Collins, Richard B. "Implied Limitations on the Jurisdiction of Indian Tribes." Washington Law Review 54 (June 1979): 479-529.

1497. Deegan, Michael N. "Indian Law--Jurisdiction--'Closing the Door to Federal Court.'" Land and Water Law Review 14 (1979): 625-634.

1498. Dein, Judith Gail. "State Jurisdiction and On-Reservation Affairs: Puyallup Tribe v. Dept. of Game." Environmental Affairs 6 (1978): 535-564.

1499. de Verges, George. "Jurisdiction: Extension of State Authority over Indian Lands--The New Mexico Cases." American Indian Law Review 3 (No. 1, 1975): 137-148.

1500. Dillingham, Brint. "The Portent of Senate Bill 1." American Indian Journal 2 (June 1976): 17-20.

1501. Dolan, Brian T. "State Jurisdiction over Non-Indian Mineral Activities on Indian Reservations." Rocky Mountain Mineral Law Institute Proceedings 21 (1975): 475-533.

1502. Eagan, Ewell E., Jr. "Federal Courts--Indian Jurisdiction--Diversity Courts May Entertain Actions between Indians That Are Not Cognizable in State Courts." Georgetown Law Journal 63 (March 1975): 989-1000.

1503. "Enforcement of State Financial Responsibility Laws within Indian Country." Arizona Law Review 17

(No. 3, 1975): 831-845.

1504. Erhart, Karl Jeffrey. "Jurisdiction over Nonmember Indians on Reservations." *Arizona State Law Journal*, 1980, pp. 727-756.

1505. Fox, Ben E. "Indian Law." *Golden Gate University Law Review* 10 (Fall 1980): 315-357.

1506. Garry, William C. "Jurisdictional Confusion on the Cheyenne River Indian Reservation: United States v. Dupris." *South Dakota Law Review* 25 (Spring 1980): 355-371.

1507. Goldberg, Carole E. "Public Law 280: The Limits of State Jurisdiction over Reservation Indians." *UCLA Law Review* 22 (1975): 535-594.

1508. Gonzalez, Gerald T. E. "Indian Sovereignty and the Tribal Right To Charter a Municipality for Non-Indians: A New Perspective for Jurisdiction on Indian Land." *New Mexico Law Review* 7 (Summer 1977): 153-223.

1509. Green, Jesse D. "Domestic Relations Jurisdiction in Montana: State ex rel. Firecrow v. District Court." *American Indian Law Review* 3 (No. 2, 1975): 459-467.

1510. Gurich, Noma D., and R. Steven Haught. "Criminal Jurisdiction over Indian Schools: Chilocco Indian School, an Example of Jurisdictional Confusion." *American Indian Law Review* 6 (No. 1, 1978): 217-229.

1511. Houston, Les. "The States and Indian Jurisdiction." *State Government* 51 (Winter 1978): 20-27.

1512. Huddleston, Carol A. "The Allocation of Criminal Jurisdiction in Indian Country--Federal, State and Tribal Relationships." *U.C.D. Law Review* 8 (1975): 431-452.

1513. Huemoeller, James L. "Indian Law--State Jurisdiction on Indian Reservations." *Land and Water Law Review* 13 (1978): 1035-1050.

1514. "Indian Law--Criminal Jurisdiction--Tribal Courts Have Criminal Jurisdiction over Non-Indians." *Brigham Young University Law Review*, 1977, pp. 506-523.

1515. "Indian Law--State Jurisdiction over Indian Reservations." *William Mitchell Law Review* 4 (1978): 454-461.

1516. Kelly, T. Christopher. "Indians--Jurisdiction--Tribal Courts Lack Jurisdiction over Non-Indian Offenders."

Wisconsin Law Review, 1979, pp. 537-569.

1517. Klein, Karen K. "Indians--Jurisdiction--Individual Consent to State Jurisdiction by Reservation Indian Ineffective." *North Dakota Law Review* 52 (Winter 1975): 419-426.

1518. Kutner, Peter B. "Can Federal Courts Remain Open When State Courts Are Closed?: *Erie R. Co. v. Tompkins* on the Indian Reservation." *North Dakota Law Review* 52 (Summer 1976): 647-683.

1519. Larson, Jeff. "Oliphant v. Suquamish Indian Tribe: A Jurisdictional Quagmire." *South Dakota Law Review* 24 (Winter 1979): 217-242.

1520. Lynaugh, Thomas J. "Developing Theories of State Jurisdiction over Indians: The Dominance of the Preemption Analysis." *Montana Law Review* 38 (1977): 63-96.

1521. Martone, Frederick J. "Of Power and Purpose." *Notre Dame Lawyer* 54 (June 1979): 829-845.

1522. Miller, Kathleen A. "Indian Law--Indian Sovereignty and Tribal Jurisdiction over Non-Indian Offenders--*Oliphant v. Schlie*." *Washington Law Review* 52 (October 1977): 989-1010.

1523. Mitchell, Carol A. "*Oliphant v. Schlie*: Tribal Criminal Jurisdiction of Non-Indians." *Montana Law Review* 38 (Summer 1977): 339-356.

1524. Murphy, James E. "Jurisdiction: The McBratney Decisions--A Pattern of Inconsistency." *American Indian Law Review* 3 (No. 1, 1975): 149-157.

1525. Nilsson, Erik D. "Indian Law." *Creighton Law Review* 13 (Summer 1980): 1372-1386.

1526. Persons, Louis D. II. "Jurisdiction: Public Law 280--Local Regulation of Protected Indian Lands." *American Indian Law Review* 6 (No. 2, 1978): 403-415.

1527. Petros, Lynne E. "The Applicability of the Federal Pollution Acts to Indian Reservations: A Case for Tribal Self-Government." *University of Colorado Law Review* 48 (Fall 1976): 63-93.

1528. Pipestem, F. Browning. "The Journey from *Ex Parte Crow Dog* to *Littlechief*: A Survey of Tribal Civil and Criminal Jurisdiction in Western Oklahoma." *American Indian Law Review* 6 (No. 1, 1978): 1-80.

1529. Ragsdale, Fred L., Jr. "Problems in the Application of Full Faith and

Credit for Indian Tribes." New Mexico Law Review 7 (Summer 1977): 133-152.

1530. Reynolds, Osborne M., Jr. "Agua Caliente Revisited: Recent Developments As to Zoning of Indian Reservations." American Indian Law Review 4 (No. 2, 1976): 249-267.

1531. Rogers, Carl Bryant. "Zoning: A Rebuttal to 'Village of Euclid Meets Agua Caliente.'" American Indian Law Review 4 (No. 1, 1976): 141-168.

1532. Rosenberg, Milton D. "Indian Law--Tribal Off-Reservation Jurisdiction." Wisconsin Law Review, 1975, pp. 1221-1251.

1533. Rubin, Ivan B. "Federal Indian Law--Criminal Jurisdiction in Indian Country." Annual Survey of American Law, 1977, pp. 517-533.

1534. Salmon, Sue. "Jurisdiction: Exhaustion of Remedies and the Status of Tribal Courts." American Indian Law Review 4 (No. 2, 1976): 295-301.

1535. Samuels, Richard A. "Tribal Court Criminal Jurisdiction over Non-Indians: Testing the Limits of Retained Sovereignty." Cornell International Law Journal 13 (Winter 1980): 89-103.

1536. Schaller, David A. "The Applicability of Environmental Statutes to Indian Lands." American Indian Journal 2 (August 1976): 15-21.

1537. Schnidman, Frank. "Indians and the Environment: An Examination of Jurisdictional Issues Relative to Environmental Management." Columbia Journal of Environmental Law 4 (Fall 1977): 1-34.

1538. Sherick, Steven Paul. "State Jurisdiction over Indians as a Subject of Federal Common Law: The Infringement-Preemption Test." Arizona Law Review 21 (1979): 85-110.

1539. Skibine, Alex. "The Courts." American Indian Journal 6 (January 1980): 10-15.

1540. Skibine, A. T., and Melanie Beth Oliviero. "The Supreme Court Decision That Jolted Tribal Jurisdiction." American Indian Journal 6 (May 1980): 2-12.

1541. Skibine, A. T., Melanie Beth Oliviero, and Ed Fagan. "Potential Solutions to Jurisdictional Problems on Reservations." American Indian Journal 6 (June 1980): 9-14.

1542. Smith, Kyle B. "Oliphant v. Suquamish Indian Tribe: A Restriction of Tribal Sovereignty." Willamette Law

Review 15 (Winter 1978): 127-142.

1543. Sutton, Imre. "Sovereign States and the Changing Definition of the Indian Reservation." Geographical Review 66 (July 1976): 281-295.

1544. "Tribal Sovereignty Sustained: Oliphant v. Schlie and Indian Court Criminal Jurisdiction." Iowa Law Review 63 (October 1977): 230-247.

1545. Vaskov, John A. "Indian Rights--What's Left? Oliphant, Tribal Courts, and Non-Indians." University of Pittsburgh Law Review 41 (Fall 1979): 75-88.

1546. Waldmeir, Peter W. "Local Land Use Regulations as State Civil Law: An Analysis of the Santa Rosa Court's Interpretation of Public Law 280." Tulsa Law Journal 12 (No. 3, 1977): 425-486.

1547. Wasserman, Richard David. "Oliphant v. Schlie: Recognition of Tribal Criminal Jurisdiction over Non-Indians." Utah Law Review, 1976, pp. 631-645.

1548. Weil, Judith H. "Federal Indian Law--Criminal Jurisdiction over Tribal Lands." Annual Survey of American Law, 1979, pp. 591-608.

1549. Wilson-Hoss, Robert D. "Jurisdiction to Zone Indian Reservations." Washington Law Review 53 (October 1978): 677-699.

1550. Ziontz, Alvin J. "Civil Rights Implications of Tribal Authority over Non-Indians within the Reservation." Indian Law Reporter 4 (1977): M6-M11.

TAXATION

1551. Ames, Marilyn. "Tribal Taxation of Non-Indian Mineral Lessees: An Undefined Inherent Power." Journal of Contemporary Law 6 (Winter 1979): 55-73.

1552. Barsh, Russel Lawrence. "Issues in Federal, State, and Tribal Taxation of Reservation Wealth: A Survey and Economic Critique." Washington Law Review 54 (June 1979): 531-586.

1553. Boyle, Gerald J. "Tax Alternatives." In Economic Development in American Indian Reservations, edited by Roxanne Dunbar Ortiz, pp. 119-128. Albuquerque: Native American Studies, University of New Mexico, 1979. Navajo Indians.

1554. "The Case for Exclusive Tribal Power to Tax Mineral Lessees of Indian Lands." University of Pennsylvania

Law Review 124 (December 1975): 491-535.

1555. Connell, Colleen K. "Balancing the Interests in Taxation of Non-Indian Activities on Indian Lands." Iowa Law Review 64 (July 1979): 1459-1516.

1556. Craig, Sandra Jo. "The Indian Tax Cases--A Territorial Analysis." New Mexico Law Review 9 (Summer 1979): 221-262.

1557. Di Pasquale, Denise, with Ann Markusen, Ronald G. Pearson, and Theodore Reynolds Smith. "Natural Resource Taxation." American University Law Review 29 (Winter 1980): 281-302.

1558. Fiske, Terry Noble, and Robert F. Wilson. "Federal Taxation of Indian Income from Restricted Indian Lands." Land and Water Law Review 10 (No. 1, 1975): 63-92.

1559. Goldberg, Carole E. "A Dynamic View of Tribal Jurisdiction To Tax Non-Indians." Law and Contemporary Problems 40 (Winter 1976): 166-189.

1560. Ihnat, Patricia A. "Tribal Sovereignty and the States' Power To Tax Indians." Arizona Law Review 22 (Spring 1980): 249-261.

1561. Kent, Robert A. "Taxation: Limitation of State Authority over Reservation Indians--The New Mexico Cases." American Indian Law Review 3 (No. 2, 1975): 479-488.

1562. McCurdy, James R. "Federal Income Taxation and the Great Sioux Nation." South Dakota Law Review 22 (Spring 1977): 296-321.

1563. Melendy, Patrick. "Tax Exemption: The Right of Urban Indians." Indian Historian 11 (Summer 1978): 29-31, 59.

1564. Molloy, Donald W. "'Must the Paleface Pay To Puff?' Confederated Salish and Kootenai v. Moe." Montana Law Review 36 (Winter 1975): 93-102.

1565. Noble, Jim, Jr. "Tribal Power To Tax Non-Indian Mineral Lessees." Natural Resources Journal 19 (October 1979): 969-995.

1566. Palmer, Michael D. "Taxation: Sales Tax Exemption of the Five Civilized Tribes." American Indian Law Review 6 (Winter 1978): 417-427.

1567. Price, Monroe E., Richard R. Purtich, and D. Gerber. "The Tax Exemption of Native Lands under Section 21 (d) of the Alaska Native Claims Settlement Act." UCLA-Alaska Law Review 6 (Fall 1976): 1-33.

1568. Skibine, A. T. "High Court Blows Political Smoke in Cigarette Tax Cases." American Indian Journal 6 (July 1980): 2-5.

1569. Stewart, Murray B. "Federal Tax Enforcement: Special Rules Applying to American Indians." Tulsa Law Journal 11 (No. 3, 1976): 330-346.

1570. Vogel, Virgil J. "Oliver Godfroy, Miami Indian, 1897-1977." Old Fort News 43 (No. 1, 1980): 19-28.

WATER RIGHTS

1571. Abrams, Robert H. "Reserved Water Rights, Indian Rights, and the Narrowing Scope of Federal Jurisdiction: The Colorado River Decision." Stanford Law Review 30 (July 1978): 1111-1148.

1572. "Adjudication of Indian and Federal Water Rights in the Federal Courts: United States v. Akin." University of Colorado Law Review 46 (Summer 1975): 555-585.

1573. Back, William Douglas, and Jeffery S. Taylor. "Navajo Water Rights: Pulling the Plug on the Colorado River?" Natural Resources Journal 30 (January 1980): 71-90.

1574. Beppler, Timothy A. "Water Law--Procedural Inconsistencies and Substantive Issues in the Federal Reserved Water Rights Doctrine--United States v. Akin." Land and Water Review 10 (No. 2, 1975): 477-487.

1575. Burness, H. S., R. G. Cummings, W. D. Gorman, and R. R. Lansford. "United States Reclamation Policy and Water Rights." Natural Resources Journal 20 (October 1980): 807-826.

1576. Chamberlain, Sue Abbey. "The Fort McDowell Indian Reservation: Water Rights and Indian Removal, 1910-1930." Journal of the West 14 (October 1975): 27-34.

1577. Clyde, Edward W. "Special Considerations Involving Indian Rights." Natural Resources Lawyer 8 (No. 2, 1975): 237-252.

1578. Dellwo, Robert D. "Recent Developments in the Northwest Regarding Indian Water Rights." Natural Resources Journal 20 (January 1980): 101-120.

1579. Dufford, Philip W. "Water for Non-Indians on the Reservation: Checkerboard Ownership and Checkerboard Jurisdiction." <u>Gonzaga Law Review</u> 15 (No. 1, 1979): 95-131.

1580. DuMars, Charles, and Helen Ingram. "Congressional Quantification of Indian Reserved Water Rights: A Definitive Solution or a Mirage?" <u>Natural Resources Journal</u> 20 (January 1980): 17-43.

1581. Ericsson, Robert J. "The Navigation Servitude and Reserved Indian Property: Does the Rule of No Compensation Apply to Indian Interests in Navigable Waters?" <u>Utah Law Review</u>, 1979, pp. 57-76.

1582. Foster, Kennith E. "The <u>Winters</u> Doctrine: Historical Perspective and Future Applications of Reserved Water Rights in Arizona." <u>Ground Water</u> 16 (May-June 1978): 186-188.

1583. Gebhart, Tim. "Who Owns the Missouri?" <u>Progressive</u> 44 (October 1980): 44-45.

1584. Griffith, Gwendolyn. "Indian Claims to Groundwater: Reserved Rights or Beneficial Interest?" <u>Stanford Law Review</u> 33 (November 1980): 103-130.

1585. Hermann, Christopher R. "The Water Rights of Klamath Indian Allottees." <u>Oregon Law Review</u> 59 (1980): 299-325.

1586. Hickey, Michael M. "Application of the Winters Doctrine: Quantification of the Madison Formation." <u>South Dakota Law Review</u> 21 (Winter 1976): 144-159.

1587. Hundley, Norris, Jr. "The Dark and Bloody Ground of Indian Water Rights: Confusion Elevated to Principle." <u>Western Historical Quarterly</u> 9 (October 1978): 455-482.

1588. "Indian Reserved Water Rights: The <u>Winters</u> of Our Discontent." <u>Yale Law Journal</u> 88 (July 1979): 1689-1712.

1589. "Indian Water Rights . . . The Attack Mounts." <u>Indian Historian</u> 12 (Summer 1979): 34-37.

1590. Laird, Michael S. "Water Rights: The <u>Winters</u> Cloud over the Rockies: Indian Water Rights and the Development of Western Energy Resources." <u>American Indian Law Review</u> 7 (No. 1, 1979): 155-169.

1591. Lamb, Micheal F. "Adjudication of Indian Water Rights: Implementation of the 1979 Amendments to the Montana Water Use Act." <u>Montana Law Review</u> 41 (Winter 1980): 73-95.

1592. Lamb, Terrence J. "Indian-Government Relations on Water Utilization in the Salt and Gila River Valleys of Southern Arizona, 1902-1914." <u>Indian Historian</u> 10 (Summer 1977): 38-45, 61.

1593. Leach, Carol S. "Federal Reserved Rights in Water: The Problem of Quanti-

fication." <u>Texas Tech Law Review</u> 9 (Fall 1977): 89-111.

1594. McCallister, Elizabeth. "Water Rights: The McCarren Amendment and Indian Tribes' Reserved Water Rights." <u>American Indian Law Review</u> 4 (No. 2, 1976): 303-310.

1595. Maynez, A. Patrick. "Pueblo Indian Water Rights: Who Will Get the Water? New Mexico v. Aamodt." <u>Natural Resources Journal</u> 18 (July 1978): 639-658.

1596. Meyers, Charles J. "Federal Groundwater Rights: A Note on <u>Cappaert v. United States</u>." <u>Land and Water Law Review</u> 13 (1978): 377-389.

1597. Morrison, Sharon M. "Comments on Indian Water Rights." <u>Montana Law Review</u> 41 (Winter 1980): 39-72.

1598. Nelson, Michael C., and Bradley L. Cooke. <u>The Winters Doctrine: Seventy Years of "Reserved" Water Rights to Indian Reservations</u>. Arid Lands Resource Information Paper No. 9. Tucson: University of Arizona Office of Arid Land Studies, 1977.

1599. Nickeson, Steve. "Floating through Lawyer Land with United States v. Akin." <u>American Indian Journal</u> 2 (May 1976): 21-24.

1600. "One Small Step for Indians." <u>Nation</u> 222 (May 29, 1976): 644.

1601. Orem, Belinda K. "Paleface, Redskin, and the Great White Chiefs in Washington: Drawing the Battle Lines over Western Water Rights." <u>San Diego Law Review</u> 17 (1980): 449-489.

1602. Palma, Jack D. II. "Considerations and Conclusions Concerning the Transferability of Indian Water Rights." <u>Natural Resources Journal</u> 20 (January 1980): 91-100.

1603. _____. "Indian Water Rights: A State Perspective after Akin." <u>Nebraska Law Review</u> 57 (No. 2, 1978): 295-318.

1604. Palmer, Gary B. "Water Development Strategies in the Colorado River Basin: Expansion versus Involution." <u>Anthropological Quarterly</u> 51 (April 1978): 99-117.

1605. Pelcyger, Robert S. "Indian Water Rights: Some Emerging Frontiers." <u>Rocky Mountain Mineral Law Institute Proceedings</u> 21 (1975): 743-755.

1606. _____. "The Winters Doctrine and the Greening of the Reservation." <u>Journal of Contemporary Law</u> 4 (Winter 1977): 19-37

1607. Price, Monroe E., and Gary D.

Weatherford. "Indian Water Rights in Theory and Practice: Navajo Experience in the Colorado River Basin." Law and Contemporary Problems 40 (Winter 1976): 97-131.

1608. _____. "Indian Water Rights in Theory and Practice: Navajo Experience in the Colorado River Basin." Public Land and Resources Law Digest 14 (No. 1, 1977): 85-119.

1609. Ranquist, Harold A. "The Winters Doctrine and How It Grew: Federal Reservation of Rights to the Use of Water." Brigham Young University Law Review, 1975, pp. 639-724.

1610. Reed, Scott W. "Should Rivers Have Running? Toward Extension of the Reserved Rights Doctrine to Include Minimum Stream Flows." Idaho Law Review 12 (1976): 153-167.

1611. Stoebner, Kerry, Vicki Camerino, and Steve Nickeson. "Alaska Native Water Rights As Affected by the Alaska Native Claims Settlement Act." American Indian Journal 4 (March 1978): 2-26.

1612. Strickland, Rennard. "American Indian Water Law Symposium." Tulsa Law Journal 15 (Summer 1980): 699-719. Participants: Robert Pelcyger, Reid Chambers, John Vance, and Ralph Keen.

1613. Taylor, Jeff, and Duane Birdbear. "State Jurisdiction to Adjudicate Indian Reserved Water Rights." Natural Resources Journal 18 (January 1978): 221-235.

1614. U.S. Bureau of Indian Affairs. Indian Water Rights. Washington: Government Printing Office, 1978.

1615. Veeder, William H. "Confiscation of Indian Winters Rights in the Upper Missouri River Basin." South Dakota Law Review 21 (Spring 1976): 282-309.

1616. _____. "Water Rights in the Coal Fields of the Yellowstone River Basin." Law and Contemporary Problems 40 (Winter 1976): 77-96.

1617. Wardlaw, Rebecca E. "The Irrigable Acres Doctrine." Natural Resources Journal 15 (April 1975): 375-384.

FISHING AND HUNTING RIGHTS

1618. Beck, Monte. "State v. Stasso: Off-Reservation Hunting Rights." Montana Law Review 39 (Summer 1978): 323-330.

1619. Boxberger, Daniel L. "The Lummi Island Reef Nets." Wassaja/The Indian Historian 13 (November 1980): 48-54.

1620. Brandimore, Kathleen. "Indian Law--Treaty Fishing Rights--the Michigan Position." Wayne Law Review 24 (March 1978): 1187-1204.

1621. "The Chippewas Want Their Rights." Time 114 (November 26, 1979): 54.

1622. Coggins, George Cameron, and William Modrcin. "Native American Indians and Federal Wildlife Law." Stanford Law Review 31 (February 1979): 375-423.

1623. Delekta, Diane H. "State Regulation of Treaty Indians' Hunting and Fishing Rights in Michigan." Detroit College of Law Review, Winter 1980, pp. 1097-1122.

1624. DeVleming, John. "The Aboriginal Hunting Right: Is the Only Good One an Extinguished One?" Idaho Law Review 13 (Summer 1977): 403-414.

1625. Evans, Alona E. "Treaties--Convention with Canada for Protection of Sockeye Salmon Fishery of Fraser River System of 1930--Political Questions." American Journal of International Law 74 (January 1980): 198-200.

1626. Fadell, Gary. "People v. LeBlanc: Indian Treaty Fishing--The Best Is Yet To Come." Detroit College of Law Review, Summer 1977, pp. 383-400.

1627. Faller, Nancy. "Washington's Fish War." Progressive 44 (September 1980): 51-53.

1628. Finnigan, Richard A. "Indian Treaty Analysis and Off-Reservation Fishing Rights: A Case Study." Washington Law Review 51 (November 1975): 61-95.

1629. Gaasholt, Oystein, and Fay Cohen. "In the Wake of the Boldt Decision: A Sociological Study." American Indian Journal 6 (November 1980): 9-17.

1630. Gartland, John C. "Sohappy v. Smith: Eight Years of Litigation over Indian Fishing Rights." Oregon Law Review 56 (1977): 680-701.

1631. Giudici, James C. "State Regulation of Indian Treaty Fishing Rights: Putting Puyallup III into Perspective." Gonzaga Law Review 13 (Fall 1977): 140-189.

1632. Gray, Janet Davis. "Fishing Vessel Association: Resolution of Indian Fishing Rights under Northwest Treaties." Willamette Law Review 16 (Summer 1980): 931-944.

1633. Isherwood, James H. III. "Indian Fishing Rights in the Pacific Northwest: Impact of the Fishery Conservation and Management Act of 1976." Environmental

Law 8 (Fall 1977): 101-130.

1634. Jones, Robert F. "Clamor along the Klamath." Sports Illustrated 50 (June 4, 1979): 30-35.

1635. Landau, Jack L. "Empty Victories: Indian Treaty Fishing Rights in the Pacific Northwest." Environmental Law 10 (Winter 1980): 413-456.

1636. McDonald, David R. "Native American Fishing/Hunting Rights: An Annotated Bibliography." Indian Historian 11 (December 1978): 57-62.

1637. Merrick, Janna Carol. "Dilemmas in American Liberalism: The Case of Indian Fishing Rights." Ph.D. dissertation, University of Washington, 1978.

1638. Moore, John H. "Racism and Fishing Rights." Nation 225 (September 17, 1977): 236-238.

1639. Nugent, Ann. The History of Lummi Fishing Rights. Bellingham, Washington: Lummi Communications, 1979.

1640. Parfit, Michael. "Fishermen at Sea in Puget Sound War of the Salmon." Smithsonian 9 (February 1979): 56-65.

1641. Pearson, Mary. "Hunting Rights: Retention of Treaty Rights after Termination--Kimball v. Callahan." American Indian Law Review 4 (No. 1, 1976): 121-133.

1642. Petty, Kenneth E. "Accommodation of Indian Treaty Rights in an International Fishery: An International Problem Begging for an International Solution." Washington Law Review 54 (March 1979): 403-458.

1643. Reiger, George. "Bury My Heart at the Western District Court." Field and Stream 80 (June 1975): 38, 102, 104.

1644. _____. "Subsistence Hunting: Fact or Fiction?" Field and Stream 84 (November 1979): 20-22, 26.

1645. Roderick, Janna. "Indian-White Relations in the Washington Territory: The Question of Treaties and Indian Fishing Rights." Journal of the West 16 (July 1977): 23-34.

1646. Schmidhauser, John R. "The Struggle for Cultural Survival: The Fishing Rights of the Treaty Tribes of the Pacific Northwest." Notre Dame Lawyer 52 (October 1976): 30-40.

1647. Starnes, Richard. "Indians and the Courts: Allies against Wildlife." Outdoor Life 159 (June 1977): 8-12, 16.

1648. Thurtell, Joel. "Troubled Waters."

Progressive 44 (September 1980): 48-50.

1649. "Washington Tribes Fight for Their Fishing Rights on a New Front." American Indian Journal 6 (March 1980): 22-25.

INDIAN DELINQUENCY AND CRIME

1650. Bloom, Joseph D. "Forensic Psychiatric Evaluation of Alaska Native Homicide Offenders." International Journal of Law and Psychiatry 3 (Spring 1980): 163-171.

1651. Chadwick, Bruce A., Joseph Stauss, Howard M. Bahr, and Lowell K. Halverson. "Confrontation with the Law: The Case of the American Indians in Seattle." Phylon 37 (July 1976): 163-171.

1652. Cockerham, William C., and Morris A. Forslund. "Attitudes toward the Police among White and Native American Youth." American Indian Law Review 3 (No. 2, 1975): 419-428.

1653. Degher, Douglas William. "Native Americans in the Justice System: An Analysis of Two Rural Washington Counties." Ph.D. dissertation, Washington State University, 1975.

1654. Eggleston, Elizabeth. "Urban Indians in Criminal Courts." University of Western Australia Law Review 12 (June 1976): 368-404.

1655. Forslund, Morris A., and Virginia A. Cranston. "A Self-Report Comparison of Indian and Anglo Delinquency in Wyoming." Criminology 13 (August 1975): 193-198.

1656. French, Laurence. "An Analysis of Contemporary Indian Justice and Correctional Treatment." Federal Probation 44 (September 1980): 19-23.

1657. French, Laurence, and Jim Hornbuckle. "An Analysis of Indian Violence: The Cherokee Example." American Indian Quarterly 3 (Winter 1977-1978): 335-356.

1658. Hall, Edwin L., and Albert A. Simkus. "Inequality in the Types of Sentences Received by Native Americans and Whites." Criminology 13 (August 1975): 199-222.

1659. Jensen, Gary F., Joseph Stauss, and V. William Harris. "Crime, Delinquency and the American Indian." Human Organization 36 (Fall 1977): 252-257.

1660. Kupferer, Harriet J., and John A. Humphrey. "Fatal Indian Violence in North Carolina." Anthropological Quarterly 48 (October 1975): 236-244.

1661. O'Brien, Michael J. "Children: Indian Juveniles in the State and Tribal

Courts of Oregon." American Indian Law Review 5 (No. 2, 1977): 343-367.

1662. Randall, Archie, and Bette Randall. "Criminal Justice and the American Indian." Indian Historian 11 (Spring 1978): 42-48.

1663. Rubin, Harold. "Legal History of an Indian: South Dakota vs. Dennis Banks. Nation 225 (August 6, 1977): 113-115.

1664. Williams, Larry Earl. "Antecedents of Urban Indian Crime." Ph.D. dissertation, Brigham Young University, 1976.

1665. Williams, Larry E., Bruce A. Chadwick, and Howard M. Bahr. "Antecedents of Self-Reported Arrest for Indian Americans in Seattle." Phylon 40 (September 1979): 243-252.

1666. Winfree, L. Thomas, and C. Taylor Griffiths. "An Examination of Factors Related to the Parole Survival of American Indians." Plains Anthropologist 20 (November 1975): 311-319.

TRIBAL LAW AND GOVERNMENT

1667. Barsh, Russel Lawrence, and J. Youngblood Henderson. "Tribal Courts, the Model Code, and the Police Idea in American Indian Policy." Law and Contemporary Problems 40 (Winter 1976): 25-60.

1668. Brakel, Samuel J. "American Indian Tribal Courts: Separate? 'Yes,' Equal? 'Probably Not.'" American Bar Association Journal 62 (August 1976): 1002-1006.

1669. Collins, Richard B., Ralph W. Johnson, and Kathy Imig Perkins. "American Indian Courts and Tribal Self-Government." American Bar Association Journal 63 (June 1977): 808-815.

1670. Fahey, Richard P. "Native American Justice: The Courts of the Navajo Nation." Judicature 59 (June-July 1975): 10-17.

1671. Fairbanks, Robert A. "The Cheyenne and Their Law: A Positivist Inquiry." Arkansas Law Review 32 (Fall 1978): 403-445.

1672. Kickingbird, Kirke. "'In Our Image . . . After Our Likeness': The Drive

for the Assimilation of Indian Court Systems." American Criminal Law Review 13 (Spring 1976): 675-700.

1673. Littlefield, Daniel F., Jr., and Lonnie E. Underhill. "The Judiciary of the Western Cherokee Nation, 1839-1876." Pacific Historian 22 (Spring 1978): 38-54.

1674. Lucke, Thomas W., Jr. "Indian Law: Recognition of a Field of Values." Indian Historian 10 (Spring 1977): 43-47.

1675. Melody, Michael Edward. "The Sacred Hoop: The Way of the Chiricahua Apache and the Teton Lakota." Ph.D. dissertation, University of Notre Dame, 1976.

1676. Park, Charles. "Enrollment: Procedures and Consequences." American Indian Law Review 3 (No. 1, 1975): 109-113.

1677. Reid, John Phillip. "The European Perspective and Cherokee Law." Appalachian Journal 2 (Summer 1975): 286-293.

1678. _____. "A Perilous Rule: The Law of International Homicide." In The Cherokee Indian Nation: A Troubled History, edited by Duane H. King, pp. 33-45. Knoxville: University of Tennessee Press, 1979.

1679. Rivers, Theodore John. "A Study of the Laws of the Ottawa Indians As Preserved in the Ottawa First Book (1850)." Kansas Historical Quarterly 42 (Autumn 1976): 225-236.

1680. Strickland, Rennard. Fire and the Spirits: Cherokee Law from Clan to Court. Norman: University of Oklahoma Press, 1975.

1681. Tejada, Susan E. M. "The IPA and Indian Tribal Governments." Civil Service Journal 17 (April-June 1977): 17-18. Intergovernmental Personnel Act.

1682. _____. "Update on Indian Tribal Governments and the IPA." Civil Service Journal 18 (January-March 1978): 11.

Legal studies pertaining to land are listed in Chapter 6. Contemporary legal affairs can be traced in Announcements, the newsletter of the Native American Rights Fund.

11
Indian Education

HISTORY OF INDIAN EDUCATION

1683. Adams, David Wallace. "Education in
Hues: Red and Black at Hampton Institute, 1878-1893." South Atlantic Quarterly 76 (Spring 1977): 159-176.

1684. _____. "The Federal Indian Boarding School: A Study of Environment and
Response, 1879-1918." Ed.D. dissertation, Indiana University, 1975.

1685. _____. "Schooling the Hopi: Federal Indian Policy Writ Small, 1887-
1917." Pacific Historical Review 48
(August 1979): 335-356.

1686. Andrew, John. "Educating the Heathen:
The Foreign Mission School Controversy
and American Ideals." Journal of American Studies 12 (December 1978): 331-
342.

1687. Barr, Thomas P. "The Pottawatomie
Baptist Manual Labor Training School."
Kansas Historical Quarterly 43 (Winter
1977): 377-431.

1688. Borden, Morton. "'To Educate the
Natives.'" American History Illustrated
9 (January 1975): 20-27.

1689. Clemmer, Janice White. "The Confederate Tribes of Warm Springs, Oregon:
Nineteenth Century Indian Education
History." Ph.D. dissertation, University of Utah, 1980.

1690. Fischer, Frances Jocelyn. "The
Third Force: The Involvement of Voluntary Organizations in the Education of
the American Indian with Special Reference to California, 1880-1933." Ph.D.
dissertation, University of California,
Berkeley, 1980.

1691. Graber, Kay, ed. Sister to the
Sioux: The Memoirs of Elaine Goodale
Eastman, 1885-91. Lincoln: University
of Nebraska Press, 1978.

1692. Havighurst, Robert J. "Indian Education since 1960." Annals of the American Academy of Political and Social

Science 436 (March 1978): 13-26.

1693. Hendrick, Irving G. "Federal Policy
Affecting the Education of Indians in
California, 1849-1934." History of
Education Quarterly 16 (Summer 1976):
163-185.

1694. Holm, Tom. "Racial Stereotypes
and Government Policies Regarding the
Education of Native Americans, 1879-
1920." In Multicultural Education and
the American Indian, pp. 15-24. Los
Angeles: American Indian Studies Center,
University of California, Los Angeles,
1979.

1695. Huff, Delores S. "Educational
Colonialism: The American Indian Ex-
perience." Harvard Graduate School of
Education Association Bulletin 20
(Spring-Summer 1976): 2-6.

1696. "Indian Americans." Research Review
of Equal Education 1 (Summer 1977):
3-17.

1697. Kersey, Harry A., Jr. "Federal
Schools and Acculturation among the
Florida Seminoles, 1927-1954." Florida
Historical Quarterly 59 (October 1980):
165-181.

1698. Kickingbird, Kirke. "A Short History
of Indian Education." American Indian
Journal 1 (December 1975): 2-15.

1699. Laurence, Robert. "Indian Education:
Federal Compulsory School Attendance
Law Applicable to American Indians: The
Treaty Making Period: 1857-1871."
American Indian Law Review 5 (No. 2,
1977): 393-413.

1700. Logsdon, Guy. "Oklahoma's First
Book: 'Istutsi in Naktsoku,' by John
Fleming." Chronicles of Oklahoma 54
(Summer 1976): 179-191. Primer in the
Creek language.

1701. McLoughlin, William G. "Parson
Blackburn's Whiskey and the Cherokee
Indian Schools, 1809-1810." Journal
of Presbyterian History 57 (Winter 1979):
427-445.

1702. Meredith, Howard L. "The Bacone School of Art." Chronicles of Oklahoma 58 (Spring 1980): 92-98.

1703. Moore, Faye Emily. "Disparate Patterns of Minority Education, 1865-1917." Ed.D. dissertation, Northern Illinois University, 1976. Compares European immigrants, blacks, and Indians.

1704. Neely, Sharlotte. "The Forced Acculturation of the Eastern Cherokees: Bureau of Indian Affairs Schools, 1892-1933." In Political Organization of Native North Americans, edited by Ernest L. Schusky, pp. 85-106. Washington: University Press of America, 1980.

1705. _____. "The Quaker Era of Cherokee Indian Education, 1880-1892." Appalachian Journal 2 (Summer 1975): 314-322.

1706. Noley, Grayson B. "Choctaw Bilingual and Bicultural Education in the 19th Century." In Multicultural Education and the American Indian, pp. 25-39. Los Angeles: American Indian Studies Center, University of California, Los Angeles, 1979.

1707. _____. "The History of Education in the Choctaw Nation from Precolonial Times to 1830." Ph.D. dissertation, Pennsylvania State University, 1979.

1708. Olson, Emma P. My Years in the Winnebago School and Community. New York: Vantage Press, 1975.

1709. Ravitch, Diane. "On the History of Minority Group Education in the United States." Teachers College Record 78 (December 1976): 213-228.

1710. Rayman, Ronald. "David Lowry and the Winnebago Indian School, 1833-1848." Journal of Presbyterian History 56 (Summer 1978): 108-119.

1711. _____. "The Winnebago Indian School Experiment in Iowa Territory, 1834-1848." Annals of Iowa 44 (Summer 1978): 359-387.

1712. Riding In, James. "The Contracting of Albuquerque Indian School." Indian Historian 11 (December 1978): 20-29.

1713. Riser, Ellen Lucille. "St. Michael's High School: A Beacon of Light." New Mexico Historical Review 55 (April 1980): 139-150.

1714. Robbins, Webster Smith. "The Administrative and Educational Policies of the United States Federal Government with Regard to the North American Indian Tribes of Nebraska from 1870 to 1970." Ed.D. dissertation, University of Nebraska-Lincoln, 1976.

1715. Roessel, Robert A., Jr. Navajo Education, 1948-1978: Its Progress and Its Problems. Rough Rock, Arizona: Navajo Curriculum Center, Rough Rock Demonstration School, 1979.

1716. Rubenstein, Bruce. "To Destroy a Culture: Indian Education in Michigan, 1855-1900." Michigan History 60 (Summer 1976): 137-160.

1717. Sharpes, Donald K. "Federal Education for the American Indian." Journal of American Indian Education 19 (October 1979): 19-22.

1718. Spear, Eloise G. "Choctaw Indian Education with Special Reference to Choctaw County, Oklahoma: An Historical Approach." Ph.D. dissertation, University of Oklahoma, 1977.

1719. Stahl, Wayne K. "The U.S. and Native American Education: A Survey of Federal Legislation." Journal of American Indian Education 18 (May 1979): 28-32.

1720. Szasz, Margaret Connell. "Federal Boarding Schools and the Indian Child: 1920-1960." South Dakota History 7 (Fall 1977): 371-384.

1721. _____. "'Poor Richard' Meets the Native American: Schooling for Young Indian Women in Eighteenth-Century Connecticut." Pacific Historical Review 49 (May 1980): 215-235.

1722. _____. "Thirty Years Too Soon: Indian Education under the Indian New Deal." Integrated Education 13 (July-August 1975): 3-9.

1723. Taylor, Anne, and Rina Swentzel. "The Albuquerque Indian School: Culture, Environment, and Change." School Arts 79 (October 1979): 12-16.

1724. Thompson, Hildegard. The Navajos' Long Walk for Education: A History of Navajo Education. Tsaile, Arizona: Navajo Community College Press, 1975.

1725. Tingey, Joseph Willard. "Indians and Blacks Together: An Experiment in Biracial Education at Hampton Institute (1878-1923)." Ed.D. dissertation, Columbia University Teachers College, 1978.

1726. Trennert, Robert A. "Peaceably If They Will, Forcibly If They Must: The Phoenix Indian School, 1890-1901." Journal of Arizona History 20 (Autumn 1979): 297-322.

1727. Walker-McNeil, Pearl Lee. "The

Carlisle Indian School: A Study of Acculturation." Ph.D. dissertation, American University, 1979.

1728. Walkingstick, Dawnena. "A Pre-Citizenship Certificate of Educational Competency." Journal of Cherokee Studies 1 (Fall 1976): 87-91.

1729. Weinberg, Meyer. A Chance to Learn: The History of Race and Education in the United States. Cambridge: Cambridge University Press, 1977. See Chapter 5, "Indian-American Children," pp. 178-229, and pp. 337-340.

MODERN INDIAN EDUCATION

General and Miscellaneous Studies

1730. Attaquin, Helen Avis. "What Are the Continuing Education Needs of the American Indian Population of Boston." Ed.D. dissertation, Boston University School of Education, 1975.

1731. Bachtold, Louise M., and Karin L. Eckvall. "Current Value Orientations of American Indians in Northern California: The Hupa." Journal of Cross Cultural Psychology 9 (September 1978): 367-375.

1732. Barta, Anita Marie. "Selected Recreational Activity Preferences of Selected Native American High School Students." Ph.D. dissertation, University of Utah, 1976.

1733. Berg, J. Otto, and Carol Ann Iantuono. "The American Indian and Career Development." College Placement 39 (Spring 1979): 49-51.

1734. Beuf, Ann H. Red Children in White America. Philadelphia: University of Pennsylvania Press, 1977.

1735. Beuke, Vernon Lee. "The Relationship of Cultural Identification to Personal Adjustment of American Indian Children in Segregated and Integrated Schools." Ph.D. dissertation, Cornell University, 1978.

1736. Blanchard, Joseph D., and Richard L. Warren. "Role Stress of Dormitory Aides at an Off-Reservation Boarding School." Human Organization 34 (Spring 1975): 41-49.

1737. Champagne, Duane, and Joy M. N. Query. "Urban Education and Training for American Indian Students: Some Correlates of Success." Urban Education 15 (April 1980): 93-101.

1738. Coleman, Ursula Rosemarie. "Parent Involvement in Preschool Education: A Reservation Head Start Program. Ph.D. dissertation, Case Western Reserve University, 1978.

1739. Cooley, Carl R. "Cultural Effects in Indian Education: An Application of Social Learning Theory." Journal of American Indian Education 17 (October 1977): 21-27.

1740. Coronado, Apolonio. "Can Adult Education Serve Indian Reservations?" Community College Review 5 (Summer 1977): 7-10.

1741. Craver, Edgar Greenleaf. "A Process for Change and Its Implementation at Mt. Edgecumbe Eskimo-Indian School, 1974-1975." Ed.D. dissertation, University of Massachusetts, 1977. Application of Longmeadow Process.

1742. Cress, Joseph N., and James P. O'Donnell. "The Self-Esteem Inventory and the Oglala Sioux: A Validation Study." Journal of Social Psychology 97 (October 1975): 135-136.

1743. Davis, Donald James. "Attitudes of American Indian Parents with Children in Traditional Minneapolis Public Schools, Compared with Attitudes of American Indian Parents with Children in Alternative Schools." Ed.D. dissertation, University of Minnesota, 1976.

1744. Davis, Thomas, and Alfred Pyatskowit. "Bicognitive Education: A New Future for the Indian Child?" Journal of American Indian Education 15 (May 1976): 14-21.

1745. Dinges, Norman G., and Albert R. Hollenbeck. "The Effect of Instructional Set on the Self-Esteem of Navajo Children." Journal of Social Psychology 104 (February 1978): 9-13.

1746. Echo Hawk, Marlene, and Oscar A. Parsons. "Leadership vs. Behavioral Problems and Belief in Personal Control among American Indian Youth." Journal of Social Psychology 102 (June 1977): 47-54.

1747. Fairweather, Donald Charles, Jr. "Administrative Planning in Indian Adult Education Based on the Socio-Economic Effects of High School versus Non-High School Graduation." Ed.D. dissertation, University of Houston, 1977.

1748. Foerster, Leona M., and Dale Little Soldier. "Learning Centers for Young Native Americans." Young Children 33 (March 1878): 53-57.

1749. Forslund, Morris A., and Betty L. Wells. "Political Learning among Members of a Racial-Ethnic Minority."

American Indian Culture and Research Journal 3 (No. 2, 1979): 1-22.

1750. Fox, Dennis R. "Perceptions of Student Rights and Responsibilities in Secondary-Level Bureau of Indian Affairs Boarding Schools." D.Ed. dissertation. Pennsylvania State University, 1977.

1751. Freeland, Franklin Ross. "A Career Awareness Instructional Program of Realistic Occupational Opportunities and Its Effect on Navajo High School Seniors." Ed.D. dissertation, New Mexico State University, 1975.

1752. Golden, Charles J., John Roraback, and Bruce Pray, Sr. "Neuropsychological Evaluation in Remedial Education for the American Indian." Journal of American Indian Education 16 (May 1977): 20-24.

1753. Gray, Clyde Thomas. "American Indian Education: Cultural Pluralism or Assimilation." Ed.D. dissertation, University of Southern California, 1975.

1754. Griffiths, Kenneth. "Support Systems for Educationally Disadvantaged Students and Assuring Practitioner Competence." Journal of Education for Social Work 13 (Spring 1977): 38-43.

1755. Gullerud, Ernest N. "Planning Professional Education Programs for Ethnic Minority Students: Native American Examples." Journal of Education for Social Work 13 (Winter 1977): 68-75.

1756. Hall, Danelle. "A Library Training Program for Native Americans." Wilson Library Bulletin 51 (May 1977): 751-754.

1757. Halverson, Vivian Beth. "Cognitive Styles of Preschool Seminole Indian Children." Ph.D. dissertation, Florida State University, 1976.

1758. Harty, Harold, and James M. Mahon. "Educational Tendencies of Student and Supervising Teachers in Preparation Programs for Native American and Mainstream Settings." Educational Research Quarterly 2 (Fall 1977): 61-69.

1759. Heyser, Richard George. "Native Americans and Libraries: A Citation-Entry Analysis." Ph.D. dissertation, Florida State University, 1977.

1760. Hiat, Albert Benjamin. "The Relationship of Socio-Cultural Variables to Selected Personality Traits among a Group of American Indians." Ph.D. dissertation, University of New Mexico, 1975.

1761. Jannusch, Marlene Rose. "The Development and Implementation of Research Techniques and Curriculum Aids Designed for the Headstart Children in the Black River Falls, Wisconsin, Winnebago Community. Ph.D. dissertation, Southern Illinois University, 1975.

1762. Jones, Irvin Joseph. "Cultural-Institutional Conflict in the Roles of Navajo School Boards Serving Two Types of School Systems in the Navajo Nation." Ph.D. dissertation, Pennsylvania State University, 1977.

1763. Lee, George Patrick. "A Comparative Study of Activities and Opinions of Navajo High School Graduates among Four Selected School Models." Ed.D dissertation, Brigham Young University, 1975.

1764. Lefley, Harriet P. "Differential Self-Concept in Indian Children as a Function of Language and Examiner." Journal of Personality and Social Psychology 31 (January 1975): 36-41.

1765. Leslie, Ernest. "Social Factors Contributing to Exceptional Navajo Children." Education and Training of the Mentally Retarded 12 (December 1977): 374-376.

1766. McCluskey, Murton Leon. "An Analysis of Selected Attitudes toward School and Knowledge of Indian Culture Held by Indian Students Enrolled in the Grand Forks, North Dakota Public Schools." Ed.D. dissertation, University of North Dakota, 1975.

1767. McLaughlin, T. F., Moneda Cady, and Phyllis Big Left Hand. "Effects of the Behavior Analysis Model of Follow Through To Increase Native American Involvement in the Classroom Educational Process." College Student Journal 14 (Spring 1980): 46-47.

1768. Martin, James Carl. "Cognitive Style and Its Relationship to Paired-Associate and Concept Identification Task Performance of Primary-Aged Indian Children." Ed.D. dissertation, Oklahoma State University, 1976.

1769. Metcalf, Ann H. R. "The Effects of Boarding School on Navajo Self-Image and Maternal Behavior." Ph.D. dissertation, Stanford University, 1975.

1770. _____. "From Schoolgirl to Mother: The Effects of Education on Navajo Women." Social Problems 23 (June 1976): 535-544.

1771. Metoyer, Cheryl Anne. "Perceptions of the Mohawk Elementary Students of Library Services Provided by the National Indian Education Association Library Project As Conducted on the Akwesasne (St. Regis) Mohawk Reservation." Ph.D.

dissertation, Indiana University, 1976.

1772. Molohon, Kathryn Theresa. "The Adjustment of Native American Students to Public Schools in the East San Francisco Bay Area." Ph.D. dissertation, University of California, Berkeley, 1977.

1773. Morris, Nancy Tucker. "A Method for Developing Multicultural Education Programs: An Example Using Cahuilla Indian Oral Narratives." Ph.D. dissertation, Iowa State University, 1976.

1774. Muller, John P. "Meeting the Needs of Exceptional Children on the Rosebud Reservation." Education and Training of the Mentally Retarded 12 (October 1977): 246-248.

1775. Multicultural Education and the American Indian. Los Angeles: American Indian Studies Center, University of California, Los Angeles, 1979.

1776. Murdock, Margaret Maier. "The Political Attitudes of Native American Children: The Arapahoe and Shoshoni of the Wind River Reservation in Wyoming." Ph.D. dissertation, Tufts University, 1978.

1777. O'Donnell, James P., and Joseph N. Cress. "Dimensions of Behavior Problems among Oglala Sioux Adolescents." Journal of Abnormal Child Psychology 3 (No. 3, 1975): 163-169.

1778. Pike, William Allison. "A Study of Self Concept as a Factor in Social Groupings of Three Indian Social Groups in Sioux City." Ed.D. dissertation, University of South Dakota, 1975.

1779. Pourier, James Emery Everette. "A Comparison of Values among Indian High Schools, Indian Dropouts and Non-Indian Teachers." Ed.D. dissertation, University of South Dakota, 1976.

1780. Ramey, Joseph H., Thomas W. Sileo, and Helen Zongolowicz. "Resource Centers for Children with Learning Disabilities." Journal of American Indian Education 14 (May 1975): 13-20.

1781. Ramirez, Bruce, and Barbara J. Smith. "Federal Mandates for the Handicapped: Implications for American Indian Children." Exceptional Children 44 (April 1978): 521-528.

1782. Rascher, Leonard Phillip. "Urban Indian Attitudes toward Indian Education." Ph.D. dissertation, Northwestern University, 1977.

1783. Red Horse, John Gregory. "An Analysis of Expectations among Significant Participants in the Indian New Careers Program in Minneapolis." Ph.D. dissertation, University of Minnesota, 1976.

1784. Reese, Kenneth M. "Obstacles to the Psychological Development of Indian Children." Family Law Quarterly 9 (Winter 1975): 573-593.

1785. Riner, Reed Douglas. "Attitudes toward Formal Education among American Indian Parents and Students in Six Communities." Ph.D. dissertation, University of Colorado at Boulder, 1977.

1786. Ross, Paul Anthony. "A Study of the Self-Concept of Academic Ability of Navajo Students in Four Selected School Environments." Ph.D. dissertation, University of Utah, 1975.

1787. Ruopp, Richard Randolph. "The NECESSITIES Case: A Policy Study and Interpretive History of a National Social Studies Curriculum Reform Project for K-12 American Indian and Native Alaskan Students, 1968-1970." Ed.D. dissertation, Harvard University, 1977. NECESSITIES is an acronym for National Education Committee for Effective Social Science Instruction and Teaching of Indian and Eskimo Students.

1788. St. Germaine, Richard Dale. "Comparative Perceptions of the Indian School Principal's Normative Role by Tribal Leaders and Principals." Ph.D. dissertation, Arizona State University, 1975.

1789. Shaughnessy, Timothy Francis. "The Attitudes of Selected Educational Groups in Arizona toward Indians." Ph.D. dissertation, Arizona State University, 1976.

1790. Smith, Frederick Downing. "A Network Analysis of a Bureau of Indian Affairs School System To Determine Factors Involved in Job Satisfaction." Ph.D. dissertation, University of Arizona, 1977.

1791. Snow, Albert J. "Ethno-Science and the Gifted." Journal of American Indian Education 16 (January 1977): 27-30.

1792. _____. "Ethno Science and the Gifted in American Indian Education." Gifted Child Quarterly 21 (Spring 1977): 53-57.

1793. Swanson, Rosemary A., and Ronald W. Henderson. "Effects of Televised Modeling and Active Participation on Rule-Governed Question Production among Native American Preschool Children." Contemporary Educational Psychology 2 (October 1977): 345-352.

1794. Tippeconnic, John W. III. "The

Relationship between Teacher Pupil Control Ideology and Elementary Student Attitudes in Navajo Schools." Ph.D. dissertation, Pennsylvania State University, 1975.

1795. Todacheeny, Frank. "Progress in Providing Services to Exceptional Children: Focusing on Parent/Community Awareness and Involvement." Education and Training of the Mentally Retarded 12 (December 1977): 377-380.

1796. Toelken, Barre. "World View, the University Establishment, and Cultural Annihilation." Journal of Ethnic Studies 2 (Winter 1975): 1-21.

1797. Van Otten, George A., and Ruth J. Narcho. "Adult Education and Land Use Planning." Journal of American Indian Education 19 (May 1980): 5-7.

1798. Van Otten, George A., and Stanley W. Swarts. "Effective Adult Education in Applied Geography on the Navajo Reservation." Journal of Geography 78 (December 1979): 277-279.

1799. Watson, John G., and Clair D. Rowe. "Training of Operative Employes." Training and Development Journal 30 (April 1976): 10-15.

1800. Whitman, Myron A., and James D. Kayotawape. "A Study Skills Course for Native American Students." Journal of College Student Personnel 16 (November 1975): 521.

1801. Wicker, Leslie Cleveland. "Racial Awareness and Racial Identification among American Indian Children As Influenced by Native-American Power Ideology and Self-Concept." Ph.D. dissertation, University of North Carolina at Greensboro, 1977.

1802. Willett, Jimmy Lee. "Historical Development of Vocational Education on the Navajo Indian Reservation." Ed.D. dissertation, University of Arkansas, 1976.

1803. Williams, Leslie Rowell. "Mending the Hoop: A Study of Roles, Desired Responsibilities and Goals of Parents of Children in Tribally Sponsored Head Start Programs." Ed.D. dissertation, Columbia University, 1975.

Language and Communication Skills

1804. Ackley, Randall. "The Navajo College-Level-Literacy Program: A Holistic Response to Language Development for the 'Outsider.'" In Minority Language and Literature: Retrospective and Perspective, edited by Dexter

Fisher, pp. 99-106. New York: Modern Language Association of America, 1977.

1805. Bartelt, H. Guillermo. "Creative ESL Composition for the Bilingual Indian Student." Journal of American Indian Education 19 (May 1980): 8-10.

1806. Battle, Edwina Larry. "A Comparison of Two Vocabulary Development Approaches on Intermediate Grade Menominee Indian Children." Ph.D. dissertation, University of Wisconsin-Madison, 1975.

1807. Begay, Joe Yazzie. "English Reading Competence of Navajo Students in Public and Bureau of Indian Affairs Schools." Ph.D. dissertation, University of Arizona, 1980.

1808. Berman, S. Sue. "Speech and Language Services on an Indian Reservation." Language, Speech, and Hearing Services in Schools 7 (January 1976): 56-60.

1809. Downey, Mary Catherine Moriarity. "A Profile of Psycholinguistic Abilities for Grades One, Two, and Three Students of the Flathead Reservation." Ed.D. dissertation, University of Montana, 1977.

1810. DuBois, Diane M. "Getting Meaning from Print: Four Navajo Students." Reading Teacher 32 (March 1979): 691-695.

1811. _____. "A Psycholinguistic Analysis of the Oral Reading Miscues Generated by a Selected Group of Navajo Speakers: A Longitudinal Study." Ph.D. dissertation, Wayne State University, 1977.

1812. Enochs, John Romily III. "The Relationship between Choctaw Teachers' and Non-Choctaw Teachers' Perceptions of Choctaw First-Graders and Student Achievement in Reading." Ed.D. dissertation, Mississippi State University, 1977.

1813. Evans, G. Edward, and Karin Abbey. Bibliography of Language Arts Materials for Native North Americans: Bilingual, English as a Second Language and Native Language Materials, 1965-1974. Los Angeles: American Indian Studies Center, University of California, Los Angeles, 1977.

1814. _____. Bibliography of Language Arts Materials for Native North Americans: Bilingual, English as a Second Language and Native Language Materials, 1975-1976, with Supplemental Entries for 1965-1974. Los Angeles: American Indian Studies Center, University of California, Los Angeles, 1979.

1815. Foerster, Leona M., and Dale Little Soldier. "Classroom Communication and the Indian Child." Language Arts 57 (January 1980): 45-49.

1816. Fox, Sandra Jean. "An Evaluation of Eight Reading Programs Implemented for Indian Students in North and South Dakota." D.Ed. dissertation, Pennsylvania State University, 1976.

1817. Giordano, Gerard. "'Congenital Verbal Deficiency' in Navajo Children: More on Testing." Reading Teacher 32 (November 1978): 132-134.

1818. Grobsmith, Elizabeth Stanley. "Lakhota Bilingualism: A Comparative Study of Language Use in Two Communities on the Rosebud Sioux Reservation." Ph.D. dissertation, University of Arizona, 1976.

1819. Guilmet, George Michael. "The Nonverbal American Indian Child in the Urban Classroom." Ph.D. dissertation, University of California, Los Angeles, 1976.

1820. Heiman, Norma L. Anderson. "The Development of Supplemental Reading Texts for Navajo Students in Elementary Education." Ed.D dissertation, Utah State University, 1977.

1821. Jackson, Joyce L. "A Study of the Oral Language Development of the Menominee Indian Preschool Children." Ed.D. dissertation, Indiana University, 1977.

1822. Liebe-Harkort, Marie-Louise. "Materials Preparation for Use in Bilingual Programs." Journal of American Indian Education 20 (October 1980): 10-15.

1823. McCarty, Teresa L. "Language Use by Yavapai-Apache Students with Recommendations for Curriculum Design." Journal of American Indian Education 20 (October 1980): 1-9.

1824. Mallett, Graham. "Using Language Experience with Junior High Native Indian Students." Journal of Reading 21 (October 1977): 25-28.

1825. Murphy, Barbara Jean. "The Identification of the Components Requisite for the Teaching of English to Primary School Navajo Students: Guidelines for English as a Second Language in Navajo/English Bilingual Education." Ed.D. dissertation, University of Massachusetts, 1978.

1826. Odle, Florence Neal. "Reading and Language Achievement of Navajo Indian Pupils." Ed.D. dissertation, University of Southern California, 1976.

1827. Pell, Sarah-Warner J. "A Communication Skills Project for Disadvantaged Aleut, Eskimo, and Indian Ninth and Tenth Graders." Journal of Reading 22 (February 1979): 404-407.

1828. Pulling, Jane Higdon. "Language Experience and Ivan Looking Horse." Language Arts 57 (January 1980): 50-52.

1829. Rosier, Paul Webb. "A Comparative Study of Two Approaches of Introducing Initial Reading to Navajo Children: The Direct Method and the Native Language Method." Ed.D. dissertation, Northern Arizona University, 1977.

1830. Roth, Edith Brill. "Lato: Lats-- Hunting in the Indian Languages." American Education 12 (August-September 1976): 10-14.

1831. Simpson, Audrey Koehler. "Oral English Usage of Six-Year-Old Crow and Northern Cheyenne Reservation Indian Children: A Descriptive Study." Ed.D. dissertation, University of Maine, 1975.

1832. Simpson-Tyson, Audrey K. "Are Native American First Graders Ready to Read?" Reading Teacher 31 (April 1978): 798-801.

1833. Spolsky, Bernard. "American Indian Bilingual Education." Linguistics 198 (October 15, 1977): 57-72.

1834. _____. "Linguistics in Practice: The Navajo Reading Study." Theory into Practice 14 (December 1975): 347-352.

1835. Stout, Steven Owen. "Sociolinguistic Aspects of English Diversity among Elementary-Aged Students from Laguna Pueblo." Ph.D. dissertation, American University, 1979.

1836. Suina-Lowery, Carletta. "Bilingual Education and the Pueblo Indians." Journal of American Indian Education 18 (January 1979): 23-27.

1837. "Talking Hands." Science and Children 13 (September 1976): 24-25. Hand positions for Plains Indian sign language.

1838. Turk, Toni Richard. "Navajo/English Bilingual-Bicultural Education: An Evaluation." Ed.D. dissertation, Brigham Young University, 1977.

1839. Wells, Bethany J., and D. Scott Bell. "A New Approach to Teaching Reading Comprehension: Using Cloze and Computer-Assisted Instruction." Educational Technology 20 (March 1980): 49-51.

1840. Wieczkiewicz, Helen C. "A Phonic Reading Program for Navajo Students." Journal of American Indian Education 18 (May 1979): 20-27.

1841. Wooden, Sharon Lee, and Jacqueline Curran Backer. "The Right to Read." Journal of American Indian Education 15 (January 1976): 1-6.

1842. Woodruff, Ross L. "The Development of the Navajo Orthography and the Translation of the Navajo New Testament." Ed.D. dissertation, Northern Arizona University, 1979.

Testing and Achievement Studies

1843. Asmussen, Johannas Mary. "Visual-Motor Perception of Sioux and Chippewa Children and the Normative Population on the Bender Gestalt Test Using the Kippitz Scoring System." Ed.D dissertation, University of Northern Colorado, 1976.

1844. Brown, Anthony D. "Cherokee Culture and School Achievement." American Indian Culture and Research Journal 4 (No. 3, 1980): 55-74.

1845. _____. "The Cross-over Effect: A Legitimate Issue in Indian Education?" In Multicultural Education and the American Indian, pp. 93-113. Los Angeles: American Indian Studies Center, University of California, Los Angeles, 1979.

1846. Chadwick, Bruce A., Howard M. Bahr, and Joseph Stauss. "Indian Education in the City: Correlates of Academic Performance." Journal of Educational Research 70 (January 1977): 135-141.

1847. Church, Avery G. "Academic Achievement, IQ, Level of Occupational Plans, and Ethnic Stereotypes for Anglos and Navahos in a Multi-Ethnic High School." Southern Journal of Educational Research 10 (Summer 1976): 184-201.

1848. Hynd, George W., and William I. Garcia. "Intellectual Assessment of the Native American Student." School Psychology Digest 8 (Fall 1979): 446-454.

1849. McAreavey, James Patrick. "An Analysis of Selected Educationally Handicapped South Dakota Sioux Indian Children's Responses to the Wechsler Intelligence Scale for Children and Wide Range Achievement Test of Reading." Ed.D. dissertation, University of Colorado, 1975.

1850. Reschly, Daniel J. "WISC-R Factor Structures among Anglos, Blacks, Chicanos, and Native-American Papagos." Journal of Consulting and Clinical Psychology 46 (June 1978): 417-422.

1851. Shipp, Patrick E. "A Comparative Study of Second and Third Grade Performance in the Eastern Navajo Agency BIA Schools." Ed.D. dissertation, Northern Arizona University, 1976.

1852. Spencer, Barbara G., Ernest Boudreaux, and John Mullins. "Using the 'Kuder E' with Choctaw Students." Journal of American Indian Education 15 (May 1976): 30-34.

1853. Talley, Tyra. "A Multifaceted Inquiry into the Personality Factors and Academic Achievement of Indian High School Students." Ed.D. dissertation, University of South Dakota, 1975.

1854. Thurber, Steven. "Changes in Navajo Responses to the Draw-a-Man Test." Journal of Social Psychology 99 (June 1976): 139-140.

Comparative Studies

1855. Cockerham, William C., and Audie L. Blevins, Jr. "Open School vs. Traditional School: Self-Identification among Native Americans and White Adolescents." Sociology of Education 49 (April 1976): 164-169. Rejoinder by Russell Thornton and Joan Marsh-Thornton, and response by Cockerham and Blevins, (July 1976): 247-48.

1856. Dawkins, Marvin Phillip. "Race and Occupational Expectations among White and Non-White College Students in the United States: A Study of Sponsored and Contest Mobility." Ph.D. dissertation, Florida State University, 1975.

1857. Day, Richard, L. Bryce Boyer, and George A. de Vos. "Two Styles of Ego Development: A Cross-Cultural, Longitudinal Comparison of Apache and Anglo School Children." Ethos 3 (Fall 1975): 345-379.

1858. Fields, Charles R. "Alaskan Natives and Caucasians: A Comparison of Educational Aspirations and Actual Enrollment." Journal of Student Financial Aid 5 (November 1975): 35-45.

1859. Gallego, Daniel Tapia. "Orientations toward Occupational Attainment and Ethnic Group Identity: A Comparison of American Indian and Caucasian High School Juniors and Seniors." Ph.D. dissertation, Utah State University, 1975.

1860. Martin, James C. "Locus of Control and Self-Esteem in Indian and White Students." Journal of American Indian Education 18 (October 1978): 23-29.

1861. Ritt, Sharon Isaacson. "Social Studies Concept Attainment of Anglo and Navajo Indian Sixth-Grade Students." Social Education 42 (November-December 1978): 616-622.

1862. _____. "Social Studies Concept Attainment of Navajo and Anglo Sixth Grade Students." Ed.D. dissertation, Northern Arizona University, 1977.

1863. Scott, Thomas B., and Max Anadon. "A Comparison of the Vocational Interest Profiles of Native American and Caucasian College Bound Students." Measurement and Evaluation in Guidance 13 (April 1980): 35-42.

1864. Tyler, John D., and David N. Holsinger. "Locus of Control Differences between Rural American Indian and White Children." Journal of Social Psychology 95 (April 1975): 149-155.

Counseling

1865. Cardell, George W., William C. Cross, and W. James Lutz. "Extending Counselor Influence into the Classroom." Journal of American Indian Education 17 (January 1978): 7-12.

1866. Dauphinais, Paul, Teresa La Fromboise, and Wayne Rowe. "Perceived Problems and Sources of Help for American Indian Students." Counselor Education and Supervision 20 (September 1980): 37-44.

1867. Ferreira, Linda Ohlsen. "Counseling Native American Children." Contemporary Education 46 (Summer 1975): 305-306.

1868. Hayes, Susanna. "The Counselor Aide: Helping Services for Native American Students." Journal of American Indian Education 18 (May 1979): 5-11.

1869. La Fromboise, Teresa, Paul Dauphinais, and Wayne Rowe. "Positive Helper Attributes." Journal of American Indian Education 19 (May 1980): 11-16.

1870. Ross, Donald David. "A Psychological and Philosophical Foundation for Counseling Amerindian College Students." Ed.D. dissertation, University of South Dakota, 1975. A collection of writings, primarily by Indians, to furnish background for counseling.

1871. Ryan, Loye Marie Johnson. "A Study of Personality Traits and Values of American Indian and Non-American Indian Counselors Trained at the University of South Dakota." Ed.D. dissertation, University of South Dakota, 1976.

1872. Winterton, Wayne. "Advisor Teaming." Journal of American Indian Education 17 (May 1978): 19-25.

Higher Education

1873. Adams, L. La Mar, H. Bruce Higley, and Leland H. Campbell. "Academic Success of American Indian Students at a Large Private University." College and University 53 (Fall 1977): 100-107.

1874. Anadon, Max Ernesto. "The American College Interest Inventory: Its Usefulness and Validity with the Native American College Student." Ph.D. dissertation, University of North Dakota, 1977.

1875. Burgess, Billy Joe. "A Study of the Attitudes, Characteristics, and Opinions of Native American Students Majoring in Liberal Arts at Haskell Indian Junior College." Ed.D. dissertation, University of Kansas, 1976.

1876. Burrough, Edna. "Our Indigenous Americans: Indian Lore and Bacone College." Daughters of the American Revolution Magazine 110 (May 1976): 536-543.

1877. Carroll, Richard E. "Academic Performance and Cultural Marginality." Journal of American Indian Education 18 (October 1978): 11-16. Haskell Indian Junior College.

1878. Chavers, Dean. "Isolation and Drainoff: The Case of the American Indian Educational Researcher." Educational Researcher 9 (October 1980): 12-15.

1879. Churchill, Ward, and Norbert S. Hill, Jr. "An Historical Survey of Tendencies in Indian Education: Higher Education." Indian Historian 12 (Winter 1979): 37-46.

1880. _____. "Indian Education at the University Level: An Historical Survey." Journal of Ethnic Studies 7 (Fall 1979): 43-58.

1881. De Lauer, Marjel. "Bridge to the Outer World." Arizona Highways 52 (September 1976): 42-47. Navajo Community College.

1882. Edwards, Eugene Daniel. "A Description and Evaluation of American Indian Social Work Training Programs." D.S.W. dissertation, University of Utah, 1976.

1883. French, Laurence, and Charles Hornbuckle. "In Our Educational System: The Need for a Multicultural Philosophy in Higher Education." Indian Historian 10 (Fall 1977): 33-39.

1884. Guyette, Susan. "Responsibility of the University in a Multi-Ethnic Society: A Pragmatic Perspective toward a Graduate Program in American Indian Studies." American Indian Culture and Research Journal 2 (Nos. 3 and 4, 1978): 24-27.

1885. "Historical Background: Indian Higher Education." American Indian Journal 2 (June 1976): 2-4.

1886. "Indian College Students' Perspective of Education." Journal of American Indian Education 15 (January 1976): 18-22.

1887. Janssen, Peter A. "Navaho C.C.'s Unfulfilled Promise." Change 7 (November 1975): 52-53.

1888. Justiz, Manuel J. "An Assessment of Institutional Philosophy and Goals at a Developing Indian Junior College." Ph.D. dissertation, Southern Illinois University, 1977. Haskell Indian Junior College.

1889. Kickingbird, Lynn. "A Case for Indian Controlled Community Colleges." American Indian Journal 2 (June 1976): 5-11.

1890. Kinsey, Mary Ann. "Indian Education at Fort Lewis College, Durango, Colorado." Ed.D. dissertation, University of Tennessee, 1975.

1891. Kolhoff, Kathleen Elizabeth. "Flaming Rainbow: From a Sioux Vision to a Cherokee Reality: A Descriptive Study of the Development of an American Indian Institution of Higher Education." Ph.D. dissertation, Union Graduate School (Ohio), 1979. Flaming Rainbow University.

1892. Leonard, Leon, James Freim, and Jay Fein. "Introducing Engineering to the American Indian." Journal of American Indian Education 14 (January 1975): 6-11.

1893. McComb, Marlin Richard. "Native American Programs as Socio-Cultural Adaptive Mechanisms to the College Environment: A Case Comparison of the University of Oregon and Oregon State University." Ph.D. dissertation, Oregon State University, 1975.

1894. Middleton, Lorenzo. "Indian College Charges Federal Harassment." Chronicle of Higher Education 19 (February 19, 1980): 4. D-Q University.

1895. _____. "Indian Tribal Colleges Accuse U.S. Bureaucrats of Delaying $85 Million Congress Authorized." Chronicle of Higher Education 19 (February 11, 1980): 1, 12.

1896. _____. "N.C. Indians Oppose Selection of a White to Head College Originally Built for Them." Chronicle

of Higher Education 18 (August 6, 1979): 1, 10.

1897. Mitchell, Irene E. "Higher Education for the Plains Indians of Western Oklahoma." Delta Kappa Gamma Bulletin 42 (Fall 1975): 27-33.

1898. Osborne, Virgus C. "An Appraisal of the Education Program for Native Americans at Brigham Young University, 1966-1974, with Curricular Recommendations." Pn.D. dissertation, University of Utah, 1975.

1899. Pace, Alfred Lawrence III. "The Education of American Indians in Community Colleges: Some Implications for Three Disciplines." Ph.D. dissertation, Washington State University, 1976.

1900. Phillips, John C. "A College of, by, and for Navajo Indians." Chronicle of Higher Education 15 (January 16, 1978): 10-12.

1901. Pope, Albert Wallace. "An Exploration of the University Environment As Perceived by Native American Freshmen." Ed.D. dissertation, University of Utah, 1977.

1902. Romero, Leo M. "The Quest for Educational Opportunity: Access to Legal and Medical Education in New Mexico." New Mexico Historical Review 53 (October 1978): 337-346.

1903. Shaffer, Gary M. "Indian Education: Accommodation or Change?" Community College Social Science Quarterly 5-6 (Summer-Fall 1975): 115-117.

1904. Webb, Robert Paul II. "A Study of the Relationship of Peer Tutoring and Academic Achievement for a Select Group of Indian Students." Ed.D. dissertation, University of Tulsa, 1976.

1905. Winchell, Dick G., Stephen Safforn, and Robert N. Porter. "Indian Self-Determination and the Community College." Journal of American Indian Education 19 (May 1980): 17-23. Scottsdale Community College.

Teacher Training

1906. Berhow, Bennett Francis. "An Evaluation of the Northern Plains Indian Teacher Corps Teacher Preparation Model." Ph.D. dissertation, University of North Dakota, 1977.

1907. Bill, Willard E. "American Indian Teacher Education." In Multicultural Education and the American Indian, pp. 129-143. Los Angeles: American In-

dian Studies Center, University of
California, Los Angeles, 1979.

1908. _____. "A Modification of the
University of Washington Teacher Evaluation Instrument To Reflect the Needs
of the American Indian." Ph.D. dissertation, University of Washington,
1978.

1909. Burke, Beverly A. "The Effect of
Teaching Communication Skills to Teachers
in an Elementary Bureau of Indian Affairs School." Ph.D. dissertation, University of Oklahoma, 1976.

1910. Galli, Marcia J. "A Transportable
Model for Cultural Awareness Inservice
Training: Rationale and Overview." In
Multicultural Education and the American
Indian, pp. 145-150. Los Angeles: Ameri-
can Indian Studies Center, University
of California, Los Angeles, 1979.

1911. Hawkins, Gene Anthony. "The Teaching
of Communication Skills to Child Care
Workers in Two Native American Organizations and Its Effects on Students."
Ph.D. dissertation, University of Oklahoma, 1977.

1912. Hayes, Susanna, and Kenneth A. Ames.
"A Program for Teachers of Native Amer-
ican Youth." Journal of American Indian
Education 15 (January 1976): 13-17.

1913. Kleinfeld, Judith. "Effective Teachers of Eskimo and Indian Students."
School Review 83 (February 1975): 301-
344.

1914. Mahan, James M., and Mary F. Smith.
"Preservice Teachers to Indian Communities." Journal of American Indian Education 18 (January 1979): 1-5.

1915. Mathieu, David J. "Adoption and
Development of Teacher Certification
Requirement." Journal of American In-
dian Education 18 (October 1978): 17-22.

1916. Morris, G. Barry. "Beliefs of
Native Teacher Trainees." Psychological Reports 38 (June 1976): 859-862.

1917. Popkewitz, Thomas S. "Reform as
Political Discourse: A Case Study."
School Review 84 (November 1975): 43-
69. Teacher Corps--Midwest Native
American Project.

Writings on Indian Education 1975

1918. Benham, William J. "A Philosophy
of Indian Education." Journal of American Indian Education 15 (October 1975):
1-3.

1919. Blei, Norbert. "Three-Day Run on a
Navajo, New Mexican Spirit Trail."

American Libraries 6 (February 1975):
96-104.

1920. Boyd, Edna McGuire. "To Light One
Candle." Delta Kappa Gamma Bulletin
42 (Fall 1975): 17-19. Textbooks for
Navajos.

1921. Breunig, Robert G. "Schools and
the Hopi Self." In The New Ethnicity:
Perspectives from Ethnology, edited
by John W. Bennett, pp. 51-58. St.
Paul: West Publishing Company, 1975.

1922. Canyon, Lena, Sandy Gibbs, and
David Churchman. "Development of a
Native American Evaluation Team."
Journal of American Indian Education
15 (October 1975): 23-28.

1923. Carpenter, Iris. "The Indian Education Act." American Education 11
(April 1975): 39-40.

1924. Carter, Ula Berniece. "Project
North America--The Teacher." Delta
Kappa Gamma Bulletin 42 (Fall 1975):
11-16. Teaching at Navajo Community
College.

1925. Chavers, Dean. "New Directions
in Indian Education." Indian Historian
8 (Winter 1975): 43-46.

1926. Churchman, David, Joan Herman,
and Teresa Hall. "To Know Both Worlds."
Journal of American Indian Education
14 (May 1975): 7-12.

1927. Colfer, Carol J. Pierce. "Bureaucrats, Budgets, and the BIA:
Segmentary Opposition in a Residential
School." Human Organization 34 (Summer 1975): 149-156.

1928. Elm, Lloyd. "Needed: A Philosophy
of Education for American Indians."
American Indian Journal 1 (November
1975): 2-5.

1929. Foerster, Leona M., and Dale Little
Soldier. "What's New--and Good--in
Indian Education Today?" Educational
Leadership 33 (December 1975): 192-198.

1930. Goodman, Elizabeth B. "New Schools
for Our Forgotten Americans." Parents'
Magazine 50 (September 1975): 46-47,
72-73.

1931. Gray, Clyde Thomas. "Cultural
Pluralism Increases in Southwestern
Schools." Journal of American Indian
Education 15 (October 1975): 13-16.

1932. Greene, H. Ross, and Harry A.
Kersey. "Upgrading Indian Education:
A Case Study of the Seminoles." School
Review 83 (February 1975): 345-361.

1933. Hobson, Arline B., and Joseph H.

Stauss. "Development of a Cross-
Cultural Seminar." Journal of American
Indian Education 14 (May 1975): 21-26.

1934. "The Indian Education Act of 1972."
Journal of American Indian Education 14
(May 1975): 5-6.

1935. "In River Falls, Wisconsin: Indian
Parents Begin Own Education." Journal
of American Indian Education 14 (January 1975): 12-14.

1936. Jones, Marie C. "To Watch Them Stand
Tall: The Sioux City PL Indian Project."
American Libraries 6 (September 1975):
494-496.

1937. Kleinfeld, Judith. "Positive Stereotyping: The Cultural Relativist in
the Classroom" Human Organization 34
(Fall 1975): 269-274.

1938. Levenson, Dorothy. "Hopi Schooling
for Two Worlds." Teacher 93 (November
1975): 63-65.

1939. Mackey, Duane. "Dimensions of Indian
Education." Journal of American Indian
Education 15 (October 1975): 8-12.

1940. Medicine, Bea. "Self-Direction in
Sioux Education." Integrated Education
13 (November-December 1975): 15-17.

1941. Patterson, Ann. "Among Arizona
Indians . . . Fewer Red Apples." Indian Historian 8 (Summer 1975): 26-31.

1942. Pyke, Beverly J., Beatrice H. White,
and Charles E. Heerman. "Akwesasne:
R2R, ABE, GED, and College Extension."
Journal of American Indian Education
14 (May 1975): 1-4.

1943. Ross, Donald D., and Joseph E.
Trimble. "Focus Is on Tribal Culture
in Understanding American Indian." Momentum 6 (October 1975): 37-39.

1944. Sim, Jessie. "Project North America." Delta Kappa Gamma Bulletin 42
(Fall 1975): 9-10.

1945. Smith, Dowell. "Bubbles and Children: A Small Ethnography of Cross-Cultural
Learning." Outlook 26 (Winter 1977):
20-27.

1946. Wells, Robert N., and Minerva White.
"Operation Kanyengehaga: An American
Cross Cultural Program." American
Indian Culture and Research Journal 1
(No. 3, 1975): 22-28.

1947. Wiles, David K. "Separate Schools
for a 'Non-Chic' Minority?" Journal
of American Indian Education 15
(October 1975): 17-22.

Writings on Indian Education 1976

1948. Alexander, M. David, and Richard
G. Salmon. "Financing Indian Education Today and Alternatives for the
Future." Journal of Education Finance
2 (Summer 1976): 33-49.

1949. Allen, Sally V. "On Educating Indians." Compact 10 (Autumn 1976): 19-
21, 26-28.

1950. Beuf, Ann H. "The Home of Whose
Brave?: Problems Confronting Native
Americans in Education." Journal of
the National Association for Women
Deans, Administrators, and Counselors
39 (Winter 1976): 70-80.

1951. "CETA Allocations for Indian Training Programs." American Indian Journal
2 (September 1976): 22-23.

1952. Cooper, Robert, and Jack Gregory.
"Can Community Control of Indian Education Work?" Journal of American Indian Education 15 (May 1976): 7-11.

1953. Deloria, Vine, Jr. "The Place of
American Indians in Contemporary Edu-
cation." American Indian Journal 2
(February 1976): 2-9.

1954. Demmert, William G., Jr. "Indian
Education: Where and Whither?" American Education 12 (August-September
1976): 6-9.

1955. _____. "Indian Education:
Where and Whither?" Education Digest
42 (December 1976): 41-44.

1956. Farris, Charles E., and Lorene
S. Farris. "Indian Children: The
Struggle for Survival." Social Work
21 (September 1976): 386-389.

1957. Fifield, Marvin, and Lonnie Farmer.
"Teacher Aides Provide Direct Instruc-
tion." Journal of American Indian
Education 16 (October 1976): 13-18.

1958. Fire, Mike, and Constance M. Baker.
"A Smile and Eye Contact May Insult
Someone." Journal of Nursing Education
15 (September 1976): 14-17.

1959. Green, Rayna, and Shirley Mahaley
Malcom. "AAAS Project on Native Americans in Science." Science 194 (November 5, 1976): 597-598.

1960. Jannusch, Marlene R., and Dolli
H. Big John. "Hochungra Headstart
Model." Journal of American Indian
Education 16 (October 1976): 1-9.
Winnebago Headstart Program.

1961. Johnston, Thomas F. "Ethnomusi-
cology Aids Alaskan Rural Education."

School Musician/Director and Teacher
48 (December 1976): 52-54.

1962. Lawrence, Ruth. "Exploring Childhood on an Indian Reservation." Children Today 5 (September-October 1976):
10-12, 34.

1963. Moorefield, Story. "Alaskan Journal." American Education 12 (August-
September 1976): 15-22.

1964. "North American Indian Traveling
College." Conservationist 30 (January
1976): 40.

1965. "The Red School House: An Alternative
Education." American Indian Journal 2
(February 1976): 10-12.

1966. "Reservations about the White Man's
Culture." Times Educational Supplement,
November 19, 1976, p. 17.

1967. Richburg, James A. "Dual Jurisdiction and Political Conflict: A Case
of the Choctaw Follow Through Program."
Journal of Research and Development in
Education 9 (Summer 1976): 91-101.

1968. Rosenfelt, Daniel M. "Toward a More
Coherent Policy for Funding Indian Education." Law and Contemporary Problems
40 (Winter 1976): 190-223.

1969. Sando, Joe S., and E. A. "Swede"
Scholer. "Programming for Native Americans." Parks and Recreation 11 (March
1976): 24-26, 53-55.

1970. Schafer, Paul J. "Education for
American Indians." Clearing House 50
(December 1976): 145-146.

1971. Short, Anthony J. "Indian Power
Saves a School." Momentum 7 (December
1976): 37-42.

1972. "Special Educational Needs of American Indian Children." Amicus 2 (December 1976): 33-36.

1973. "This Land Was Their Land." Humanities 6 (Autumn 1976): 7-8.

1974. Tippeconnic, John W. III. "The
Center of Indian Education at ASU:
A Report by the New Director." Journal
of American Indian Education 16 (October 1976): 10-12.

1975. Viers, Gerald R. "Media on the
Ramah Navajo Reservation." Audiovisual
Instruction 21 (February 1976): 12-14.

Writings on Indian Education 1977

1976. Arkell, R. N. (Bob). "Native Education: Searching for Alternatives."
Journal of American Indian Education

17 (October 1977): 28-30.

1977. Benham, William J. "Residential
Schools at the Crossroads." Journal of
American Indian Education 16 (January
1977): 20-26.

1978. Brewer, Annemarie. "On Indian
Education." Integrated Education 15
(May-June 1977): 21-23.

1979. Coburn, Joe. "A Community-Based
Indian Curriculum Development Program."
Educational Leadership 34 (January
1977): 284-287.

1980. Croft, Carolyn. "The First American: Last in Education." Journal of
American Indian Education 16 (January
1977): 15-19.

1981. Dearmin, Evalyn Titus. "Project
Paiute." Journal of American Indian
Education 17 (October 1977): 1-10.

1982. Esping, Mardel. "Students Write
about Their Artwork." School Arts
76 (February 1977): 36-38.

1983. "Faye Knoki: Retired Navajo Back
with the Kids!" Instructor 87 (September 1977): 16.

1984. Foerster, Leona M., and Dale Little
Soldier. "Trends in Early Childhood
Education for Native American Pupils."
Educational Leadership 34 (February
1977): 373-378.

1985. Hikel, J. Steven. "Cross-Cultural
Education in Alaska: Not How but Why?
Phi Delta Kappan 58 (January 1977):
403-404.

1986. Hirschi, Melvin, and Thomas Glass.
"Athabascans Get a School." Journal
of American Indian Education 16 (May
1977): 16-19.

1987. "International Conference on Op-
pression of Native Americans." Interracial Books for Children Bulletin 8
(No. 8, 1977): 10-11.

1988. Mahan, James Mark, and Mary Kathryn
Criger. "Culturally Oriented Instruction for Native American Students."
Integrated Education 15 (March-April
1977): 9-13.

1989. Messinger, Carla J. S. "Native
Americans, Like Your Kids, Aren't
'Wild Indians.'" Instructor 86 (April
1977): 31.

1990. Peterson, Kenneth. "Indian in
Education: One Community's Experience."
Journal of Education 159 (February
1977): 23-42. Cass Lake, Minnesota.

1991. Van Dyne, Larry. "New Wealth, Old

Anger among Alaska's 'Natives.'" Chronicle of Higher Education 15 (November 21, 1977): 7-8.

1992. Wardle, Francis. "Do They Still Kill Cowboys?" Early Years 8 (October 1977): 32-33.

1993. Zastrow, Leona M. "Two Native Americans Speak on Art Values and the Value of Art." Journal of American Indian Education 16 (May 1977): 25-30.

Writings on Indian Education 1978

1994. Bachtold, Louise M., and Olivia Rangel de Jackson. "Hupa Indians: A Culturally-Based Preschool." Children Today 7 (November-December 1978): 22-23, 26-27.

1995. Bowd, Alan D. "Eight Prevalent Myths about Indian Education." Education Canada 18 (Summer 1978): 4-7, 47.

1996. Elsey, Katherine J. "Under the Turquoise Sky." Delta Kappa Gamma Bulletin 44 (Winter 1978): 11-18.

1997. Green, Rayna. "Math Called Key to Indian Self-Determination." Science 201 (August 4, 1978): 433.

1998. Lawerence, Gay. "Indian Education: Why Bilingual-Bicultural?" Education and Urban Society 10 (May 1978): 305-320.

1999. McLester-Greenfield, Owana. "Educated or Indian? (Either/Or)." In The Worlds between Two Rivers: Perspectives On American Indians in Iowa, edited by Gretchen M. Bataille and others, pp. 90-98. Ames: Iowa State University Press, 1978.

2000. Mahan, James M., and Mary F. Smith. "Non-Indians in Indian Schools." Journal of American Indian Education 17 (January 1978): 1-6.

2001. "Respect My Child: He Has a Right To Be Himself." Media and Methods 15 (September 1978): 34-35.

2002. Sharpes, Donald K. "A Curriculum Model." Journal of American Indian Education 17 (January 1978): 25-27.

2003. Smith, Frederick D. "An Anthropological Perspective of Native American Cultural Studies." Journal of American Indian Education 17 (May 1978): 8-12.

2004. Villegas, Gregory. "Cultural Identity." Social Education 42 (February 1978): 162, 164.

2005. Vorih, Lillian, and Paul Rosier. "Rock Point Community School: An Example of a Navajo-English Bilingual Elementary School Program." TESOL Quarterly 12 (September 1978): 263-269.

2006. Wade, Arnold, and John Anderson. "A New Start in Indian Education." Journal of American Indian Education 18 (October 1978): 1-5.

2007. Wanatee, Adeline. "Education, the Family, and the Schools." In The Worlds between Two Rivers: Perspectives on American Indians in Iowa, edited by Gretchen M. Bataille and others, pp. 100-103. Ames: Iowa State University Press, 1978.

2008. Witt, Linda. "Navajo Educator Don McCabe Frets That He'll Be Cut Off at the Cross-Cultural Pass." People Weekly 10 (July 17, 1978): 57-58.

Writings on Indian Education 1979

2009. Andreoli, Andrew. "Implementation Problems with Present Multicultural Education Policies." In Multicultural Education and the American Indian, pp. 77-79. Los Angeles: American Indian Studies Center, University of California, Los Angeles, 1979.

2010. Antell, Lee. "Quality Education for the Indian Child." Compact 13 (Summer 1979): 18, 30.

2011. Dupris, Joseph C. "The National Impact of Multicultural Education: A Renaissance of Native American Culture through Tribal Self-Determination and Indian Control of Education." In Multicultural Education and the American Indian, pp. 43-54. Los Angeles: American Indian Studies Center, University of California, Los Angeles, 1979.

2012. Forbes, Jack. "Traditional Native American Philosophy and Multicultural Education." In Multicultural Education and the American Indian, pp. 3-13. Los Angeles: American Indian Studies Center, University of California, Los Angeles, 1979.

2013. French, Laurence. "The Educational Dilemma Facing Urban Indians." Journal of American Indian Education 18 (January 1979): 28-32.

2014. Gipp, G. E. "Help for Dana Fast Horse and Friends." American Education 15 (August-September 1979): 18-21.

2015. Gunsky, Frederic R. "Multicultural Education: Implications for American Indian People." In Multicultural Education and the American Indian, pp. 69-75. Los Angeles: American Indian Studies Center, University of California, Los Angeles, 1979.

2016. Hurst, C. O. "A Pow-wow on Early Childhood Education." Early Years 9 (February 1979): 24-27.

2017. Hutchinson, Jerry E. "Perceptions of an Educational Environment." Journal of American Indian Education 19 (October 1979): 12-18.

2018. Miller, Brian P. "The Design of an American Indian Community Education and Leadership Development Center." Journal of American Indian Education 18 (January 1979): 11-14.

2019. Moorefield, Story. "Two Programs under the Indian Education Act." American Education 15 (August-September 1979): 37-38.

2020. Noley, Grayson. "Summary and Critique of the Report on Indian Education of the American Indian Policy Review Commission." In New Directions in Federal Indian Policy: A Review of the American Indian Policy Review Commission, pp. 57-73. Los Angeles: American Indian Studies Center, University of California, Los Angeles, 1979.

2021. O'Neil, Floyd. "Multiple Sources and Resources for the Development of Social Studies Curriculum for the American Indian." In Multicultural Education and the American Indian, pp. 153-156. Los Angeles: American Indian Studies Center, University of California, Los Angeles, 1979.

2022. Ousterhout, Ann. "Alaska's Unique Dropout Problems." Journal of American Indian Education 18 (January 1979): 6-10.

2023. Rosson, Robert W. "Values and American Indian Leadership Styles." In Multicultural Education and the American Indian, pp. 117-127. Los Angeles: American Indian Studies Center, University of California, Los Angeles, 1979.

2024. Shaughnessy, Timothy, and Eddie F. Brown. "Developing Indian Content in Social Work Education: A Community-Based Curriculum Model." In Multicultural Education and the American Indian, pp. 157-169. Los Angeles: American Indian Studies Center, University of California, Los Angeles, 1979.

Writings on Indian Education 1980

2025. Boloz, Sigmund A., and Carl G. Foster. "The Reservation Administrator." Journal of American Indian Education 19 (January 1980): 24-28.

2026. Boudreaux, Ernest. "A Minimum Competency Assessment." Journal of American Indian Education 19 (January 1980): 8-12.

2027. Darou, Wes G. "Experiencing Native American Culture." Counseling and Values 25 (October 1980): 3-17.

2028. "Dr. Gipp Justifies Recent OIE Action." American Indian Journal 6 (October 1980): 14-23. Interview with Gerald Gipp.

2029. "Educational Needs Assessment Inventory Announced." Journal of American Indian Education 19 (May 1980): 29-31.

2030. Foster, Carl G., and Sigmund A. Boloz. "The BIA School Administrator and Effective Leadership." Journal of American Indian Education 19 (May 1980): 24-28.

2031. French, Laurence. "Native American Prison Survival Schools." Lifelong Learning: The Adult Years 3 (February 1980): 4-7, 31.

2032. Hone, Emily. "Indian Arts for Indian Students." Design 81 (May-June 1980): 15-19.

2033. Ivie, Stanley D. "National Policy and Indian Education: Should It Be Multicultural?" Peabody Journal of Education 57 (July 1980): 268-275.

2034. Miller, Brian P. "Program Definitions and Priorities." Journal of American Indian Education 20 (Ocober 1980): 30-33.

2035. Reilly, Robert T. "Wind River Changes Its Course: The St. Stephens Experience." Phi Delta Kappan 62 (November 1980): 200-202.

2036. Smith, Jeanette C. "When Is a Disadvantage a Handicap?" Journal of American Indian Education 19 (January 1980): 13-18.

2037. Smith, Jeanne A. "Glass Walls." English Journal 69 (April 1980): 56-59.

2038. Smith, Murray R. "Archaeology as an Aid in Cross-Cultural Science Education." Journal of American Indian Education 19 (January 1980): 1-7.

2039. Taylor, Anne, and Rina Swentzel. "Albuquerque Indian School: A Cooperative Renovation Project." Education Digest 45 (January 1980): 50-53.

TEACHING ABOUT INDIANS

2040. Arrington, Ruth M. "Some American Indian Voices: Resources in Intercultural Rhetoric and Interpretation." Speech Teacher 24 (September 1975): 191-194.

2041. Berardi, Anne L. "Native American

Literature." English Journal 64 (January 1975): 71-72.

2042. Churchill, Ward. "National Patterns in Contemporary Indian Studies Programs." In Multicultural Education and the American Indian, pp. 55-65. Los Angeles: American Indian Studies Center, University of California, Los Angeles, 1979.

2043. Clemmer, Janice White. "A Portrayal of the American Indian in Utah State Approved United States History Textbooks." Ph.D. dissertation, University of Utah, 1979.

2044. Costo, Rupert. "Fact from Fiction." Indian Historian 10 (Winter 1977): 31-36.

2045. DeAngelis, Edith Gladys. "The American Indian: An Introduction to the Culture and Life Activities: Resources for Educators." Ed.D. dissertation, Boston University School of Education, 1977.

2046. Dorris, Michael. "Why I'm Not Thankful for Thanksgiving." Interracial Books for Children Bulletin 9 (No. 7, 1978): 6-9.

2047. Evans, Richard M., and Michael B. Husband. "Indian Studies in the Classroom." Journal of American Indian Education 15 (October 1975): 4-7.

2048. Garcia, Jesus. "The American Indian: No Longer a Forgotten American in U.S. History Texts Published in the 1970s." Social Education 44 (February 1980): 148-152, 164.

2049. _____. "Images of Named White and Non-White Ethnic Groups As Presented in Selected Eighth Grade United States History Textbooks." Ed.D. dissertation, University of California, Berkeley, 1977.

2050. _____. "Native Americans in U.S. History Textbooks: From Bloody Savages to Heroic Chiefs." Journal of American Education 17 (January 1978): 15-19.

2051. Gregory, Jack, and Rennard Strickland. "Indian Studies Must Be More Than an Academic Wild West Show." In Indians of the Lower South: Past and Present, edited by John K. Mahon, pp. 42-50. Pensacola: Gulf Coast History and Humanities Conference, 1975.

2052. Hauptman, Laurence M. "Mythologizing Westward Expansion: Schoolbooks and the Image of the American Frontier before Turner." Western Historical Quarterly 8 (July 1977): 269-282.

2053. Heinrich, June Sark. "Native Americans: What Not To Teach." Interracial

Books for Children Bulletin 8 (Nos. 4-5, 1977): 26-27.

2054. Hirschfelder, Arlene B. "The Treatment of Iroquois Indians in Selected American History Textbooks." Indian Historian 8 (Fall 1975): 31-39.

2055. Husband, Michael B. "Reflections on Teaching American Indian History." Journal of American Indian Education 16 (January 1977): 7-14.

2056. Kidwell, Clara Sue. "Native American Studies: Academic Concerns and Community Service." American Indian Culture and Research Journal 2 (Nos. 3-4, 1978): 4-9.

2057. Kirkness, Verna J. "Prejudice about Indians in Textbooks." Journal of Reading 20 (April 1977): 595-600.

2058. Ladevich, Laurel, and Thom Swiss. "Resources for the Study of Native Americans." Media and Methods 13 (May-June 1977): 50-56.

2059. Little, Wesley, and Betty Little. "Bridges to the Past: Wind River's Native Culture Program." Childhood Education 54 (March 1978): 242-245.

2060. LoGuidice, Thomas. "A Ratinale for Ethnic Studies." In Indians of the Lower South: Past and Present, edited by John K. Mahon, pp. 65-76. Pensacola: Gulf Coast History and Humanities Conference, 1975.

2061. McHargue, Georgess. "Countering Old Myths." American Libraries 6 (March 1975): 166-167.

2062. Moore, Robert G., ed. Stereotypes, Distortions, and Omissions in U.S. History Textbooks: A Content Analysis for Detecting Racism and Sexism. New York: Council on Interracial Books for Children, 1977.

2063. Morris, Joann S. "Indian Portrayal in Teaching Materials." In Multicultural Education and the American Indian, pp. 83-92. Los Angeles: American Indian Studies Center, University of California, Los Angeles, 1979.

2064. "Native Americans: One Teacher's Approach to Bridging Two Worlds." Instructor 87 (February 1978): 74-76.

2065. Otis, Morgan G., Jr. "A Native American Studies Program: An Institutional Approach." Indian Historian 9 (Winter 1976): 14-18.

2066. _____. "Textbooks and the People Known as American Indians." Indian Historian 10 (Fall 1977): 40-46.

2067. Peterson, John. "The Effects of Past Indian-White Contacts on Contemporary Studies." In Indians of the Lower South: Past and Present, edited by John K. Mahon, pp. 51-64. Pensacola: Gulf Coast History and Humanities Conference, 1975.

2068. Purcell, L. Edward. "The Unknown Past: Sources for History Education and the Indians of Iowa." Indian Historian 9 (Summer 1976): 13-18.

2069. _____. "The Unknown Past: Sources for History Education and the Indians of Iowa." In The Worlds between Two Rivers: Perspectives on American Indians in Iowa, edited by Gretchen M. Bataille and others, pp. 16-25. Ames: Iowa State University Press, 1978.

2070. Ramsey, Patricia G. "Beyond 'Ten Little Indians' and Turkeys: Alternative Approaches to Thanksgiving." Young Children 34 (September 1979): 28-34.

2071. Smith, Jacklyn. "'Unlearning Indian Stereotypes': A Classroom Experience." Interracial Books for Children Bulletin 9 (No. 7, 1978): 14-15.

2072. Sorber, Edna C., Jon A. Halstead, and Ruth A. Thrun. "American Indian Speaking: An Intercultural, Interdisciplinary Approach." Speech Teacher 24 (September 1975): 181-190.

2073. "Study Shows Children's Books Still Stereotype Indians." Inequality in Education, No. 23 (September 1978): 69.

2074. Swanson, Charles H. "The Treatment of the American Indian in High School History Texts." Indian Historian 10 (Spring 1977): 28-37.

2075. Thornton, Russell. "American Indian Studies as an Academic Discipline." American Indian Culture and Research Journal 2 (Nos. 3-4, 1978): 10-19.

2076. _____. "American Indian Studies as an Academic Discipline." Journal of Ethnic Studies 5 (Fall 1977): 1-15.

2077. Townsend, Mary Jane. "Taking Off the War Bonnet: American Indian Literature." Language Arts 53 (March 1976): 236-244.

2078. Washburn, Wilcomb E. "American Indian Studies: A Status Report." American Quarterly 27 (August 1975): 263-274.

2079. Wilson, Raymond. "Native Americans in College Textbooks." Wassaja/The Indian Historian 13 (June 1980): 44-47.

2080. Wood, Jeremy. "Non-Indian High School Education Has Serious Flaws." American Indian Journal 6 (October 1980): 24-26.

12
Indian Health

HISTORICAL STUDIES

2081. Allen, Virginia R. "Agency Physicians to the Southern Plains Indians, 1868-1900." Bulletin of the History of Medicine 49 (Fall 1975): 318-330.

2082. _____. "'When We Settle Down, We Grow Pale and Die': Health in Western Indian Territory." Oklahoma State Medical Association Journal 70 (June 1977): 227-232.

2083. _____. "The White Man's Road: The Physical and Psychological Impact of Relocation on the Southern Plains Indians." Journal of the History of Medicine and Allied Sciences 30 (April 1975): 148-163.

2084. Blair, Margaret Berry, and R. Palmer Howard. "Scalpel in a Saddlebag: The Story of a Physician in Indian Territory: Virgil Berry, MD." Oklahoma State Medical Association Journal 71 (November 1978): 427-434; (December 1978): 460-467.

2085. Boyd, Robert T. "Another Look at the 'Fever and Ague' of Western Oregon." Ethnohistory 22 (Spring 1975): 135-154.

2086. Crosby, Alfred W. "God . . . Would Destroy Them, and Give Their Country to Another People. . . ." American Heritage 29 (October-November 1978): 38-43.

2087. Dollar, Clyde D. "The High Plains Smallpox Epidemic of 1837-38." Western Historical Quarterly 8 (January 1977): 15-38.

2088. Forrest, Herbert J. "Malaria and the Union Mission to the Osage Indians, 1820-1837." Oklahoma State Medical Association Journal 69 (July 1976): 322-327.

2089. Hauptman, Laurence M. "Smallpox and American Indians: Depopulation in Colonial New York." New York State Journal of Medicine 79 (November 1979): 1945-1949.

2090. Howard, R. Palmer, and Virginia E. Allen. "Stress and Death in the Settlement of Indian Territory." Chronicles of Oklahoma 54 (Fall 1976): 352-359.

2091. Keehn, Pauline A. The Effect of of Epidemic Diseases on the Natives of North America: An Annotated Bibliography. London: Survival International, 1978.

2092. Newman, Marshall T. "Aboriginal New World Epidemiology and Medical Care, and the Impact of Old World Disease Imports." American Journal of Physical Anthropology 45 (November 1976): 667-672.

2093. Porvaznik, John. "Washington Matthews, M.D.: The Navajo Years." New England Journal of Medicine 296 (May 5, 1977): 1042-1044.

2094. Putney, Diane Therese. "Fighting the Scourge: American Indian Morbidity and Federal Policy, 1897-1928." Ph.D. dissertation, Marquette University, 1980.

2095. Salmon, Roberto Marino. "The Disease Complaint at Bosque Redondo (1864-68)." Indian Historian 9 (Summer 1976): 2-7.

2096. Sarafian, Winston L. "Smallpox Strikes the Aleuts." Alaska Journal 7 (Winter 1977): 46-49.

2097. Sayre, James W., and Robert F. Sayre. "American Children and the 'Children of Nature.'" American Journal of Diseases of Children 130 (July 1976): 716-723.

2098. Schlesier, Karl H. "Epidemics and Indian Middlemen: Rethinking the Wars of the Iroquois, 1609-1653." Ethnohistory 23 (Spring 1976): 129-145.

2099. Tessendorf, K. C. "Red Death on the Missouri." American West 14 (January 1977): 48-53. Smallpox epidemic of 1837.

2100. Wier, James A. "The Army Doctor and the Indian." Denver Westerners' Roundup 31 (September 1975): 3-14.

GENERAL STUDIES AND COMMENTS

2101. Christmas, June Jackson. "How Our Health System Fails Minorities." Civil Rights Digest 10 (Fall 1977): 3-11.

2102. "Conference on American Indian Science and Health Education." Science 196 (April 1, 1977): 46-47.

2103. Downey, Gregg W. "An American Travesty." Modern Health Care 5 (February 1976): 22-31.

2104. Fuchs, Michael, and Rashid Bashshur. "Use of Traditional Indian Medicine among Urban Native Americans." Medical Care 13 (November 1975): 915-927.

2105. Gallerito, Cecilia. "Indian Health, Federally or Tribally Determined?: Health Recommendations of the American Indian Policy Review Commission." In New Directions in Federal Indian Policy: A Review of the American Indian Policy Review Commission, pp. 29-43. Los Angeles : American Indian Studies Center, University of California, Los Angeles, 1979.

2106. Kaltenbach, Charles. "Health Problems of the Navajos." Integrated Education 15 (March-April 1977): 36.

2107. Larson, Janet Karsten. "'And Then There Were None.'" Christian Century 94 (January 26, 1977): 61-63.

2108. "McGrath Demonstration Project." American Journal of Public Health 65 (October supplement, 1975): 38-39.

2109. Payne, Diana. "Indian Health Legislation--To Amend a Century of Neglect." American Indian Journal 2 (August 1976): 23-24.

2110. Rice, Jon F., Jr. "Health Conditions of Native Americans in the Twentieth Century." Indian Historian 10 (Fall 1977): 14-18.

2111. Spake, Amanda. "Death on the Reservation." Progressive 41 (February 1977): 27-30.

2112. Spivey, Gary H., and Norbert Hirschhorn. "A Migrant Study of Adopted Apache Children." Johns Hopkins Medical Journal 140 (February 1977): 43-46.

HEALTH SERVICES AND PROGRAMS

Health Services

2113. Bell, Cathy. "The Navajo Patient: Illumination of Cultural Differences." Colorado Medicine 77 (April 1980): 127-130.

2114. Camazine, Scott M. "Traditional and Western Health Care among the Zuni Indians of New Mexico." Social Science and Medicine, Medical Anthropology 14B (February 1980): 73-80.

2115. Cooley, Richard C., Don Ostendorf, and Dorothy Bickerton. "Outreach Services for Elderly Native Americans." Social Work 24 (March 1979): 151-153.

2116. Dauble, Darcy Ann. "Establishing the Health Science Library in the Rural, Cross-Cultural Setting." Journal of Nursing Education 16 (November 1977): 33-37.

2117. Davis, Scott, and Stephen J. Kunitz. "Hospital Utilization and Elective Surgery on the Navajo Indian Reservation." Social Science and Medicine, Medical Anthropology 12B (October 1978): 263-272.

2118. Dillingham, Brint. "Indian Health Service and the Health Information System." American Indian Journal 3 (April 1977): 16-18.

2119. _____. "Indian Women and IHS Sterilization Practices." American Indian Journal 3 (January 1977): 27-28.

2120. _____. "Sterilization of Native Americans." American Indian Journal 3 (July 1977): 16-19.

2121. _____. "Sterilization Update." American Indian Journal 3 (September 1977): 25.

2122. Fannin, Paul J. "Indian Health Care: A Real Health Care Crisis." Arizona Medicine 32 (September 1975): 741-747.

2123. Freed, James R., and Allan S. Bernstein. "Utilization of Emergency Dental Services by Rural, Nonreservation Indians." Journal of Public Health Dentistry 35 (Summer 1975): 165-169.

2124. Friedman, Emily. "The Possible Dream: The Navajo Nation Health Foundation." Hospitals 53 (October 16, 1979): 81-84.

2125. Giacalone, Joseph J., and James I. Hudson. "A Health Status Assessment System for a Rural Navajo Population." Medical Care 13 (September 1975): 722-735.

2126. Haynes, Terry L. "Some Factors Related to Contraceptive Behavior among

Wind River Shoshone and Arapahoe Females." Human Organization 36 (Spring 1977): 72-76.

2127. "Health Care via TV in a Rural Area." U.S. News and World Report 83 (December 26, 1977): 79-80.

2128. Helmick, Edward, Paul A. Nutting, and William Thomas McClure. "Evaluation of Alaska Native Ambulatory Health Services, I: Examination of Health Systems Performance." Alaska Medicine 20 (May 1978): 33-36.

2129. Horn, Beverly M. "An Ethnoscientific Study To Determine Social and Cultural Factors Affecting American Indian Women during Pregnancy." Ph.D. dissertation, University of Washington, 1975.

2130. Hostetter, C. L., and J. D. Felsen. "Multiple Variable Motivators Involved in the Recruitment of Physicians for the Indian Health Service." Public Health Reports 90 (July-August 1975): 319-324.

2131. Isaacs, Hope L. "American Indian Medicine and Contemporary Health Problems, I: Toward Improved Health Care for Native Americans, Comparative Perspective on American Indian Medicine Concepts." New York State Journal of Medicine 78 (April 1978): 824-829.

2132. Kane, Robert L., and P. Douglas McConatha. "The Men in the Middle: A Dilemma of Minority Health Workers." Medical Care 13 (September 1975): 736-743.

2133. Kniep-Hardy, Mary, and Margaret A. Burkhardt. "Nursing the Navajo." American Journal of Nursing 77 (January 1977): 95-96.

2134. Levin, Richard H. "The Indian Health Service Medical Care Program: A Guide for Advocates." Clearinghouse Review 10 (December 1976): 681-698.

2135. Mail, Patricia D. "Hippocrates Was a Medicine Man: The Health Care of Native Americans in the Twentieth Century." Annals of the American Academy of Political and Social Science 436 (March 1978): 40-49.

2136. Miller, Mark, Judith Miller, and Chris Szechenyi. "Native American Peoples on the Trail of Tears Once More." America 139 (December 9, 1978): 422-425. Sterilization on reservations.

2137. Montgomery, Theodore A. "Health Care for the Underprivileged in the Land of Affluence: California Native Americans." Pediatrics 62 (September 1978): 377-381.

2138. Mulligan, Wallace J. "Letter: 'Western' Health Care for Southwest Indians." New England Journal of Medicine 295 (August 12, 1976): 454.

2139. _____. "The Navajo Nation Health Foundation: The Sequel to Salsbury." Arizona Medicine 33 (January 1976): 52-54.

2140. Oughtred, Orville W. "Recollections of Two Weeks Providing Medical Care to the Navajo." Michigan Medicine 78 (June 1979): 325.

2141. Primeaux, Martha. "Caring for the American Indian Patient." American Journal of Nursing 77 (January 1977): 91-94.

2142. _____. "American Indian Health Care Practices: A Cross-Cultural Perspective." Nursing Clinics of North America 12 (March 1977): 55-65.

2143. Ranck, Lee. "Improving Indian Health Services." Engage/ Social Action 7 (June 1979): 4-8, 41-43.

2144. Rhoades, Everett R. "Barriers to Health Care: The Unique Problems Facing American Indians." Civil Rights Digest 10 (Fall 1977): 25-31.

2145. Schneiter, Harry E. "Michigan Indians Need Much in Health Care." Michigan Medicine 75 (December 1976): 688-689.

2146. Serven, James E. "A Dividend from the Space Program: NASA Technology Pays Off in Arizona." Arizona Highways 51 (February 1975): 46-47.

2147. Simmons, Bradford. "Surgical Services in a Navajo Indian Hospital." Western Journal of Medicine 125 (November 1976): 407-410.

2148. Slemenda, Charles W. "Sociocultural Factors Affecting Acceptance of Family Planning Services by Navajo Women." Human Organization 37 (Summer 1978): 190-194.

2149. Staub, Henry P. "American Indian Medicine and Contemporary Health Problems, III: American Indians, New Opportunity for Health Care." New York State Journal of Medicine 78 (June 1978): 1137-1141.

2150. Staub, Henry P., Robert A. Hoekelman, Stephen J. Bien, and George A. Drazek. "Health Supervision of Infants on the Cattaraugus Indian Reservation, New York." Clinical Pediatrics 15 (January 1976): 44, 49-52.

2151. Wagner, Bill. "Lo, The Poor and

Sterilized Indian." *America* 136 (January 29, 1977): 75.

2152. Williams, Henry. "A Perspective on Health on the Navajo Indian Reservation." *Journal of the Tennessee Medical Association* 70 (July 1977): 475-480.

2153. Winslow, Kate. "Health." *American Indian Journal* 6 (January 1980): 21-23.

Diet and Nutrition

2154. Bosco, Dominick. "White Man's Food Bad Medicine for Indian." *Prevention* 28 (January 1976): 75-82.

2155. Horner, Mary R., Christine M. Olson, and Dorothy J. Pringle. "Nutritional Status of Chippewa Head Start Children in Wisconsin." *American Journal of Public Health* 67 (February 1977): 185-186.

2156. Krech, Shepard III. "Nutritional Evaluation of a Mission Residential School Diet: The Accuracy of Informant Recall." *Human Organization* 37 (Summer 1978): 186-190.

2157. Lukaczer, Moses. "School Breakfasts and Indian Children's Health." *Journal of American Indian Education* 15 (January 1976): 7-12.

2158. Miller, Mary Beth. "Reservations Begin Their Own Food Distribution Programs." *Food and Nutrition* 10 (August 1980): 4-11.

2159. "Nutrition Program Aids California's Older Native Americans." *Aging*, Nos. 263-264 (September-October 1976): 1-12.

2160. Willett, Rose Marie. "A Historical Assessment of the Food Sources of the Navajo Indian." Ed.D. dissertation, University of Arkansas, 1976.

Health Education

2161. Betts, William A. "A Method of Allocating Resources for Health Education Services by the Indian Health Service." *Public Health Reports* 91 (May-June 1976): 256-260.

2162. Booker, John M., and Jasper L. McPhail. "American Indians in U.S. Medical Education: Trends and Prospects." *Journal of Medical Education* 54 (August 1979): 651-652.

2163. Brodt, William. "Implications for Training Curriculums from a Task Inventory Survey of Indian Community Health Representatives." *Public Health Reports* 90 (November-December 1975): 552-560.

2164. McPhail, Jasper L. "American Indian

School of Medicine." *Arizona Medicine* 31 (April 1977): 270-272.

2165. Owens, Mitchell V., and Harry M. Deliere. "Graduate Education Program in Public Health for American Indians." *Public Health Reports* 94 (June 1979): 287.

2166. Weiss, Lawrence, William H. Wiese, and Alan B. Goodman. "Scholarship Support for Indian Students in the Health Sciences: An Alternative Method to Address Shortages in the Underserved Area." *Pulic Health Reports* 95 (May-June 1980): 243-246.

DISEASES AND MEDICAL PROBLEMS

Diseases

2167. Barry, Tom. "Bury My Lungs at Red Rock." *Progressive* 43 (February 1979): 25-28.

2168. Ludlam, Joel A. "Prevalence of Trachoma among Navajo Indian Children." *American Journal of Optometry and Physiological Optics* 55 (February 1978): 116-118.

2169. McShane, Damian, and Jeanette Mitchell. "Middle Ear Disease, Hearing Loss and Educational Problems of American Indian Children." *Journal of American Indian Education* 19 (October 1979): 7-11.

2170. Nickoloff, Elia George. "The Hearing-Impaired American Indian in the Vocational Rehabilitation Process." Ed.D. dissertation, University of Arizona, 1975.

Studies on particular diseases among American Indians can be located in *Index Medicus*.

Mental Health

2171. Borunda, Patrick, and James H. Shore. "Neglected Minority--Urban Indians and Mental Health." *International Journal of Social Psychiatry* 24 (Autumn 1978): 220-224.

2172. Burchell, Linda Nichole. "Native American Healing in Psychotherapy." Ph.D. dissertation, Union Graduate School, 1977.

2173. Favazza, Armando R., and Mary Owen. *Anthropological and Cross-Cultural Themes in Mental Health: An Annotated Bibliography, 1925-1974.* Columbia: University of Missouri Press, 1977.

2174. French, Laurence, and Jim Hornbuckle. "Indian Stress and Violence: A Psycho-Cultural Perspective."

Journal of Alcohol and Drug Education
25 (Fall 1979): 36-43.

2175. Gordon, Donald. "A Recent History of Mental Health Administration on the Fort Sand Reservation." *Papers in Anthropology* 17 (Spring 1976): 37-43.

2176. Jipson, Frederick Jerome. "Prevalence of Mental Retardation among School Populations in Pima County, Arizona." Ed.D. dissertation, University of Arizona, 1975.

2177. Kahn, Marvin, and others. "The Papago Psychology Service: A Community Mental Health Program on an American Indian Reservation." *American Journal of Community Psychology* 3 (June 1975): 81-97.

2187. McDonald, Thomas. "Group Psychotherapy with Native-American Women." *International Journal of Group Psychotherapy* 25 (October 1975): 410-420.

2179. Mala, Theodore A. "Status of Mental Health for Alaska Natives." *Alaska Medicine* 21 (January 1979): 1-3.

2180. Miller, Maurice W., and Don Ostendorf. "Community Programs for Native Americans: Mental Health Programs." In *Drinking Behavior among Southwestern Indians*, edited by Jack O. Waddell and Michael W. Everett, pp. 213-216. Tucson: University of Arizona Press, 1980.

2181. Ostendorf, Donald, and Carl A. Hammerschlag. "An Indian-Controlled Mental Health Program." *Hospital and Community Psychiatry* 28 (September 1977): 682-685.

2182. Rhoades, Everett R., and others. "Mental Health Problems of American Indians Seen in Outpatient Facilities of the Indian Health Service, 1975." *Public Health Reports* 95 (July-August 1980): 329-335.

2183. Signell, Karen A. "Following the Blackfoot Indians: Toward Democratic Administration of a Community Mental Health Center." *Community Mental Health Journal* 11 (Winter 1975): 430-449.

2184. Tyler, John D., and Steven F. Dreyer. "Planning Primary Prevention Strategy." *American Journal of Community Psychology* 3 (March 1975): 69-76.

2185. Westermeyer, Joseph. "Erosion of Indian Mental Health in Cities." *Minnesota Medicine* 59 (June 1976): 431-433.

Alcoholism and Drug Abuse

2186. Albaugh, Bernard, and Patricia Albaugh. "Alcoholism and Substance Sniffing among the Cheyenne and Arapaho Indians of Oklahoma." *International Journal of the Addictions* 14 (No. 7, 1979): 1001-1007.

2187. Beltrame, Thomas, and David V. McQueen. "Urban and Rural Indian Drinking Patterns: The Special Case of the Lumbee." *International Journal of the Addictions* 14 (No. 4, 1979): 533-548.

2188. Brod, Thomas M. "Alcoholism as a Mental Health Problem of Native Americans: A Review of the Literature." *Archives of General Psychiatry* 32 (November 1975): 1385-1391.

2189. Brown, Donald N. "Drinking as an Indicator of Community Disharmony: The People of Taos Pueblo." In *Drinking Behavior among Southwestern Indians*, edited by Jack O. Waddell and Michael W. Everett, pp. 83-102. Tucson: University of Arizona Press, 1980.

2190. Cockerham, William C. "Drinking Attitudes and Practices among Wind River Reservation Indian Youth." *Journal of Studies on Alcohol* 36 (March 1975): 321-326.

2191. _____. "Patterns of Alcohol and Multiple Drug Use among Rural White and American Indian Adolescents." *International Journal of the Addictions* 12 (Nos. 2-3, 1976-1977): 272-285.

2192. Cockerham, William C., and Morris A. Forslund. "Drug Use among White and American Indian High School Youth." *International Journal of the Addictions* 11 (No. 2, 1976): 209-220.

2194. Cooley, Richard. "Community Programs for Native Americans: Alcoholism Programs." In *Drinking Behavior among Southwestern Indians*, edited by Jack O. Waddell and Michael W. Everett, pp. 205-213. Tucson: University of Arizona Press, 1980.

2195. Cooper, Margaret Baba. "Task Force Eleven of the American Indian Policy Review Commission: A Developmental Overview." In *New Directions in Federal Indian Policy: A Review of the American Policy Review Commission*, pp. 53-55. Los Angeles: American Indian Studies Center, University of California, Los Angeles, 1979.

2196. Crompton, Don Walter. "The Biographical Inventory as a Predictive Instrument in the Selection of Indians for Training as Paraprofessional Alcoholism Counselors." D.S.W. dissertation, University of Utah, 1976.

2197. Escalante, Fernando. "Group Pressure and Excessive Drinking among Indians." In *Drinking Behavior among*

Southwestern Indians, edited by Jack O. Waddell and Michael W. Everett, pp. 183-204. Tucson: University of Arizona Press, 1980.

2198. Everett, Michael W. "Drinking as a Measure of Proper Behavior: The White Mountain Apaches." In Drinking Behavior among Southwestern Indians, edited by Jack O. Waddell and Michael W. Everett, pp. 148-177. Tucson: University of Arizona Press, 1980.

2199. Everett, Michael, Jack O. Waddell, and Dwight B. Heath, eds. Cross-Cultural Approaches to the Study of Alcohol: An Interdisciplinary Perspective. The Hague: Mouton Publishers, 1976.

2200. Ferguson, Frances N. "Similarities and Differences among a Heavily Arrested Group of Navajo Indian Drinkers in a Southwestern American Town." In Cross-Cultural Approaches to the Study of Alcohol: An Interdisciplinary Perspective, edited by Michael Everett, Jack O. Waddell, and Dwight B. Heath, pp. 161-171. The Hague: Mouton Publishers, 1976.

2201. _____. "Stake Theory as an Explanatory Device in Navajo Alcoholism Treatment Response." Human Organization 35 (Spring 1976): 65-78.

2202. Forslund, Morris A. "Drinking Problems of Native American and White Youth." Journal of Drug Education 9 (No. 1, 1979): 21-27.

2203. _____. "Functions of Drinking for Native American and White Youth." Journal of Youth and Adolescence 7 (September 1978): 327-332.

2204. French, Laurence, and Renitia Bertoluzzi. "The Drunken Indian Stereotype and the Eastern Cherokees." Appalachian Journal 2 (Summer 1975): 332-344.

2205. French, Laurence, and Jim Hornbuckle. "Alcoholism among Native Americans: An Analysis." Social Work 25 (July 1980): 275-280.

2206. Fuller, Lauren L. "Alcohol Beverage Control: Should the Remaining Reservations Repeal Prohibition under 18 U.S.C. 1161?" American Indian Law Review 3 (No. 2, 1975): 429-444.

2207. Guyette, Susan. "Suggestions for Priority Alcohol and Drug Abuse Research: A Comment on the Recommendations of Task Force Eleven of the American Indian Policy Review Commission." In New Directions in Federal Indian Policy: A Review of the American Indian Policy Review Commission, pp. 45-52. Los Angeles: American Indian Studies Center, University of California, Los Angeles, 1979.

2208. Heidenreich, C. Adrian. "Alcohol and Drug Use and Abuse among Indian-Americans: A Review of Issues and Sources." Journal of Drug Issues 6 (Summer 1976): 256-272.

2209. Hill, Thomas W. "Drunken Comportment of Urban Indians: 'Time-out' Behavior?" Journal of Anthropological Research 34 (Fall 1978): 442-467.

2210. _____. "'Feeling Good' and 'Getting High': Alcohol Use of Urban Indians." Ph.D. dissertation, University of Pennsylvania, 1976.

2211. Hobfall, S. E., D. Kelso, and W. J. Peterson. "The Anchorage Skid Row." Journal of Studies on Alcohol 41 (January 1980): 94-99.

2212. Hoffmann, Helmut, and Avis A. Noem. "Adjustment of Chippewa Indian Alcoholics to a Predominantly White Treatment Program." Psychological Reports 37 (December 1975): 1284-1286.

2213. _____. "Alcoholism and Abstinence among Relatives of American Indian Alcoholics." Journal of Studies on Alcohol 36 (January 1975): 165.

2214. Joyce, Kevin. "Alcohol and the Indians." Medical Times 103 (June 1975): 124-127, 133-137.

2215. Leatham, Raymond Claude. "A Study of the Relationship between Self-Concept Variables and Different Lengths of Sobriety for Male American Indian Alcoholics and Male American Indian Non-Alcoholics." Ed.D. dissertation, University of South Dakota, 1975.

2216. Leland, Joy. "Alcohol, Anthropologists, and Native Americans." Human Organization 38 (Spring 1979): 94-99.

2217. _____. "Drinking Styles in an Indian Settlement: A Numerical Folk Taxonomy." Ph.D. dissertation, University of California, Irvine, 1975.

2218. _____. Firewater Myths: North American Indian Drinking and Alcohol Addiction. New Brunswick, New Jersey: Rutgers Center for Alcohol Studies, 1976.

2219. Locklear, Herbert H. "American Indian Alcoholism: Program for Treatment." Social Work 22 (May 1977): 202-207.

2220. Loder, Richard Robert. "The American Indian Bar as Gate Keeper: An Exploratory Study in Syracuse, New York." Ph.D. dissertation, Syracuse University, 1978.

2221. May, Philip A. "Alcohol Beverage Control: A Survey of Tribal Alcohol Statutes." American Indian Law Review 5 (Summer 1977): 217-228.

2222. _____. "Alcohol Legalization and Native Americans: A Sociological Inquiry." Ph.D. dissertation, University of Montana, 1976.

2223. _____. "Explanations of Native American Drinking: A Literature Review." Plains Anthropologist 22 (August 1977): 223-232.

2224. Oetting, E. R., Ruth Edwards, G. S. Goldstein, and Velma Garcia-Mason. "Drug Use among Adolescents of Five Southwestern Native American Tribes." International Journal of the Addictions 15 (April 1980): 439-445.

2225. Popham, Robert E. "Psychocultural Barriers to Successful Alcoholism Therapy in an American Indian Patient." Journal of Studies on Alcohol 40 (July 1979): 656-676. Comment by Joy Leland, pp. 737-742.

2226. Price, John A. "An Applied Analysis of North American Indian Drinking Patterns." Human Organization 34 (Spring 1975): 17-26.

2227. Schottstaedt, Mary F., and John W. Bjork. "Inhalant Abuse in an Indian Boarding School." American Journal of Psychiatry 134 (November 1977): 1290-1293.

2228. Stratton, Ray, Arthur Zeiner, and Alfonso Paredes. "Tribal Affiliation and Prevalence of Alcohol Problems." Journal of Studies on Alcohol 39 (July 1978): 1166-1177.

2229. Streit, Fred, and Mark J. Nicolich. "Myths versus Data on American Indian Drug Abuse." Journal of Drug Education 7 (No. 2, 1977): 117-122.

2230. Tamminen, Armas W., Marlowe H. Smaby, Robert E. Powless, and Moy F. Gum. "Preparing Native American Counselors for the Chemically Dependent Native American." Counselor Education and Supervision 19 (June 1980): 310-317.

2231. Topper, Martin D. "Drinking as an Expression of Status: Navajo Male Adolescents." In Drinking Behavior among Southwestern Indians, edited by Jack O. Waddell and Michael W. Everett, pp. 103-147. Tucson: University of Arizona Press, 1980.

2232. Waddell, Jack O. "Drinking as a Means of Articulating Social and Cultural Values: Papagos in an Urban Setting." In Drinking Behavior among Southwestern Indians, edited by Jack O. Waddell and Michael W. Everett, pp. 37-82. Tucson: University of Arizona Press 1980.

2233. _____. "For Individual Power and Social Credit: The Use of Alcohol among Tucson Papagos." Human Organization 34 (Spring 1975): 9-15.

2234. _____. "Similarities and Variations in Alcohol Use in Four Native American Societies in the Southwest." In Drinking Behavior among Southwestern Indians, edited by Jack O. Waddell and Michael W. Everett, pp. 227-237. Tucson: University of Arizona Press, 1980.

2235. _____. "The Use of Intoxicating Beverages among the Native Peoples of the Aboriginal Greater Southwest." In Drinking Behavior among Southwestern Indians, edited by Jack O. Waddell and Michael W. Everett, pp. 1-32. Tucson: University of Arizona Press, 1980.

2236. Waddell, Jack O., and Michael W. Everett, eds. Drinking Behavior among Southwestern Indians: An Anthropological Perspective. Tucson: University of Arizona Press, 1980.

2237. Westermeyer, Joseph. "Use of a Social Indicator System To Assess Alcoholism among Indian People in Minnesota." American Journal of Drug and Alcohol Abuse 3 (No. 3, 1976): 447-456.

2238. Whitley, Gary P. "Reservation versus Nonreservation American Indians' Loci of Control and Consumption of Alcohol." Psychological Reports 46 (April 1980): 431-434.

2239. Williams, John Robert. "A Comparison of the Self-Concepts of Alcoholic and Non-Alcoholic Males of Indian and Non-Indian Ancestry in Terms of Scores on the Tennessee Self Concept Scale." Ed.D. dissertation, University of South Dakota, 1975.

2240. Wilson, Lawrence G., and James H. Shore. "Evaluation of a Regional Indian Alcohol Program." American Journal of Psychiatry 132 (March 1975): 255-258.

2241. Winn, W. "American Indian Alcoholism: Etiology and Implications for Effective Treatment." Alaska Medicine 20 (May 1978): 30-32.

2242. Wood, Ron. "Community Programs for Native Americans: Urban Alcoholism Programs." In Drinking Behavior among Southwestern Indians, edited by Jack O. Waddell and Michael W. Everett, pp. 217-221. Tucson: University of Arizona Press, 1980.

Suicide

2243. Blanchard, Joseph D., and Samuel Roll. "A Psychological Autopsy of an Indian Adolescent Suicide with Implications for Community Service." <u>Suicide and Life-Threatening Behavior</u> 6 (Spring 1976): 3-10.

2245. Shore, James H. "American Indian Suicide--Fact and Fantasy." <u>Psychiatry</u> 38 (February 1975): 86-91.

13
Social and Economic Developments

ACCULTURATION AND ASSIMILATION

All aspects of Indian-white relations touch on acculturation and assimilation. Singled out here are a few illustrative studies.

2246. Barry, Edward E., Jr. "From Buffalo to Beef: Assimilation on Fort Belknap Reservation." Montana, the Magazine of Western History 26 (January 1976): 38-51.

2247. Fairbanks, William Louis II. "The Acculturation of the Pomo Indians of Northern California." Ph.D dissertation, University of California, Santa Barbara, 1975.

2248. Freeman, Daniel M. A. "Psychoanalysis, Folklore, and Processes of Socialization." Journal of the American Psychoanalytic Association 25 (1977): 235-252.

2249. French, Laurence. "Social Problems among Cherokee Females: A Study of Cultural Ambivalence and Role Identity." American Journal of Psychoanalysis 36 (Summer 1976): 163-169.

2250. Hicks, George L. "The Same North and South: Ethnicity and Change in Two American Indian Groups." In The New Ethnicity: Perspectives from Ethnology, edited by John W. Bennett, pp. 75-94. St. Paul: West Publishing Company, 1975. Catawba and Monhegan Indians.

2251. Johnston, Thomas F. "Alaskan Native Adjustment and the Role of Eskimo and Indian Music." Journal of Ethnic Studies 3 (Winter 1976): 21-36.

2252. Lefley, Harriet P. "Acculturation, Child-Rearing, and Self-Esteem in Two North American Indian Tribes." Ethos 4 (Fall 1976): 385-401. Miccosukee and Seminole Indians.

2253. Wilson, Gilbert L. "The Ordeal of Getting Civilized." Natural History 89 (April 1980): 40, 44-48. Reprint from issue of January-February 1926.

2254. Younger, J. Milton, and George Eaton

Simpson. "The Integration of Americans of Indian Descent." Annals of the American Academy of Political and Social Science 436 (March 1978): 137-151.

URBANIZATION

2255. Beaulieu, David L. "A Critical Review of the Urban Indian Task Force of the American Indian Policy Review Commission." In New Directions in Federal Indian Policy: A Review of the American Indian Policy Review Commission, pp. 75-85. Los Angeles: American Indian Studies Center, University of California, Los Angeles, 1979.

2256. Borman, Leonard. "American Indians: The Reluctant Urbanites." Center Magazine, March-April 1977, pp. 44-45.

2257. Bramstedt, Wayne G. A Bibliography of North American Indians in the Los Angeles Metropolitan Area--The Urban Indian Capital. Monticello, Illinois: Vance Bibliographies, 1979.

2258. _____. "Corporate Adaptations of Urban Migrants: American Indian Voluntary Associations in the Los Angeles Metropolitan Area." Ph.D. dissertation, University of California, Los Angeles, 1977.

2259. _____. North American Indians in Towns and Cities: A Bibliography. Monticello, Illinois: Vance Bibliographies, 1979.

2260. Chadwick, Bruce A., and Joseph H. Stauss. "The Assimilation of American Indians into Urban Society: The Seattle Case." Human Organization 34 (Winter 1975): 359-369.

2261. Clinton, Lawrence, Bruce A. Chadwick, and Howard M. Bahr. "Urban Relocation Reconsidered: Antecedents of Employment among Indian Males." Rural Sociology 40 (Summer 1975): 117-133.

2262. DeRosier, Arthur H., Jr. "The Past Continues: Indian Relocation in the 1950s." In Forked Tongues and Broken Treaties, edited by Donald E. Worcester, pp. 451-464. Caldwell, Idaho: Caxton Printers, 1975.

2263. Dobyns, Henry F., Richard W. Stoffle, and Kristine Jones. "Native American Urbanization and Socio-Economic Integration in the Southwestern United States." Ethnohistory 22 (Spring 1975): 155-179.

2264. Fiske, Shirley Jeanette. "Navajo Cognition in the Urban Milieu: An Investigation of Social Categories and Use of Address Terms." Ph.D. dissertation, Stanford University, 1975.

2265. Guillemin, Jeanne. Urban Renegades: The Cultural Strategy of American Indians. New York: Columbia University Press, 1975. Micmacs in Boston.

2266. Gundlach, James H., and Alden E. Roberts. "Native American Indian Migration and Relocation: Success or Failure." Pacific Sociological Review 21 (January 1978): 117-128.

2267. Gundlach, James H., P. Nelson Reid, and Alden E. Roberts. "Migration, Labor Mobility, and Relocation Assistance: The Case of the American Indian." Social Service Review 51 (September 1977): 464-473.

2268. Hansen, Karen Tranberg. "American Indians and Work in Seattle: Associations, Ethnicity and Class." Ph.D. dissertation, University of Washington, 1979.

2269. Harper, Chris J. "Problems, Like Birds of Prey, Stalk America's Urban Indians." Planning 41 (October 1975): 5-6.

2270. Husband, Michael, and Gary Koerselman. "The American Indian in Sioux City: A Historical Overview." In The Worlds between Two Rivers: Perspectives on American Indians in Iowa, edited by Gretchen M. Bataille and others, pp. 104-111. Ames: Iowa State University Press, 1978.

2271. Huyghe, Patrick, and David Konigsberg. "Bury My Heart at New York City." New York 12 (February 19, 1979): 53-57.

2272. Johnston, Francis E., John I. McKigney, Sharol Hopwood, and Jean Smelker. "Physical Growth and Development of Urban Native Americans: A Study in Urbanization and Its Implications for Nutritional Status." American Journal of Clinical Nutrition 31 (June 1978): 1017-1027.

2273. Kerri, James Nwannukwu. "'Push' and 'Pull' Factors: Reasons for Migration as a Factor in Amerindian Urban Adjustment." Human Organization 35 (Summer 1976): 215-220.

2274. Lave, Charles A., James V. Mueller, and Theodore D. Graves. "The Economic Payoff of Different Kinds of Education: A Study of Urban Migrants in Two Societies." Human Organization 37 (Summer 1978): 157-162.

2275. Lazewski, Tony. "American Indian Migration to and within Chicago, Illinois." Ph.D. dissertation, University of Illinois at Urbana-Champaign, 1976.

2276. Makofsky, Abraham. "Tradition and Change in the Lumbee Indian Community of Baltimore." Maryland Historical Magazine 75 (March 1980): 55-71.

2277. Margon, Arthur. "Indians and Immigrants: A Comparison of Groups New to the City." Journal of Ethnic Studies 4 (Winter 1977): 17-28.

2278. Miller, Nancy Brown. "Utilization of Services for the Developmentally Disabled by American Indian Families in Los Angeles." Ph.D. dissertation, University of California, Los Angeles, 1978.

2279. Palmer, James O. "A Geographical Investigation of the Effects of the Bureau of Indian Affairs' Employment Assistance Program upon the Relocation of Oklahoma Indians, 1967-1971." Ph.D. dissertation, University of Oklahoma, 1975.

2280. Paredes, J. Anthony. "Chippewa Townspeople." In Anishinabe: 6 Studies of Modern Chippewa, edited by J. Anthony Paredes, pp. 324-396. Tallahassee: University Presses of Florida, 1980.

2281. Phillips, George Harwood. "Indians in Los Angeles, 1781-1875: Economic Integration, Social Disintegration." Pacific Historical Review 49 (August 1980): 427-451.

2282. Price, John A. "The Development of Urban Ethnic Institutions by U.S. and Canadian Indians." Ethnic Groups 1 (No. 2, 1976): 107-131.

2283. Red Horse, John G., Ronald Lewis, Marvin Feit, and James Decker. "Family Behavior of Urban American Indians." Social Casework 59 (February 1978): 67-72.

2284. Simmons, James L. "One Little, Two Little, Three Little Indians: Counting American Indians in Urban Society." Human Organization 36 (Spring 1977): 76-79.

2285. Snake, Reuben. "Urbanization of the American Indian: One Man's View." In The Worlds between Two Rivers: Perspectives on American Indians in Iowa, edited by Gretchen M. Bataille and others, pp. 84-88. Ames: Iowa State University Press, 1978.

2286. Sorkin, Alan L. The Urban American Indian. Lexington, Massachusetts: D.C. Heath and Company, 1978.

2287. Stauss, Joseph H. "A Critique of the Task Force Eight Final Report to the American Indian Policy Review Commission: Urban and Rural Non-Reservation Indians." In New Directions in Federal Indian Policy: A Review of the American Indian Policy Review Commission, pp. 87-98. Los Angeles: American Indian Studies Center, University of California, Los Angeles, 1979.

2288. Stauss, Joseph H., and Bruce A. Chadwick. "Urban Indian Adjustment." American Indian Culture and Research Journal 3 (No. 2, 1979): 23-38.

2289. Steele, C. Hoy. "Urban Indian Identity in Kansas: Some Implications for Research." In The New Ethnicity: Perspectives from Ethnology, edited by John W. Bennett, pp. 167-178. St. Paul: West Publishing Company, 1975.

2290. Stull, Donald D. "New Data on Accident Victim Rates among Papago Indians: The Urban Case." Human Organization 36 (Winter 1977): 395-398.

2291. Tax, Sol. "The Impact of Urbanization on American Indians." Annals of the American Academy of Political and Social Science 436 (March 1978): 121-136.

2292. Tyler, S. Lyman. "The Recent Urbanization of the American Indian." In Essays on the American West, 1973-1974, edited by Thomas G. Alexander, pp. 43-62. Charles Redd Monographs in Western History, No. 5. Provo: Brigham Young University Press, 1975.

2293. "Urban Indians Enter the Political Arena." American Indian Journal 6 (August 1980): 15-18. Interview with Gregory Frazier.

2294. Weibel, Joan Crofut. "Native Americans in Los Angeles: A Cross-Cultural Comparison of Assistance Patterns in an Urban Environment." Ph.D. dissertation, University of California, Los Angeles, 1977.

ECONOMIC DEVELOPMENT

General and Miscellaneous Studies

2295. Anders, Gary C. "Dependence and Underdevelopment: The Political Economy of Cherokee Native Americans." Ph.D. dissertation, University of Notre Dame, 1978.

2296. _____. "Theories of Underdevelopment and the American Indian." Journal of Economic Issues 14 (September 1980): 681-701.

2297. "Apache Capitalism." Forbes 120 (August 15, 1977): 105.

2298. "Arguing for a Separation of Powers." American Indian Journal 6 (September 1980): 12-17. Interview with Ernie Stevens.

2299. Bailey, Lynn R. If You Take My Sheep . . . : The Evolution and Conflicts of Navajo Pastoralism, 1630-1868. Pasadena, California: Westernlore Publications, 1980.

2300. Barsh, Russel L., and James Youngblood Henderson. "Tribal Administration of Natural Resource Development." North Dakota Law Review 52 (Winter 1975): 307-347.

2301. Blevins, Winfred. "The World's First Solar Villages Are Waiting To See." Smithsonian 10 (November 1979): 157-167. Papago use of solar energy.

2302. Boles, Joann Ferguson. "The Development of the Navaho Rug, 1890-1920, As Influenced by Trader J.L. Hubbell." Ph.D. dissertation, Ohio State University, 1977.

2303. Brickey, James, and Catherine Brickey. "Reindeer, Cattle of the Arctic." Alaska Journal 5 (Winter 1975): 16-24.

2304. Burt, Larry W. "Factories on Reservations: The Industrial Development Programs of Commissioner Glenn Emmons, 1953-1960. Arizona and the West 19 (Winter 1977): 317-332.

2305. "The Cheyennes Drive for Clean Air Rights." Business Week, No. 2477, April 4, 1977, p. 29.

2306. Clemmer, Richard O. "Pine Nuts, Cattle, and the Ely Chain: Rip-off Resource Replacement vs. Homeostatic Equilibrium" In Selected Papers from the 14th Great Basin Anthropological Conference, edited by Donald R. Tuohy, pp. 61-75. Socorro, New Mexico, 1978.

2307. Culbertson, Harold James. "Values and Behaviors: An Exploratory Study of Differences between Indians and Non-Indians." Ph.D. dissertation, University of Washington, 1977.

2308. Davies, Bruce. "Will the Circle

Be Unbroken." American Indian Journal 2 (May 1976): 11-14.

2309. DeMallie, Raymond J. "Pine Ridge Economy: Cultural and Historical Perspective." In American Indian Economic Development, edited by Sam Stanley, pp. 237-312. The Hague: Mouton Publishers, 1978.

2310. Duncan, Kate C. "American Indian Lace Making." American Indian Art Magazine 5 (Summer 1980): 28-35, 80.

2311. "EDA Indian Programs Reviewed." American Indian Journal 1 (November 1975): 22-23. Economic Development Administration.

2312. Ellis, Michael George. "The Navajo: A Comparative Systems Study of Economic Conflict." Ph.D. dissertation, University of California, Riverside, 1975.

2313. Erlich, Richard. "Sovereignty and the Tribal Economy." American Indian Journal 6 (November 1980): 21-26.

2314. Furman, Necah. "Technological Change and Industrialization among the Southern Pueblos." Ethnohistory 22 (Winter 1975): 1-14.

2315. Goodman, Lowell Robert. "Regional Economic Development: The Action Indian Reservations." Ph.D. dissertation, University of Illinois at Urbana-Champaign, 1975.

2316. Green, Gary Irwin. "A Systems Analysis of Puget Sound Commercial, Indian, and Recreational Salmon Fishing." Ph.D. dissertation, University of Washington, 1976.

2317. Grover, J. Z., and Mark W. Nykanen. "Fairchild and the Navajos." Progressive 39 (May 1975): 32-33.

2318. Haas, Albert, Jr. "Another Bad Deal for the Indians." Business and Society Review 12 (Winter 1974-1975): 56-57.

2319. Hackenberg, Robert A. "Colorado Basin Development and Its Potential Impact on Tribal Life." Human Organization 35 (Fall 1976): 303-311.

2321. Harris, James J. The North Dakota Indian Reservation Economy: A Descriptive Study. Grand Forks: Bureau of Business and Economic Research, University of North Dakota, 1975.

2322. _____. "An Overview of the North Dakota Indian Economy." North Dakota Quarterly 44 (Autumn 1976): 52-66.

2323. Harrold, Paul Thomas. "A Program To Assist in the Development of the Economic Conditions of the United Sioux Tribes of South Dakota." Ed.D. dissertation, University of Northern Colorado, 1975.

2324. Henderson, Al. "Tribal Enterprises: Will They Survive?" In Economic Development in American Indian Reservations, edited by Roxanne Dunbar Ortiz, pp. 114-118. Albuquerque: Native American Studies, University of New Mexico, 1979. Navajo Indians.

2325. Hess, Bill. "Seeking the Best of Two Worlds." National Geographic 157 (February 1980): 272-290. Apache Indians.

2326. "Indian Country Vacations." Better Homes and Gardens 56 (July 1978): 169-170, 173-180.

2327. "Indians Want a Bigger Share of Their Wealth." Business Week, May 3, 1976, pp. 100-102.

2328. Jett, Stephen C. "History of Fruit Tree Raising among the Navajo." Agricultural History 51 (October 1977): 681-701.

2329. Johnson, Helen W. American Indians in Transition. Washington: Economic Development Division, Economic Research Service, U.S. Department of Agriculture, 1975.

2330. Kunitz, Stephen J. "Economic Variation on the Navajo Reservation." Human Organization 36 (Summer 1977): 186-193.

2331. _____. "Underdevelopment and Social Services on the Navajo Reservation." Human Organization 36 (Winter 1977): 398-406.

2332. Lamphere, Louise. "Traditional Pastoral Economy." In Economic Development in American Indian Reservations, edited by Roxanne Dunbar Ortiz, pp. 78-90. Albuquerque: Native American Studies, University of New Mexico, 1979. Navajo Indians.

2333. "A Landmark Case." Newsweek 91 (March 20, 1978): 90. Indian monopoly of handcraft selling.

2334. Lawson, Michael L. "The Navajo Indian Irrigation Project: Muddied Past, Clouded Future." Indian Historian 9 (Winter 1976): 19-29.

2335. Libecap, Gary D., and Ronald N. Johnson. "Legislating Commons: The Navajo Tribal Council and the Navajo Range." Economic Inquiry 18 (January 1980): 69-86.

2336. Lukaczer, Moses. The Federal Buy

Indian Program: Promise versus Performance. Reseda, California: Mojave Books, 1976.

2337. Mann, James. "Business Breakout for America's Indians." U.S. News and World Report 86 (May 28, 1979): 68-71.

2338. Manuel, Henry F., Juliann Ramon, and Bernard L. Fontana. "Dressing for the Window: Papago Indians and Economic Development." In American Indian Economic Development, edited by Sam Stanley, pp. 511-577. The Hague: Mouton Publishers, 1978.

2339. Michael, Robert Elias. "The Economic Problems of the Rio Grande Pueblos." Ph.D. dissertation, University of New Mexico, 1976.

2340. Ortiz, Roxanne Dunbar. "Sources of Underdevelopment." In Economic Development in American Indian Reservations, edited by Roxanne Dunbar Ortiz, pp. 61-75. Albuquerque: Native American Studies, University of New Mexico, 1979.

2341. Ortiz, Roxanne Dunbar, ed. Economic Development in American Indian Reservations. Albuquerque: Native American Studies, University of New Mexico, 1979.

2342. Owens, Nancy Jean. "Indian Reservations and Bordertowns: The Metropolis-Satellite Model Applied to the Northwestern Navahos and the Umatillas." Ph.D. dissertation, University of Oregon, 1976.

2343. Pratt, Raymond B. "Tribal Sovereignty and Resource Exploitation." Southwest Economy and Society 4 (Spring 1979): 38-74.

2344. Reno, Philip. "The Navajos: High, Dry and Penniless." Nation 220 (March 29, 1975): 359-363.

2345. _____. "Planning Indian Economic Development." In Economic Development in American Indian Reservations, edited by Roxanne Dunbar Ortiz, pp. 145-150. Albuquerque: Native American Studies, University of New Mexico, 1979.

2346. Robbins, Lynn A. "Structural Changes in Navajo Government Related to Development." In Economic Development in American Indian Reservations, edited by Roxanne Dunbar Ortiz, pp. 129-134. Albuquerque: Native American Studies, University of New Mexico, 1979.

2347. Ruby, Robert H., and John A. Brown. "Early Twentieth Century Blue-Print for Transportation and Electrical Utilities on and near the Spokane Indian Reservation." Idaho Yesterdays 20 (Spring 1976): 28-36.

2348. Ruffing, Lorraine Turner. "Dependence and Underdevelopment." In Economic Development in American Indian Reservations, edited by Roxanne Dunbar Ortiz, pp. 91-113. Albuquerque: Native American Studies, University of New Mexico, 1979. Navajo Indians.

2349. _____. "Navajo Economic Development: A Dual Perspective." In American Indian Economic Development, edited by Sam Stanley, pp. 15-86. The Hague: Mouton Publishers, 1978.

2350. _____. "Navajo Economic Development Subject to Cultural Constraints." Economic Development and Cultural Change 24 (April 1976): 611-621.

2351. Sailors, William M., and Robert T. Patton. "Measuring the Effectiveness of Training Programs for Tribal Enterprises Management." American Indian Journal 2 (November 1976): 15-17.

2352. Schusky, Ernest L. "Development by Grantsmanship: Economic Planning on the Lower Brule Sioux Reservation." Human Organization 34 (Fall 1975): 227-236.

2353. Sorkin, Alan L. "The Economic and Social Status of the American Indian, 1940-1970." Journal of Negro Education 45 (Fall 1976): 432-447.

2354. _____. "Economic Basis of Indian Life." Annals of the American Academy of Political and Social Science 436 (March 1978): 1-12.

2355. Stanley, Sam, ed. American Indian Economic Development. The Hague: Mouton Publishers, 1978.

2356. Stevens, Susan McCulloch. "Passamaquoddy Economic Development in Cultural and Historical Perspective." In American Indian Economic Development, edited by Sam Stanley, pp. 313-408. The Hague: Mouton Publishers, 1978.

2357. Stoffle, Richard W. "Reservation-Based Industry: A Case from Zuni, New Mexico." Human Organization 34 (Fall 1975): 217-226.

2358. Stoffle, Richard W., Cheryl A. Last, and Michael J. Evans. "Reservation-Based Tourism: Implications of Tourist Attitudes for Native American Economic Development." Human Organization 38 (Fall 1979): 300-306.

2359. Tomlinson, Kenneth Y. "Scalping at Crow Creek." Reader's Digest 115 (October 1979): 199-200. Failure of EDA tourism developments.

2360. "Tribes Eligible for Revenue Sharing

Money." <u>American Indian Journal</u> 1 (December 1975): 20-22.

2361. Trosper, Ronald L. "American Indian Relative Ranching Efficiency." <u>American Economic Review</u> 68 (September 1978): 503-516.

2362. Wade, Edwin Lewis. "The History of the Southwest Indian Ethnic Art Market." Ph.D. dissertation, University of Washington, 1976.

2363. Wahrhaftig, Albert L. "Making Do with the Dark Meat: A Report on the Cherokee Indians in Oklahoma." In <u>American Indian Economic Development</u>, edited by Sam Stanley, pp. 409-510. The Hague: Mouton Publishers, 1978.

2364. Watson, John G., and Clair D. Rowe. "A Company Seeks Profits with a Sioux Indian Tribe." <u>Harvard Business Review</u> 54 (July-August 1976): 7-8, 10.

2365. Weiss, Lawrence David. "The Development of Capitalism in Navajo Nation." Ph.D. dissertation, State University of New York at Binghamton, 1979.

2366. Willard, Lawrence F. "Passamaquoddy Uprising." <u>Yankee</u> 40 (October 1976): 82-87, 162-169.

2367. "Will Fairchild Really Pull Out of Shiprock?" <u>Business Week</u>, March 17, 1975, p. 28.

2368. Williams, David C. "Spending Patterns of Navajo Families." <u>New Mexico Business</u> 28 (March 1975): 3-10.

2369. Winslow, Kate. "The Last Stand?" <u>American Indian Journal</u> 6 (September 1980): 2-11. Navajo economic development.

2370. Young, Robert Allan. "Regional Development and Rural Proverty in the Navajo Indian Area." Ph.D. dissertation, University of Wisconsin-Madison, 1976.

Mineral and Energy Resources

2371. Alverez, Frank H., and J. Kevin Poorman. "Real Property: Congressional Control of Allotted Mineral Interests." <u>American Indian Law Review</u> 3 (No. 1, 1975): 159-167.

2372. Anderson, Alison. "An Expendable People: Power and Water in the American South West." <u>Ecologist</u> 5 (August-September 1975): 237-240.

2373. Barry, Tom. "An Energy Dichotomy for the 80's." <u>American Indian Journal</u> 6 (February 1980): 18-20.

2374. _____. "The Energy Drive Finds Resistance in the Jemez Mountains." <u>American Indian Journal</u> 6 (August 1980): 19-22.

2375. _____. "Navajos and National Nuclear Policy." <u>Southwest Economy and Society</u> 4 (Spring 1979): 21-32.

2376. Books, Richard K. "Oil and Gas: The Effect of Oklahoma Conservation Laws on Federal and Indian Lands." <u>Oklahoma Law Review</u> 29 (Fall 1976): 994-1002.

2377. Broad, William J. "The Osage Oil Cover-up." <u>Science</u> 208 (April 4, 1980): 32-35.

2378. "Charles Lipton on Indian Mineral Leases." <u>American Indian Journal</u> 2 (May 1976): 9-10.

2379. "A Crow Indian Threat to Western Strip Mines." <u>Business Week</u>, October 13, 1975, p. 37.

2380. Demaret, Kent. "There's Fuel in Them Thar Hills, and Peter MacDonald's Indians May Now Get Theirs." <u>People Weekly</u> 12 (September 3, 1979): 26-29. Council of Energy Resources Tribes.

2381. Dillingham, Brint. "Exxon, Uranium, and the Navajo Nation." <u>American Indian Journal</u> 3 (March 1977): 27.

2382. Fialka, John J. "The Indians, the Royalties, and the BIA." <u>Civil Rights Digest</u> 10 (Winter 1978): 14-31.

2383. "Fuel Powwow." <u>Time</u> 114 (August 20, 1979): 17. Council of Energy Resources Tribes.

2384. Gedicks, Al. "Copper Country Chippewas: A Tribe Joins the Third World." <u>Nation</u> 222 (May 15, 1976): 582-584.

2385. "The Great Indian Oil Scam." <u>Newsweek</u> 96 (December 22, 1980): 67-68.

2386. Henderson, Al. "Aneth Community: Oil Crisis in Navajoland." <u>Indian Historian</u> 12 (Winter 1979): 33-36.

2387. Johansen, Bruce. "Uranium Rush in Black Hills, S.D." <u>Nation</u> 228 (April 14, 1979): 393-396.

2388. Leubben, Thomas E. <u>American Indian Natural Resources: Oil and Gas</u>. Washington: Institute for the Development of Indian Law, 1980.

2389. _____. "Mining Agreements with Indian Tribes." <u>American Indian Journal</u> 2 (May 1976): 2-8.

2390. Levy, Jerrold E. "Who Benefits

from Energy Resource Development: The Special Case of Navajo Indians." Social Science Journal 17 (January 1980): 1-19.

2391. Levy, Robert. "Damson and the Indians." Dun's Review 106 (November 1975): 77-79. Oilman Barrie M. Damson and Blackfeet Indians.

2392. Lipton, Charles J. "The Pros and Cons of Petroleum Agreements." American Indian Journal 6 (February 1980): 2-10.

2393. Loble, Henry. "Interstate Water Compacts and Mineral Development (with Emphasis on the Yellowstone River Compact)." Rocky Mountain Mineral Law Institute Proceedings 21 (1975): 777-800.

2394. MacDonald, Peter. "Navajo Natural Resources." In American Indian Environments: Ecological Issues in Native American History, edited by Christopher Vecsey and Robert W. Venables, pp. 162-170. Syracuse: Syracuse University Press, 1980.

2395. McGee, Patti Palmer. "Indian Lands: Coal Development: Environmental/Economic Dilemma for the Modern Indian." American Indian Law Review 4 (No. 2, 1976): 279-288.

2396. "Navajo Sheiks." Economist 269 (October 28, 1978): 51.

2397. O'Gara, Geoffrey. "Canny CERT Gets Respect, Money Problems." Wassaja/The Indian Historian 13 (June 1980): 24-28.

2398. "An 'OPEC' Right in America's Own Back Yard." U.S. News and World Report 81 (August 2, 1976): 29-30.

2399. "A Petroleum Geologist Branches Out in a Burgeoning Field." American Indian Journal 6 (February 1980): 21-24. Interview with Curtis Canard.

2400. Richardson, Douglas. "What Happens after the Lease Is Signed." American Indian Journal 6 (February 1980): 11-17.

2401. Robbins, Lynn Arnold. "Navajo Energy Politics." Social Science Journal 16 (April 1979): 93-119.

2402. Ruffing, Lorraine Turner. "Agenda for Action." American Indian Journal 6 (July 1980): 14-22. Mining claims on reservations.

2403. _____. "Fighting the Sub-Standard Lease." American Indian Journal 6 (June 1980): 2-8.

2404. _____. "Navajo Mineral Development." Indian Historian 11 (Spring 1978): 28-41.

2405. _____. "Strategy for Assessing Indian Control over Mineral Development." In Economic Development in American Indian Reservations, edited by Roxanne Dunbar Ortiz, pp. 136-144. Albuquerque: Native American Studies, University of New Mexico, 1979.

2406. Saugstad, Kathryn. "Indian Coal Authorities: The Concept of Federal Preemption and Independent Tribal Coal Development on the Northern Great Plains." North Dakota Law Review 53 (1977): 469-497.

2407. Scott, Wilfred. "Energy Resource Tribes Have More To Offer the Nation Than the Usual Hot Air." Wassaja/The Indian Historian 13 (September 1980): 13-16.

2408. Shenk, Phil. "The Frontier Days Are Here Again: The Impact of the Energy Crisis on Native Americans." Sojourners 7 (January 1978): 20-23.

2409. Simonds, Jerome H. "The Acquisition of Rights To Prospect for and Mine Coal from Tribal and Allotted Indian Lands." Rocky Mountain Mineral Law Institute Proceedings 21 (1975): 125-162.

2410. Stephenson, Barbara. "EIS for Uranium Mining Operation on Indian Lands Ruled Inadequate." Natural Resources Journal 18 (April 1978): 397-401. Environmental Impact Statement.

2411. Toole, K. Ross. The Rape of the Great Plains: Northwest America, Cattle and Coal. Boston: Little, Brown and Company, 1976. Chapters 2 and 3 deal with Indians.

2412. "U.S. Indians Demand a Better Energy Deal." Business Week, December 19, 1977, p. 53.

2413. Viers, Becky J. Miles. "Environmental Law: Uranium Mining on the Navajo Reservation." American Indian Law Review 7 (No. 1, 1979): 115-124.

Agriculture

2414. Harvey, Cecil L. Agriculture of the American Indian: A Select Bibliography. Washington: United States Department of Agriculture, 1979.

2415. Norton, George W. "A Model for Indian Reservation Agricultural Development: The Case of the Sisseton-Wahpeton Sioux." Ph.D. dissertation, University of Minnesota, 1979.

2416. Norton, George W., K. William Easter, and Terry L. Roe. "American

Indian Farm Planning: An Analytical Approach to Tribal Decision Making." American Journal of Agricultural Economics 62 (November 1980): 689-699.

2417. Stahl, Robert John. "Farming among the Kiowa, Comanche, Kiowa Apache and Wichita." Ph.D. dissertation, University of Oklahoma, 1978.

2418. Vlasich, James A. "Pueblo Indian Agriculture, Irrigation, and Water Rights." Ph.D. dissertation, University of Utah, 1980.

2419. _____. "Transitions in Pueblo Agriculture, 1938-1948." New Mexico Historical Review 55 (January 1980): 25-46.

2420. Wessel, Thomas R. "Agriculture on the Reservations: The Case of the Blackfeet, 1885-1935." Journal of the West 18 (October 1979): 17-24.

Forestry

2421. Dillsaver, Joe D. "Natural Resources: Federal Control over Indian Timber." American Indian Law Review 5 (No. 2, 1977): 415-422.

2422. Fox, Franklin George, Jr. "Bureau of Indian Affairs' Timber Sales Policies: Economic Impacts on the Flathead Indian Reservation." Ph.D. dissertation, University of Washington, 1977.

2423. Mater, Milton H., and Jean Mater. "American Indian Forests." American Forests 82 (July 1976): 36-39, 56.

2424. Nafziger, Rich. "A Violation of Trust?: Federal Management of Indian Timber Lands." Indian Historian 9 (Fall 1976): 15-23.

Labor and Employment

2425. Chadwick, Bruce A., and Howard M. Bahr. "Factors Associated with Unemployment among American Indians in the Pacific Northwest." Phylon 39 (December 1978): 356-368.

2426. Fay, Keith LaVerne. Developing Indian Employment Opportunities. Washington: U.S. Department of the Interior, Bureau of Indian Affairs, 1976.

2427. Henderson, Eric. "Skilled and Unskilled Blue Collar Navajo Workers: Occupational Diversity in an American Indian Tribe." Social Science Journal 16 (April 1979): 63-80.

2428. Mooney, Kathleen A. "Urban and Reserve Coast Salish Employment: A Test of Two Approaches to the Indian's Niche in North America." Journal of Anthropological Research 32 (Winter 1976): 390-410.

2429. Robbins, Lynn A. "Navajo Labor and the Establishment of a Voluntary Workers Association." Journal of Ethnic Studies 6 (Fall 1978): 97-112.

2430. _____. "Navajo Workers and Labor Unions." Southwest Economy and Society 3 (Spring 1978): 4-23.

2431. Smith, Jackie. "Creating Jobs in an Indian Community." Growth and Change 8 (October 1977): 33-37.

Housing

2432. Berkey, Curtis, and Loretta Lehman. "HUD Publishes Proposed Indian Housing Rules." American Indian Journal 1 (November 1975): 20-21.

2433. Brooks, Loie. "Indian Housing: Special Problems Require Special Techniques." Journal of Housing 34 (June 1977): 292.

2434. Dimas, Joe. "Cooperative Effort Brings Home Repair Program to the Navajos of Canoncito." Aging, No. 263 (September-October 1976): 9.

2435. Esber, George Salem, Jr. "The Study of Space in Advocacy Planning with the Tonto Apaches of Payson, Arizona." Ph.D. dissertation, University of Arizona, 1977.

2436. "Indian Housing Demonstration Involves Resident Training for Fire Safety." Journal of Housing 34 (June 1977): 296.

2437. Mills, C. P., Jr. "Effective Management Puts an Indian Housing Authority on the Road to Sound Practices." Journal of Housing 36 (June 1979): 310-311.

2438. Ormiston, George. "Management Innovations for Indian Housing: HUD Demonstration Program Seeks to Provide Training, Assistance." Journal of Housing 34 (June 1977): 293-295.

2439. Schaller, David A. "Congress Votes Home Insulation Aid for Low-Income Indian Households." American Indian Journal 2 (December 1976): 27-28.

2440. Willard, William. The Agency Camp Project." Human Organization 36 (Winter 1977): 352-362.

14
Indians and Indian Groups

Although organization of this bibliography is not primarily by tribal groups, some studies are best classified by region or tribe. Included are general works about Indians of each region or tribe and specialized studies about tribes that do not fit into other classifications. Biographical studies are also given here, and a few special classifications are included after the tribal sections. Use the index to locate items about particular tribes classified under such topics as education or economic development.

GENERAL ARCHEOLOGICAL AND ETHNOLOGICAL WORKS

Listed here are general works dealing with Indian prehistory and with ethnological descriptions of Indian tribes. These publications furnish background for Indian-white relations, and some of them have sections on white contact.

2441. America's Fascinating Indian Heritage. Pleasantville, New York: Reader's Digest Association, 1978.

2442. Brown, Vinson. Peoples of the Sea Wind: The Native Americans of the Pacific Coast. New York: Macmillan Publishing Company, 1977.

2443. Castile, George Pierre. North American Indians: An Introduction to the Chichimeca. New York: McGraw-Hill Company, 1979.

2444. Garbarino, Merwyn S. Native American Heritage. Boston: Little, Brown and Company, 1976.

2445. Highwater, Jamake. Indian America. New York: David McKay Company, 1975. A Fodor's Modern Guide.

2446. Howard, James H. "The Culture-Area Concept: Does It Diffract Anthropological Light?" Indian Historian 8 (Spring 1975): 22-26.

2447. Hudson, Herschel C. "Cultural and Social Dimensions of North American

Indians." Ph.D. dissertation, Indiana University, 1979.

2448. Snow, Dean R. The Archaeology of North America: American Indians and Their Origins. London: Thames and Hudson, 1976.

2449. _____. Native American Prehistory: A Critical Bibliography. Bloomington: Indiana University Press, 1979.

2450. Spencer, Robert F., and others. The Native Americans: Ethnology and Backgrounds of the North American Indians. New York: Harper and Row, 1977.

2451. Spicer, Edward H. "American Indians." In Harvard Encyclopedia of American Ethnic Groups, edited by Stephan Thernstrom, Ann Orlov, and Oscar Handlin, pp. 58-114. Cambridge; Harvard University Press, 1980.

2452. Sturtevant, William C., ed. Handbook of North American Indians. 20 volumes projected. Washington: Smithsonian Institution, 1978--.

INDIANS OF THE EAST AND NORTHEAST

General and Miscellaneous Studies

2453. Apes, William. Indian Nullification of the Unconstitutional Laws of Massachusetts Relative to the Marshpee Tribe: Or the Pretended Riot Explained. Stanfordville, New York: Earl M. Coleman, 1979. Reprint of 1835 edition.

2454. Boissevain, Ethel. The Narragansett People. Phoenix: Indian Tribal Series, 1975.

2455. Brodeur, Paul "The Mashpees." New Yorker 54 (November 6, 1978): 62-150.

2456. Campbell, Paul R., and Glenn W. LaFantasie. "Scattered to the Winds of Heaven--Narragansett Indians,

1676-1880." Rhode Island History 37 (August 1978): 66-83.

2457. Ceci, Lynn. "The Effect of European Contact and Trade on the Settlement Pattern of Indians in Coastal New York, 1524-1665: The Archeological and Documentary Evidence." Ph.D. dissertation, City University of New York, 1977.

2458. Clark, Wayne. "The Origin of the Piscataway and Related Indian Cultures." Maryland Historical Magazine 75 (March 1980): 8-22.

2459. Colee, Philip Sauve. "The Housatonic-Stockbridge Indians: 1734-1749." Ph.D. dissertation, State University of New York at Albany, 1977.

2460. Currier, Coburn Leo, Jr. "Wabanaki Ethnic-History, Five Centuries of Becoming Indian: An Ethnohistorical Approach to Ethnicity." Ph.D. dissertation, Washington State University, 1978.

2461. Hill, Rick, and Jim Wake. "The Native American Center for the Living Arts in Niagara Falls." American Indian Art Magazine 5 (Summer 1980): 22-25.

2462. Hutchins, Francis G. Mashpee: The Story of Cape Cod's Indian Town. West Franklin, New Hampshire: Amarta Press, 1979.

2463. Lahrman, Dolores M., and Ross S. Johnson. "A Delaware Indian's Reservation: Samuel Cassman vs. Goldsmith C. Gilbert." Indiana Magazine of History 71 (June 1975): 103-123.

2464. Levitas, Gloria. "No Boundary Is a Boundary: Conflict and Change in a New England Indian Community." Ph.D. dissertation, Rutgers University, 1980. Gay Head, Massachusetts.

2465. McQuaid, Kim. "William Apes, Pequot: An Indian Reformer in the Jackson Era." New England Quarterly 50 (December 1977): 605-625.

2466. Morrison, Kenneth M. "The People of the Dawn: The Abnaki and Their Relations with New England and New France, 1600-1727." Ph.D. dissertation, University of Maine, 1975.

2467. Porter, Frank W. III. Indians in Maryland and Delaware: A Critical Bibliography. Bloomington: Indiana University Press, 1979.

2468. Ray, Roger B. The Indians of Maine and the Atlantic Provinces: A Bibliographical Guide. Portland: Maine Historical Society, 1977.

2469. Ronda, Jeanne, and James P. Ronda.

"'As They Were Faithful': Chief Hendrick Aupaumut and the Struggle for Stockbridge Survival, 1757-1830." American Indian Culture and Research Journal 3 (No. 3, 1979): 43-55.

2470. Russell, Howard S. Indian New England before the Mayflower. Hanover, New Hampshire: University Press of New England, 1980.

2471. Sherwood, Mary P. "Indian Island at Old Town." Thoreau Journal Quarterly 7 (October 1975): 10-15. Penobscot settlement in Maine.

2472. Snow, Dean R. "The Ethnohistoric Baseline of the Eastern Abenaki." Ethnohistory 23 (Summer 1976): 291-306.

2473. Tooker, Elisabeth. The Indians of the Northeast: A Critical Bibliography. Bloomington: Indiana University Press, 1978.

2474. Trigger, Bruce G., ed. Northeast. Volume 15 of Handbook of North American Indians, edited by William C. Sturtevant. Washington: Smithsonian Institution, 1978.

2475. Weslager, C. A. The Delaware Indian Westward Migration, with the Texts of Two Manuscripts (1821-22) Responding to General Lews Cass's Inquiries about Lenape Culture and Language. Wallingford, Pennsylvania: Middle Atlantic Press, 1978.

2476. _____. The Delawares: A Critical Bibliography. Bloomington: Indiana University Press, 1978.

Iroquois Indians

2477. Abrams, George H. J. The Seneca People. Phoenix: Indian Tribal Series, 1976.

2478. Aquila, Richard. "Down the Warrior's Path: The Causes of the Southern Wars of the Iroquois." American Indian Quarterly 4 (August 1978): 211-221.

2479. _____. "The Iroquois Restoration: A Study of Iroquois Power, Politics, and Relations with Indians and Whites, 1700-1744." Ph.D. dissertation, Ohio State University, 1977.

2480. Armstrong, William H. Warrior in Two Camps: Ely S. Parker, Union General and Seneca Chief. Syracuse: Syracuse University Press, 1978.

2481. Boyce, Douglas W. "Did a Tuscarora Confederacy Exist?" In Four Centuries of Southern Indians, edited by Charles M. Hudson, pp. 28-45. Athens: University of Georgia Press, 1975.

2482. Bradley, James Wesley. "The Onondaga Iroquois, 1500-1655: A Study in Acculturative Change and Its Consequences." Ph.D. dissertation, Syracuse University, 1979.

2483. Burton, Bruce A. "A Film on the Founding of the Five Nations Confederacy." *International Journal of Instructional Media* 7 (No. 2, 1979-1980): 109-113.

2484. Corkran, David H. *The Iroquois Frontier*. 2 volumes. Ann Arbor, Michigan: University Microfilms International, 1979. Reproduced from typed manuscript.

2485. Daum, Raymond Witham. "A Film Study of Some Aspects of Urban and Rural Communities of a Twentieth-Century American Indian Group: The Mohawks of Caughnawaga and New York City." Ed.D. dissertation, Columbia University Teachers College, 1976.

2486. Fenton, William N. "'Aboriginally Yours,' Jesse J. Cornplanter, Hah-Yonh-Wonh-Ish, The Snipe: Seneca, 1889-1957." In *American Indian Intellectuals*, edited by Margot Liberty, pp. 117-195. St. Paul: West Publishing Company, 1978.

2487. _____. "Frederick Starr, Jesse Cornplanter and the Cornplanter Medal for Iroquois Research." *New York History* 61 (April 1980): 186-199.

2488. Foley, Denis. "An Ethnohistoric and Ethnographic Analysis of the Iroquois from the Aboriginal Era to the Present Suburban Era." Ph.D. dissertation, State University of New York at Albany, 1975.

2489. Geier, Philip Otto III. "A Peculiar Status: A History of Oneida Indian Treaties and Claims: Jurisdictional Conflict within the American Government, 1775-1920." Ph.D. dissertation, Syracuse University, 1980.

2490. Grinde, Donald A., Jr. *The Iroquois and the Founding of the American Nation*. San Francisco: Indian Historian Press, 1977.

2491. Hauptman, Laurence M. "Alice Jemison: Seneca Political Activist, 1901-1964." *Indian Historian* 12 (Summer 1979): 15-22, 60-62.

2492. _____. "The Iroquois School of Art: Arthur C. Parker and the Seneca Arts Project, 1935-1941." *New York History* 60 (July 1979): 283-312.

2493. _____. "Refugee Havens: The Iroquois Villages of the Eighteenth Century." In *American Indian Environments: Ecological Issues in Native American History*, edited by Christopher Vecsey and Robert W. Venables, pp. 128-139. Syracuse: Syracuse University Press, 1980.

2494. Hertzberg, Hazel W. "Arthur C. Parker: Seneca, 1881-1955." In *American Indian Intellectuals*, edited by Margot Liberty, pp. 129-138. St. Paul: West Publishing Company, 1978.

2495. Hollister, Frederica, in collaboration with Mary Templeton. "The Indians of the Long House." *Delta Kappa Gamma Bulletin* 42 (Fall 1975): 23-26.

2496. Jacobs, Wilbur. "Descanosora: A Note on Cadwallader Colden's Concept of the Iroquois." *Indian Historian* 8 (Summer 1975): 55-56.

2497. Lewis, Ann. "Separate Yet Sharing." *Conservationist* 30 (January 1976): 17

2498. Miles, George. "A Brief Study of Joseph Brant's Political Career in Relation to Iroquois Political Structure." *American Indian Journal* 2 (December 1976): 12-20.

2499. O'Donnell, James H. III. "Joseph Brant." In *American Indian Leaders: Studies in Diversity*, edited by R. David Edmunds, pp. 21-40. Lincoln: University of Nebraska Press, 1980.

2500. _____. "Logan's Oration: A Case Study in Ethnographic Authentication." *Quarterly Journal of Speech* 65 (April 1979): 150-156.

2501. Shimony, Annemarie. "Alexander General, 'Deskahe': Cayuga-Oneida, 1889-1965." In *American Indian Intellectuals*, edited by Margot Liberty, pp. 159-175. St. Paul: West Publishing Company, 1978.

2502. Snyder, Charles M., ed. *Red and White on the New York Frontier, a Struggle for Survival: Insights from the Papers of Erastus Granger, Indian Agent 1807-1819*. Harrison, New York: Harbor Hill Books, 1978.

2503. Tarbell, Phillip H. "From Lake Champlain to Eagle Bay." *Conservationist* 30 (January 1976): 12-16.

2504. Tooker, Elisabeth. "Ely S. Parker: Seneca, ca. 1828-1895." In *American Indian Intellectuals*, edited by Margot Liberty, pp. 15-30. St. Paul: West Publishing Company, 1978.

2505. Venables, Robert W. "Iroquois Environments and 'We the People of the United States': Gemeinschaft and Gesellschaft in the Apposition of Iroquois, Federal, and New York State

Sovereignties." In American Indian Environments: Ecological Issues in Native American History, edited by Christopher Vecsey and Robert W. Venables, pp. 81-127. Syracuse: Syracuse University Press, 1980.

2506. Williams, Ted C. The Reservation. Syracuse: Syracuse University Press, 1976. Stories of life on the Tuscarora Indian Reservation.

INDIANS OF THE NORTH CENTRAL REGION

General and Miscellaneous Studies

2507. Bataille, Gretchen M. "The American Indian in Iowa: A Selected Bibliography." In The Worlds between Two Rivers: Perspectives on American Indians in Iowa, edited by Gretchen M. Bataille and others, pp. 126-144. Ames: Iowa State University Press, 1978.

2508. Bataille, Gretchen M., David M. Gradwohl, and Charles L. P. Silet, eds. The Worlds between Two Rivers: Perspectives on American Indians in Iowa. Ames: Iowa State University Press, 1978.

2509. Bigony, Beatrice A. "A Brief History of Native Americans in the Detroit Area." Michigan History 61 (Summer 1977): 135-163.

2510. Blaine, Martha Royce. The Ioway Indians. Norman: University of Oklahoma Press, 1979.

2511. Buchman, Randall, ed. The Historic Indian in Ohio. Ohio American Revolution Bicentennial Conference Series, No. 3. Columbus: Ohio Historical Society, 1976.

2512. Cash, Joseph H., and Gerald W. Wolff. The Ottawa People. Phoenix: Indian Tribal Series, 1976.

2513. Clark, Jerry E. The Shawnee. Lexington: University Press of Kentucky, 1977.

2514. Edmunds, R. David. "Old Briton." In American Indian Leaders: Studies in Diversity, edited by R. David Edmunds, pp. 1-20. Lincoln: University of Nebraska Press, 1980.

2515. Fixico, Don. "The Black Hawk-Keokuk Controversy." In Indian Leaders: Oklahoma's First Statesmen, edited by H. Glenn Jordan and Thomas M. Holm, pp. 64-78. Oklahoma City: Oklahoma Historical Society, 1979.

2516. Gradwohl, David Mayer. "The Native American Experience in Iowa: An Archaeological Perspective." In The Worlds between Two Rivers: Perspectives on American Indians in Iowa, edited by

Gretchen M. Bataille and others, pp. 26-53. Ames: Iowa State University Press, 1978.

2517. Hauser, Raymond E. "The Illinois Indian Tribe: From Autonomy and Self-Sufficiency to Dependency and Depopulation." Journal of the Illinois State Historical Society 69 (May 1976): 127-138.

2518. Haygood, William Converse. "Red Child, White Child: The Strange Disappearance of Casper Partridge." Wisconsin Magazine of History 58 (Summer 1975): 259-312.

2519. Herzberg, Stephen J. "The Menominee Indians: From Treaty to Termination." Wisconsin Magazine of History 60 (Summer 1977): 267-329.

2520. Koehler, Michael D. "Jim Thorpe: Legend and Legacy." Journal of American Indian Education 15 (May 1976): 3-6.

2521. Lurie, Nancy Oestreich. Wisconsin Indians. Madison: State Historical Society of Wisconsin, 1980.

2522. McAnulty, Sarah. "Angel DeCora: American Indian Artist and Educator." Nebraska History 57 (Summer 1976): 143-199. Winnebago Indian.

2523. McTaggart, Fred. Wolf That I Am: In Search of the Red Earth People. Boston: Houghton Mifflin Company, 1976. Mesquaki Indians.

2524. Neff, Ronald L., and Jay A. Weinstein. "Iowa's Indians Come of Age." Society 12 (January-February 1975): 22-26, 60.

2525. Nielsen, George R. The Kickapoo People. Phoenix: Indian Tribal Series, 1975.

2526. Osoinach, Harrison Kirkland. "Indian Politics and Culture in Rural Northern Michigan." Ph.D. dissertation, University of Michigan, 1976.

2527. Ourada, Patricia K. The Menominee Indians: A History. Norman: University of Oklahoma Press, 1979.

2528. Peterson, Jacqueline. "Prelude to Red River: A Social Portrait of the Great Lakes Metis." Ethnohistory 25 (Winter 1978): 41-67.

2529. Rogers, Virginia. "The Indians and the Metis: Genealogical Sources on Minnesota's Earliest Settlers." Minnesota History 46 (Fall 1979): 286-296.

2530. Schultz, George A. "Kennekuk, the

Kickapoo Prophet." Kansas History 3
(Spring 1980): 38-46.

2531. Spindler, George D., and Louise S.
Spindler. "Identity, Militancy, and
Cultural Congruence: The Menominee and
Kainai." Annals of the American Academy
of Political and Social Science 436
(March 1978): 73-85.

2532. Tanner, Helen Hornbeck. "The Glaize
in 1792: A Composite Indian Community."
Ethnohistory 25 (Winter 1978): 15-39.

2533. Unrau, William E. The Emigrant Indians of Kansas: A Critical Bibliography.
Bloomington: Indiana University Press,
1979.

2534. Vogel, John J. Indians of Ohio and
Wyandot County. New York: Vantage Press,
1975.

2535. Wanatee, Donald. "The Lion, Fleur-
de-lis, the Eagle, or the Fox: A Study
of Government." In The Worlds between
Two Rivers: Perspectives on American
Indians in Iowa, edited by Gretchen M.
Bataille and others, pp. 74-83. Ames:
Iowa State University Press, 1978.
Mesquakie Indians.

2536. Waseskuk, Bertha. "Mesquakie His-
tory--As We Know It." In The World
between Two Rivers: Perspectives on
American Indians in Iowa, edited by
Gretchen M. Bataille and others, pp. 54-
61. Ames: Iowa State University Press,
1978.

2537. Zanger, Martin. "Red Bird." In
American Indian Leaders: Studies in
Diversity, edited by R. David Edmunds,
pp. 64-87. Lincoln: University of
Nebraska Press, 1980. Winnebago Indian.

Chippewa Indians

2538. Danziger, Edmund Jefferson, Jr.
The Chippewas of Lake Superior. Norman:
University of Oklahoma Press, 1979.

2539. Kah-Ge-Ga-Gah-Bowh. "The End of the
Trail." Saturday Evening Post 248
(July-August 1976): 25. Reprint of a
statement by George Copway.

2540. Paredes, J. Anthony. "Anishinabe,
a People." In Anishinabe: 6 Studies
of Modern Chippewa, edited by J. Anthony
Paredes, pp. 397-410. Tallahassee:
University Presses of Florida, 1980.

2541. Paredes, J. Anthony, ed. Anishinabe:
6 Studies of Modern Chippewa. Tallahassee: University Presses of Florida,
1980.

2542. Pelto, Gretel H. "Chippewa People
and Politics in a Reservation Town."

In Anishinabe: 6 Studies of Modern
Chippewa, edited by J. Anthony Paredes,
pp. 242-323. Tallahassee: University
Presses of Florida, 1980.

2543. Roufs, Timothy G. The Anishinabe
of the Minnesota Chippewa Tribe.
Phoenix: Indian Tribal Series, 1975.

2544. Smith, Donald B. "Who Are the
Mississauga?" Ontario History 67
(September 1975): 211-222.

2545. Tanner, Helen Hornbeck. The Ojibwas:
A Critical Bibliography. Bloomington:
Indiana University Press, 1976.

Potawatomi Indians

2546. Cash, Joseph H. The Potawatomi
People (Citizen Band). Phoenix:
Indian Tribal Series, 1976.

2547. Clifton, James A. "Billy Caldwell's
Exile in Early Chicago." Chicago
History 6 (Winter 1977-1978): 218-228.

2548. _____. "Merchant, Soldier,
Broker, Chief: A Corrected Obituary of
Captain Billy Caldwell." Journal of
the Illinois State Historical Society
71 (August 1978): 185-210.

2549. _____. "Personal and Ethnic
Identity on the Great Lakes Frontier:
The Case of Billy Caldwell, Anglo-
Canadian." Ethnohistory 25 (Winter
1978): 69-94.

2550. _____. A Place of Refuge for
All Time: Migration of the American
Potawatomi into Upper Canada, 1830-1850.
Ottawa: National Museum of Canada, 1975.

2551. _____. The Prairie People:
Continuity and Change in Potawatomi
Indian Culture, 1665-1965. Lawrence:
Regents Press of Kansas, 1977.

2552. Conway, Thomas G. "An Indian
Politician and Entrepreneur in the Old
Northwest." Old Northwest 1 (March
1975): 51-62. Billy Caldwell.

2553. Edmunds, R. David. The Potawatomis:
Keepers of the Fire. Norman: University of Oklahoma Press, 1978.

2554. _____. "Redefining Red Patriot-
ism: Five Medals of the Potawatomis."
Red River Valley Historical Review 5
(Spring 1980): 13-24.

2555. "The Prairie Potawatomie Resistance
to Allotment." Indian Historian 9
(Fall 1976): 27-31.

INDIANS OF THE SOUTH AND SOUTHEAST

General and Miscellaneous Studies

2556. Barbour, Philip L. The Riddle of the Powhatan 'Black Boyes.'" *Virginia Magazine of History and Biography* 88 (April 1980): 148-154.

2557. Bilotta, James D. "Manifest Destiny and the Five Civilized Tribes." *Indian Historian* 10 (Summer 1977): 23-33.

2558. Campbell, Janet. "The First Americans' Tribute to the First President." *Chronicles of Oklahoma* 57 (Summer 1979): 190-195.

2559. Coe, Joffre L. "The Indian in North Carolina." *North Carolina Historical Review* 56 (Spring 1979): 158-161.

2560. Covington, James W. "Trail Indians of Florida." *Florida Historical Quarterly* 58 (July 1979): 37-57.

2561. Cox, Gail Diane. "An American Princess in London." *American History Illustrated* 13 (October 1978): 4-7, 47-50. Pocahontas.

2562. Downs, Ernest C. "The Struggle of the Louisiana Tunica Indians for Recognition." In *Southeastern Indians since the Removal Era*, edited by Walter L. Williams, pp. 72-89. Athens: University of Georgia Press, 1979.

2563. Downs, Ernest C., and Jenna Whitehead, eds. "The Houma Indians: Two Decades in a History of Struggle." *American Indian Journal* 2 (March 1976): 2-18. Letters, 1921-1940.

2564. Feest, Christian F., ed. "Another French Account of Virginia Indians by John Lederer." *Virginia Magazine of History and Biography* 83 (April 1975): 150-159.

2565. Ferguson, Robert. "An Overview of Southeastern Indian Culture." In *Indians of the Lower South: Past and Present*, edited by John K. Mahon, pp. 37-41. Pensacola: Gulf Coast History and Humanities Conference, 1975.

2566. Garrow, Patrick H. *The Mattamuskeet Documents: A Study in Social History*. Raleigh: North Carolina Division of Archives and History, 1975.

2567. Gover, Kevin. "Oklahoma Tribes: A History." *American Indian Journal* 3 (June 1977): 2-19.

2568. Graebner, Laura Baum. "Agriculture among the Five Civilized Tribes, 1840-1906." *Red River Valley Historical Review* 3 (Winter 1978): 45-60.

2569. Herndon, Paul C. "The Civilized Tribes and Settlement South of the Ohio." *Our Public Lands* 28 (Winter 1978): 20-22.

2570. Hollingsworth, Dixon. *Indians on the Savannah River*. Sylvania, Georgia: Partridge Pond Press, 1976.

2571. Hoover, Herbert T. *The Chitimacha People*. Phoenix: Indian Tribal Series, 1975.

2572. "The Houma Indians since 1940; An Update on Educational Struggles of the Houma Indian People." *American Indian Journal* 2 (April 1976): 16-17.

2573. Hudson, Charles M. "The Catawba Indians of South Carolina: A Question of Ethnic Survival." In *Southeastern Indians since the Removal Era*, edited by Walter L. Williams, pp. 110-120. Athens: University of Georgia Press, 1979.

2574. _____. *The Southeastern Indians*. Knoxville: University of Tennessee Press, 1976.

2575. Hudson, Charles M., ed. *Four Centuries of Southern Indians*. Athens: University of Georgia Press, 1975.

2576. Jamail, Milton H. "Indians on the Border." *Indian Historian* 10 (Summer 1977): 34-37. Kickapoo Indians at Eagle Pass, Texas.

2577. Johnson, Bobby H. *The Coushatta People*. Phoenix: Indian Tribal Series, 1976.

2578. Jones, A. Bruce. "A Historical Perspective about the Indians of North Carolina and an Overview of the Commission of Indian Affairs." *North Carolina Historical Review* 56 (Spring 1979): 177-187.

2579. Mahon, John K., ed. *Indians of the Lower South: Past and Present*. Pensacola: Gulf Coast History and Humanities Conference, 1975.

2580. Merrell, James H. "Cultural Continuity among the Piscataway Indians of Colonial Maryland." *William and Mary Quarterly*, 3d series 36 (October 1979): 548-570.

2581. "The Miccosukees Strive To Be Self-Sufficient." *Delta Kappa Gamma Bulletin* 42 (Fall 1975): 20-22.

2582. Mossiker, Frances. *Pocahontas: The Life and the Legend*. New York: Alfred A. Knopf, 1976.

2583. Nackman, Mark E. "The Indians of Texas in the Nineteenth Century: A

Cross-Section of American Indian Cultures." <u>Texas Quarterly</u> 18 (Summer 1975): 56-75.

2584. Perdue, Theda. <u>Nations Remembered: An Oral History of the Five Civilized Tribes, 1865-1907</u>. Westport, Connecticut: Greenwood Press, 1980.

2585. Porter, Frank W. III. "Behind the Frontier: Indian Survivals in Maryland." <u>Maryland Historical Magazine</u> 75 (March 1980): 42-54.

2586. _____. "A Century of Accommodation: The Nanticoke Indians in Colonial Maryland." <u>Maryland Historical Magazine</u> 74 (June 1979): 175-192.

2587. Roark-Calnek, Sue N. "Indian Way in Oklahoma: Transactions in Honor and Legitimacy." Ph.D. dissertation, Bryn Mawr College, 1977. Delaware Indians.

2588. Rountree, Helen C. "Change Came Slowly: The Case of the Powhatan Indians of Virginia." <u>Journal of Ethnic Studies</u> 3 (Fall 1975): 1-19.

2589. _____. "The Indians of Virginia: A Third Race in a Biracial State." In <u>Southeastern Indians since the Removal Era</u>, edited by Walter L. Williams, pp. 27-48. Athens: University of Georgia Press, 1979.

2590. Roy, Ewell P., and Don Leary. "Economic Survey of American Indians in Louisiana." <u>American Indian Journal</u> 3 (January 1977): 11-16.

2591. Satz, Ronald N. <u>Tennessee's Indian Peoples: From White Contact to Removal, 1540-1840</u>. Knoxville: University of Tennessee Press, 1979.

2592. Servies, James A. "Notes on the Literature of the Gulf Coast Indians." In <u>Indians of the Lower South: Past and Present</u>, edited by John K. Mahon, pp. 6-24. Pensacola: Gulf Coast History and Humanities Conference, 1975.

2593. Speck, Frank G. "The Houma Indians in 1940." <u>American Indian Journal</u> 2 (January 1976): 4-15.

2594. Stanley, Samuel. "The End of the Natchez Indians." <u>History Today</u> 28 (September 1978): 612-618.

2595. Stanton, Max E. "Southern Louisiana Survivors: The Houma Indians." In <u>Southeastern Indians since the Removal Era</u>, edited by Walter L. Williams, pp. 90-109. Athens: University of Georgia Press, 1979.

2596. Strickland, Rennard. <u>The Indians in Oklahoma</u>. Norman: University of

Oklahoma Press, 1980.

2597. Wetmore, Ruth Y. <u>First on the Land: The North Carolina Indians</u>. Winston-Salem, North Carolina: John F. Blair, Publisher, 1975.

2598. _____. "The Role of the Indian in North Carolina History." <u>North Carolina Historical Review</u> 56 (Spring 1979): 162-176.

2599. Williams, Walter L. "Patterns in the History of the Remaining Southeastern Indians, 1840-1975." In <u>Southeastern Indians since the Removal Era</u>, edited by Walter L. Williams, pp. 193-207. Athens: University of Georgia Press, 1979.

2600. _____. "Southeastern Indians before Removal: Prehistory, Contact, Decline." In <u>Southeastern Indians since the Removal Era</u>, edited by Walter L. Williams, pp. 3-24. Athens: University of Georgia Press, 1979.

2601. Williams, Walter L., ed. <u>Southeastern Indians since the Removal Era</u>. Athens: University of Georgia Press, 1979.

2602. Williams, Walter L., and Thomas R. French. "Bibliographic Essay." In <u>Southeastern Indians since the Removal Era</u>, edited by Walter L. Williams, pp. 211-241. Athens: University of Georgia Press, 1979.

Cherokee Indians

2603. Agnew, Brad. "The Cherokee Struggle for Lovely's Purchase." <u>American Indian Quarterly</u> 2 (Winter 1975-1976): 347-361.

2604. Bridgers, Ben Oshel. "A Legal Digest of the North Carolina Cherokee." <u>Journal of Cherokee Studies</u> 4 (Winter 1979): 21-43.

2605. Brown, Kent R. "Fact and Fiction: 'The Trail of Tears.'" <u>Journal of American Indian Education</u> 16 (January 1977): 1-6. Assessment of outdoor drama sponsored by Cherokee National Historical Society.

2606. _____. "Re-creating History: The Trail of Tears." <u>Players Magazine</u> 51 (December-January 1976): 58-65.

2607. Butler, Brian M. "The Red Clay Council Ground." <u>Journal of Cherokee Studies</u> 2 (Winter 1977): 140-153.

2608. Campbell, Janet, and Archie Sam. "The Primal Fire Lingers." <u>Chronicles of Oklahoma</u> 53 (Winter 1975-1976): 463-475.

2609. Carpenter, Iris. "The Tallest Indian." American Education 12 (August-September 1976): 23-25. Sequoyah.

2610. Conser, Walter H., Jr. "John Ross and the Cherokee Resistance Campaign, 1833-1838." Journal of Southern History 44 (May 1978): 191-212.

2611. Davis, Kenneth Penn. "Chaos in the Indian Country: The Cherokee Nation, 1828-35." In The Cherokee Indian Nation: A Troubled History, edited by Duane H. King, pp. 129-147. Knoxville: University of Tennessee Press, 1979.

2612. Dickens, Roy S., Jr. "The Origins and Development of Cherokee Culture." In The Cherokee Indian Nation: A Troubled History, edited by Duane H. King, pp. 3-32. Knoxville: University of Tennessee Press, 1979.

2613. Douthitt, Roy Lee. "Sociocultural Change and Schooling: A Case Study of an Eastern Cherokee Community." Ph.D. dissertation, Florida State University, 1980.

2614. Evans, E. Raymond. "Following the Rainbow: The Cherokees in the California Gold Fields." Journal of Cherokee Studies 2 (Winter 1977): 170-175.

2615. _____. "Highways to Progress: Nineteenth Century Roads in the Cherokee Nation." Journal of Cherokee Studies 2 (Fall 1977): 394-400.

2616. _____. "Notable Persons in Cherokee History: Bob Benge." Journal of Cherokee Studies 1 (Fall 1976): 98-106.

2617. _____. "Notable Persons in Cherokee History: Dragging Canoe." Journal of Cherokee Studies 2 (Winter 1977): 176-189.

2618. _____. "Notable Persons in Cherokee History: Ostenaco." Journal of Cherokee Studies 1 (Summer 1976): 41-54.

2619. _____. "Notable Persons in Cherokee History: Stephen Foreman." Journal of Cherokee Studies 2 (Spring 1977): 230-239.

2620. Evans, J. P. "Sketches of Cherokee Characteristics." Journal of Cherokee Studies 4 (Winter 1979): 10-20. Written in 1835.

2621. Fenton, William N. "Cherokee and Iroquois Connections Revisited." Journal of Cherokee Studies 3 (Fall 1978): 239-249.

2622. Finger, John R. "The Saga of Tsali: Legend versus Reality." North Carolina Historical Review 56 (Winter 1979): 1-18.

2623. Fink, Kenneth Ernest. "A Cherokee Notion of Development." Ph.D. dissertation, Union Graduate School (Ohio), 1978.

2624. Fogelson, Raymond D. The Cherokees: A Critical Bibliography. Bloomington: Indiana University Press, 1978.

2625. Franks, Kenny A. Stand Watie and the Agony of the Cherokee Nation. Memphis State University Press, 1979.

2626. French, Laurence. "Emerging Social Problems among the Qualla Cherokee." Appalachian Notes 3 (No. 2, 1975): 17-23.

2627. _____. "Tourism and Indian Exploitation: A Social Indictment." Indian Historian 10 (Fall 1977): 19-24.

2628. Goodwin, Gary C. Cherokees in Transition: A Study of Changing Culture and Environment Prior to 1775. Chicago: Department of Geography, University of Chicago, 1977.

2629. Hammond, Sue. "Socioeconomic Reconstruction in the Cherokee Nation, 1865-1870." Chronicles of Oklahoma 56 (Summer 1978): 158-170.

2630. Hewes, Leslie. Occupying the Cherokee Country of Oklahoma. University of Nebraska Studies, new series, No. 57. Lincoln: University of Nebraska, 1978.

2631. Iobst, Richard W. "William Holland Thomas and the Cherokee Claims." In The Cherokee Indian Nation: A Troubled History, edited by Duane H. King, pp. 181-201. Knoxville: University of Tennessee Press, 1979.

2632. Jackson, Gilliam. "Cultural Identity for the Modern Cherokees." Appalachian Journal 2 (Summer 1975): 280-283.

2633. Jordan, Janet Etheridge. "Politics and Religion in a Western Cherokee Community: A Century of Struggle in a White Man's World." Ph.D. dissertation, University of Connecticut, 1975.

2634. Kelly, James C. "Notable Persons in Cherokee History: Attakullakulla." Journal of Cherokee Studies 3 (Winter 1978): 2-34.

2635. _____. "Oconostota." Journal of Cherokee Studies 3 (Fall 1978): 221-238.

2636. King, Duane H. "Long Island of the Holston: Sacred Cherokee Ground." Journal of Cherokee Studies 1 (Fall 1976): 113-127.

2637. _____. "The Origin of the Eastern Cherokees as a Social and Political

Entity." In The Cherokee Indian Nation: A Troubled History, edited by Duane H. King, pp. 164-180. Knoxville: University of Tennessee Press, 1979.

2638. King, Duane H., ed. The Cherokee Indian Nation: A Troubled History. Knoxville: University of Tennessee Press, 1979.

2639. King, Duane H., and E. Raymond Evans. "The Death of John Walker, Jr.: Political Assassination or Private Vengeance?" Journal of Cherokee Studies 1 (Summer 1976): 4-16.

2640. _____. "Tsali: The Man behind the Legend." Journal of Cherokee Studies 4 (Fall 1979): 194-201.

2641. King, Duane H., and E. Raymond Evans, eds. "History in the Making: Cherokee Events As Reported by Contemporary Newspapers." Journal of Cherokee Studies 4 (Spring 1979): 53-118.

2642. Kinsey, Ron R. "A New Vision of Sequoyah." Masterkey 53 (January-March 1979): 4-9.

2643. Lillard, Roy G. "The Story of Nancy Ward, 1738-1822." Daughters of the American Revolution Magazine 110 (January 1976): 42-43, 158.

2644. Littlefield, Daniel F., Jr., and Lonnie E. Underhill. "The Granger Movement in the Cherokee Nation." Red River Valley Historical Review 4 (Winter 1979): 14-25.

2645. Littlejohn, Hawk. "The Reawakening of the Cherokees." Appalachian Journal 2 (Summer 1975): 276-279.

2646. Lowery, George. "Notable Persons in Cherokee History: Sequoyah or George Gist." Journal of Cherokee History 2 (Fall 1977): 385-393. Written in 1835; introduction and transcription by John Howard Payne.

2647. Luebke, Barbara F. "Elias Boudinott, Indian Editor: Editorial Columns from the Cherokee Phoenix." Journalism History 6 (Summer 1979): 48-53.

2648. McLoughlin, William G. "Cherokee Anomie, 1794-1809: New Roles for Red Men, Red Women, and Black Slaves." In Uprooted Americans: Essays to Honor Oscar Handlin, edited by Richard L. Bushman and others, pp. 125-160. Boston: Little, Brown and Company, 1979.

2649. _____. "Thomas Jefferson and the Beginning of Cherokee Nationalism." William and Mary Quarterly, 3d series 32 (October 1975): 547-580.

2650. McLoughlin, William G., and Walter H.

Conser, Jr. "The Cherokees in Transition: A Statistical Analysis of the Federal Cherokee Census of 1835." Journal of American History 64 (December 1977): 678-703.

2651. Mathes, Valerie L. "Chief John Ross." Masterkey 54 (April-June 1980): 67-71.

2652. Meredith, Howard L. "Emmet Starr's Manuscript Essay on the Texas Cherokees." Indian Historian 10 (Winter 1977): 14-16.

2653. _____. "Will Rogers' Roots." Chronicles of Oklahoma 57 (Fall 1979): 259-268.

2654. Meredith, Howard L., and Virginia E. Milam. "A Cherokee Vision of Eloh." Indian Historian 8 (Winter 1975): 19-23.

2655. "Military Intelligence Report on N.C. Cherokees in 1838." Journal of Cherokee Studies 4 (Fall 1979): 202-240.

2656. Miner, H. Craig. "Dennis Bushyhead." In American Indian Leaders: Studies in Diversity, edited by R. David Edmunds, pp. 192-205. Lincoln: University of Nebraska Press, 1980.

2657. Mooney, James. Historical Sketch of the Cherokees. Chicago: Aldine Publishing Company, 1975. Reprinted from the 19th Annual Report of the Bureau of American Ethnology.

2658. Morgan, James F. "The Cherokee Scrip Issuance of 1862." Chronicles of Oklahoma 54 (Fall 1976): 393-400.

2659. Moulton, Gary E. "Chief John Ross and the Internal Crises of the Cherokee Nation." In Indian Leaders: Oklahoma's First Statesmen, edited by H. Glenn Jordan and Thomas M. Holm, pp. 114-125. Oklahoma City: Oklahoma Historical Society, 1979.

2660. _____. "Chief John Ross: The Personal Dimension." Red River Valley Historical Review 2 (Summer 1975): 220-239.

2661. _____. "John Ross." In American Indian Leaders: Studies in Diversity, edited by R. David Edmunds, pp. 88-106. Lincoln: University of Nebraska Press, 1980.

2662. _____. John Ross, Cherokee Chief. Athens: University of Georgia Press, 1978.

2663. _____. "'Voyage to the Arkansas': New Letters of John Ross." Tennessee Historical Quarterly 35 (Spring 1976): 46-50.

2664. Neely, Sharlotte. "Acculturation and Persistence among North Carolina's Eastern Band of Cherokee Indians." In Southeastern Indians since the Removal Era, edited by Walter L. Williams, pp. 154-173. Athens: University of Georgia Press, 1979.

2665. Pearson, Anthony A. "John Hunter and Two Cherokee Indians." Journal of the Medical Association of Georgia 68 (June 1978): 449-455.

2666. Perdue, Theda. "People without a Place--Aboriginal Cherokee Bondage." Indian Historian 9 (Summer 1976): 31-37.

2667. _____. "Rising from the Ashes: The Cherokee Phoenix as an Ethnohistorical Source." Ethnohistory 24 (Summer 1977): 207-218.

2668. Persico, V. Richard, Jr. "Early Nineteenth-Century Cherokee Political Organization." In The Cherokee Indian Nation: A Troubled History, edited by Duane H. King, pp. 92-109. Knoxville: University of Tennessee Press, 1979.

2669. Purrington, Burton L. "Introduction: Reassessing Cherokee Studies." Appalachian Journal 2 (Summer 1975): 252-257.

2670. Reed, Gerard. "Postremoval Factionalism in the Cherokee Nation." In The Cherokee Indian Nation: A Troubled History, edited by Duane H. King, pp. 148-163.

2671. Reid, John Phillip. A Better Kind of Hatchet: Law, Trade, and Diplomacy in the Cherokee Nation during the Early Years of European Contact. University Park: Pennsylvania State University Press, 1976.

2672. Riley, Sam G. "The Cherokee Phoenix: The Short Unhappy Life of the First American Indian Newspaper." Journalism Quarterly 53 (Winter 1976): 666-671.

2673. _____. "A Note of Caution--The Indian's Own Prejudice, As Mirrored in the First Native American Newspaper." Journalism History 6 (Summer 1979): 44-47. Cherokee Phoenix.

2674. Royce, Charles C. The Cherokee Nation of Indians. Chicago: Aldine Publishing Company, 1975. Reprinted from the Fifth Annual Report of the Bureau of American Ethnology, 1883-1884.

2675. Schroedl, Gerald F. "Louis-Philippe's Journal and Archaeological Investigations at the Overhill Cherokee Town of Toqua." Journal of Cherokee Studies 3 (Fall 1978): 206-219.

2676. Smith, Betty Anderson. "Distribution of Eighteenth-Century Cherokee Settlements." In The Cherokee Indian Nation: A Troubled History, edited by Duane H. King, pp. 46-60. Knoxville: University of Tennessee Press, 1979.

2677. Snell, William R. "The Councils at Red Clay Council Ground, Bradley County, Tennessee, 1832-1837." Journal of Cherokee Studies 2 (Fall 1977): 344-355.

2678. Strickland, Rennard, and Jack Gregory. "Emmet Starr, Heroic Historian: Cherokee, 1870-1930." In American Indian Intellectuals, edited by Margot Liberty, pp. 105-114. St. Paul: West Publishing Company, 1978.

2679. Strickland, William. "Cherokee Rhetoric: A Forceful Weapon." Journal of Cherokee Studies 2 (Fall 1977): 375-384.

2680. Sturtevant, William C. "Louis-Philippe on Cherokee Architecture and Clothing in 1797." Journal of Cherokee Studies 3 (Fall 1978): 198-205.

2681. Tanner, Helen Hornbeck. "Cherokees in the Ohio Country." Journal of Cherokee Studies 3 (Spring 1978): 94-102.

2682. Wahrhaftig, Albert L. "Institution Building among Oklahoma's Traditional Cherokees." In Four Centuries of Southern Indians, edited by Charles M. Hudson, pp. 132-147. Athens: University of Georgia Press, 1975.

2683. Wahrhaftig, Albert, and Jane Lukens-Wahrhaftig. "New Militants or Resurrected State? The Five County Northeastern Oklahoma Cherokee Organization." In The Cherokee Nation: A Troubled History, edited by Duane H. King, pp. 223-246. Knoxville: University of Tennessee Press, 1979.

2684. Wardell, Morris L. A Political History of the Cherokee Nation, 1838-1907. With "In Search of Cherokee History," a Bibliographical Foreword to the Second Printing, by Rennard Strickland. Norman: University of Oklahoma Press, 1977. Reprint of 1938 edition.

2685. Williams, Walter L. "The Merger of Apaches with Eastern Cherokees: Qualla in 1893." Journal of Cherokee Studies 2 (Spring 1977): 240-245.

2686. Wilms, Douglas C. "Cherokee Acculturation and Changing Land Use Practice." Chronicles of Oklahoma 56 (Fall 1978): 331-343.

2687. _____. "A Note on the District Boundaries of the Cherokee Nation, 1820." Appalachian Journal 2 (Summer

1975): 284-285.

2688. Witthoft, John. "Observations on Social Change among the Eastern Cherokees." In The Cherokee Indian Nation: A Troubled History, edited by Duane H. King, pp. 202-222. Knoxville: University of Tennessee Press, 1979.

Chickasaw Indians

2689. Alexander, Franklin David. "The Chickasaw Indian Tribe and Self-Determination: A Study of Organization and Organizational Change." Ph.D. dissertation, University of Oklahoma, 1978.

2690. Gibson, Arrell Morgan. "The Colberts: Chickasaw Nation Elitism." In Indian Leaders: Oklahoma's First Statesmen, edited by H. Glenn Jordan and Thomas M. Holm, pp. 79-100. Oklahoma City: Oklahoma Historical Society, 1979.

Choctaw Indians

2691. Baird, W. David. "Peter Pitchlynn and the Reconstruction of the Choctaw Republic, 1834-1850." In Indian Leaders: Oklahoma's First Statesmen, edited by H. Glenn Jordan and Thomas M. Holm, pp. 12-28. Oklahoma City: Oklahoma Historical Society, 1979.

2692. Goss, Charles Wayne. "The French and the Choctaw Indians, 1700-1763." Ph.D. dissertation, Texas Tech University, 1977.

2693. Gregory, Hiram F. "Jena Band of Louisiana Choctaw." American Indian Journal 3 (February 1977): 2-16.

2694. Kidwell, Clara Sue, and Charles Roberts. The Choctaws: A Critical Bibliography. Bloomington: Indiana University Press, 1980.

2695. Kinnaird, Lawrence, and Lucia B. Kinnaird. "Choctaws West of the Mississippi, 1766-1800." Southwestern Historical Quarterly 83 (April 1980): 349-370.

2696. Lujan, Philip, and L. Brooks Hill. "The Mississippi Choctaw: A Case Study of Tribal Identity Problems." American Indian Culture and Research Journal 4 (No. 3, 1980): 37-53.

2697. McKee, Jesse O., and Jon A. Schlenker. The Choctaws: Cultural Evolution of a Native American Tribe. Jackson: University Press of Mississippi, 1980.

2698. Penman, John T. "Historic Choctaw Towns of the Southern Division." Journal of Mississippi History 40 (May 1978): 133-141.

2699. Peterson, John H., Jr. "Louisiana Choctaw Life at the End of the Nineteenth Century." In Four Centuries of Southern Indians, edited by Charles M. Hudson, pp. 101-112. Athens: University of Georgia Press, 1975.

2700. _____. "Three Efforts at Development among the Choctaws of Mississippi." In Southeastern Indians since the Removal Era, edited by Walter L. Williams, pp. 142-153. Athens: University of Georgia Press, 1979.

2701. Schlenker, Jon A. "An Historical Analysis of the Family Life of the Choctaw Indians." Southern Quarterly 13 (July 1975): 323-334.

2702. Thompson, Bobby, and John H. Peterson, Jr. "Mississippi Choctaw Identity: Genesis and Change." In The New Ethnicity: Perspectives from Ethnology, edited by John W. Bennett, pp. 179-196. St. Paul: West Publishing Company, 1975.

Creek Indians

2703. Clark, Carter Blue. "Opothleyahola and the Creeks during the Civil War." In Indian Leaders: Oklahoma's First Statesmen, edited by H. Glenn Jordan and Thomas M. Holm, pp. 49-63. Oklahoma City: Oklahoma Historical Society, 1979.

2704. Culbertson, Gilbert M. "The Creek Indians in East Texas." East Texas Historical Journal 14 (No. 2, 1976): 20-25.

2705. Green, Michael D. "Alexander McGillivray." In American Indian Leaders: Studies in Diversity, edited by R. David Edmunds, pp. 41-63. Lincoln: University of Nebraska Press, 1980.

2706. _____. The Creeks: A Critical A Critical Bibliography. Bloomington: Indiana University Press, 1979.

2707. Megehee, Mark K. "Creek Nativism since 1865." Chronicles of Oklahoma 56 (Fall 1978): 282-297.

2708. Paredes, J. Anthony. "Back from Disappearance: The Alabama Creek Indian Community." In Southeastern Indians since the Removal Era, edited by Walter L. Williams, pp. 123-141. Athens: University of Georgia Press, 1979.

2709. _____. "The Folk Culture of the Eastern Creek Indians: Synthesis and Change." In Indians of the Lower South: Past and Present, edited by Jack K. Mahon, pp. 93-111. Pensacola: Gulf Coast History and Humanities Conference, 1975.

2710. Paredes, J. Anthony, and Sandra K. Joos. "Economics, Optimism, and Community History: A Comparison of

Rural Minnesotans and Eastern Creek Indians." Human Organization 39 (Summer 1980): 142-152.

2711. Romine, Dannye. "Alexander Mc-Gillivray: Shrewd Scot, Cunning Indian." Southern Humanities Review 9 (Fall 1975): 409-421.

2712. Todd, Helen. Tomochichi: Indian Friend of the Georgia Colony. Atlanta: Cherokee Publishing Company, 1977.

Lumbee Indians

2713. Blu, Karen I. The Lumbee Problem: The Making of an American Indian People. Cambridge: Cambridge University Press, 1980.

2714. Dial, Adolph L. "Lumbee Indians." In Indians of the Lower South: Past and Present, edited by John K. Mahon, pp. 77-92. Pensacola: Gulf Coast History and Humanities Conference, 1975.

2715. Dial, Adolph, and David K. Eliades. The Only Land I Know: A History of the Lumbee Indians. San Francisco: Indian Historian Press, 1975.

2716. Evans, W. McKee. "The North Carolina Lumbees: From Assimilation to Revitalization." In Southeastern Indians since the Removal Era, edited by Walter L. Williams, pp. 49-71. Athens: University of Georgia Press, 1979.

Seminole Indians

2717. Carter, L. Edward. "The Seminole Nation after Leaving Florida, 1855-1860." Chronicles of Oklahoma 55 (Winter 1977-1978): 433-453.

2718. Garbarino, Merwyn S. "Independence and Dependency among the Seminole of Florida." In Political Organization of Native North Americans, edited by Ernest L. Schusky, pp. 141-162. Washington: University Press of America, 1980.

2719. Jahoda, Gloria. "Seminole." Florida Historical Quarterly 55 (October 1976): 129-133.

2720. Kersey, Harry A., Jr. "The Case of Tom Tiger's Horse: An Early Foray into Indian Rights." Florida Historical Quarterly 53 (January 1975): 306-318.

2721. _____. "Private Societies and the Maintenance of Seminole Tribal Integrity, 1899-1957." Florida Historical Quarterly 56 (January 1978): 297-316.

2722. _____. "Those Left Behind: The Seminole Indians of Florida." In Southeastern Indians since the Removal

Era, edited by Walter L. Williams, pp. 174-190. Athens: University of Georgia Press, 1979.

2723. King, Robert Thomas. "Clan Affiliation and Leadership among the Twentieth Century Florida Indians." Florida Historical Quarterly 55 (October 1976): 138-152.

2724. _____. "The Florida Seminole Polity, 1858-1978." Ph.D. dissertation, University of Florida, 1978.

2725. Work, Susan. "The 'Terminated' Five Tribes of Oklahoma: The Effect of Federal Legislation and Administrative Treatment on the Government of the Seminole Nation." American Indian Law Review 6 (No. 1, 1978): 81-141.

INDIANS OF THE PLAINS

General and Miscellaneous Studies

2726. Baird, W. David. The Quapaw People. Phoenix: Indian Tribal Series, 1975.

2727. Bedford, Denton R. "The Fight at 'Mountains on Both Sides.'" Indian Historian 8 (Fall 1975): 13-23.

2728. _____. "First Thunder of the Rocky Boys." Indian Historian 10 (Winter 1977): 37-43.

2729. DeMallie, Raymond J. "Joseph N. Nicollet's Account of the Sioux and Assiniboin in 1839." South Dakota History 5 (Fall 1975): 343-359.

2730. Dempsey, Hugh A. "Sylvester Long, Buffalo Child Long Lance: Catawba-Cherokee and Adopted Blackfoot, 1891-1932." In American Indian Intellectuals, edited by Margot Liberty, pp. 197-203. St. Paul: West Publishing Company, 1978.

2731. Edmunds, R. David. The Otoe-Missouria People. Phoenix: Indian Tribal Series, 1976.

2732. Ewers, John C. "Richard Sanderville, Blackfoot Indian Interpreter: Blackfoot, ca. 1873-1951." In American Indian Intellectuals, edited by Margot Liberty, pp. 117-126. St. Paul: West Publishing Company, 1978.

2733. Foley, William E., and Charles David Rice. "The Return of the Mandan Chief." Montana, the Magazine of Western History 29 (July 1979): 2-15.

2734. Green, Norma Kidd. "The Make Believe White Man's Village." Nebraska History 56 (Summer 1975): 242-247. Omaha Indians.

2735. Haines, Francis. The Plains Indians. New York: Thomas Y. Crowell Company, 1976.

2736. Hoebel, E. Adamson. The Plains Indians: A Critical Bibliography. Bloomington: Indiana University Press, 1977.

2737. Hughes, J. Donald. American Indians in Colorado. Boulder, Colorado: Pruett Publishing Company, 1977.

2738. Klein, Alan Michael. "Adaptive Strategies on the Plains: The 19th Century Cultural Sink." Ph.D. dissertation, State University of New York at Buffalo, 1977. A Marxist analysis dealing with four northern plains tribes and two fur companies.

2739. McGinnis, Anthony. "Intertribal Conflict on the Northern Plains and Its Suppression, 1738-1889." Journal of the West 18 (April 1979): 49-60.

2740. Mathes, Valerie. "Portrait for a Western Album.: American West 16 (May-June 1979): 38-39. Indian Dr. Susan La Flesche.

2741. Meyer, Roy W. The Village Indians of the Upper Missouri: The Mandans, Hidatsas, and Arikaras. Lincoln: University of Nebraska Press, 1977.

2742. Newcomb, W. W., Jr. The People Called Wichita. Phoenix: Indian Tribal Series, 1976.

2743. Ruffin, Thomas F. "The Tragic Trail." North Louisiana Historical Association Journal 7 (Fall 1975): 1-11. Quapaw Indians.

2744. Siry, Joseph Vincent. "When the River Flows Upstream: The Appearance, Adaptation and Extinction of the Nu-Mah-ka-kee People." Indian Historian 11 (Spring 1978): 6-14. Mandan Indians.

2745. Springer, W. F. "The Omaha Indians: What They Ask of the United States Government." Indian Historian 9 (Winter 1976): 30-33. Address given in 1928.

2746. Taylor, Colin. The Warriors of the Plains. New York: Arco Publishing Company, 1975.

2747. Unrau, William E. The Kaw People. Phoenix: Indian Tribal Series, 1975.

2748. _____. "The Mixed-Blood Connection: Charles Curtis and Kaw Detribalization." In Kansas and the West: Bicentennial Essays in Honor of Nyle H. Miller, edited by Forrest R. Blackburn and others, pp. 151-161. Topeka:

Kansas State Historical Society, 1976.

2749. _____. "Removal, Death, and Legal Reincarnation of the Kaw People. Indian Historian 9 (Winter 1976): 2-9.

2750. Voget, Fred W. "Adaptation and Cultural Persistence among the Crow Indians of Montana." In Political Organization of Native North Americans, edited by Ernest L. Schusky, pp. 163-187. Washington: University Press of America, 1980.

2751. Wood, W. Raymond. "David Thompson at the Mandan-Hidatsa Villages, 1797-1798: The Original Journals." Ethnohistory 24 (Fall 1977): 329-342.

Cheyenne and Arapaho Indians

2752. Berthrong, Donald J. "Black Kettle, a Friend of Peace." In Indian Leaders: Oklahoma's First Statesmen, edited by H. Glenn Jordan and Thomas M. Holm, pp. 29-48. Oklahoma City: Oklahoma Historical Society, 1979.

2753. _____. The Cheyenne and Arapaho Ordeal: Reservation and Agency Life in the Indian Territory, 1875-1907. Norman: University of Oklahoma Press, 1976.

2754. Fowler, Loretta. "Oral Historian or Ethnologist? The Career of Bill Shakespeare: Northern Arapahoe, 1901-1975." In American Indian Intellectuals, edited by Margot Liberty, pp. 227-240. St. Paul: West Publishing Company, 1978.

2755. Hoig, Stan. The Peace Chiefs of the Cheyennes. Norman: University of Oklahoma Press, 1980.

2756. Marquis, Thomas B. The Cheyennes of Montana. Edited by Thomas D. Weist. Algonac, Michigan: Reference Publications, 1978.

2757. Marriott, Alice, and Carol K. Rachlin. Dance around the Sun: The Life of Mary Little Bear Inkanish, Cheyenne. New York: Thomas Y. Crowell Company, 1977.

2758. Miller, Gene C. "Some Aspects of Cheyenne History with Attention Paid to Commerce." American Indian Journal 3 (March 1977): 2-12.

2759. Powell, Peter J. The Cheyennes, Ma'heo'o's People: A Critical Bibliography. Bloomington: Indiana University Press, 1980.

2760. _____. "They Drew from Power: An Introduction to Northern Cheyenne Ledger Book Art." In Montana: Past and

Present, pp. 1-54. Los Angeles: William Andrews Clark Memorial Library, University of California, Los Angeles, 1976.

2761. Roberts, Gary L. "The Shame of Little Wolf." Montana, the Magazine of Western History 28 (July 1978): 36-47.

2762. Shaw, Virginia. "The End of the Cheyenne-Arapaho Alliance." Red River Valley Historical Review 5 (Winter 1980): 56-73.

2763. Swanson, Evadene Burris. "Friday: Roving Arapaho." Annals of Wyoming 47 (Spring 1975): 59-68.

2764. Thunderbird, Chief (Richard Davis). "Two Boys from El Llano Estacado." Masterkey 50 (April-June 1976): 68-72.

2765. Weist, Tom. A History of the Cheyenne People. Billings, Montana: Montana Council for Indian Education, 1977.

Comanche Indians

2766. Hagan, William T. "Quanah Parker." In American Indian Leaders: Studies in Diversity, edited by R. David Edmunds, pp. 175-191. Lincoln: University of Nebraska Press, 1980.

2767. _____. United States-Comanche Relations: The Reservation Years. New Haven: Yale University Press, 1976.

2768. Jordan, H. Glenn, and Peter MacDonald, Jr. "Quanah Parker: Patriot or Opportunist." In Indian Leaders: Oklahoma's First Statesmen, edited by H. Glenn Jordan and Thomas M. Holm, pp. 158-175. Oklahoma City: Oklahoma Historical Society, 1979.

2769. Lester, Marianne. "Indian Powerhouse." American Home 79 (July 1976): 10-11, 66. LaDonna Harris.

Kiowa Indians

2770. Momaday, N. Scott. The Names. New York: Harper and Row, 1976. Memoir of his early years.

2771. Pate, J'Nell. "Kiowa Defiance: Chiefs Satanta and Satank and the War on the Southern Plains." In Indian Leaders: Oklahoma's First Statesmen, edited by H. Glenn Jordan and Thomas M. Holm, pp. 126-140. Oklahoma City: Oklahoma Historical Society, 1979.

2772. Watkins, T. H. "Chief Satanta, I Presume?" American Heritage 29 (October-November 1978): 66-71.

2773. Worcester, Donald. "Satanta." In American Indian Leaders: Studies in Diversity, edited by R. David Edmunds, pp. 107-130. Lincoln: University of Nebraska Press, 1980.

Osage Indians

2774. Bailey, Garrick. "John Joseph Mathews: Osage, 1894--." In American Indian Intellectuals, edited by Margot Liberty, pp. 205-214. St. Paul: West Publishing Company, 1978.

2775. Burrill, Robert M. "The Osage Pasture Map." Chronicles of Oklahoma 53 (Summer 1975): 204-211.

2776. Liberty, Margot. "Francis La Flesche, the Osage Odyssey: Omaha, 1857-1932." In American Indian Intellectuals, edited by Margot Liberty, pp. 45-59. St. Paul: West Publishing Company, 1978.

2777. Thomas, James. "The Osage Removal to Oklahoma." Chronicles of Oklahoma 55 (Spring 1977): 46-55.

2778. Wilson, Raymond, ed. "Dr. Charles A. Eastman's Report on the Economic Conditions of the Osage Indians in Oklahoma, 1924." Chronicles of Oklahoma 55 (Fall 1977): 343-345.

2779. Wilson, Terry P. "Claremore, the Osage, and the Intrusion of Other Indians, 1800-1824." In Indian Leaders: Oklahoma's First Statesmen, edited by H. Glenn Jordan and Thomas M. Holm, pp. 141-157. Oklahoma City: Oklahoma Historical Society, 1979.

Pawnee Indians

2780. Blaine, Garland James, and Martha Royce Blaine. "Pa-re-su A-ri-ra-ke: The Hunters That Were Massacred." Nebraska History 58 (Fall 1977): 343-358.

2781. Blaine, Martha Royce. The Pawnees: A Critical Bibliography. Bloomington: Indiana University Press, 1980.

2782. Parks, Douglas R. "James R. Murie, Pawnee Ethnographer: Pawnee, 1862-1921." In American Indian Intellectuals, edited by Margot Liberty, pp. 75-89. St. Paul: West Publishing Company, 1978.

2783. Tyson, Carl N. The Pawnee People. Phoenix: Indian Tribal Series, 1976.

2784. Wishart, David J. "The Dispossession of the Pawnee." Annals of the Association of American Geographers 69 (September 1979): 382-401.

Ponca Indians

2785. Cash, Joseph H., and Gerald W. Wolff. The Ponca People. Phoenix: Indian Tribal Series, 1975.

2786. Heerman, Charles E. "The Poncas and Community Control." *Integrated Education* 13 (July 1975): 32-36.

2787. _____. "The Poncas . . . A People in the Process of Becoming." *Journal of American Indian Education* 14 (May 1975): 27-31.

2788. Jacobs, Kenneth Roy. "A History of the Ponca Indians to 1882." Ph.D. dissertation, Texas Tech University, 1977.

Sioux Indians

2789. Anderson, Gary Clayton. "Early Dakota Migration and Intertribal War: A Revision." *Western Historical Quarterly* 11 (January 1980): 17-36.

2790. _____. "The Santee Dakota: A Study in Sovereignty and Economic Dependency." Ph.D. dissertation, University of Toledo, 1978.

2791. Carroll, Peter. "Portrait for a Western Album." *American West* 16 (January-February 1979): 30-31 Black Elk, Lakota Holy Man.

2792. Clow, Richmond L. "The Rosebud Sioux: The Federal Government and the Reservation Years, 1878-1940." Ph.D. dissertation, University of New Mexico, 1977.

2793. _____. "The Sioux Nation and Indian Territory: The Attempted Removal of 1876." *South Dakota History* 6 (Fall 1976): 456-473.

2794. DeMallie, Raymond J. "George Bushotter, the First Lakota Ethnographer: Teton Sioux, 1864-1892." In *American Indian Intellectuals*, edited by Margot Liberty, pp. 91-102. St. Paul: West Publishing Company, 1978.

2795. Eastman, Elaine Goodale. "Pagan Interlude: A New England Woman's Memories of an 1889 Hunting Trip with the Sioux-- and Its Tragic Ending." Edited by Kay Graber. *American West* 15 (March-April 1978): 4-9, 69-71.

2796. Ewers, John C. "Five Strings to His Bow: The Remarkable Career of William (Lone Star) Dietz." *Montana, the Magazine of Western History* 27 (January 1977): 2-13.

2797. Feaver, George. "Vine Deloria." *Encounter* 44 (April 1975): 33-46.

2798. Fielder, Mildred. *Sioux Indian Leaders*. Seattle: Superior Publishing Company, 1975.

2799. Hanson, James Austin. *Metal Weapons, Tools, and Ornaments of the Teton Dakota Indians*. Lincoln: University of Nebraska Press, 1975.

2800. Hinman, Eleanor H. "Oglala Sources on the Life of Crazy Horse." *Nebraska History* 57 (Spring 1976): 1-51.

2801. Hoover, Herbert T. *The Sioux: A Critical Bibliography*. Bloomington: Indiana University Press, 1979.

2802. _____. "Sitting Bull." In *American Indian Leaders: Studies in Diversity*, edited by R. David Edmunds, pp. 152-174. Lincoln: University of Nebraska Press, 1980.

2803. _____. "Yankton Sioux Experience in the 'Great Indian Depression,' 1900-1930." In *The American West: Essays in Honor of W. Eugene Hollon*, edited by Ronald Lora, pp. 53-71. Toledo: University of Toledo, 1980.

2804. Jacobson, Clair. "A History of the Yanktonai and Hunkpatina Sioux." *North Dakota History* 47 (Winter 1980): 4-24.

2805. *The Killing of Chief Crazy Horse: Three Eyewitness Views*. Commentary by Carroll Friswold. Edited, with introduction, by Robert A. Clark. Glendale, California: Arthur H. Clark Company, 1976.

2806. Lawrence, Elizabeth. "Sitting Bull and Custer." *By Valor and Arms* 1 (Summer 1975): 13-29.

2807. Lawson, Michael L. "The Oahe Dam and the Standing Rock Sioux." *South Dakota History* 6 (Spring 1976): 203-228.

2808. Lewis, T. H. "The Changing Practice of the Oglala Medicine Man." *Plains Anthropologist* 25 (August 1980): 265-267.

2809. Mails, Thomas E., assisted by Dallas Chief Eagle. *Fools Crow*. New York: Doubleday and Company, 1979. Memoirs of Frank Fools Crow.

2810. Marken, Jack W., and Herbert T. Hoover. *Bibliography of the Sioux*. Metuchen, New Jersey: Scarecrow Press, 1980.

2811. Miller, David Reed. "Charles Alexander Eastman, the 'Winner': From Deep Woods to Civilization: Santee Sioux, 1858-1939." In *American Indian Intellectuals*, edited by Margot Liberty, pp. 61-73. St. Paul: West Publishing Company, 1978.

2812. Milligan, Edward A. *Dakota Twilight: The Standing Rock Sioux, 1874-1890*. Hicksville, New York: Exposition Press, 1976.

2814. Ortiz, Roxanne Dunbar, ed. *The Great Sioux Nation: Sitting in Judgment* on America. New York: American Indian Treaty Council Information Center, and Berkeley, California: Moon Books, 1977.

2815. Rothstein, David. "Intergroup Contact and Socio-Cultural Change." Ph.D. dissertation, University of Oregon, 1976. History of white-Teton Sioux contact, 1800-1910.

2816. Schusky, Ernest L. The Forgotten Sioux: An Ethnohistory of the Lower Brule Reservation. Chicago: Nelson-Hall, 1975.

2817. Sneve, Virginia Driving Hawk. They Led a Nation. Edited by N. Jane Hunt. Portraits by Loren Zephier. Sioux Falls, South Dakota: Brevet Press, 1975.

2818. Stanley, George F. G. "Displaced Red Men: The Sioux in Canada." In One Century Later: Western Canadian Reserve Indians since Treaty 7, edited by Ian A. L. Getty and Donald B. Smith, pp. 55-81. Vancouver: University of British Columbia Press, 1978.

2819. Stensland, Anna Lee. "Charles Alexander Eastman: Sioux Storyteller and Historian." American Indian Quarterly 3 (Autumn 1977): 199-208.

2820. Taylor, Allan R. "Note Concerning Lakota Sioux Terms for White and Negro." Plains Anthropologist 21 (February 1976): 63-65.

2821. White, Richard. "The Winning of the West: The Expansion of the Western Sioux in the Eighteenth and Nineteenth Centuries." Journal of American History 65 (September 1978): 319-343.

2822. Wilson, Raymond. "Dr. Charles Alexander Eastman (Ohiyesa), Santee Sioux." Ph.D. dissertation, University of New Mexico, 1977.

2823. _____. "The Writings of Ohiyesa--Charles Alexander Eastman, M.D., Santee Sioux." South Dakota History 6 (Winter 1975): 55-73.

2824. Wozniak, John S. Contact, Negotiation and Conflict: An Ethnohistory of the Eastern Dakota, 1819-1839. Washington: University Press of America, 1978.

INDIANS OF THE SOUTHWEST

General and Miscellaneous Studies

2825. Alison, Kathy. "Life among the Papago." Arizona Highways 51 (September 1975): 4-10.

2826. Blaine, Peter, Sr., as told to

Michael S. Adams. "Pete Blaine Goes to Washington." Journal of Arizona History 21 (Summer 1980): 189-208.

2827. Brewer, Sam Aaron, Jr. "The Yaqui Indians of Arizona: Trilingualism and Cultural Change." Ph.D. dissertation, University of Texas at Austin, 1976.

2828. Bronson, Leisa. "The Long Walk of the Yavapai." Wassaja/The Indian Historian 13 (March 1980): 37-43.

2829. Conrad, David E. "Whipple at Zuni." In The American West: Essays in Honor of W. Eugene Hollon, edited by Ronald Lora, pp. 25-51. Toledo: University of Toledo, 1980. Amiel Weeks Whipple.

2830. Crampton, C. Gregory. The Zunis of Cibola. Salt Lake City: University of Utah Press, 1977.

2831. Culp, Georgia Laird. "The Chemehuevis." Desert Magazine 38 (March 1975): 18-21, 38.

2832. Dobyns, Henry F., and Robert C. Euler. Indians of the Southwest: A Critical Bibliography. Bloomington: Indiana University Press, 1980.

2833. _____. The Walapai People. Phoenix: Indian Tribal Series, 1976.

2834. Dutton, Bertha P. Indians of the American Southwest. Englewood Cliffs, New Jersey: Prentice-Hall, 1975.

2835. Euler, Robert C. "The Havasupai of the Grand Canyon." American West 16 (May-June 1979): 12-17, 65.

2836. Henrick, Hilton, and James St. Leger. "The Pima River of Life." Aging, Nos. 263-264 (September-October 1976): 13-17.

2837. Hirst, Stephen. Life in a Narrow Place. Photographs by Terry and Lynthia Eiler. New York: David McKay Company, 1976. Havasupai Indians of the Grand Canyon.

2838. Iverson, Peter. "Carlos Montezuma." In American Indian Leaders: Studies in Diversity, edited by R. David Edmunds, pp. 206-220. Lincoln: University of Nebraska Press, 1980.

2839. Kelley, Jane Holden. Yaqui Women: Contemporary Life Histories. Lincoln: University of Nebraska Press, 1978.

2840. Laird, W. David. Hopi Bibliography: Comprehensive and Annotated. Tucson: University of Arizona Press, 1977.

2841. Lamb, Neven P. "Papago Indian

Admixture and Mating Patterns in a Mining Town: A Genetic Cauldron." *American Journal of Physical Anthropology* 42 (January 1975): 71-79.

2842. Ortiz, Alfonso, ed. *Southwest*. Volume 9 of *Handbook of North American Indians*, edited by William C. Sturtevant. Washington: Smithsonian Institution, 1979.

2843. Page, James K., Jr. "A Rare Glimpse into the Evolving Way of the Hopi." *Smithsonian* 6 (November 1975): 90-94, 96-101.

2844. Pandey, Triloki Nath. "Flora Zuni-- A Portrait: Zuni, 1897. In *American Indian Intellectuals*, edited by Margot Liberty, pp. 217-225. St. Paul: West Publishing Company, 1978.

2845. Roth, George Edwin. "Incorporation and Changes in Ethnic Structure: The Chemehuevi Indians." Ph.D. dissertation, Northwestern University, 1976.

2846. Spicer, Edward H. *The Yaquis: A Cultural History*. Tucson: University of Arizona Press, 1980.

2847. Yava, Albert. *Big Falling Snow: A Tewa-Hopi Indian's Life and Times and the History and Traditions of His People*. Edited by Harold Courlander. New York: Crown Publishers, 1978.

Apache Indians

2848. Ball, Eve, with Nora Henn and Lynda Sanchez. *Indeh: An Apache Odyssey*. Provo, Utah: Brigham Young University Press, 1980.

2849. Brown, Dee. "Geronimo." *American History Illustrated* 15 (June 1980): 12-20; (July 1980): 36-45.

2850. Debo, Angie. "Apaches as Southeastern Indians." In *Indians of the Lower South: Past and Present*, edited by John K. Mahon, pp. 143-158. Pensacola: Gulf Coast History and Humanities Conference, 1975.

2851. _____. *Geronimo: The Man, His Time, His Place*. Norman: University of Oklahoma Press, 1976.

2852. Dubois, Betty Lou. "The Mescalero Apache." *Journal of American Indian Education* 15 (May 1976): 22-27.

2853. Kessel, William Burkhardt. "White Mountain Apache Religious Cult Movements: A Study in Ethnohistory." Ph.D. dissertation, University of Arizona, 1976.

2854. Locke, Raymond Friday. "Apaches, the Children of Cochise." *Mankind* 6

(November 1979): 8-13, 42-44.

2855. Melody, Michael Edward. *The Apaches: A Critical Bibliography*. Bloomington: Indiana University Press, 1977.

2856. Myres, Sandra L. "The Apaches." In *Forked Tongues and Broken Treaties*, edited by Donald E. Worcester, pp. 383-423. Caldwell, Idaho: Caxton Printers, 1975.

2857. Opler, Morris E. "Applied Anthropology and the Apaches." *Papers in Anthropology* 16 (Fall 1975): 1-77.

2858. _____. "The Indian Consolidation Policy and the Chiricahua Apache." *Papers in Anthropology* 17 (Spring 1976): 43-50.

2859. Thrapp, Dan L. "Cochise." *Arizona Highways* 54 (October 1978): 38-46.

2860. _____. "A Man Called Geronimo.' *Arizona Highways* 52 (May 1976): 2-11.

2861. Tiller, Veronica Velarde. "A History of the Jicarilla Apache Tribe." Ph.D. dissertation, University of New Mexico, 1976.

2862. Turcheneske, John Anthony, Jr. "Disaster at White Tail: The Fort Sill Apaches' First Ten Years at Mescalero, 1913-1923." *New Mexico Historical Review* 53 (April 1978): 109-132.

2863. _____. "'It Is Right That They Should Set Us Free': The Role of the War and Interior Departments in the Release of the Apache Prisoners of War, 1909-1913." *Red River Valley Historical Review* 4 (Summer 1979): 4-32.

2864. Worcester, Donald E. *The Apaches: Eagles of the Southwest*. Norman: University of Oklahoma Press, 1979.

2865. _____. "The Apaches in the History of the Southwest." *New Mexico Historical Review* 50 (January 1975): 25-44.

Navajo Indians

2866. Adams, William Y., and Lorraine T. Ruffing. "Shonto Revisited: Measures of Social and Economic Change in a Navajo Community, 1955-1971." *American Anthropologist* 79 (March 1977): 58-83.

2867. Ashley, Yvonne. "'That's the Way We Were Raised': An Oral Interview with Ada Damon." *Frontiers, a Journal of Women Studies* 2 (Summer 1977): 59-62.

2868. Benally, Clyde J. "The Navajos."

In The Peoples of Utah, edited by Helen Z. Papanikolas, pp. 13-27. Salt Lake City: Utah State Historical Society, 1976.

2869. Blanchard, Kendall A. The Economics of Sainthood: Religious Change among the Rimrock Navajos. Rutherford, New Jersey: Fairleigh Dickinson University Press, 1977.

2870. Conn, Stephen. "Mid-Passage--The Navajo Tribe and Its First Legal Revolution." American Indian Law Review 6 (No. 2, 1978): 329-370.

2871. Correll, J. Lee. Through White Men's Eyes, a Contribution to Navajo History: A Chronological Record of the Navajo People from Earliest Times to the Treaty of June 1, 1868. Window Rock, Arizona: Navajo Heritage Center, 1976.

2872. DesGeorge, Herbert E. "The Long Walk." Rio Grande History, No. 10 (1979): 17-20.

2873. Dresner, Stewart. "Lonely Navajo Indians." Geographical Magazine 50 (December 1977): 200-207.

2874. George, Barbara D. "The Navajos in a Complex Society." Journal of American Indian Education 18 (January 1979): 15-22.

2875. Iverson, Peter James. "The Evolving Navajo Nation: Dine Continuity within Change." Ph.D. dissertation, University of Wisconsin-Madison, 1975.

2876. _____. The Navajos: A Critical Bibliography. Bloomington: Indiana University Press, 1976.

2877. _____. "Peter MacDonald." In American Indian Leaders: Studies in Diversity, edited by R. David Edmunds, pp. 222-241. Lincoln: University of Nebraska Press, 1980.

2878. Kunitz, Stephen J., and John C. Slocumb. "The Changing Sex Ratio of the Navajo Tribe." Social Biology 23 (Spring 1976): 33-44.

2879. Laughter, Albert. "Navajo Ranger Interprets: Our People, Our Past." National Geographic 156 (July 1979): 80-85.

2880. Light, Ronald, and Bradley Henio. "The Role of Media in Ramah Navajo Society." Audiovisual Instruction 22 (December 1977): 10-12.

2881. Locke, Raymond Friday. The Book of the Navajo. Los Angeles: Mankind Publishing Company, 1976.

2882. Magers, Pamela Carroll. "Navajo

Settlement in Canyon del Muerto." Ph.D. dissertation, University of Arizona, 1976.

2883. Mitchell, Frank. Navajo Blessingway Singer: The Autobiography of Frank Mitchell, 1881-1967. Edited by Charlotte J. Frisbie and David P. McAllester. Tucson: University of Arizona Press, 1978.

2884. Parman, Donald L. The Navajos and the New Deal. New Haven: Yale University Press, 1976.

2885. Rada, Stephen Edward. "An Analysis of KTDB-FM Ramah Navajo Radio." Ph.D. dissertation, University of Texas at Austin, 1976.

2886. Trafzer, Clifford E. "Sam Day and His Boys: Good Neighbors to the Navajos." Journal of Arizona History 18 (Spring 1977): 1-22.

2887. United States Commission on Civil Rights. The Navajo Nation: An American Colony. Report written by Carol J. McCabe and Hester Lewis. Washington, 1975.

2888. Ward, Albert E., and David M. Brugge. "Changing Contemporary Navajo Burial Practice and Values." Plateau 48 (Summer 1975): 31-42.

2889. Wilson, Raymond. "Establishing Canyon de Chelly National Monument: A Study in Navajo and Government Relations." New Mexico Historical Review 51 (April 1976): 109-120.

2890. Wyckoff, Theodore. "The Navajo Nation Tomorrow--51st State, Commonwealth, or . . . ?" American Indian Law Review 5 (No. 2, 1977): 267-297.

2891. Young, Robert W. A Political History of the Navajo Tribe. Tsaile, Arizona: Navajo Community College Press, 1978.

Pueblo Indians

2892. Erdoes, Richard. The Rain Dance People: The Pueblo Indians, Their Past and Present. New York: Alfred A. Knopf, 1976.

2893. Frost, Richard H. "The Romantic Inflation of Pueblo Culture." American West 17 (January-February 1980): 5-9, 56-60.

2894. McCluney, Eugene B. "The Eastern Pueblos." In Forked Tongues and Broken Treaties, edited by Donald E. Worcester, pp. 425-448. Caldwell, Idaho: Caxton Printers, 1975.

2895. Minge, Ward Alan. Acoma: Pueblo in

the Sky. Albuquerque: University of
New Mexico Press, 1976.

2896. Sando, Joe S. The Pueblo Indians.
San Francisco: Indian Historian Press,
1976.

2897. Scott, Sandy. "Margaret Garnaat,
Pueblo Librarian: 'Just Learning Things
Day by Day.'" American Libraries 7
(June 1976): 378-379.

CALIFORNIA INDIANS

2898. Bachtold, Louise M. "Hupa Indians:
An Historical Perspective." Children
Today 7 (November-December 1978): 23-26.

2899. Bean, Lowell John. "Morongo Indian
Reservation: A Century of Adaptive
Strategies." In American Indian Economic
Development, edited by Sam Stanley, pp.
159-236. The Hague: Mouton Publishers,
1978.

2900. Bean, Lowell John, and Sylvia Brakke
Vane. California Indians, Primary Resources: A Guide to Manuscripts, Artifacts, Documents, Serials, Music and Il-
lustrations. Ramona, California: Ballena Press, 1977.

2901. Bidwell, Annie E. K. Rancho Chico
Indians. Edited by Dorothy J. Hill.
Chico, California: Bidwell Mansion Co-
operating Association, 1980.

2902. Burrows, Jack. "Walker." American
West 16 (May-June 1979): 40-45, 70-71.
Biography of a Miwok Indian.

2903. Campbell, C. W. "The Wild Man of
Oroville." American History Illustrated
12 (June 1977): 18-27. Ishi.

2904. Carrico, Richard L. "San Diego
Indians and the Federal Government: Years
of Neglect, 1850-1865." Journal of San
Diego History 26 (Summer 1980): 164-184.

2905. Castillo, Ed. "Petition to Congress
on Behalf of the Yosemite Indians."
Journal of California Anthropology 5
(Winter 1978): 271-277.

2906. Coffer, William E. "Genocide among
the California Indians." Indian Historian
10 (Spring 1977): 8-15.

2907. Cook, Sherburne F. The Conflict
between the California Indian and White
Civilization. Berkeley: University of
California Press, 1976. Reprint of
Ibero-Americana series.

2908. Costo, Rupert. "Erros Multiply in
Smithsonian Handbook on California."
Indian Historian 12 (No. 3, 1979): 2-5.

2909. Cummins, Marjorie W. The Tache-

Yokuts, Indians of the San Joaquin
Valley: Their Lives, Songs, and Stories.
Second edition, revised. Fresno, Cali-
fornia: Pioneer Publishing Company, 1979.

2910. Day, R. Morris. "The Dissident
Chief." In Forked Tongues and Broken
Treaties, edited by Donald E. Worcester,
pp. 329-352. Caldwell, Idaho: Caxton
Printers, 1975. Modoc Indians.

2911. Faulk, Odie B. The Modoc People.
Phoenix: Indian Tribal Series, 1976.

2912. Frazer, Robert W., ed. "Lovell's
Report on the Cahuilla Indians, 1854."
Journal of San Diego History 22 (Win-
ter 1976): 4-10. Christopher S. Lovell.

2913. Garner, Van Hastings. "The Treaty
of Guadalupe Hidalgo and the California
Indians." Indian Historian 9 (Winter
1976): 10-13.

2914. Guest, Francis F. "An Examination
of the Thesis of S. F. Cook on the
Forced Conversion of Indians in the
California Missions." Southern California Quarterly 61 (Spring 1979): 1-77.

2915. Heizer, Robert F. The Indians of
California: A Critical Bibliography.
Bloomington: Indiana University Press,
1976.

2916. Heizer, Robert F., ed. California.
Volume 8 of Handbook of North American
Indians, edited by William C. Sturtevant. Washington: Smithsonian Institution, 1978.

2917. _____. Some Last Century Accounts
of the Indians of Southern California.
Ramona, California: Ballena Press, 1976.

2918. Heizer, Robert F., and Albert B.
Elsasser. A Bibliography of California
Indians: Archaeology, Ethnography,
Indian History. New York: Garland
Publishing, 1977.

2919. _____. The Natural World of
the California Indians. Berkeley:
University of California Press, 1980.

2920. Heizer, Robert F., and Alfred L.
Kroeber. "For Sale: California at 47
Cents per Acre." Journal of California
Anthropology 3 (Winter 1976): 38-65.
Testimony before the Indian Claims Com-
mission in 1946.

2921. Heizer, Robert F., and Theodora
Kroeber, eds. Ishi, the Last Yaki: A
Documentary History. Berkeley: Uni-
versity of California Press, 1979.

2922. Heizer, Robert F., Karen M. Nissen,
and Edward D. Castillo. California
Indian History: A Classified and Annotated Guide to Source Materials.

Ramona, California: Ballena Press, 1975.

2923. Hill, Dorothy. The Indians of Chico Rancheria. Sacramento: California Department of Parks and Recreation, 1978.

2924. Hoover, Robert Linville. "Ethnohistoric Salinan Acculturation." Ethnohistory 24 (Summer 1977): 261-268.

2925. Kroeber, Theodora. Ishi in Two Worlds: A Biography of the Last Wild Indian in North America. Deluxe illustrated edition. Berkeley: University of California Press, 1976.

2926. Miller, Virginia P. Ukomno'm: The Yuki Indians of Northern California. Socorro, New Mexico: Ballena Press, 1979.

2927. _____. "Whatever Happened to the Yuki?" Indian Historian 8 (Fall 1975): 6-12.

2928. Norton, Jack. When Our Worlds Cried: Genocide in Northwestern California. San Francisco: Indian Historian Press, 1979.

2929. Oandasan, William. Bibliography of the Tribe of the Covelo Indian Community in Round Valley of Northern California and Related Topics. Occasional Papers Series, No. 3. Chicago: Newberry Library Center for the History of the American Indian, 1980.

2930. Peterson, Robert M. A Case Study of a Northern California Indian Tribe: Cultural Change to 1860. San Francisco: R and E Research Associates, 1977. Nisenan Indians.

2931. Phillips, George Harwood. Chiefs and Challengers: Indian Resistance and Cooperation in Southern California. Berkeley: University of California Press, 1975.

2932. Powers, Stephen. The Northern California Indians. Edited by Robert F. Heizer. Berkeley: University of California, Department of Anthropology, 1975. Articles originally published in 1872-1877.

2933. Rawls, James J. "Gold Diggers: Indian Miners in the California Gold Rush." California Historical Quarterly 55 (Spring 1976): 28-45.

2934. Roth, George. "The Calloway Affair of 1880: Chemehuevi Adaptation and Chemehuevi-Mohave Relations." Journal of California Anthropology 4 (Winter 1977): 273-286.

2935. Weber, Francis J., ed. "Rumblings at Pala." Journal of San Diego History 21 (Fall 1975): 38-42. Report of Charles

Maltby, Superintendent of Indian Affairs for California, concerning troubles among mission Indians at Temecula in 1866.

2936. Young, Lucy. "Lucy's Story." Family Heritage 1 (October 1978): 146-151. Memoirs of a Wylackie Indian.

BASIN-PLATEAU INDIANS

2937. Anderson, Irving W. "Sacajawea, Sacagawea, Sakakawea?" South Dakota History 8 (Fall 1978): 303-311.

2938. Bluth, John Frederick. "Confrontation with an Arid Land: The Incursion of Gosiutes and Whites into Utah's Central West Desert, 1800-1978." Ph.D. dissertation, Brigham Young University, 1978.

2939. Cairns, Robert. "The Changing Times of the Northern Utes." Orange Disc 22 (May-June 1976): 20-25.

2940. Chuinard, E. G. "The Actual Role of the Bird Woman: Purposeful Member of the Corps or Casual 'Tag Along'?" Montana, the Magazine of Western History 26 (July 1976): 18-29.

2941. Clark, Ella E., and Margot Edmonds. Sacagawea of the Lewis and Clark Expedition. Berkeley: University of California Press, 1979.

2942. Collins, Thomas W. "Behavioral Change and Ethnic Maintenance among the Northern Ute: Some Political Considerations." In The New Ethnicity: Perspectives from Ethnology, edited by John W. Bennett, pp. 59-74. St. Paul: West Publishing Company, 1975.

2943. Deloria, Vine, Jr. "The Western Shoshones." American Indian Journal 2 (January 1976): 16-20.

2944. Fowler, Catherine S. "Sarah Winnemucca, Northern Paiute, ca. 1844-1891." In American Indian Intellectuals, edited by Margot Liberty, pp. 33-42. St. Paul: West Publishing Company, 1978.

2945. Gehm, Katherine. Sarah Winnemucca: Most Extraordinary Woman of the Paiute Nation. Phoenix: O'Sullivan, Woodside and Company, 1975.

2946. Johnson, Edward C. Walker-River Paiutes: A Tribal History. Schurz, Nevada: Walker River Paiute Tribe, 1975.

2947. Johnson, Thomas Hoevet. "The Enos Family and Wind River Shoshone Society: A Historical Analysis." Ph.D. dissertation, University of Illinois at Urbana-Champaign, 1975.

2948. Laudenschlager, David D. "The Utes in South Dakota, 1906-1908." South Dakota History 9 (Summer 1979): 233-247.

2949. Lynch, Robert N. "Cowboys and Indians: An Ethnohistorical Portrait of Indian-White Relations on Ranches in Western Nevada." In Selected Papers from the 14th Great Basin Anthropological Conference, edited by Donald R. Tuohy, pp. 51-57. Socorro, New Mexico, 1978.

2950. Madsen, Brigham D. The Lemhi: Sacajawea's People. Caldwell, Idaho: Caxton Printers, 1979.

2951. Morrison, Dorothy Nafus. Chief Sarah: Sarah Winnemucca's Fight for Indian Rights. New York: Atheneum, 1980.

2952. O'Neil, Floyd A. "The Utes, Southern Paiutes, and Gosiutes." In The Peoples of Utah, edited by Helen Z. Papanikolas, pp. 27-59. Salt Lake City: Utah State Historical Society, 1976.

2953. Richey, Elinor. "Sagebrush Princess with a Cause: Sarah Winnemucca." American West 12 (November 1975): 30-33, 57-63.

2954. Schroer, Blanche. "Boat-Pusher or Bird Woman? Sacagawea or Sacajawea?" Annals of Wyoming 52 (Spring 1980): 46-54.

2955. "Shoshone-Bannock." Idaho Heritage, October 1977, pp. 40-47. Includes brief articles by Mark N. Trahant, Clyde A. Hall, Alan Abromowitz, and Anna Lee Townsend.

2956. "Shoshone-Paiute." Idaho Heritage, October 1977, pp. 29-32. Statements by Thurman Welbourne and Anna Primo.

2957. Stoffle, Richard W., and Michael J. Evans. "Resource Competition and Population Change: A Kaibab Paiute Ethnohistorical Case." Ethnohistory 23 (Spring 1976): 173-197.

2958. Wright, Peter M. "Washakie." In American Indian Leaders: Studies in Diversity, edited by R. David Edmunds, pp. 131-151. Lincoln: University of Nebraska Press, 1980.

INDIANS OF THE PACIFIC NORTHWEST AND ALASKA

2959. Ackerman, Robert E. The Kenaitze People. Phoenix: Indian Tribal Series, 1975.

2960. "Alaska: Historical Summary." American Indian Journal 3 (May 1977): 2-6.

2961. "Alaska Native Villages." American Indian Journal 3 (May 1977): 7-9.

2962. Allard, William Albert. "Chief Joseph." National Geographic 151 (March 1977): 408-434.

2963. Bartlett, Grace. "Ollokot and Joseph." Idaho Yesterdays 21 (Spring 1977): 22-30.

2964. Beckman, Stephen Dow. The Indians of Western Oregon: This Land Was Theirs. Coos Bay, Oregon: Arago Books, 1977.

2965. Blinman, Eric, Elizabeth Colson, and Robert Heizer. "A Makah Epic Journey: Oral History and Documentary Sources." Pacific Northwest Quarterly 68 (October 1977): 153-163.

2966. Boyer, David S. "Warm Springs Indians Carve Out a Future." National Geographic 155 (April 1979): 494-505.

2967. Brown, Ellsworth Howard. "The History of the Flathead Indians in the Nineteenth Century." Ph.D. dissertation, Michigan State University, 1975.

2968. Cox, Thomas R. "Tribal Leadership in Transition: Chief Peter Moctelme of the Coeur d'Alenes." Idaho Yesterdays 23 (Spring 1979): 2-9.

2969. Day, R. Morris. "Thief Treaties and Lie-Talk Councils." In Forked Tongues and Broken Treaties, edited by Donald E. Worcester, pp. 354-381. Caldwell, Idaho: Caxton Printers, 1975.

2970. Deloria, Vine, Jr. Indians of the Pacific Northwest from the Coming of the White Man to the Present Day. Garden City, New York: Doubleday and Company, 1977.

2971. _____. "The Lummi Indian Community: The Fishermen of the Pacific Northwest." In American Indian Economic Development, edited by Sam Stanley, pp. 87-158. The Hague: Mouton Publishers, 1978.

2972. Drury, Clifford M. Chief Lawyer of the Nez Perce Indians, 1796-1876. Glendale, California: Arthur H. Clark Company, 1979.

2973. _____. "Lawyer, Head Chief of the Nez Perce, 1848-1875." Idaho Yesterdays 22 (Winter 1979): 2-12.

2974. Faust, Richard. "Native Peoples of the Pacific Basin: An Ethnographic Setting." Journal of the West 15 (April 1976): 15-32.

2975. Fisher, Robin. "Arms and Men on the Northwest Coast, 1774-1825." BC Studies, No. 29 (Spring 1976): 3-18.

2976. Geoffroy, William T. "Coeur d'Alene."

Idaho Heritage, October 1977, pp. 36-37. Includes interview with Bernard LaSarte, tribal chairman.

2977. Grumet, Robert Steven. *Native Americans of the Northwest Coast: A Critical Bibliography*. Bloomington: Indiana University Press, 1979.

2978. Gunkel, Alexander. "Culture in Conflict: A Study of Contrasted Interrelations and Reactions between Euroamericans and the Wallawalla Indians of Washington State." Ph.D. dissertation, Southern Illinois University at Carbondale, 1978.

2979. Halpin, Marjorie Myers. "William Beynon, Ethnographer: Tsimshian, 1888-1958." In *American Indian Intellectuals*, edited by Margot Liberty, pp. 141-156. St. Paul: West Publishing Company, 1978.

2980. Hays, H. R. *Children of the Raven: The Seven Indian Nations of the Northwest Coast*. New York: McGraw-Hill, 1975.

2981. Hinckley, Ted C. "'We Are More Truly Heathen Than the Natives': John G. Brady and the Assimilation of Alaska's Tlingit Indians." *Western Historical Quarterly* 11 (January 1980): 37-55.

2982. Jones, Dorothy M. "Strategy Straddling: A Community Organization Dilemma in an Alaskan Native Village." *Human Organization* 36 (Spring 1977): 22-33.

2983. Klein, Laura Frances. "Tlingit Women and Town Politics." Ph.D. dissertation, New York University, 1975.

2984. "Kootenai." *Idaho Heritage*, October 1977, pp. 33-35. Includes interview with Joe Mathias and brief articles by Josephine Shottanana and Margaret Friedlander.

2985. Nadeau, Josephine E. "Ripon: Ethnic and General Development." *Pacific Historian* 19 (Winter 1975): 385-394. Yokut Indians.

2986. "Nez Perces." *Idaho Heritage*, October 1977, pp. 24-28. Contains material by Allen Slickpoo and Richard Ellenwood.

2987. Patton, Robert T., Elizabeth C. Patton, and Sandra Cultee. "Where Are the Lummi Management Graduates Today?" *American Indian Journal* 1 (October 1975): 8-11.

2988. Powell, Jay, and Vickie Jensen. *Quileute: An Introduction to the Indians of La Push*. Seattle: University of Washington Press, 1976.

2989. Roberts, Natalie Andrea. "A History of the Swinomish Tribal Community." Ph.D. dissertation, University of Washington, 1975.

2990. Ruby, Robert H., and John A. Brown. *The Chinook Indians: Traders of the Lower Columbia River*. Norman: University of Oklahoma Press, 1976.

2991. _____. *Myron Eells and the Puget Sound Indians*. Seattle: Superior Publishing Company, 1976.

2992. Schneider, William Samuel. "Beaver, Alaska: The Story of a Multi-Ethnic Community." Ph.D. dissertation, Bryn Mawr College, 1976.

2993. Schuster, Helen Hersh. "Yakima Indian Traditionalism: A Study in Continuity and Change." Ph.D. dissertation, University of Washington, 1975.

2994. Thompson, Albert W. "Coeur d'Alene: The Names Applied to Tribe and Lake." *Idaho Yesterdays* 21 (Winter 1978): 11-28.

2995. Townsend, Joan B. "Mercantilism and Societal Change: An Ethnohistoric Examination of Some Essential Variables." *Ethnohistory* 22 (Winter 1975): 21-32. Russian-American Company mercantilism in Alaska.

2996. Walker, Deward E., Jr. *Indians of Idaho*. Moscow: University Press of Idaho, 1978.

2997. White, Richard. "Indian Land Use and Environmental Change, Island County, Washington: A Case Study." *Arizona and the West* 17 (Winter 1975): 327-338.

2998. Woodcock, George. *Peoples of the Coast: The Indians of the Pacific Northwest*. Bloomington: Indiana University Press, 1977.

INDIAN BIOGRAPHY

Listed here are publications that provide biographies of more than one Indian. Individual Indian biographies are listed under appropriate tribes or regions.

2999. Capps, Benjamin. *The Great Chiefs*. New York: Time-Life Books, 1975.

3000. Churchill, Ward, Norbert S. Hill, Jr., and Mary Jo Barlow. "An Historical Overview of Twentieth Century Native American Athletics." *Indian Historian* 12 (No. 4, 1979): 22-32.

3001. *Dictionary of Indians of North America*. 3 volumes. St. Clair Shores, Michigan: Scholarly Press, 1980.

3002. Dockstader, Frederick J. *Great North American Indians: Profiles in Life and Leadership*. New York: Van Nostrand Reinhold Company, 1977.

3003. Edmunds, R. David, ed. American Indian Leaders: Studies in Diversity. Lincoln: University of Nebraska Press, 1980.

3004. Jordan, H. Glenn, and Thomas M. Holm, eds. Indian Leaders: Oklahoma's First Statesmen. Oklahoma City: Oklahoma Historical Society, 1979.

3005. Liberty, Margot, ed. American Indian Intellectuals. 1976 Proceedings of the American Ethnological Society. St. Paul: West Publishing Company, 1978.

3006. Smith, William F., Jr. "American Indian Autobiographies." American Indian Quarterly 2 (Autumn 1975): 237-245.

OTHER TOPICS

Demography

3007. Cook, Sherburne F. The Indian Population of New England in the Seventeenth Century. Berkeley: University of California Press, 1976.

3008. _____. The Population of the California Indians, 1769-1970. Foreword by Woodrow Borah and Robert F. Heizer. Berkeley: University of California Press, 1976.

3009. Crosby, Alfred W. "Virgin Soil Epidemics as a Factor in the Aboriginal Depopulation in America." William and Mary Quarterly, 3d series 33 (April 1976): 289-299.

3010. Denevan, William M., ed. The Native Population of the Americas in 1492. Madison: University of Wisconsin Press, 1976.

3011. Dobyns, Henry F. "The Decline of Mescalero Apache Indian Population from 1873 to 1913." Papers in Anthropology 18 (Fall 1977): 61-69.

3012. _____. Native American Historical Demography: A Critical Bibliography. Bloomington: Indiana University Press, 1976.

3013. Doran, Michael F. "Population Statistics of Nineteenth Century Indian Territory." Chronicles of Oklahoma 53 (Winter 1975-1976): 492-515.

3014. Gundlach, James Howard. "The Transition of Native American Indian Fertility: 1960 to 1970." Ph.D. dissertation, University of Texas at Austin, 1976.

3015. Johansson, S. Ryan, and S. H. Preston. "Tribal Demography: The Hopi and Navaho Population As Seen through Manuscripts

from the 1900 U.S. Census." Social Science History 3 (Fall 1978): 1-33.

3016. Liberty, Margot. "Population Trends among Present-Day Omaha Indians." Plains Anthropologist 20 (August 1976): 225-230.

3017. Martin, Calvin. "Wildlife Diseases as a Factor in the Depopulation of the North American Indian." Western Historical Quarterly 7 (January 1976): 47-62.

3018. Meister, Cary W. "Demographic Consequences of Euro-American Contact of Selected American Indian Populations and Their Relationship to the Demographic Transition." Ethnohistory 23 (Spring 1976): 161-172.

3019. _____. "The Misleading Nature of Data in the Bureau of the Census Subject Report on 1970 American Indian Population." Indian Historian 11 (December 1978): 12-19.

3020. Passel, Jeffrey S. "Provisional Evaluation of the 1970 Census Count of American Indians." Demography 13 (August 1976): 397-409.

3021. Posey, Darrell A. "Entomological Considerations in Southeastern Aboriginal Demography." Ethnohistory 23 (Spring 1976): 147-160.

3022. Rogers, C. Jean, and Teresa E. Gallion. "Characteristics of Elderly Pueblo Indians in New Mexico." Gerontologists 18 (October, part 1, 1978): 482-487.

3023. Smith, David G. "Effect of Emigration on the Structure and Growth of a Southwestern Indian Reservation Population." Social Biology 23 (Spring 1976): 21-32.

3024. Stanley, Sam, and Robert K. Thomas. "Current Demographic and Social Trends among North American Indians." Annals of the American Academy of Political and Social Science 436 (March 1978): 111-120.

3025. Thornton, Russell. "Implications of Catlin's American Indian Population Estimates for Revision of Mooney's Estimate." American Journal of Physical Anthropology 49 (July 1978): 11-13.

3026. Ubelaker, Douglas H. "The Sources and Methodology for Mooney's Estimates of North American Indian Populations." In The Native Population of the Americas in 1492, edited by William M. Denevan, pp. 243-288. Madison: University of Wisconsin Press, 1976.

Indian Women

3027. Blicksilver, Edith. "Traditionalism vs. Modernity: Leslie Silko on American Indian Women." *Southwest Review* 64 (Spring 1979): 149-160.

3028. Dalsimer, Marlyn Hartzell. "Women and Family in the Oneida Community, 1837-1881." Ph.D. dissertation, New York University, 1975.

3029. Hanson, Wynne. "The Urban Indian Woman and Her Family." *Social Casework* 61 (October 1980): 476-483.

3030. Kidwell, Clara Sue. "The Power of Women in Three American Indian Societies." *Journal of Ethnic Studies* 6 (Fall 1978): 113-121.

3031. Mathes, Valerie Sherer. "A New Look at the Role of Women in Indian Society." *American Indian Quarterly* 2 (Summer 1975): 131-139.

3032. Medicine, Beatrice. "The Role of Women in Native American Societies: A Bibliography." *Indian Historian* 8 (Summer 1975): 50-54.

3033. Miller, Dorothy L. "Native American Women: Leadership Images." *Integrated Education* 16 (January-February 1978): 37-39.

3034. Ortiz, Roxanne Dunbar. "Colonialism and the Role of Women: The Pueblos of New Mexico." *Southwest Economy and Society* 4 (Winter 1978-1979): 28-46.

3035. Starr, Michael L. "She Did Not Head a Movement." *American History Illustrated* 15 (August 1980): 44-47.

3036. Westermeyer, Joseph. "Sex Roles at the Indian-Majority Interface in Minnesota." *International Journal of Social Psychiatry* 24 (Autumn 1978): 189-194.

3037. Wood, Beth, and Tom Barry. "The Story of Three Navajo Women." *Integrated Education* 16 (March-April 1978): 33-35.

3038. Young, Mary E. "Women, Civilization, and the Indian Question." In *Clio Was a Woman: Studies in the History of American Women*, edited by Mabel E. Deutrich and Virginia C. Purdy, pp. 98-110. Washington: Howard University Press, 1980. Uses Cherokees as a case study.

Indians and Blacks

3039. Crowe, Charles. "Indians and Blacks in White America." In *Four Centuries of Southern Indians*, edited by Charles M. Hudson, pp. 148-169. Athens: University of Georgia Press, 1975.

3040. Doran, Michael F. "Negro Slaves of the Five Civilized Tribes." *Annals of the Association of American Geographers* 68 (September 1978): 335-350.

3041. Gammon, Tim. "Black Freedmen and the Cherokee Nation." *Journal of American Studies* 11 (December 1977): 357-364.

3042. _____. "The Black Freedmen of the Cherokee Nation." *Negro History Bulletin* 40 (July-August 1977): 733-735.

3043. Geist, Christopher D. "Slavery among the Indians: An Overview." *Negro History Bulletin* 38 (October 1975): 465-467.

3044. Halliburton, Janet. "Black Slavery in the Creek Nation." *Chronicles of Oklahoma* 56 (Fall 1978): 298-314.

3045. Halliburton, R., Jr. "Black Slave Control in the Cherokee Nation," *Journal of Ethnic Studies* 3 (Summer 1975): 23-35.

3046. _____. "Black Slavery among the Cherokees." *American History Illustrated* 11 (October 1976): 12-19.

3047. _____. *Red over Black: Black Slavery among the Cherokee Indians*. Westport, Connecticut: Greenwood Press, 1977.

3048. Katz, William Loren. "Black and Indian Cooperation and Resistance to Slavery." *Freedomways* 17 (No. 3, 1977): 164-174.

3049. Kremer, Gary R. "For Justice and a Fee: James Milton Turner and the Cherokee Freedmen." *Chronicles of Oklahoma* 58 (Winter 1980-1981): 377-391.

3050. Littlefield, Daniel F., Jr. *Africans and Creeks: From the Colonial Period to the Civil War*. Westport, Connecticut: Greenwood Press, 1979.

3051. _____. *Africans and Seminoles: From Removal to Emancipation*. Westport, Connecticut: Greenwood Press, 1977.

3052. _____. *The Cherokee Freedmen: From Emancipation to American Citizenship*. Westport, Connecticut: Greenwood Press, 1978.

3053. _____. *The Chickasaw Freedmen: A People without a Country*. Westport, Connecticut: Greenwood Press, 1980.

3054. Littlefield, Daniel F., Jr., and Mary Ann Littlefield. "The Beams Family: Free Blacks in Indian Territory."

Journal of Negro History 41 (January 1976): 16-35.

3055. Littlefield, Daniel F., Jr., and Lonnie E. Underhill. "Slave 'Revolt' in the Cherokee Nation, 1842." *American Indian Quarterly* 3 (Summer 1977): 121-131.

3056. Perdue, Theda. "Cherokee Planters: The Development of Plantation Slavery before Removal." In *The Cherokee Indian Nation: A Troubled History*, edited by Duane H. King, pp. 110-128. Knoxville: University of Tennessee Press, 1979.

3057. _____. *Slavery and the Evolution of Cherokee Society, 1540-1866.* Knoxville: University of Tennessee Press, 1979.

3058. Smith, C. Calvin. "The Oppressed Oppressors: Negro Slavery among the Choctaw Indians of Oklahoma." *Red River Valley Historical Review* 2 (Summer 1975): 240-253.

Indians and the Environment

3059. Cortner, Hanna J. "The Navajo Environmental Protection Commission: Developing the Capabilities for Environmental Impact Assessment and Regulation." *Indian Historian* 9 (Fall 1976): 32-37.

3060. Costo, Rupert. "The American Indian and Environmental Issues." *Wassaja/The Indian Historian* 13 (June 1980): 51-55.

3061. Jacobs, Wilbur R. "Indians as Ecologists and Other Environmental Themes in American Frontier History." In *American Indian Environments: Ecological Issues in Native American History*, edited by Christopher Vecsey and Robert W. Venables, pp. 46-64. Syracuse: Syracuse University Press, 1980.

3062. Lyons, Oren. "An Iroquois Perspective." In *American Indian Environments: Ecological Issues in Native American History*, edited by Christopher Vecsey and Robert W. Venables, pp. 171-174. Syracuse: Syracuse University Press, 1980.

3063. Mitchell, Joseph D. "The American Indian: A Fire Ecologist." *American Indian Culture and Research Journal* 2 (No. 2, 1978): 26-31.

3064. Smaby, Beverly P. "The Mormons and the Indians: Conflicting Ecological Systems in the Great Basin." *American Studies* 16 (Spring 1975): 35-48.

3065. Vecsey, Christopher. "American Indian Environmental Religions." In *American Indian Environments: Ecological Issues in Native American History*, edited

by Christopher Vecsey and Robert W. Venables, pp. 1-37. Syracuse: Syracuse University Press, 1980.

3066. Vecsey, Christopher, and Robert W. Venables, eds. *American Indian Environments: Ecological Issues in Native American History*. Syracuse: Syracuse University Press, 1980.

3067. White, Richard. "Indian Land Use and Environmental Change: Island County, Washington, a Case Study." *Arizona and the West* 17 (Winter 1975): 327-338.

3068. Zimmerman, David R. "Can Indians and Environmentalists Find Common Ground?" *Progressive* 40 (December 1976): 27-29.

Peyote

3069. Anderson, Edward F. *Peyote: The Divine Cactus*. Tucson: University of Arizona Press, 1980. Contains an extensive bibliography, pp. 211-242.

3070. Brito, Silvester John. "The Development and Change of the Peyote Ceremony through Time and Space." Ph.D. dissertation, Indiana University, 1975.

3071. Jackson, Barbara D. "A Peyote Community in Northern Minnesota." In *Anishinabe: 6 Studies of Modern Chippewa*, edited by J. Anthony Paredes, pp. 127-193. Tallahassee: University Presses of Florida, 1980.

3072. La Barre, Weston. *The Peyote Cult*. 4th edition enlarged. Hamden, Connectcut: Archon Books, 1975. Includes "Peyote Studies, 1963-73," pp. 251-285.

3073. _____. "Peyotl and Mescaline." *Journal of Psychedelic Drugs* 11 (January-June 1979): 33-39.

3074. McRae, William E. "Peyote Rituals of the Kiowas." *Southwest Review* 60 (Summer 1975): 217-233.

3075. Morgan, George Robert. "Man, Plant, and Religion: Peyote Trade on the Mustang Plains of Texas." Ph.D. dissertation, University of Colorado, 1976.

3076. Moses, L. G. "James Mooney and the Peyote Controversy." *Chronicles of Oklahoma* 56 (Summer 1978): 127-144.

3077. Pascarosa, Paul, and Sanford Futterman. "Ethnopsychedelic Therapy for Alcoholics: Observations in the Peyote Ritual of the Native American Church." *Journal of Psychedelic Drugs* 8 (July-September 1976): 215-221.

3078. "The Peyote Cure." *Human Behavior* 4 (April 1975): 45-46.

3079. Wachtel, David. "Peyotism: Ritual, History, Legality." Wassaja/The Indian Historian 13 (November 1980): 38-44.

3080. Wagner, Roland M. "Pattern and Process in Ritual Syncretism: The Case of Peyotism among the Navajo." Journal of Anthropological Research 31 (Summer 1975): 162-181.

3081. _____. "Some Pragmatic Aspects of Navaho Peyotism." Plains Anthropologist 20 (August 1975): 197-205.

15
Special Topics

INDIAN CAPTIVITIES

3082. Axtell, James. "The White Indians of Colonial America." William and Mary Quarterly, 3d series 32 (January 1975): 55-88.

3083. Carey, Larry Lee. "A Study of the Indian Captivity Narrative as a Popular Literary Genre, ca. 1675-1875." Ph.D. dissertation, Michigan State University, 1978.

3084. Denn, Robert J. "Captivity Narratives of the American Revolution." Journal of American Culture 2 (Winter 1980): 575-582.

3085. Gherman, Dawn Lander. "From Parlour to Tepee: The White Squaw on the American Frontier." Ph.D. dissertation, University of Massachusetts, 1975. Draws some material from captivity narratives.

3086. Haberly, David T. "Women and Indians: The Last of the Mohicans and the Captivity Tradition." American Quarterly 28 (Fall 1976): 431-443.

3087. Heard, Joseph Norman. "The Assimilation of Captives on the American Frontier in the Eighteenth and Nineteenth Centuries." Ph.D. dissertation, Louisiana State University, 1977.

3088. Kolodny, Annette. "Review Essay." Early American Literature 14 (Fall 1969): 228-235. Reviews Narratives of North American Indian Captivities and a preliminary introduction to them by Wilcomb E. Washburn.

3089. Levernier, James Arthur. "Indian Captivity Narratives: Their Functions and Forms." Ph.D. dissertation, University of Pennsylvania, 1975.

3090. Levernier, James, and Hennig Cohen, eds. The Indians and Their Captives. Westport, Connecticut: Greenwood Press, 1977.

3091. Narratives of North American Indian Captivities. 111 volumes. New York: Garland Publishing, 1975-1879. Reprints of captivity narratives from the Newberry Library collections primarily.

3092. Stanford, Ann. "Mary Rowlandson's Journey to Redemption." Ariel 7 (July 1976): 27-37.

CONCEPTS AND IMAGES OF THE INDIAN

Images of the Indian

3093. Baird, W. David. "The Quest for a Red-Faced White Man: Reservation Whites View Their Indian Wards." In Red Men and Hat Wearers: Viewpoints in Indian History, edited by Daniel Tyler, pp. 113-131. Boulder, Colorado: Pruett Publishing Company, 1976.

3094. Barry, Roxana. "Rousseau, Buffalo Bill and the European Image of the American Indian." Art News 74 (December 1975): 58-61.

3095. Belting, Natalia Maree. "The Native American as Myth and Fact." Journal of the Illinois State Historical Society 69 (May 1976): 119-126.

3096. Berkhofer, Robert F., Jr. The White Man's Indian: Images of the American Indian from Columbus to the Present. New York: Alfred A. Knopf, 1978.

3097. Briggs, Harold. "Indians!: A Whole Movement of Native Opera Romanticized the American Stage." Opera News 40 (June 1976): 22-24, 51.

3098. Chiapelli, Fredi, Michael J. B. Allen, and Robert L. Benson, eds. First Images of America: The Impact of the New World on the Old. 2 volumes. Berkeley: University of California Press, 1976.

3099. Comstock, W. Richard. "On Seeing with the Eye of the Native European." In Seeing with a Native Eye: Essays on Native American Religion, edited by Walter Holden Capps, assisted by Ernst F. Tonsing, pp. 58-78. New York: Harper and Row, 1976.

3100. Drinnon, Richard. <u>Facing West:</u> <u>The Metaphysics of Indian-Hating and</u> <u>Empire-Building</u>. Minneapolis: University of Minnesota Press, 1980.

3101. Fishman, Laura Schrager. "How Noble the Savage? The Image of the American Indian in French and English Travel Accounts, ca. 1550-1680." Ph.D. dissertation, City University of New York, 1979.

3102. Green, Rayna D. "The Pocahontas Perplex: The Image of Indian Women in American Culture." <u>Massachusetts Review</u> 16 (Autumn 1975): 698-714.

3103. _____. "Traits of Indian Character: The 'Indian' Anecdote in American Vernacular Tradition." <u>Southern Folklore Quarterly</u> 39 (No. 3, 1975): 233-262.

3104. Howard, James H. "The Native American Image in Western Europe." <u>American Indian Quarterly</u> 4 (February 1978): 33-56.

3105. Hoxie, Frederick E. "Red Man's Burden." <u>Antioch Review</u> 37 (Summer 1979): 326-342. Images of the Indian at the world's fairs of Philadelphia, Chicago, St. Louis, and San Francisco.

3106. Hoy, James F. "The Indian through the Eyes of <u>The Cattlemen</u>." <u>Indian Historian</u> 12 (Summer 1979): 41-46, 62.

3107. "Indian Images." <u>Human Behavior</u> 7 (October 1978): 36. In children's books.

3108. Kaufman, Donald L. "The Indian as Media Hand-Me-Down." <u>Colorado Quarterly</u> 23 (Spring 1975): 489-504.

3109. Kenneson, Susan Reyner. "Through the Looking-Glass: A History of Anglo-American Attitudes towards the Spanish-Americans and Indians of New Mexico." Ph.D. dissertation, Yale University, 1978.

3110. Kerber, Linda K. "The Abolitionist Perception of the Indian." <u>Journal of American History</u> 62 (September 1975): 271-295.

3111. Leo, John Robert. "Riding Geronimo's Cadillac: <u>His Own Story</u> and the Circumstancing of Text." <u>Journal of American Culture</u> 1 (Winter 1978): 818-837.

3112. Mahon, John K., panel moderator. "The White Man's Image of the Indian: A Rebuttal." In <u>Indians of the Lower South: Past and Present</u>, edited by John K. Mahon, pp. 25-36. Pensacola: Gulf Coast History and Humanities Conference, 1975.

3113. Meyer, Larry L. "Welsh Indians and Other Anglo Fables," <u>American West</u> 12 (May 1975): 42-47.

3114. Miller, David Harry, and William W. Savage, Jr. "Ethnic Stereotypes and the Frontier: A Comparative Study of Roman and American Experience." In <u>The Frontier: Comparative Studies</u>, edited by David Harry Miller and Jerome O. Steffen, pp. 109-137. Norman: University of Oklahoma Press, 1977.

3115. Moriarty, Francis J. "Some European Myths: The Case of America." <u>Indiana Social Studies Quarterly</u> 28 (Winter 1975-1976): 107-127.

3116. Muldoon, James. "The Indian as Irishman." <u>Essex Institute Historical Collections</u> 111 (October 1975): 267-289.

3117. Murphy, Sharon. "American Indians and the Media: Neglect and Stereotype." <u>Journalism History</u> 6 (Summer 1979): 39-43.

3118. Plumb, J. H. "America: Illusion and Reality." <u>American Heritage</u> 27 (August 1976): 14-25.

3119. Porter, H. C. <u>The Inconstant Savage: England and the North American Indian, 1500-1660</u>. London: Gerald Duckworth and Company, 1979.

3120. Rawls, James Jabus. "Images of the California Indians: American Attitudes toward the Indians of California, 1808-1873." Ph.D. dissertation, University of California, Berkeley, 1975.

3121. Savage, William W., Jr., ed. <u>Indian Life: Transforming an American Myth</u>. Norman: University of Oklahoma Press, 1977.

3122. Scholder, Fritz. <u>Indian Kitsch: The Use and Misuse of Indian Images</u>. Flagstaff, Arizona: Northland Press, 1979.

3123. Shaughnessy, Tim. "White Stereotypes of Indians." <u>Journal of American Indian Education</u> 17 (January 1978): 20-24.

3123a. Sheehan, Bernard W. <u>Savagism and Civility: Indians and Englishmen in Colonial Virginia</u>. Cambridge: Cambridge University Press, 1980.

3124. Sullivan, Marjorie, and John S. Goodell. "Media Use in the Study of Minorities." <u>Emporia State Research Studies</u> 24 (Fall 1975): 5-63.

3125. Trigger, Bruce G. "Archaeology and the Image of the American Indian." <u>American Antiquity</u> 45 (October 1980): 662-676.

3126. Trillin, Calvin. "U.S. Journal:

Hanover, N.H.: The Symbol Is a Symbol."
New Yorker 55 (May 7, 1979): 132-140.
Dartmouth College Indian symbol.

3127. Wenrick, Jon S. "Indians in Alma-
nacs (1783-1815)." Indian Historian 8
(Winter 1975): 36-42.

3128. White, John R. "Playboy Blacks vs.
Playboy Indians: Differential Minority
Stereotyping in Magazine Cartoons."
American Indian Culture and Research
Journal 3 (No. 2, 1979): 39-55.

3129. Wilson, Charles Reagan. "Racial
Reservations: Indians and Blacks in Amer-
ican Magazines, 1865-1900." Journal of
Popular Culture 10 (Summer 1976): 70-79.

3130. _____. "Shamans and Charlatans:
The Popularization of Native American
Religion in Magazines, 1865-1900." In-
dian Historian 12 (No. 3, 1979): 6-13.

3131. Wolf, Bobi. "Karl May." Pacific
Historian 24 (Fall 1980): 301-311.

Indians in Literature

3132. Anderson, Brenda Jean. "The North
American Indian in Theatre and Drama
from 1605 to 1970." Ph.D. dissertation,
University of Illinois at Urbana-
Champaign, 1978.

3133. Anderson, Marilyn J. "The Best of
Two Worlds: The Pocahontas Legend As
Treated in Early American Drama."
Indian Historian 12 (Summer 1979): 54-
59, 64.

3134. _____. "The Image of the Indian
in American Drama during the Jacksonian
Era, 1829-1845." Journal of American
Culture 1 (Winter 1978): 800-810.

3135. _____. "Ponteach: The First
American Problem Play." American Indian
Quarterly 3 (Autumn 1977): 225-241.

3136. Arner, Robert D. "The Quest for
Freedom: Style and Meaning in Robert
Beverley's History and Present State of
Virginia." Southern Literary Journal 8
(Spring 1976): 79-98.

3137. Ashliman, D. L. "The American Indian in German Travel Narratives and
Literature." Journal of Popular Culture
10 (Spring 1977): 833-839.

3138. Barnett, Louise K. The Ignoble
Savage: American Literary Racism, 1790-
1890. Westport, Connecticut: Greenwood
Press, 1975.

3139. _____. "Nineteenth-Century Indian
Hater Fiction: A Paradigm for Racism."
South Atlantic Quarterly 74 (Spring
1975): 224-236.

3140. Barry, Nora Baker. "The Bear's
Son Folk Tale in When the Legends Die
and House Made of Dawn." Western
American Literature 12 (Winter 1978):
275-287.

3141. Beaver, Harold. "Parkman's Crack-up:
A Bostonian on the Oregon Trail." New
England Quarterly 48 (March 1975):
84-103.

3142. Beidler, Peter G. Fig Tree John:
An Indian in Fact and Fiction. Tucson:
University of Arizona Press, 1977.

3143. _____. "The Popularity of Dan
Cushman's Stay Away, Joe among American
Indians." Arizona Quarterly 33
(Autumn 1977): 216-240.

3144. Beidler, Peter G., and Marion F.
Egge. The American Indian in Short
Fiction: An Annotated Bibliography.
Metuchen, New Jersey: Scarecrow Press,
1979.

3145. Berkman, Brenda. "The Vanishing
Race: Conflicting Images of the American Indian in Children's Literature,
1880-1930." North Dakota Quarterly 44
(Spring 1976): 31-40.

3146. Black, Nancy B., and Bette S.
Weidman, eds. White on Red: Images of
the American Indian. Port Washington,
New York: Kennikat Press, 1976.

3147. "A Book Ignites an Indian Uprising."
Time 115 (May 5, 1980): 98. The novel
Hanta Yo.

3148. Brown, Richard William. "Characteristics and Concepts of American Indians
in Children's Fictional Literature
Published between 1963 and 1973."
Ed.D. dissertation, Temple University,
1978.

3149. Butler, Michael D. "Narrative
Structure and Historical Process in
The Last of the Mohicans." American
Literature 48 (May 1976): 117-139.

3150. Cata, Juanita Opal. "The Portrait
of American Indians in Children's
Fictional Literature." Ph.D. dissertation, University of New Mexico, 1977.

3151. Cohen, Lester H. "What's in a
Name" The Presence of the Victim in
The Pioneers." Massachusetts Review
16 (Autumn 1975): 688-698.

3152. Doyle, James. "Mennonites and
Mohawks: The Universalist Fiction of
J.L.E.W. Shecut." Mennonite Quarterly
Review 51 (January 1977): 22-30.

3153. Easy, Peter. "The Treatment of
American Indian Materials in Contemporary

American Poetry." Journal of American Studies 12 (April 1978): 81-98.

3154. Elliott, Karen Sue. "The Portrayal of the American Indian Woman in a Select Group of American Novels." Ph.D. dissertation, University of Minnesota, 1979.

3155. Fleck, Richard F., ed. "Further Selections from the 'Indian Notebooks.'" Thoreau Journal Quarterly 9 (January 1977): 2-23.

3156. Grose, Burl Donald. "'Here Come the Indians': An Historical Study of the Representations of the Native American upon the North American Stage, 1808-1969." Ph.D. dissertation, University of Missouri-Columbia, 1979.

3157. Gura, Philip F. "Thoreau's Maine Woods Indians: More Representative Men." American Literature 49 (November 1977): 366-384.

3158. Hanson, Elizabeth Irene. "The Indian Metaphor in the American Renaissance." Ph.D. dissertation, University of Pennsylvania, 1977.

3159. "Hanta Yo: A Gross Insult Is Offered to Indian People." Wassaja/The Indian Historian 13 (November 1980): 15-23.

3160. Harris, Helen L. "Mark Twain's Response to the Native American." American Literature 46 (January 1975): 495-505.

3161. Hoilman, Grace Dona Gubler. "Voices and Images of the American Indian in Literature for Young People." Ph.D. dissertation, Ball State University, 1980.

3162. "An Indian Epic." Newsweek 93 (April 16, 1979): 86, 90. Novel Hanta Yo.

3163. Jacobs, Wilbur R. "Robert Beverley: Colonial Ecologist and Indian Lover." In Essays in Early American Literature Honoring Richard Beale Davis, edited by J. A. Leo Lemay, pp. 91-99. New York: Burt Franklin and Company, 1977.

3164. Jamison, Blanche Noma Miller. "The Western American Indian: Cross-Cultural Literary Attitudes, 1830-1975." Ed.D. dissertation, East Texas State University, 1978.

3165. Jenkins, William Warren. "Three Centuries in the Development of the Pocahontas Story in American Literature: 1608-1908." Ph.D. dissertation, University of Tennessee, 1977.

3166. Kelley, James Richard. "The Bloody Loam." Ph.D. dissertation, State University of New York at Stony Brook, 1976. Indians in the writings of Francis Parkman and Henry David Thoreau.

3167. Kelly, William Patrick III. "The Leatherstocking Tales: Fiction and the American Historical Experience." Ph.D. dissertation, Indiana University, 1977.

3168. Krefft, James Harvey. "The Yoknapatawpha Indians: Fact and Fiction." Ph.D. dissertation, Tulane University, 1976.

3169. Lane, Lauriat, Jr. "Thoreau's Autumnal Indian." Canadian Review of American Studies 6 (Fall 1975): 228-236.

3170. Lawson, Lewis A. "Old Fish Hawk: From Stereotype to Archetype." American Indian Quarterly 3 (Winter 1977-1978): 321-333.

3171. Lutz, Hartmut. "The Image of the American Indian in German Literature." Interracial Books for Children Bulletin 10 (Nos. 1-2, 1979): 17-18.

3172. McCullough, Joseph B., and Robert K. Dodge. "The Puritan Myth and the Indian in the Early American Novel." Pembroke Magazine, No. 7 (1976): 237-244.

3173. McNutt, James C. "Mark Twain and the American Indian: Earthly Realism and Heavenly Idealism." American Indian Quarterly 4 (August 1978): 223-242.

3174. McWilliams, Wilson Carey. "Natty Bumppo and the Godfather." Colorado Quarterly 24 (Autumn 1975): 133-144.

3175. Mansfield-Kelley, Deane. "Oliver La Farge and the Indian Woman in American Literature." Ph.D. dissertation, University of Texas at Austin, 1979.

3176. Martin, Terence. "Surviving on the Frontier: The Doubled Consciousness of Natty Bumppo." South Atlantic Quarterly 75 (Autumn 1976): 447-459.

3177. Medicine, Bea. "Hanta Yo: A New Phenomenon." Indian Historian 12 (Summer 1979): 2-5.

3178. Moen, Ole O. "The Voice of Siouxland: Man and Nature in Frederick Manfred's Writing." Ph.D. dissertation, University of Minnesota, 1978.

3179. Mitchell, Lee Clark. "The Vanishing Wilderness and Its Recorders: Developing Apprehensions about 'Progress' in Nineteenth-Century American Literature." Ph.D. dissertation, University of Washington, 1975.

3180. Moore, L. Hugh. "Francis Parkman on the Oregon Trail: A Study in Cultural Prejudice." Western American Literature 12 (Fall 1977): 185-197.

3181. Mulvey, Kathleen A. "The Growth, Development, and Decline of the Popularity of American Indian Plays before the Civil War." Ph.D. dissertation, New York University, 1978.

3182. Pitcher, Edward W. R. "The Un-American Fiction of The American Moral and Sentimental Magazine, with a Comment on the 'Captivity Narrative.'" Early American Literature 14 (Winter 1979-1980): 312-315.

3183. Rans, Geoffrey. "Inaudible Man: The Indian in the Theory and Practice of White Fiction." Canadian Review of American Studies 8 (Fall 1977): 103-115.

3184. Rose, Alan Henry. Demonic Vision: Racial Fantasy and Southern Fiction. Hamden, Connecticut: Archon Books, 1976.

3185. Rucker, Mary E. "Natural, Tribal, and Civil Law in Cooper's The Prairie." Western American Literature 12 (Fall 1977): 215-222.

3186. Sayre, Robert F. Thoreau and the American Indians. Princeton: Princeton University Press, 1977.

3187. Scheick, William J. The Half-Blood: A Cultural Symbol in 19th-Century American Fiction. Lexington: University Press of Kentucky, 1979.

3188. _____. "The Half-Breed in Snelling's Tales of the Northwest." Old Northwest 2 (June 1976): 141-151.

3189. Schneider, Jack Ward. "Patterns of Cultural Conflict in Southwestern Indian Fiction." Ph.D. dissertation, Texas Tech University, 1977.

3190. Sears, Priscilla Flagg. "A Pillar of Fire to Follow: American Indian Dramas, 1808-1859." Ph.D. dissertation, Tufts University, 1975.

3191. Sonnichsen, C. L. "The Ambivalent Apache." Western American Literature 10 (August 1975): 99-114.

3192. Stensland, Anna Lee. "The Indian Presence in American Literature." English Journal 66 (March 1977): 37-41.

3193. _____. Literature by and about the American Indian: An Annotated Bibliography. 2nd edition. Urbana, Illinois: National Council of Teachers of English, 1979.

3194. Stoodt, Barbara D., and Sandra Ignizio. "The American Indian in Children's Literature." Language Arts 53 (January 1976): 17-21.

3195. Sullivan, Sherry Ann. "The Indian in American Fiction 1820-1850." Ph.D. dissertation, University of Toronto, 1979.

3196. Tanselle, G. Thomas. "The Birth and Death of Alknomook." Newberry Library Bulletin 6 (May 1979): 389-401.

3197. Taylor, Allan R. "The Literary Offences of Ruth Beebe Hill." American Indian Culture and Research Journal 4 (No. 3, 1980): 75-85.

3198. Teunissen, John J., and Evelyn J. Hinz. "Anti-Colonial Satire in Roger Williams' A Key into the Language of America." Ariel 7 (July 1976): 5-26.

3199. Thomson, Peggy. "Ruth Hill Became Indian To Write Epic of the Sioux." Smithsonian 9 (December 1978): 111-128.

3200. Trimmer, Joseph F. "Native Americans and the American Mix: N. Scott Momaday's House Made of Dawn." Indiana Social Studies Quarterly 28 (Autumn 1975): 75-91.

3201. Troy, Anne. "The Indian in Adolescent Novels." Indian Historian 8 (Winter 1975): 32-35.

3202. Velie, Alan R. "Cain and Abel in N. Scott Momaday's House Made of Dawn." Journal of the West 17 (April 1978): 55-62.

Indians in Painting and Sculpture

3203. "Artists of the Sante Fe." American Heritage 27 (February 1976): 57-72.

3204. Boynton, Searles R. "The Pomo Indian Portraits of Grace Carpenter Hudson." American West 14 (September-October 1977): 20-29.

3205. Brandon, William. "Indian Anangka." Massachusetts Review 17 (Spring 1976). 145-164. Essay accompanying lithographs by Leonard Baskin.

3206. Campbell, Janet, and Kenny A. Franks. "The Wilderness Legacy of James Otto Lewis." Chronicles of Oklahoma 54 (Winter 1976-1977): 474-488.

3207. Catlin, George. Letters and Notes on the North American Indians. Edited and with an introduction by Michael MacDonald Mooney. New York: Clarkson N. Potter, 1975.

3208. Coke, Van Deren. "Southwest

Bouguereau." Art News 74 (February 1975): 68-70.

3209. Dallas, Sandra. "Winold Reiss Portraits of Plains Indians." American Artist 42 (November 1978): 54-59, 117-119.

3210. DuPont, John J. "Frederic Remington, 1861-1909." Conservationist 31 (March-April 1977): 10-18.

3211. Dykshorn, Jan M. "William Fuller's Crow Creek and Lower Brule Paintings." South Dakota History 6 (Fall 1976): 411-420.

3212. Hassrick, Royal B. "George Catlin's Indian Gallery." American West 15 (January-February 1978): 20-33.

3213. Herndon, Paul C. "They Painted the West II: George Catlin--Artist on Crusade." Our Public Lands 28 (Summer 1978): 18-22.

3214. _____. "They Painted the West III: Karl Bodmer--Artist for Hire." Our Public Lands 29 (Spring 1979): 19-22.

3215. Highwater, Jamake. "Indian Peacepaint: Canvas of a Culture." Saturday Review, November 25, 1978, pp. 30-31.

3216. Hutchinson, James. "A Florida Artist Views the Seminoles." Florida Historical Quarterly 55 (October 1976): 134-137.

3217. Johnson, Patricia. "The Artist's Life--The Indian's World." American History Illustrated 13 (Janaury 1979): 39-46. Seth Eastman.

3218. Kroeber, Theodora, Albert B. Elsasser, and Robert F. Heizer. Drawn from Life: California Indians in Pen and Brush. Socorro, New Mexico: Ballena Press, 1977.

3219. Locke, Raymond Friday. "George Catlin and the Mandans." Mankind 6 (August 1978): 8-13, 44-45.

3220. McPike, Dan. "Artist on a Military Expedition." Gilcrease Magazine of American History and Art 20 (No. 1, 1979): 16-23. George Catlin.

3221. Maximilian, Alexander Philip. "A Great Painter, A Royal Naturalist on Wild Missouri." Smithsonian 7 (October 1976): 58-67.

3222. Millichap, Joseph R. "George Catlin's 'Life amongst the Indians.'" American History Illustrated 12 (August 1977): 5-9, 43-48.

3223. Nelson, Mary Carroll. "George Carlson: Sculptor on Location." American Artist 42 (November 1978): 88-93, 124-127.

3224. Newcomb, William R., Jr., with Mary S. Carnahan. German Artist on the Texas Frontier: Friedrich Richard Petri. Austin: University of Texas Press, 1978.

3225. Page, Jean Jepson. "Frank Blackwell Mayer: Painter of the Minnesota Indian." Minnesota History 46 (Summer 1978): 66-74.

3226. Pearson, Anthony A. "John Hunter and Two Cherokee Indians: History through Art." Annals of the Royal College of Surgeons of England 58 (September 1976): 374-381.

3227. Russell, Charles M. "Paper Talk": Charlie Russell's American West. Edited by Brian W. Dippie. New York: Alfred A. Knopf, 1979.

3228. Samuels, Peggy, and Harold Samuels. The Illustrated Biographical Encyclopedia of Artists of the American West. Garden City, New York: Doubleday and Company, 1976.

3229. Schoonover, Cortlandt. Frank Schoonover, Illustrator of the North American Frontier. New York: Watson-Guptill Publications, 1976.

3230. Sellers, Charles Coleman. "'Good Chiefs and Wise Men': Indians as Symbols of Peace in the Art of Charles Willson Peale." American Art Journal 7 (November 1975): 10-18.

3231. Silliman, Lee. "William de la Montange Cary." American West 17 (September-October 1980): 34-47.

3232. Taylor, Ted. "Jo Mora: Artist of the Spanish and Indian West." American Wdst 16 (March-April 1979): 16-30.

3233. Thomas, Davis, and Karin Ronnefeldt, eds. People of the First Man: Life among the Plains Indians in Their Final Days of Glory: The Firsthand Account of Prince Maximilian's Expedition up the Missouri River, 1833-34. Watercolors by Karl Bodmer. New York: E.P. Dutton and Company, 1976.

3234. _____. "Winter at Fort Clark: Maximilian and Bodmer among the Tribes of the Upper Missouri, 1833-1834." American West 14 (January-February 1977): 36-47.

3235. Truettner, William H. The Natural Man Observed: A Study of Catlin's Indian Gallery. Washington: Smithsonian Institution Press, 1979.

3236. Viola, Herman J. "Charles Bird King's Indian Gallery." Art News 75 (December 1976): 67-70.

3237. _____. "How Did an Indian Chief Really Look?" Smithsonian 8 (June

1977): 100-104.

3238. _____. The Indian Legacy of Charles Bird King. Washington: Smithsonian Institution Press, and New York: Doubleday and Company, 1976.

3239. Wyman, Walker D. "A Dedication to the Memory of Frederic Remington, 1861-1909." Arizona and the West 19 (Spring 1977): 1-4.

Photographs of Indians

3240. Bigart, Robert, and Clarence Woodcock. "The Rinehart Photographs: A Portfolio." Montana, the Magazine of Western History 29 (October 1979): 24-37.

3241. Blackman, Margaret B. "Posing the American Indian." Natural History 89 (October 1980): 68-75.

3242. Buechel, Eugene. "Scenes from the Dakota Missions: Rosebud and Pine Ridge Photographs, 1922-1942." Critic 34 (Summer 1976): 48-53. Photographs by Buechel, with introductory commentary by David Wing.

3243. Canavor, Natalie. "Shows We've Seen." Popular Photography 87 (August 1980): 68, 174, 194, 199. Work of Edward S. Curtis.

3244. Curtis, Edward Sheriff. Visions of a Vanishing Race. Text by Florence Curtis Graybill and Victor Boesen. New York: Thomas Y. Crowell Company, 1976.

3245. Farber, Joseph C. Native Americans: 500 Years After. Text by Michael Dorris. New York: Thomas Y. Crowell Company, 1975.

3246. Gray, John S. "Itinerant Frontier Photographers, and Images Lost, Strayed or Stolen." Montana, the Magazine of Western History 28 (April 1978): 2-15. Discussion of five photographers: William R. Pywell, John H. Fouch, Stanley J. Morrow, Orlando Scott Goff, and David F. Barry.

3247. Holm, Bill, and George Irving Quimby. Edward S. Curtis in the Land of the War Canoes: A Pioneer Cinematographer in the Pacific Northwest. Seattle: University of Washington Press, 1980.

3248. Horse Capture, George P. "The Camera Eye of Sumner Matteson and the People Who Fooled Them All." Montana, the Magazine of Western History 27 (July 1977): 58-71. Fort Belknap, 1904.

3249. Ivers, Louise Harris. "Early Photographs of Indian Pueblos in New Mexico." Masterkey 51 (July-September 1977): 85-100.

3250. Johnson, Christopher S. "E. Jane Gay and the Nez Perces." Harvard Magazine 82 (March-April 1980): 50-51.

3251. Johnston, Patricia Condon. "The Indian Photographs of Roland Reed." American West 15 (March-April 1978): 44-57.

3252. Kramer, Hilton. "Exotics in the White Man's World." New York Times Magazine, February 5, 1978, pp. 16-18. Work of F. A. Rinehart.

3253. McHugh, Joseph J. "Indians and a Telltale Lens." America 133 (December 27, 1975): 475-476. Photographs by Eugene Buechel.

3254. Maye, Patricia. "John Running, Faces of the Southwest." Modern Photography 42 (January 1978): 96-101.

3255. Nadel, Norman. "Curtis Recovered." Horizon 23 (August 1980): 40-49.

3256. Palmquist, Peter E. "Mirror of Our Conscience: Surviving Photographic Images of California Indians Produced before 1860." Journal of California Anthropology 5 (Winter 1978): 163-178.

3257. "The Red Earth People in 1905: A Photographic Essay." In The Worlds between Two Rivers: Perspectives on American Indians in Iowa, edited by Gretchen M. Bataille and others, pp. 62-73. Ames: Iowa State University Press, 1978. Photographs by Duren J.H. Ward.

3258. Ritzenthaler, Robert E., and Leo Johnson. "The Artistry of Sumner W. Matteson." American Indian Art Magazine 5 (Winter 1979): 60-67.

3259. Roberts, Gary L. "In Search of Little Wolf . . . A Tangled Photographic Record." Montana, the Magazine of Western History 28 (July 1978): 48-61.

3260. Scully, Julia. "Seeing Pictures." Modern Photography 39 (April 1975): 10, 120, 123.

3261. "Sitting Bull Collection." South Dakota History 5 (Summer 1975): 245-265.

3262. Weinberger, Caspar, Jr. "Classic Images of Dying Nations Enjoy a Rebirth." Smithsonian 6 (April 1975): 82-89. Photographs of Edward S. Curtis.

Indians in Movies

3263. Bataille, Gretchen, and Charles L.P. Silet. "The Entertaining Anachronism: Indians in American Film." In The Kaleidoscopic Lens: How Hollywood Views Ethnic Groups, edited by Randall M. Miller, pp. 36-53. Englewood, New

Jersey: Jerome S. Ozer, 1980.

3264. _____. "The Indian in American Film: A Checklist of Published Materials on Popular Images of the Indian in the American Film." Journal of Popular Film 5 (No. 2, 1976): 171-182.

3265. Bataille, Gretchen M., and Charles L. P. Silet, eds. The Pretend Indians: Images of Native Americans in the Movies. Ames: Iowa State University Press, 1980.

3266. Bernstein, Gene M. "Robert Altman's Buffalo Bill and the Indians or Sitting Bull's History Lesson: A Self-Portrait in Celluloid." Journal of Popular Culture 13 (Summer 1979): 17-25.

3267. Churchill, Ward, Norbert Hill, and Mary Ann Hill. "Media Stereotyping and Native Response: An Historical Overview." Indian Historian 11 (December 1978): 45-56, 63.

3268. Harrington, John. "Understanding Hollywood's Indian Rhetoric." Canadian Review of American Studies 8 (Spring 1977): 77-88.

3269. Hartman, Hedy. "A Brief Review of the Native American in American Cinema." Indian Historian 9 (Summer 1976): 27-29.

3270. Kendall, Martha. "Forget the Masked Man: Who Was His Indian Companion?" Smithsonian 8 (September 1977): 113-120.

3271. Sheff, David, and Jack Fincher. "A Growing War over 'Hanta Yo' Pits Chief Lame Deer and Wojo vs. Ruth Beebe Hill and David Wolper." People Weekly 12 (June 23, 1980): 82+.

3272. Silet, Charles L. P. "The Image of the American Indian in Film." In The Worlds between Two Rivers: Perspectives on American Indians in Iowa, edited by Gretchen M. Bataille and others, pp. 10-15. Ames: Iowa State University Press, 1978.

3273. Siminoski, Ted. "Sioux versus Hollywood: The Image of Sioux Indians in American Films." Ph.D. dissertation, University of Southern California, 1979.

IDEAS ON RACE

3274. Berg, Philip L. "Racism and the Puritan Mind." Phylon 36 (March 1975): 1-7.

3275. Bieder, Robert E. "Scientific Attitudes toward Indian Mixed-Bloods in Early Nineteenth Century America." Journal of Ethnic Studies 8 (Summer 1980): 17-30.

3276. Dyer, Thomas G. Theodore Roosevelt and the Idea of Race. Baton Rouge: Louisiana State University Press, 1980.

3277. Hoover, Dwight W. The Red and the Black. Chicago: Rand McNally, 1976.

3278. Horsman, Reginald. "Scientific Racism and the American Indian in the Mid-Nineteenth Century." American Quarterly 27 (May 1975): 152-168.

3279. Kirsch, George B. "Jeremy Belknap and the Problem of Blacks and Indians in Early America." Historical New Hampshire 34 (Fall-Winter 1979): 202-222.

3280. Meek, Ronald L. Social Science and the Ignoble Savage. Cambridge: Cambridge University Press, 1976.

3281. Rader, Brian Farmer. "The Political Outsiders: Blacks and Indians in a Rural Oklahoma County." Ph.D. dissertation, University of Oklahoma, 1977.

3282. Sanders, Ronald. Lost Tribes and Promised Lands: The Origins of American Racism. Boston: Little, Brown and Company, 1978.

3283. Takaki, Ronald T. Iron Cages: Race and Culture in Nineteenth-Century America. New York: Alfred A. Knopf, 1979.

CONTRIBUTIONS OF INDIANS TO AMERICAN LIFE

3284. Brinegar, Bonnie. "Choctaw Place-Names in Mississippi." Mississippi Folklore Register 11 (Fall 1977): 142-150.

3285. Brown, Janet W. "Native American Contributions to Science, Engineering, and Medicine." Science 189 (July 4, 1975): 38-40.

3286. Flexner, Stuart Berg. I Hear America Talking: An Illustrated Treasury of American Words and Phrases. New York: Van Nostrand Reinhold Company, 1976. Indians, pp. 194-203.

3287. Jeffries, Theodore W. "On the Transmission of Indian Pharmaceutical Knowledge to Physicians." Pharmacy in History 18 (No. 1, 1976): 28-30.

3288. Johansen, Bruce Elliot. "Franklin, Jefferson, and American Indians: A Study in the Cross-Cultural Communication of Ideas." Ph.D. dissertation, University of Washington, 1979.

3289. Jones, Evan. "Indian Food: A Rich Harvest." Saturday Review, November 25, 1978, pp. 32-34.

3290. Powless, Robert E. "All People, All Tribes, All Nations." Conservationist 30 (January 1976): 10-11.

3291. Skelly, Madge. Amer-Ind Gestural Code Based on Universal American Indian Hand Talk. New York: Elsevier North Holland, 1979.

3292. Szasz, Margaret C., and Ferenc M. Szasz. "The American Indian and the Classical Past." Midwest Quarterly 17 (October 1975): 58-70.

3293. Vogel, Virgil J. "American Indian Influence on the American Pharmacopeia." American Indian Culture and Research Journal 2 (No. 1, 1977): 3-7.

3294. Zychowicz, Marlene Jane. "American Indian Teachings as a Philosophical Base for Counseling and Psychotherapy." Ed.D. dissertation, Northern Illinois University, 1975.

PERSONS CONCERNED WITH INDIAN AFFAIRS

Anthropologists and Ethnologists

3295. Archabal, Nina Marchetti. "Frances Densmore: Pioneer in the Study of American Indian Music." In Women of Minnesota: Selected Biographical Essays, edited by Barbara Stuhler and Gretchen Kreuter, pp. 94-115. St. Paul: Minnesota Historical Society Press, 1977.

3296. Blanchard, Kendall. "The Expanded Responsibilities of Long Term Informant Relationships." Human Organization 36 (Spring 1977): 66-69.

3297. Brown, Dee. "Perspectives on the Past." American History Illustrated 12 (February 1978): 19. Work of Henry Rowe Schoolcraft.

3298. Clemmer, Richard O. "Advocacy, Anthropology, and Accuracy: An Additional Rejoinder to Wilcomb Washburn." Journal of Ethnic Studies 8 (Summer 1980): 95-113.

3299. Cohen, Fay G. "The American Indian Movement and the Anthropologist: Issues and Implications of Consent." In Ethics and Anthropology: Dilemmas in Fieldwork, edited by Michael Al Rynkiewich and James P. Spradley, pp. 81-94. New York: John Wiley and Sons, 1976.

3300. Colby, William Munn. "Route to Rainy Mountain: A Biography of James Mooney, Ethnologist." Ph.D. dissertation, University of Wisconsin-Madison, 1977.

3301. Cushing, Frank Hamilton. Zuni: Selected Writings of Frank Hamilton Cushing. Edited by Jesse Green. Lincoln: University of Nebraska Press, 1979.

3302. Fletcher, Maurine S. "Nordenskiold and the Natives." Journal of Arizona History 20 (Autumn 1979): 345-370.

3303. Fogelson, Raymond D. "Major John Norton as Ethno-Ethnologist." Journal of Cherokee Studies 3 (Fall 1978): 250-255.

3304. Hertzberg, Hazel Whitman. "Nationality, Anthropology, and Pan-Indianism in the Life of Arthur C. Parker." Proceedings of the American Philosophical Society 123 (February 20, 1979): 47-72.

3305. Hinsley, Curtis Matthew, Jr. "The Development of a Profession: Anthropology in Washington, D.C., 1846-1903." Ph.D. dissertation, University of Wisconsin-Madison, 1976.

3306. Hudson, Charles. "James Adair as Anthropologist." Ethnohistory 24 (Fall 1977): 311-328.

3307. Hyatt, Marshall. "The Emergence of a Discipline: Franz Boas and the Study of Man." Ph.D. dissertation, University of Delaware, 1979.

3308. Jorgensen, Joseph G., and Richard O. Clemmer. "On Washburn's 'On the Trail of the Activist Anthropologist': A Rejoinder to a Reply." Journal of Ethnic Studies 8 (Summer 1980): 85-94.

3309. Kelly, Lawrence C. "Anthropology and Anthropologists in the Indian New Deal." Journal of the History of the Behavioral Sciences 16 (January 1980): 6-24.

3310. Liberty, Margot. "American Indians and American Anthropology." In American Indian Intellectuals, edited by Margot Liberty, pp. 1-33. St. Paul: West Publishing Company, 1978.

3311. Low, Jean. "George Thornton Emmons." Alaska Journal 7 (Winter 1977): 2-11.

3312. Mark, Joan. "Frank Hamilton Cushing and an American Science of Anthropology." Perspectives in American History 10 (1976): 449-486.

3313. _____. "Vita: Alice Fletcher, Activist Anthropologist, 1838-1923." Harvard Magazine 82 (March-April 1980): 34-35.

3314. Marsden, Michael T. "Henry Rowe Schoolcraft: A Reappraisal." Old Northwest 2 (June 1976): 153-182.

3315. Moses, Lester George. "James Mooney, U.S. Ethnologist: A Biography." Ph.D. dissertation, University of New Mexico, 1977.

3316. Oberweiser, David. "The Indian Education of Lewis H. Morgan." Indian Historian 12 (Winter 1979): 23-28.

3317. Paredes, J. Anthony. "New Uses for Old Ethnography: A Brief Social History of a Research Project with the Eastern Creek Indians, or How To Be an Applied Anthropologist without Really Trying." Human Organization 35 (Fall 1976): 315-320

3318. Porter, Frank W. III. "Anthropologists at Work: A Case Study of the Nanticoke Indian Community." American Indian Quarterly 4 (February 1978): 1-18.

3319. Reiger, John F. "A Dedication to the Memory of George Bird Grinnell, 1849-1938." Arizona and the West 21 (Spring 1979): 1-4.

3320. Sherwood, John. "Life with Cushing: Farewell to Desks." Smithsonian 10 (August 1979): 96-113. Frank H. Cushing.

3321. Trimble, Joseph E. "The Sojourner in the American Indian Community: Methodological Issues and Concerns." Journal of Social Issues 33 (Fall 1977): 159-174.

3322. Washburn, Wilcomb E. "On the Trail of the Activist Anthropologist: Response to Jorgensen and Clemmer." Journal of Ethnic Studies 7 (Spring 1979): 89-99.

3323. Wolf, Ronald Howard. "The Influence of Cultural Anthropology upon American History As Reflected in the American Indian Case." Ed.D. dissertation, Columbia University Teachers College, 1977.

Other Persons

3324. Angie Debo: A Biographical Sketch and a Bibliography of Her Published Works. Stillwater, Oklahoma: Department of History and Edmon Low Library of Oklahoma State University, 1980.

3325. Clark, LaVerne Harrell. "A Dedication to the Memory of Mari Sandoz." Arizona and the West 18 (Winter 1976): 311-314.

3326. Colley, Charles C. "The Papers of Carl T. Hayden: Arizona's 'Silent Senator' on Record." Journal of the West 14 (October 1975): 5-14. Senator Hayden and Indian affairs.

3327. Debo, Angie. "To Establish Justice." Western Historical Quarterly 7 (October 1976): 405-412.

3328. Fleck, Richard F. "John Muir's Evolving Attitudes toward Native American Cultures." American Indian Quarterly 4 (February 1978): 19-31.

3329. Guentzel, Richard Dale. "Alexander Ramsey: First Territorial and Second State Governor of Minnesota." Ph.D. dissertation, University of Nebraska-Lincoln, 1976.

3330. McDermott, John Dishon. "A Dedication to the Memory of George E. Hyde, 1882-1968." Arizona and the West 17 (Summer 1975): 103-106.

3331. Ortiz, Alfonso. "D'Arcy McNickle (1904-1977): Across the River and up the Hill." American Indian Journal 4 (April 1978): 12-16.

3332. Phillips, Joseph Wilson. "Jedediah Morse: An Intellectual Biography." Ph.D. dissertation, University of California, Berkeley, 1978. Contains information on Morse's Indian work.

3333. Richards, Kent D. Isaac I. Stevens: Young Man in a Hurry. Provo, Utah: Brigham Young University Press, 1979.

3334. Turcheneske, John A., Jr. "John G. Bourke--Troubled Scientist." Journal of Arizona History 20 (Autumn 1979): 323-344.

3335. Underhill, Lonnie E., and Daniel F. Littlefield, Jr., eds. Hamlin Garland's Observations on the American Indian, 1895-1905. Tucson: University of Arizona Press, 1976.

3336. Yost, Nellie Snyder. Buffalo Bill: His Family, Friends, Fame, Failures, and Fortunes. Chicago: Swallow Press, 1979.

INDIAN WRITINGS

3337. Allen, Paula Gunn. "The Sacred Hoop: A Contemporary Indian Perspective on American Indian Literature. Cross Currents 26 (Summer 1976): 144-163.

3338. Bannan, Helen M. "Spider Woman's Web: Mothers and Daughters in Southwestern Native American Literature." In The Lost Tradition: Mothers and Daughters in Literature, edited by E.M. Broner and Cathy N. Davidson, pp. 286-279. New York: Frederick Ungar Publishing Company, 1980.

3339. Bataille, Gretchen M. "An Approach to the Study of American Indian Literature at the College Level." D.A. dissertation, Drake University, 1977.

3340. Beidler, Peter G. "Animals and Human Development in the Contemporary American Indian Novel." Western American Literature 14 (Summer 1979): 133-148.

3341. Beidler, Peter G., ed. Special

Symposium Issue on James Welch's <u>Winter in the Blood</u>. <u>American Indian Quarterly</u> 4 (May 1978).

3342. Berner, Robert L. "N. Scott Momaday: Beyond Rainy Mountain." <u>American Indian Culture and Research Journal</u> 3 (No. 1, 1979): 57-67.

3343. Buller, Galen. "New Interpretations of Native American Literature: A Survival Technique." <u>American Indian Culture and Research Journal</u> 4 (Nos. 1-2, 1980): 165-177.

3344. Cook, Liz. "American Indian Literatures in Servitude." <u>Indian Historian</u> 10 (Winter 1977): 3-6.

3345. Dorris, Michael. "Native American Literature in an Ethnohistorical Context." <u>College English</u> 41 (October 1979): 147-162. Response by Jarold Ramsey, 41 (April 1980): 933-935.

3346. Espey, David B. "Endings in Contemporary American Indian Fiction." <u>Western American Literature</u> 13 (Summer 1978): 133-139.

3347. Hogan, Linda. "The Nineteenth Century Native American Poets." <u>Wassaja/ The Indian Historian</u> 13 (November 1980): 24-29.

3348. Jacobson, Angeline. <u>Contemporary Native American Literature: A Selected and Partially Annotated Bibliography</u>. Metuchen, New Jersey: Scarecrow Press, 1977. Works of Indian authors, 1960 to mid-1976.

3349. Larson, Charles R. <u>American Indian Fiction</u>. Albuquerque: University of New Mexico Press, 1978.

3350. _____. "Indian Fiction: A Tribal Vision." <u>Saturday Review</u>, November 25, 1978, p. 28.

3351. Ludovici, Paola. "The Struggle for an Ending: Ritual and Plot in Recent American Indian Literature." Ph.D. dissertation, American University, 1979.

3352. McTaggart, Fred. "American Indian Literature: Contexts for Understanding." In <u>The Worlds between Two Rivers: Perspectives on American Indians in Iowa</u>, edited by Gretchen M. Bataille and others, pp. 2-9. Ames: Iowa State University Press, 1978.

3353. Marken, Jack W. <u>The American Indian: Language and Literature</u>. Arlington Heights, Illinois: AHM Publishing Corporation, 1978. A Goldentree Bibliography.

3354. Nabokov, Peter, ed. <u>Native American Testimony: An Anthology of Indian and</u>

White Relations, First Encounter to Dispossession. New York: Thomas Y. Crowell, 1978.

3355. Ortiz, Simon J. "Literature." <u>American Indian Journal</u> 6 (January 1980): 32-35.

3356. Peyer, Bernd C. "A Bibliography of Native American Prose Prior to the 20th Century." <u>Wassaja/The Indian Historian</u> 13 (September 1980): 23-25.

3357. Ramsey, Jarold. "The Teacher of Modern American Indian Writing as Ethnographer and Critic." <u>College English</u> 41 (October 1979): 163-169.

3358. Rhodes, Geri Marlane. "Shared Fire: Reciprocity in Contemporary American Indian and Related Literature." Ph.D. dissertation, University of New Mexico, 1976.

3359. Roemer, Kenneth M. "Bear and Elk: The Nature(s) of Contemporary Indian Poetry." <u>Journal of Ethnic Studies</u> 5 (Summer 1977): 69-79.

3360. Ruoff, A. LaVonne. "History in <u>Winter in the Blood</u>: Background and Bibliography." <u>American Indian Quarterly</u> 4 (No. 2, 1978): 169-172. Novel by James Welch.

3361. Velie, Alan R. "James Welch's Poetry." <u>American Indian Culture and Research Journal</u> 3 (No. 1, 1979): 19-38.

3362. Whitney, Blair. "American Indian Literature of the Great Lakes." <u>Great Lakes Review</u> 11 (Winter 1976): 43-53.

3363. Zachrau, Thekla. "N. Scott Momaday: Towards an Indian Identity." <u>American Indian Culture and Research Journal</u> 3 (No. 1, 1979): 39-56.

ON THE WRITING OF INDIAN HISTORY

3364. Axtell, James. The Ethnohistory of Early America: A Review Essay." <u>William and Mary Quarterly</u>, 3d series 35 (January 1978): 110-144.

3365. Beaulieu, David L., ed. <u>Breaking Barriers: Perspectives on the Writing of Indian History</u>. Occasional Papers Series, No. 1. Chicago: Newberry Library, 1978.

3366. DeMallie, Raymond J. "Sioux Ethnohistory: A Methodological Critique." <u>Journal of Ethnic Studies</u> 4 (Fall 1976): 77-84. Review of Ernest L. Schusky, <u>The Forgotten Sioux</u>.

3367. Dobyns, Henry F. "Ethnohistory and Human Resource Development." <u>Ethno-</u>

history 25 (Spring 1978): 103-120.

3368. Edmunds, R. David. "The Indian in the Mainstream: Indian Historiography for Teachers of American History Surveys." History Teacher 8 (February 1975): 242-264.

3369. Gilbert, Arthur N. "The American Indian and United States Diplomatic History." History Teacher 8 (February 1975): 229-241.

3370. Hagan, William T. "Archival Captive--The American Indian." American Archivist 41 (April 1978): 135-142.

3371. Horsman, Reginald. "Recent Trends and New Directions in Native American History." In The American West: New Perspectives, New Dimensions, edited by Jerome O. Steffen, pp. 124-151. Norman: University of Oklahoma Press, 1979.

3372. Jacobs, Wilbur R. "Native American History: How It Illuminates Our Past." American Historical Review 80 (June 1975): 595-609.

3373. Jennings, Francis. "A Growing Partnership: Historians, Anthropologists, and American Indian History." History Teacher 14 (November 1980): 87-104.

3374. Magnaghi, Russell M. "Herbert E. Bolton and Sources for American Indian Studies." Western Historical Quarterly 6 (January 1975): 33-46.

3375. Martin, Calvin. "Ethnohistory: A Better Way To Write Indian History." Western Historical Quarterly 9 (January 1978): 41-56.

3376. Nash, Gary B. "Whither Indian History?" Journal of Ethnic Studies 4 (Fall 1976): 69-76.

3377. Ortiz, Alfonso. "Some Concerns Central to the Writing of 'Indian' History." Indian Historian 10 (Winter 1977): 17-22.

3378. Prucha, Francis Paul. "Books on American Indian Policy: A Half-Decade of Important Work, 1970-1975." Journal of American History 63 (December 1976): 658-669.

3379. _____. "Doing Indian History." In Indian-White Relations: A Persistent Paradox, edited by Jane F. Smith and Robert M. Kvasnicka, pp. 1-10. Washington: Howard University Press, 1976.

3380. _____. "New Approaches to the Study of the Administration of Indian Policy." In Research in the Administration of Public Policy, edited by Frank B. Evans and Harold T. Pinkett, pp. 147-152. Washington: Howard University Press, 1975.

3381. Rusco, Mary. "The People Write Their History: The Intertribal Council Project." Nevada Historical Society Quarterly 21 (Summer 1978): 143-148.

3382. Schwerin, Karl H. "The Future of Ethnohistory." Ethnohistory 23 (Fall 1976): 322-341.

MISCELLANEOUS STUDIES

3383. Axtell, James. "Who Invented Scalping?" American Heritage 28 (April 1977): 96-99.

3384. Axtell, James, and William C. Sturtevant. "The Unkindest Cut, or Who Invented Scalping?" William and Mary Quarterly, 3d series 37 (July 1980): 451-472.

3385. Bonney, Rachel Ann. "Forms of Supratribal Indian Interaction in the United States." Ph.D. dissertation, University of Arizona, 1975.

3386. Brito, Silvester John. "The Indian Cowboy in the Rodeo Circuit." Journal of Ethnic Studies 5 (Spring 1977): 51-57.

3387. Carroll, Michael P. "Revitalization Movements and Social Structure: Some Quantitative Tests." American Sociological Review 40 (June 1975): 389-401.

3388. Finster, David. "Museums and Medicine Bundles." Indian Historian 8 (Fall 1975): 40-48.

3389. Foster, Henry H. "Indian and Common Law Marriages." American Indian Law Review 3 (Summer 1975): 83-102.

3390. French, Larry, and Jim Hornbuckle. "The Historical Influence of the Eastern Indians on Contemporary Pan Indianism." Indian Historian 10 (Spring 1977): 23-27.

3391. Gilman, Carolyn. "Grand Portage Ojibway Indians Give British Medals to Historical Society." Minnesota History 47 (Spring 1980): 26-32.

3392. Grinde, Donald, Jr. "Native American Slavery in the Southern Colonies." Indian Historian 10 (Spring 1977): 38-42.

3393. Horvath, Steven M., Jr. "Indian Slaves for Spanish Horses." Museum of the Fur Trade Quarterly 14 (Winter 1978): 4-5.

3394. LaCourse, Richard. "An Indian Perspective: Native American Journalism, an Overview." Journalism History 6

(Summer 1979): 34-38.

(March 1975): 10-13.

3395. Lurie, Nancy Oestreich. "American Indians and Museums: A Love-Hate Relationship." Old Northwest 2 (September 1976): 235-251.

3396. Magnaghi, Russell M. "The Role of Indian Slavery in Colonial St. Louis." Bulletin of the Missouri Historical Society 31 (July 1975): 264-272.

3397. McNamara, Brooks. "Health or Money Restored: The Great Era of the Indian Medicine Show." American West 12

3398. _____. Step Right Up. Garden City, New York: Doubleday and Company, 1976. Wild West Shows.

3399. Moses. L. G. "James Mooney and Wovoka: An Ethnologist's Visit with the Ghost Dance Prophet." Nevada Historical Society Quarterly 23 (Summer 1980): 71-86.

3400. Viola, Herman J. "American Indian Cultural Resources Training Program at the Smithsonian Institution." American Archivist 41 (April 1978): 143-146.

Index

Reference is to the serial numbers of the items in the bibliography except where page is specifically designated. The term <u>Indian</u> has been used in preference to <u>American Indian</u> or <u>Native American</u> except where the latter terms are part of an official name or title.

Baptist missions, 1223, 1253, 1259-1262, 1687
Barbour, Philip L., 2556
Baris, Allan, 1486
Barker, Raleigh E., 684
Barlow, Mary Jo, 3000
Barnett, Louise K., 3138-3139
Barnitz, Albert, 981-982
Barnitz, Jennie, 981-982
Barr, Thomas P., 1687
Barry, David F., 3246
Barry, Edward E., Jr., 2246
Barry, Nora Baker, 3140
Barry, Roxana, 3094
Barry, Tom, 2167, 2373-2375, 3037
Barsh, Russel Lawrence, 180, 1367-1370, 1469, 1487-1488, 1552, 1667, 2300
Barta, Anita Marie, 1732
Bartelt, H. Guillermo, 1805
Bartlett, Grace, 2963
Barton, Thomas, 171
Basin-plateau Indians, 2937-2958
Baskin, Leonard, 3205
Bataille, Gretchen M., 2507-2508, 3263-3265, 3339
Battle, Edwina Larry, 1806
Battle: Adobe Walls, 977; Beecher Island, 973; Big Hole, 1042; Cibecue, 1046, 1051; Dog Canyon, 1052; Hay Camp, 1049; Little Big Horn, 290, 1007-1036; Mackinac Island, 909; Point Pleasant, 877; Rosebud, 995; Spillman Creek, 984; Summit Springs, 984; Tippecanoe, 902; Warbonnet Creek, 994, 1000; Washita, 966, 972; White Bird Canyon, 1038-1039; Whitestone Hill, 960; Wounded Knee, 1060-1067
Batzle, Peter, 573
Bean, Lowell John, 2899-2900
Beaulieu, David L., 2255, 3365
Beaver, Harold, 3141
Beaver, Jennifer B., 1455
Beaver, R. Pierce, 1220
Beaver, Alaska, 2992
Beck, Monte, 1618
Beckman, Stephen Dow, 2964
Bedford, Denton R., 2727-2728
Bee, Robert L., 105, 437, 560
Beecher Island, Battle of, 973
Beeton, Beverly, 217
Begay, Harold G., 1415
Begay, Joe Yazzie, 1807
Behnkte, Henry, 957
Beidler, Peter G., 3142-3144, 3340-3341
Bekken, James M., 685
Belknap, Jeremy, 3279
Bell, Cathy, 2113
Bell, D. Scott, 1839
Bell, William Gardner, 1124
Bellevue, Nebraska, 1203
Belting, Natalia Maree, 3095
Beltrame, Thomas, 2187
Benally, Clyde, J., 2868
Bendell, Herman, 676
Bender Gestalt Test, 1843
Benge, Bob, 2616
Benham, William J., 1918, 1977
Benner, Judith Ann, 1125
Bennett, Robert L., 644
Bennington, Vermont, 883
Benson, Robert L., 3098

Benteen, Frederick W., 963
Bentley, Charles A., 963
Benton, Thomas Hart, 920
Bent's Fort, 1186, 1188, 1212
Beppler, Timothy A., 1574
Berardi, Anne L., 2041
Berens, John F., 331
Berg, J. Otto, 1733
Berg, Maclyn P., 1127-1128
Berg, Philip L., 3274
Berhow, Bennett Francis, 1906
Berkey, Curtis, 343-345, 728, 1371-1372, 1389, 1421, 1489, 2432
Berkhofer, Robert F., Jr., 3096
Berkman, Brenda, 3145
Berlin, Irving N., 1470
Berman, Howard R., 1416
Berman, S. Sue, 1808
Berner, Robert L., 3342
Bernstein, Allan S., 2123
Bernstein, Gene M., 3266
Berry, James Jesse, 1187
Berry, Mary Clay, 757
Berry, Thomas, 474
Berry, Virgil, 2084
Berry, Wendell, 475
Berthrong, Donald J., 795, 837, 2752-2753
Bertoluzzi, Renitia, 2204
Best, J.J., 678
Betts, William A., 2161
Beuf, Ann H., 1734, 1950
Beuke, Vernon Lee, 1735
Beverley, Robert, 3136, 3163
Beynon, William, 2979
Bible, 1235
Bibliographic Guide to North American History, 76
Bibliography: agriculture, 2414; Apache Indians, 2855; California Indians, 2915, 2918, 2922; Cherokee Indians, 2624, 2684; Cheyenne Indians, 2759; Chippewa Indians, 2545; Choctaw Indians, 2694; Christian Church and Indians, 1223; community development, 68; contemporary North American Indians, 64; Covelo Indian community, 2929; Creek Indians, 2706; Debo, Angie, 3324; Delaware Indians, 2476; demography, 3012; diseases, 2091; dissertataions, 81-82; ethnology, 61; fishing and hunting rights, 1636; Hopi Indians, 2840; Indian justice, 1339; Indian materials, 59-74; Indian policy, 60, 72; Indians in southern colonies, 173; Indian-white relations, 71; Iowa Indians, 2507; Kansas Indians, 2533; land tenure, 749; language arts materials, 1813-1814; law, 1336; literature, 3144, 3193; Maine Indians, 2468; Maryland and Delaware Indians, 2467; minority studies, 69; mental health, 2173; missions, 1236; Navajo Indians, 2876; northeast Indians, 2473; Pacific Northwest Indians, 2977; Pawnee Indians, 2781; periodical literature, 77; peyote, 3069; Plains Indians, 2736; prehistory, 2449; social science research, 73; sociology of American Indians, 74; southeastern Indians, 2602; Southern Baptist Church and Indians, 1223; southwestern Indians, 2832; urban